D0918211

Last, the contributors confron
tions of analysis. How should a.......
conducted? What levels of analysis are suitable for the question at hand? Are the data
units suitably chosen to permit answers to
questions at this level of analysis? What tools
might be useful in searching through the
data? Each chapter focuses on a specific issue, analyzing the conceptual issues involved. They tend to clarify the considerations rather than to attempt definitive
answers, since there are no generally relevant conclusions to these difficult issues.

Although research in social interaction
analysis is now at an all-time high, conceptual confusion has remained a serious problem. The editors and contributors to this
volume, in bringing together a literate and
comprehensive review of these central conceptual issues, hope that their concerted effort will contribute to the enhancement of
interdisciplinary research in this important
area.

Michael E. Lamb is Assistant Professor of
Psychology and a Research Scientist in the
Center for Human Growth and Develop-
ment at the University of Michigan. Stephen
J. Suomi is Assistant Professor of Psychology
and Associate Director of the Primate Lab-
oratory at the University of Wisconsin-
Madison. Gordon R. Stephenson is Assistant
Scientist at the Wisconsin Regional Primate
Center.

SOCIAL INTERACTION ANALYSIS
Methodological Issues

SOCIAL INTERACTION ANALYSIS

Methodological Issues

Edited by
MICHAEL E. LAMB
STEPHEN J. SUOMI
GORDON R. STEPHENSON

The University of Wisconsin Press

516855

Published 1979

The University of Wisconsin Press

Box 1379, Madison, Wisconsin 53701

/

The University of Wisconsin Press, Ltd.

1 Gower St., London WC1E 6HA, England

Copyright © 1979

The Board of Regents of the University of Wisconsin System

All rights reserved

First printing

Printed in the United States of America

For LC CIP information see the colophon

ISBN 0-299-07590-7

HM
1111
S6267
1979

CONTENTS

v

CONTRIBUTORS

Heidelise Als. Children's Hospital Medical Center, Boston, MA.

Roger Bakeman. Department of Psychology, Georgia State University, Atlanta, GA.

Nicholas Blurton Jones. Institute of Child Health, University of London, London, England.

T. Berry Brazelton. Children's Hospital Medical Center, Boston, MA.

John M. Gottman. Department of Psychology, University of Illinois, Urbana-Champaign, ILL.

Willard W. Hartup. Institute of Child Development, University of Minnesota, Minneapolis, MN.

Michael E. Lamb. Department of Psychology and Center for Human Growth and Development, University of Michigan, Ann Arbor, MI.

Emil W. Menzel, Jr. Department of Psychology, State University of New York, Stony Brook, N.Y.

Dennis Moore. Oregon Social Learning Center, Eugene, OR.

Ross D. Parke. Department of Psychology, University of Illinois, Champaign-Urbana, ILL.

Gerald R. Patterson. Oregon Social Learning Center, Eugene, OR.

Thomas G. Power. Department of Psychology, University of Illinois, Champaign-Urbana, ILL.

Leonard A. Rosenblum. Department of Psychiatry, Downstate Medical Center, Brooklyn, N.Y.

Michael J. A. Simpson. Sub-Department of Animal Behaviour, Cambridge University, Madingley, England.

Gordon R. Stephenson. Wisconsin Regional Primate Center, University of Wisconsin, Madison, WI.

Stephen J. Suomi. Primate Laboratory, Department of Psychology, University of Wisconsin, Madison, WI.

Edward Tronick. Department of Psychology, University of Massachusetts, Amherst, MA.

Robert H. Woodson. Institute of Child Health, University of London, London, England.

PREFACE

We have brought together in this volume a group of papers in which various methodological and conceptual issues concerning the observation of social interaction are scrutinized. These chapters grew out of the deliberations of a Study Group, financially supported by the Society for Research in Child Development under a grant from the Foundation for Child Development, which met in Madison, Wisconsin, in July 1977. The needs for both the Study Group and this volume appear self-evident. In recent years, there have occurred quantum advances in the sophistication of the devices whereby observational data can be gathered and reduced, and equivalent advances in the statistical techniques whereby these data can be analyzed, evaluated, and interpreted. Unfortunately, these developments have proliferated too rapidly for researchers in the field to keep abreast of them. Of researchers, there are indeed many. The observation of social behavior has become a topic of interest to developmental and clinical psychologists, zoologists, behavioral pediatricians, and anthropologists. Unfortunately, regardless of the analytic sophistication evinced by some investigators, much of the work in the area has been marred by a lack of conceptual clarity and the absence of clearly articulated plans about the level of analysis to be employed and the type of questions to be addressed.

This volume is designed to serve three purposes. First, we have included several chapters describing new or underemployed analytic or data acquisition techniques whose adoption would, in our opinion, be of benefit to many of the research fields identified above. Second, we have included chapters in which programs of research are described in detail by their intellectual progenitors. Our hope is that these exemplary descriptions will prove of heuristic benefit to other investigators. The rest of the chapters articulate in some detail the conceptual issues that must be addressed by researchers if their investigations are to be theoretically and conceptually revealing. The authors concerned often stake out clearly conflicting positions regarding these issues, and the conflicts help to underscore and clarify the importance of the issue themselves.

The audience for which this volume is intended is fairly diverse. We believe that the issues discussed in the chapters that follow are of importance to anyone conducting or contemplating research in the area of social interaction. Although the discussion may be especially helpful to graduate students in developmental psychology, zoology, anthropology, and related fields, we would like to believe (having ourselves benefitted from the insights provided by the contributors) that the material will be of interest to more experienced investigators in these fields as well.

A number of individuals and organizations played a crucial role in making the Study Group and this volume possible. To the following we owe special thanks. First, as noted earlier, the Society for Research in Child Development and the Foundation for Child Development underwrote both the Study Group expenses and a portion of the publication costs in an effort to ensure that the book was published at a reasonable price. Second, Karen Suomi undertook responsibility for the smooth administration and coordination of the Study Group. A reservation fiasco and a strike by hotel personnel would have vitiated the conference itself had she not assumed this managerial role! Margaret Tresch Owen reviewed and commented on the draft chapters. Karen Kraemer and Helen LeRoy helped edit the chapters and typed them in preparation for publication, while Cindy Neff prepared the Author and Subject Indexes.

Ann Arbor, Michigan   Michael E. Lamb
Madison, Wisconsin   Stephen J. Suomi
    July, 1978   Gordon R. Stephenson

SOCIAL INTERACTION
ANALYSIS
Methodological Issues

1.

Issues in the study
of social interaction:
An introduction

MICHAEL E. LAMB

This volume is not a compendium of instructions specifying how
social interaction should be studied. Instead, it comprises a series
of discussions of the problems shared by researchers in this area.
This somewhat unusual focus has been a consistent and over-riding
consideration throughout the months between the book's inception and
its final publication. When Drs. Suomi, Stephenson, and I began
organizing the workshop from which this volume emerged, we were
motivated largely by dissatisfaction with the data gathering and
found that the conference participants shared our discontent. In
fact, no one was willing to participate in an enterprise billed as
a public declaration of the way in which research should be conducted.
Instead, all perceived the need for a discussion of the central
issues with which researchers in the area grapple. The present
volume is the product of our workshop and of the months of writing
that succeeded our deliberations.

The focus of several of the chapters (those of Gottman,
Stepehenson, and Gottman and Bakeman, for instance) is upon data
gathering and analysis techniques. The techniques described in
these chapters are not explained elsewhere in an equivalently
accessible fashion, and we hope that the inclusion of these descriptions will facilitate the utilization of these powerful procedures
and devices. The justification for inclusion of the other chapters
is rather different. The authors of each take an issue or set of
issues of substantive importance and then proceed to discuss the
topic in depth--supplementing their presentations with illustrative
data. Our goal in these chapters as well as in the present chapter
is to review the issues that have to be accorded preconsideration
if the study of social interaction is to be maximally fruitful.

The common characteristic of these issues is that none have
straightforward and generally relevant answers. Instead, the

1

resolution of each issue is dependent on the purpose and predictions of the individual study. The accomplished and thoughtful researcher must be ever mindful of this fact. Before initiating a study, s/he will weigh the options carefully, and not adopt a strategy simply because it is currently in vogue or because it promises the speediest (and perhaps most superficial) results.

During the last decade, the study of social interaction has become remarkably popular among psychologists, zoologists, and anthropologists. For most of them, interest in studying interaction is a derived concern--a concern developed from the assumption that the social environment in which an individual lives dramatically affects that individual's behavior. From this, it follows that one must focus upon the interaction through which the social environment exerts its influence. In addition, scientists such as Stephenson propose that by studying interaction we may come to understand the meaning of an individual's behavior to those around it. The study of interaction thus becomes a technique whereby to translate nonverbal communications, especially those among members of another species, or among preverbal humans. For a final group of social scientists, myself included, interest in social interaction derives from the assumption that a child's social experiences partially determine how that individual will later behave. Being able to describe the formative interactions thus becomes essential if we are to understand the course and process of social and personality development.

Whatever the specific interests of the scientist, however, there are three types of issues that demand attention before a program of research is launched. In the sections that follow we will deal with each of these issues in turn: what behaviors shall be recorded, how should they be recorded, and how should the resulting data be reduced. Needless to say, resolution of all issues presumes prior definition of the guiding theoretical framework and the focal empirical questions. In a final substantive section, I will discuss several factors that necessarily limit our ability to infer causal relationships from the analysis of sequences of social interaction. Our relative ignorance about the situational determinants of interaction and our past unwillingness to consider complex and indirect modes of influence properly underscores, at the close of the chapter, how unsophisticated social scientists remain.

DEGREE OF REFINEMENT IN THE BEHAVIORAL DESCRIPTION

We are not concerned, of course, with the specific behaviors recorded, for that will vary from study to study. Our question here is simply: How fine or gross should the data units be? In a study of parent-infant interaction, for example, should the researcher distinguish between "full smile", "half-smile", "bright-face", "coo", and "babble" or should s/he record all of these as instances of "positive distal signals"? Either decision has attendant risks. If only a few gross categories are recorded, it is possible that the researcher will fail to observe the meshing of the subjects' behavior because s/he is confusing (i.e., failing to distinguish

among) behavioral units that are assigned different meanings by
the interactants. The researcher may conclude incorrectly that the
parent fails to respond to 75% of the infant's signals, never
realizing that the adult is vocalizing in response to every coo.

Adopting a highly refined inventory has its attendant problems
too. If the researcher devises an inventory comprising a large
number of refined behavioral distinctions, s/he may distinguish
among several behaviors that are morphologically different, but
are perceived as semantically similar by the interactants. More
importantly, the researcher may classify as a behavior unit a motor
act such as "raises eyebrows" to which no consistent response can
be found. If s/he had considered "raises eyebrows", "raises corners
of mouth", and "face brightens" as *components* of one unit--a smile--
the partner's actual responsiveness would have been apparent to the
investigator.

For most research questions, the behavior units should be
roughly equivalent to the unit of meaning. They need not approximate
the smallest units of meaning, but the researcher is well advised
to be consistent when devising a behavior inventory. If some of
the units are superordinate categories like "aggressive behavior",
for example, then the other units should be equivalently inclusive.
"Positive reinforcement" would be appropriate whereas "smile"
would not be. Patterson and Moore provide an excellent discussion
of this topic in their chapter. They illustrate very clearly that
the researcher should avoid employing a coding system that makes
finer discriminations than the focal interactants typically make.
Patterson and his colleagues, for instance, have learned a great
deal about the antecedents and consequences of aggressive behavior
in children despite the fact that their coding scheme appears to
be relatively crude.

The *"unit of meaning* rule", of course, presupposes fairly
extensive knowledge of the social group under question. This
knowledge is usually not available to the researcher. In their
contribution, Woodson and Blurton Jones reiterate a traditional
concern of the ethologists that choosing in advance which behaviors
to record (and thus which to ignore) involves an implicit assumption
that the researcher knows which behaviors are important to the
subjects. Ethologists are unwilling to accept this assumption.
They propose that the researcher must first describe the organism's
behavioral repertoire carefully and *without preconception,* allowing
the data to instruct one regarding the direction in which subsequent
investigation should proceed. In our present ignorance, Woodson
and Blurton Jones propose, social scientists have no alternative
but to record as much as they can in as refined a fashion as
possible.

Perhaps the dispute between Patterson and Moore, on the one
hand, and Woodson and Blurton Jones, on the other, can be viewed
as the consequence of divergent responses to the question: "How
comfortable does the researcher feel assessing what a behavior means
to someone else?" The ethologists' unease can surely be traced to
their involvement in animal behavior research where there is every
justification for caution in assigning meanings to behaviors and
in "chunking" complex behaviors into units. Many primatologists

remain wary of making *a priori* decisions about the relative importance and meaning of elemental behaviors in their subjects'
repertoire.

Similar problems are encountered by anthropologists, who often
feel too ignorant about the foreign culture's social structure to
define gross meaning units. Finally, students of infancy are
unwilling to assume that the baby assigns meaning to the behavior
of others in the same way that adults do. In fact, coming to
define the baby's units is one of the central and general problems in research on infancy! We have yet to learn what infants
know about their social world, what aspects of interaction are
most salient to them, and how these change as infants become older
and more sophisticated. Unfortunately, then, assumptions about
the meaning of behavior are dubious in the three areas of investi-
gation--animal behavior, anthropology, and infant social behavior--
that are of central concern to most of the scientists studying
social interaction!

Concerns about how finely behavior should be described have
become exceptionally vexing with the widespread availability of
sophisticated equipment permitting researchers to conduct, at slow
speed, refined analyses as precise as those obtainable from the
frame-by-frame scoring of the behavior of each individual. As
indicated earlier, the danger here is that the researcher may
categorize the behavior more finely than the interactants do. In
other words, s/he may subdivide the smallest meaningful behavioral
units into subunits that, on their own, communicate no meaningful
message between the interactants. In such cases, it becomes
necessary for the researcher to reconstruct meaningful behavioral
units from the parts s/he recorded, perhaps learning in the process
just how subunits may be combined into units of meaning. Als,
Tronick, and Brazelton present elegent examples of the uses to
which this strategy can be applied. In addition to elucidating the
relationships among different levels of analysis, these authors
also indicate that one can combine the information concerning two
individuals into a form that tells one, not about the individuals,
but about the time-course and quality of their interaction.

"Level of analysis" questions are also central to Suomi's
chapter, in which we are presented with evidence indicating that
group differences in social behavior can be completely obscured
when the level of analysis is too crude, and can be rendered
increasingly apparent as more sophisticated levels of analysis
are employed in place of the less refined approaches.

HOW TO RECORD BEHAVIOR?

There are three types of issues involved here, and the range
of options available to the researcher confronting either of these
issues has multiplied with the onset of the electronic age.

The first question is a practical one. To record behavior with
the desired degree of refinement, is it necessary to view and review
the data several times--perhaps at reduced speed--or will a single
pass suffice? If multiple viewings are necessary, the researcher

has no option but to film the interaction. In some situations,
though, the practical problems (e.g., carrying a videocamera and
recorder through impassable jungle terrain) and the costs involved
lead to a redefinition of the research question in order to eliminate
the need for filming. Unless one needs to score sequences of
behavior on multiple occasions--whether to assure refined coding
or to assess reliability--it is usually best to score the behavior
directly, without an intermediate filming. This is so because a
good deal of critical contextual information is often absent from
film records.

The discussion in the preceeding paragraph refers not to the
final coding of behavior so much as to the need for intermediate
storage of as rich a description (e.g., a film record) of the raw
data as possible. That record then has to be scored or coded.
Until a few years ago, the job usually involved having a scorer note
on an analysis pad how often a given behavior occurred within a given
time frame. While this technique remains suitable for most problems,
it is tedious and often unreliable in that it requires the scorer
to take his/her eyes off the subject in order to make a notation.
Perhaps most importantly, furthermore, paper-and-pencil scoring
techniques usually do not permit the scorer to record the exact
time at which a behavior occurred--neither in real time (i.e.,
time of day) or relative to the preceeding, simultaneous, and
succeeding behaviors of the target subject or its interactant.
By contrast, most of the new electronic data acquisition aids that
Sidowski described record the time of each entry, and so make it
possible for the researcher to specify the latency between one
behavior and the next, or between the onset of a behavior and its
termination. Nevertheless, one caution is necessary. No machine,
however sophisticated, can surpass the reliability of its operator.
It can recall only the time at which an entry was made, and the
entry time is rendered variably inaccurate by the unreliability
of the observer's reaction time. The likelihood of inaccurate
ascription of simultaneity or sequence is elevated when two observers are sources of information that is later combined. There
will inevitably be uncertainty about the true sequence of behaviors
separated from one another in the record by less than about 1.0
second.

Besides the potential for information about timing, one further
reason why most researchers have switched from paper-and-pencil
to electronic data recorders is the fact that most systems offer
automated data reduction, relieving the researchers and their
assistants of these tedious chores while also assuring more accurate
computations.

At the conference, Sidowski evaluated the systems currently available. Without reviewing the options in detail, I wish to emphasize two
considerations of which any potential investor ought to be aware.
First, implementing an electronic data-encoding system comprises a
costly undertaking, and the decisions concerned should not be taken
lightly. It is especially important that the scientist think about
the relative effectiveness of the available systems for both present
and anticipated future needs. The systems are by no means equivalently flexible, which means that a system ideally suited for one
study may be cumbersome or inappropriate when addressed to another

issue. Lack of flexibility can be a major disadvantage simply because of the costs of installation, implementation, and training.

Second, it is important to understand that a data-gathering aid is only a tool that facilitates or expedites a researcher's task, perhaps making possible analyses that would otherwise be impossible or prohibitively expensive. It does not relieve the user of the responsibility for determining which analyses should be conducted, nor for interpreting the resultant findings. Even today, too many investigators appear to believe that scientific responsibility for the conduct of the study can be assumed by a machine. Just record the data, they assume, and the computer will provide the answers. At that point, it will be easy to identify the questions! Fortunately, this assumption is invalid. Few behavioral phenomena are so translucent that the puzzles surrounding them can be solved without extensive and thoughtful investigation.

Many electronic aids permit the observer to note the occurrence of each behavior and have its time recorded automatically. This is known as an *event sampling procedure*. By contrast, many paper-and-pencil techniques involve a *time-sampling procedure* in which the observer notes whether, within the predetermined time frame, each of the behaviors did or did not occur. Two types of information are lost when this procedure is employed: the actual number of times the behavior occurred within the time frame, and the temporal relationships among the behaviors that occurred within the same frame. Further information about the incidence of behaviors is lost when a time-to-observe/time-to-record sampling procedure is employed (i.e., observer watches for 20 seconds, then spends 10 seconds writing down what was observed).

When the scientist is studying a large group of subjects both event sampling and time sampling become impossible, so a modification known as *scan sampling* is employed. In this procedure, the observer scans the group for evidence of an interesting interaction (e.g., courting and copulation), and then focuses upon that interaction, recording as much as possible about it while temporarily ignoring the rest of the group. When the interaction ends, the observer again begins to scan the group.

Two of the chapters in this volume directly address issues relating to sampling strategy. Simpson discusses the reliability and validity questions that any sampling procedure poses, while Gottman and Bakeman discuss a time-series analysis procedure that assumes the raw data are coded in a time-sampled format.

WHAT TO DO WITH BEHAVIOR RECORDS?

When research in this area began, investigators felt comfortable describing the social experience of an individual simply by tabulating the frequencies of occurrence of a set of criterial behaviors. Although many researchers (including myself) still adopt this strategy for addressing some questions, scientists have, in the main, become dissatisfied with this strategy. Its major deficiency is the fact that it disregards all information concerning the timing, sequence, and variable density of the individual's behavior and its relation to the behavior of the interactive partner. Inevitably, this realization leads to questions about the value of the information that is being sacrificed.

Clearly, the sacrifice is a substantial one. It seems unlikely that any smile from A to B conveys the same message in all circumstances. Rather, its meaning in B's eyes is highly dependent on its relationship to A's ongoing activity and its temporal relationship to B's own social behavior. For many sophisticated questions about social interaction, it is necessary to take into account the behavior of all the participants, and analyze the actions of every one in the context of each others' behavior.

In the early attempts at the analysis of interaction, many investigators tried to capture sequencing information by computing contingent probabilities--equations quantifying the likelihood that each instance of a given behavior by A would be followed by one of a given range of responses by individual B. (For example, $p\, X_B/Y_A$ represents the probability that B will emit behavior X given that A has performed behavior Y.) If $p\, X_B/Y_A = 1.0$, it would mean that A's Ys were always followed by B's Xs. If it were also the case that Xs followed Ys only, then one could conclude that Y was a specific elictor of X, and that B was highly attuned and sensitive to A's behavior. The technique and uses of contingent probability or sequence analyses are described by Gottman and Bakeman.

When the data units have been carefully chosen, contingent probabilities can comprise important information. The most useful probabilities are those in which the scientist focuses on the relationships between specific behaviors whose temporal relationship is defined as important on theoretical grounds. Thus, for example, a salient dimension of the rearing environment--the sensitivity of a caretaker to a baby's cries--may be elucidated by computing the probability that the baby's cries will elicit responses within a specified period. (In most cases, the size of this "window" is of critical importance.) This statistic may permit informative comparisons among caretaker-infant dyads. In addition, the information value of the statistic could be enhanced by determining which responses occurred most frequently in different families or situations, and which were most effective in soothing infants (in general or in particular).

The important thing to note about contingent probability analyses is that they comprise a data-reduction not a data-analysis procedure. They provide statistics that can be used in hypothesis-testing roles but they are merely descriptive statistics. The major difference between figures representing (say) the number of times that a baby smiles at its mother and the responsiveness of the mother to the infant's smiles is that the latter statistic describes the dyad, whereas the former statistic describes one individual's social behavior. In both cases, however, the raw figures themselves are not informative: They are only meaningful when viewed in relative rather than absolute terms and are most likely to be revealing when group differences are obtained, or when individual differences are systematically related to earlier (or later) characteristics of the dyad or of either interactant. Unfortunately, the ascendance to popularity of interactional analysis has produced a spate of publications whose sole and common finding has been that interaction does indeed take place.

This is a wholly unsatisfactory finding, of course, because it has never been in dispute.

Contingent probability analyses have yet to be used as extensively as one might expect, but they are becoming increasingly popular. Consequently, it is important to appreciate that the technique has one major conceptual deficiency. Although few scientists would dispute the claim that an action may occur in response to a behavior or interaction sequence that occurred some time ago, a contingent probability analysis explicitly disavows this, operating instead upon the assumption that the elicitor of a behavior (if indeed there is one) is the immediately preceeding behavior of the partner. This deficiency is remedied to some extent in lag sequence analysis--a procedure that permits the researcher to vary systematically the size of the lag between "stimulus" and "response" in order to describe and understand the flow of interaction better. Sackett provided an accounting of lag sequence analysis in his presentation. Gottman discusses spectral analysis--a little-used technique that can facilitate a scientist's decision about what size "lag" to employ in lag sequence analysis while also providing visual representation of the synchrony or asynchrony of a dyad's functioning.

As typically employed, both contingent probability analysis and lag sequence analysis seek temporal relationships among individual behaviors rather than clusters of behaviors. Most of those working in this area, however, recognize that the eliciting stimulus is likely to be a pattern of behaviors rather than a single behavior. This problem may be addressed by trying to define complex behavior units rather than discrete behavior units, and by searching for interaction patterns that might be viewed as complex units in later analyses. This is tedious research, but it offers the best hope of insightful analyses of interaction.

The issues discussed in the last few paragraphs have one further implication for the investigator undertaking a study in this area. The description of interaction and the comprehension of social communication are facilitated when the scientist is able to explore the data by slicing the behavioral record in different ways. This requirement increases the importance of flexibility in the encoding/reduction process. In his chapter, Stephenson describes a software system that is designed to ensure maximum flexibility while minimizing the mechanical demands upon the observer in order to enhance the accuracy, reliability, and refinement of the behavior coding process.

BEYOND THE DYAD

In their usual applications, the sequence analysis procedures identified in the preceeding section are useful for the analysis of dyadic interaction only. How should one proceed if the social system of interest is a triad rather than a dyad? Bakeman and his colleagues (see Gottman and Bakeman's chapter) employ a technique of data recording that could be useful in this context. Instead of using an event sampling procedure (scoring X each time it occurs, scoring Y each time it occurs, etc.), Bakeman and associates use a time

sampling strategy. The record for each time frame specifies *both*
what B did and what A did. ("No scorable behavior" (0) would thus
be a legitimate category.) If, for example, B smiled(s) at A in
the first one-second frame, and A cooed (c) back in the next, the
two frame entries would be:

$$T_1, [S_B:O_A]; T_2 [O_B:C_A].$$

The unit of analysis then becomes the frame entry, and there is
theoretically no limit to the number of individuals whose behavior
is recorded in each frame. Since all possible permutations must
be accommodated, however, the procedure rapidly evolves into one
in which there are so many different frame entry units that it is
difficult to identify interactional sequences. This problem is,
of course, exaccerbated when one is trying to analyze interactions
within triads or even larger social groups. In addition, there
is the problem common to all time-sampling procedures. Data
concerning timing are rendered inaccurate, simultaneity and
sequence may thus be confused, and so the estimates of contingent
probability are necessarily affected.

Questions concerning our ability to analyze interaction in
groups larger than dyads have elicited less attention than their
manifest significance demands. In their chapter, Parke, Power, and
Gottman discuss some of the conceptual issues that have to be
considered in studying triads. Their concern is not with the
mechanics of data analysis so much as with questions about the
inference or identification of causal relationships within a group
of individuals. Their discussion highlights the fact that elucidation of the patterns of social influence demands the integration
of information from many different levels of analysis and aspects
of relationships. In addition, they illustrate that effects are
seldom unidirectional: typically, the effect that A has on B
changes B's behavior toward A (and C), changing their behavior
toward B, and so on. One implication of this is that influences
can be both directly mediated (i.e., B affects A) and indirectly
mediated (e.g., C affects A via her effect on B's behavior toward
A). The direct unidirectional influence pattern within dyads--
a pattern that absorbs the preponderance of professional attention--
is in reality just one of a large range of possible influence
patterns. Unfortunately, social scientists have barely initiated
the research that would add substance to the conceptual scheme
sketched out by Parke and his colleagues.

EFFECTS OF THE SOCIAL AND PHYSICAL ENVIRONMENT

The issues raised by Parke, Power, and Gottman lead to more
general questions about the effects of the social and physical
environment upon the interaction between or among the individuals
who comprise the focal group (be it a dyad, a triad, or a larger
group). Although most researchers would like to believe that the
interactions they observe are reliable and representative, it is
increasingly apparent that the patterns of interaction, even though
they may be characteristic of a dyad, are heavily influenced by the

context in which they are observed. A context-free observation is an unattainable goal. The concept of "the dyad" is itself a convenient fiction representing the fact that two people are being observed by a third. If the group being observed is larger (a family, or a troop of monkeys) then each of the individuals in the group may affect the behavior of the others. In my later chapter, I present the findings of several studies demonstrating that "the social context" indeed affects the extent of dyadic interaction, and that the nature of the effect differs depending upon the age of the focal interactants, and the sex, age, and specific identity of the persons who represent "the social context".

The physical context also affects social interaction, often by limiting the types of interaction that can occur. In his chapter, Rosenblum presents a taxonomy of the physical environments in which nonhuman primates are typically observed. The effects of the physical context are obviously of concern to students of animal behavior, who frequently study animals in laboratory conditions that bear little resemblance to the natural ecology of the species concerned. They are also of increasing interest to developmental and social psychologists, however, for their experiments too are often conducted in artificially constructed environments that are unfamiliar to and unnatural for their subjects. It is not necessary, of course, that either discipline eschew laboratory studies entirely. Rather, researchers must be aware of the effects that the environment *may* have on the phenomena under review, and must take these effects into account when interpreting their findings. The more one learns about situational effects, the more one comes to understand the species itself, for it seems that the effects (at least those that have been explored) are lawful and orderly rather than random and unpredictable.

CONCLUSION

Such, then, are the issues that confront the scientist as s/he prepares to undertake a study of social interaction--whatever the species under examination and whatever the specific questions to be addressed. Clearly, the topics span a remarkably diverse array of concerns indeed. The reader will be reminded frequently, furthermore, that we are only beginning to define and refine the issues. We are not yet ready to present definitive or even tentative resolutions. With the compilation of these chapters and the publication of this book, we hope to focus attention on the problems, thereby making prospective researchers more self-conscious of their assumptions and their decisions. There are no simple pithy answers, and there are no attractive short-cuts, but there are considerations that can help transform a trivial study into a productive and revealing endeavor. If we can effect a change in the priority assigned to these considerations, we will have achieved our goal.

2.
Levels of analysis in the study of social interaction: An historical perspective

WILLARD W. HARTUP

Direct observation is the methodological cornerstone of the natural sciences. Nevertheless, the invention of systematic methods for observing social interaction occurred relatively recently. Although zoologists and ethnographers have utilized observational methods since the beginnings of their disciplines, major advances were made as late as the 1920s when empirically-based categories were derived, sampling strategies were devised, and methods established for training observers so that reliable measures could be maintained.

Quantification was a primary objective. In the words of one investigator:

> "We know but little regarding the changes that appear with advancing age in frequency or duration of outbursts of anger, the conditions making for increased irritability, or the methods of training best suited to bring about improvement in self-control among children. Here we are obliged to depend almost completely upon individual experience and judgment, together with whatever accumulation of folkwisdom has been handed down from generation to generation. Although we should not decry as worthless this knowledge, which has met the test of time, its limitations must nevertheless be admitted . . . In the mental as well as the physical world real advance is contingent upon the accumulation of a body of scientific knowledge based upon controlled experimentation or, where experiment is impossible, upon the assembling of objective records organized and summarized in such a way that conclusions are warranted (Goodenough, 1931, p. 3).

11

Unable to systematize long-standing impressions about the
ontogeny of social behavior, research workers in child development were extremely active in their initial work with observational methods. Paper-and-pencil techniques, which served to
advance the study of mental development earlier in the century,
were nearly useless in the study of social development. Interviews, projective techniques, Guess-Who tests, and sociometry
similarly revealed their limitations and/or weaknesses. Most
investigators now agree that no accumulation of facts about social
behavior and development is complete without measurement of events
in the process of occurring. Sometimes, the needed facts can be
obtained in natural (i.e., typical) settings; at other times,
standardized (i.e., atypical) settings will do. But, invariably,
the forms and functions of social activity can only be understood
via direct observation of the relevant events.

This essay includes brief discussions about the uses of observational methods by research workers in child development, the
problem of parametric choice in observational research, and the
issue of levels of analysis. The main argument centers on the
thesis that multiple modes of analysis should be used more frequently in research. Too often, the contentions of the "lumpers" and
the "splitters" suggest that molar and molecular classification
systems are incompatible or that their simultaneous use constitutes a categorical exercise with little substantive yield. Too
often, armchair analysis determines that response rates, rather
than latencies or intensities, adequately represent the range
of psychological manifestations involved in social activity. Both
the child development and the animal behavior literatures are replete
with examples in which recombinant techniques have elucidated
important dynamics in social behavior. Indeed, it is difficult
to understand how an appreciation of the functions, ontogenesis,
and management of social behavior can be obtained without the
use of multiple measures at many different levels of analysis.

THE USES OF OBSERVATIONAL DATA

Individual Differences

Observational methods have been used extensively to study
individual differences. Attention in the early child development
literature was given to individual differences in aggression
(Goodenough, 1931), cooperation (Parten, 1932), quarrels (Dawe,
1934), ascendance (Jack, 1934), sympathy (Murphy, 1937), and their
interrelations (Arrington, 1932). Controversy rages concerning
the best classification schemes with which to search for continuities and changes in individual differences in social activity. While
long-term continuities have been difficult to demonstrate at both
molecular and molar levels of analysis (Mischel, 1968), the
possibility remains that, when behavior constellations are considered in context (i.e., when behavior is studied in relation to
effectance in adaptation), continuities can be demonstrated.

Behavior Morphology

Direct observation has been used, abeit infrequently, to examine the morphology of children's social behavior. Mostly, behavior items in the early research were assumed to represent larger, functional classes of social behavior such as "sympathy," "dependency," or "aggression." Behavior configurations within these classes, either among individual children or among children of various ages, were not studied extensively. Goodenough (1931) was interested in morphological issues; her studies revealed changes in the behaviors associated with anger ranging from "undirected" flailing during the first year to focussed acts accompanied by increased utilization of language during the preschool years. Certain motor components (e.g., stamping and hitting) were noted more regularly among older children than among younger ones, and non-violent "after reactions" (e.g., whining, sulking, and moodiness) emerged in episodes of anger only during the elementary school years. This investigation was exceptional in its emphasis on behavioral organization and re-organization occurring in relation to chronological age.

The manner in which certain acts (e.g., crying, puckering, frowning, hitting, and laughing) combine to produce certain consequences has been recognized now as a major issue in socialization research. McGrew (1972) was able to determine empirically that, among nursery school children, certain behaviors are exhibited significantly more frequently in agonistic and quasi-agonistic interaction than in nonagonistic interaction: backs, beats, beats up, body oppose, chase, fall, flee, flinch, forearm raise, forearm sweep, freeze, laugh, pull, punch, play face, push, vocalize, and wrestle. Such observations assist in establishing the motoric and verbal substructure of early agonism, as well as the broader "functions" of the activity in child development. Of course, agonism is more than the sum of these bits and pieces: contextual factors such as the physical environment, eliciting events, and social values must also be weighed in order to establish the meaning of these configurations. Moreover, interrelations in agonistic activity change with age. Hitting and verbal insults transmit different social messages at different ages (Hartup, 1974), thereby complicating the search for adaptive functions.

The Ecology of Social Behavior

Observational methods have long been used to study the ecology of social behavior. Early investigators found that possessions were the most frequent elicitors of social conflict from 18 months through the sixth year (Dawe, 1934); that physical space constrains aggressive interaction (Jersild & Markey, 1935); and that mixed-age conditions elicit more altruism than same-age conditions (Murphy, 1937). Social relations were recognized as contextual variables, too. Authoritarian adult leadership styles produce more interpersonal aggression than democratic leadership styles (Lippitt & White, 1943); modeling effects are altered by the relationship existing between model and observer (Hartup & Coates, 1967; Hetherington, 1967); and, when children watch humorous cartoons, the frequency of laughing, smiling, looking, and talking is greater between friends than between acquaintances; behavioral concordance is greater between friends than between non-friends; and dominance interactions are more likely to be mutually-directed than individually-directed (Foot, Chapman, & Smith, 1977; Brady-Smith, Newcomb, & Hartup, 1978). Currently, the observational literature contains extensive information on a wide variety of contextual factors in social activity although the objectives of the investigators have varied widely.

Social Learning

Direct observation has been used to study behavior maintenance and change (i.e., social learning). Patterson, Littman, and Bricker (1967) were able to correlate accelerations in the frequency of aggression in peer interaction in the nursery school with the display, by the victim, of *cries, passivity, withdrawal,* and *telling the teacher.* Decelerations in aggression rates were associated with counter-aggression. In family interaction, negative reinforcement (i.e., the cessation of aversive stimulation) seems to be a major correlate of increases in aggression (Patterson, in press). Such contingencies do not lead to clear-cut conclusions about the determinants of social behavior since cessation of aversive stimulation and increases in aggression may have a common cause rather than be causally-linked. But field experimentation, involving planned interventions *in situ,* augments the explanatory power of naturally-occurring contingencies. Field experiments are used increasingly in child development research, although their full potential has not been realized (Hartup, 1973; Parke, in press).

Summary and Comment

Observational studies have been applied to some of the key issues in the development sciences: continuities in individual differences, elucidation of behavior functions, and the analysis of childhood socialization. For many years, observational studies were regarded as "dust bowl" efforts intended to *describe* the nature of social interaction rather than *explain* it. Such an evaluation was never accurate, and does not characterize the present field. Given that the issues being addressed in observational research today are among the most important issues in the field, efforts must continue toward the perfection of techniques for studying social behavior in the process of occurring.

SOCIAL ACTS: WHICH PARAMETERS TO USE?

The basic elements in the social world are *social acts.* Social acts occur between individuals, or occur in relation to some stimulus which has derived its significance through association with individuals or their surrogates. To designate some acts as social and some acts as non-social is a taxonomic exercise of still un-certain value. No common properties characterize the myriad elici-tors of social activity. Different classes of persons (.eg., care-takers, peers) possess unique characteristics, as do the different individuals within a class (e.g., mother, father, and grandmother among caretakers). But children classify the individuals with whom they interact in a manner which is unknown. Is a class defined for a child in terms of one or more properties that distinguish its members from nonmembers? Or, are classes defined in terms of the proportion of their properties that are shared? (See Rheingold and Eckerman, 1975.) The newborn infant may possess behavioral biases that maximize the probability of its responding in a particular way to a social stimulus (e.g., the nipple), but it may be mere tauto-logy to classify such actions as *social* actions. Nevertheless, the heuristic value of the distinction between social and nonsocial acts seems undiminished in the behavioral sciences.

Frequencies

Social acts may be examined in terms of their frequency, latency, amplitude, duration, density, and sequence. Frequencies have been most widely used in the literature; other measures have been used relatively rarely. Frequencies, from which rate measures are derived, have dominated the literature for two main reasons: a) to determine the presence or absence of an act, either in terms of its onset or its ongoing occurrence, involves a conceptually-straightforward judgment; and b) rate of occurrence is widely believed to be correlated with the strength of the internal response disposition or the frequency of prior reinforcement—i.e., the measure is theoretically-relevant. But latency measures and response amplitudes have been assumed traditionally to be indica-tors of response strength, too (cf. Woodworth & Schlossberg, 1954). Why are such measures so little used? Duration and density measures are used infrequently because they are not clearly linked to any theory of social action. But why are latencies and intensities avoided?

Latencies

To date, latency measures have been used most regularly in studies of internalization—in studies of "self-control," "inhibi-tion," and "resistance to temptation." Here, as elsewhere in the psychological literature, investigators have turned to latency measures when response competition or conflict is believed to be tied dynamically to the social act. Latencies can be used to study individual differences involving minimal conflict (Hull, 1943) but, in actual practice, studies in which latencies have been used to index "acquisition" or "appetitive motivation" are rare.
Exemplifying the conventional use of response latencies in

observational research, Hartup, Moore, and Sager (1963) employed
latency of orientation to inappropriate-sex toys as a normative
measure of avoidance activity in sex-role development. These
latencies were longer among elementary school children than among
nursery school children, and greater age differences were observed
among boys than among girls. Based on the usual assumtions about
the manifestations expressed in response latencies, we concluded
that avoidance of sex-inappropriate activities increases with age
and is stronger among boys than among girls. Since these latencies
also were longer in the presence of an adult experimenter than in
her absence, regardless of the subject's age, the evidence suggested that avoidance of sex-appropriate activity is not entirely under
internal control in either early or middle childhood. Response
rates were also recorded, and were found to be inversely correlated
with the response latencies (-.48 for boys, -.45 for girls); the
statistical analysis of these measures indicated that the older
children manipulated the inappropriate-sex toys less frequently
than the younger children did. Are frequency scores redundant,
then, with the latency scores? Would results based solely on
frequency scores provide convincing evidence for normative avoidance? It is doubtful. The latencies are more convincing since their
basis is a span of time in which the subject does *not* engage in
the "inappropriate" activity. At the same time, the latency scores
alone would not show fully the extent to which avoidance learning
is manifest in sex-role behavior. The two moderately-correlated
measures, taken together, reveal more about the manifestations of
avoidance than either measure alone.

Latencies have proved to be useful measures in numerous
other studies of resistance to deviation--both laboratory and field
investigations. Walters and his associates (Walters, Leat, & Mezei,
1963; Walters & Parke, 1964; Walters, Parke, & Cane, 1965) examined
latencies to the first "deviation" in a temptation situation with
attractive but forbidden toys. In this instance, it was assumed
that response suppression induced by punishment training would be
indexed by the response latency to the first deviation. As it
turned out, these latencies were sensitive to the experimental
manipulations but no more so than two other measures: a) rate of
deviant response, and b) deviation densities--i.e., the total time
spent in contact with the forbidden toys. (Although intercorrelations were not reported, it appears that the three measures were
positively correlated.) Again, the use of latencies strengthens
the argument that the experimental procedures induced suppression
of resistance to deviation. But, most important, the use of
multiple measures shows the manifestations of the social learning
to be pervasive.

Intensities

Measures of response magnitude, although theoretically
linked to the motivational dimensions of the social act, are
rarely used in child development research. Basic scaling studies
have not been done and many investigators have found it

difficult to judge reliably either affective intensities as revealed
in facial expression (Oster & Ekman, in press) or intensities in
motor activity. Frequently, the occurrence of intense vocalizations
or vigorous motor activity (e.g., crying or clinging) will be used
along with other criteria to index a major social activity like the
quality of the child's relation to the caretaker (cf. Ainsworth,
1972). But intensities alone are seldom used to measure individual
differences in social interaction.

Some exceptions: Walters and Brown (1964) proposed a theory
of aggressive socialization which states that training in high-
intensity responses would predispose a child to aggression. A
discrimination task was constructed wherein certain subjects were
trained to make high-intensity aggressive responses to a Bobo doll
while others were trained to make low-intensity responses. The
theory was tested in posttraining playground observations focussed
on intense aggressive acts in physical contact games (e.g., hitting,
kneeing, kicking, pulling, and pushing). Only frequency scores
were used in the analysis because an objective technique for
assessing the intensity of the aggressive responses could not be
derived. The authors conceded that, owing to this dilemma, their
study was less than an ideal test of the high-magnitude theory.
Their main thesis, though, is scarcely arguable, since discriminations based on response magnitude are central achievements in
aggressive socialization; children must discriminate early between
"love taps" and "the real thing."

Intensity measures are needed to advance the study of emotional
development. Traditionally, measurement in this area has been
dominated by psychophysiological methods--not very successfully.
But Kobasigawa (1965) demonstrated vicarious emotional arousal
in first grade children through measurement of the pressure
exerted on a plunger, and advances also can be found in recent
studies of individual differences in affective states in infancy
(Oster & Ekman, in press), affective reactions to strangers
(Morgan & Riciutti, 1969), affective reactions to aggressive television programs (Ekman, Liebert, Friesen, Harrison, Zlatchin, Malm-
strom, & Baron, 1972), and the relation between affect and learning
(Masters, Barden, & Ford, 1978). These researchers found that the
intensity of positive induced affect, as rated from photographs of
the subjects' faces, was positively correlated with performance on
a post-induction discrimination learning task; intensity of negative
emotion was found to be negatively associated with task performance.
Such exceptions notwithstanding, the assessment of intensities in
social activity remains a primitive act.

Duration Measures

Duration measures are not easily linked to the processes of
socialization. Two types of these measures can be identified:
a) the length of time required for a behavior unit to "run-off;"
and b) the proportion of observed time in which the subject engages
in a designated class of social behavior. The second measure can
be called a density score since it consists of the number of social

acts multiplied by the average duration of an individual act. In most instances, duration and density scores are modestly corre- lated--or not at all. Liebert and Baron (1972), in their studies of the effects of exposure to aggressive television shows, counted the number of seconds each child displayed certain classes of aggressive activity. The correlation between average density scores was .30 ($p < .05$). Since duration measures are relatively uncommon in the observational literature, the relation between durations and densities in most social situations is unknown.

Duration measures are especially uncommon in their applica- tion to behavior units that "run-off" rapidly. Measurement of the duration of a glance or a blow is a difficult task even when videocameras and electronic event recorders are used. In many instances, the duration of single, short units of social activity would not be a theoretically-relevant variable. Response durations are necessary, though, to distinguish between such social acts as glances and stares, comfort and distress vocaliza- tions, and touching and clinging. Such social acts are common attachment activities and cannot be fully understood without measure- ment of their duration.

With behavior units involving sequences or repetitions of molecular units, duration measures become more feasible. Even so, few examples can be located in the observational literature. As mentioned, Liebert and Baron (1972) clocked the duration of each aggressive response in their observations of school children who had watched either aggressive or nonaggressive television shows. Statistical analysis showed that the average duration of aggressive responses was longer among subjects who had watched the aggressive shows; frequencies of aggression did not differ. Thus, it was largely as a result of the longer response durations associated with the aggressive shows that density of aggression (i.e., total time engaged in aggressive activity) was observed to be greater under those conditions.

Goodenough (1931) showed that close scrutiny of response durations can assist in the developmental analysis of aggression. While the average duration of the entire aggressive sequence did not vary with chronological age, the duration of sub-units within sequences did. Violent sub-units were longer in the anger outbursts of younger children than similar sub-units in the outbursts of older children. Less violent "after reactions" were longer in duration among the older subjects, with the average duration of these reactions being twice as long among children over the age of four than among younger children. Frequency scores could illuminate some of these changes but, clearly, the duration scores better reveal the nature of the developmental progression.

Very long behavior units are also amenable to duration analysis. Horowitz (1962) found that children exposed to pictures of best friends, as compared to children exposed to picture of neutral peers or a light stimulus, voluntarily remained longer in the situa- tion. Here, the duration measure suggests that motivational mani- festations derive from socialization in the peer group. Elsewhere,

the duration of longer behavior units has been used to measure
dependency motivation (Gewirtz, 1956), audience anxiety (Levin,
Baldwin, Gallwey, & Paivio, 1960), and exploratory motivation
(Rheingold & Eckerman, 1969).

Densities

Density measures are more common than duration measures in the
observational literature. As mentioned, Walters and associates
(cf. Walters & Parke, 1964) used total number of seconds during
which a child touched or manipulated a "forbidden" toy as an index
of resistance to deviation, and Liebert and Baron (1972) regarded
the total duration of the child's aggressive responses as the
measure which captured the greatest amount of information about the
effects of aggressive television on social behavior. These results
indicate that density may be theoretically-linked to avoidance
learning and to disinhibition--maybe even to acquisition. Exact
conclusions, however, concerning the manifestations measured by
response densities cannot be drawn from the existing literature
because the use of density measures remains rare.

Sequences

Another dimension of social activity derives from its sequential
nature. Sequences may be studied within the ongoing behavior stream
of single individuals or within two or more behavior streams involving many individuals. Sequential analysis, in its most rudimentary
form, consists of counting instances in which particular sequences
occur within a given time; in some instances, it may involve the
analysis of events following each other in ordinal sequence without
reference to the clock. Other discussions, in this volume and elsewhere (cf. Sackett, 1978), concern the exquisitely difficult problems
of sequential analysis. Suffice to say here that certain properties
of social activity, including the presence of accelerating and decelerating functions, cannot be studied without attention to sequential ordering. Situational elicitors of social activity cannot be
identified without sequential analysis, nor can the natural conditions associated with response termination. Regardless of the
psychological mechanism manifested--acquisition, extinction, inhibition, response competition, or catharsis--terminating conditions as
well as eliciting conditions can be studied *in situ* only with
sequential analysis.

Comment

No "user's guide" exists to assist the novice investigator in
making choices from among the measures available. We could use one.
Currently, one must search through scores of studies to discover an
instance in which the investigator reports a correlation between
latency scores and density scores (see Liebert & Baron, 1972) or
between frequency scores and latency scores (see Hartup, Moore, &
Sager, 1963). The circumstances under which latencies may be regarded

as manifestations of inhibition or disinhibition are not clearly
catalogued; the conditions under which rate measures may be regarded as indices of more-or-less stable traits or dispositions are not
specified; and the meaning of response amplitudes in many situations is unknown. Unfortunately, validation studies are not regarded as particularly interesting in psychological science, so the
behavioral manifestations measured by latencies, rates, durations,
and densities have never been systematically studied. The literature contains much lore about these matters, but investigators could
use a catalogue of their stock-in-trade and clearer notions about
its validity.

Research workers should be sensitive to the implications of
their parametric choices. Is the ubiquitous use of rate measures
justified? What does it mean to use a density or duration measure?
Our observation manuals are nearly silent on such matters. Hutt
and Hutt (1970) write:

> "If we focus primarily upon the morphology of the
> behavior, we may count the frequency with which
> different motor patterns are recruited, measure
> the total amount of time spent in particular postures
> or in making particular movements, compute the mean
> duration of such movements, and calculate their
> velocity. If we focus upon the functional aspect of
> behavior (i.e., what are its effects upon the environ-
> ment), we may count the number of stimuli sampled,
> measure the total amount of time spent in contact with
> a particular stimulus, compute the mean duration of
> contacts with each stimulus, and calculate the rate
> of change effected in a particular stimulus... In
> practice a complete analysis of behavior will consist
> of a conjunction of the two classes of measurement, a
> particular action being related to its environmental
> consequences (pp. 33-34)."

Perhaps. But a compendium of empirical support for these recommen-
dations does not exist.

Current conventions in multivariate research can also be questioned. Frequently, multivariate designs are used to cover the
investigator's bets rather than to explore the psychological manifestations involved in social activity. Measures are assumed *a
priori* to be interchangeable. When effects are not uniform, null
findings are ignored. To be sure, speculation *post hoc* cannot
explain such variations but, sometimes, these very "inconsistencies"
are suggestive. Thus, in her validation study of the picture sociometric technique, Horowitz (1972) found that children would produce
greater numbers of exposures to pictures of best friends than to
pictures of neutral peers (frequency scores) and would persist
longer at the task (a duration measure). On the other hand, rate-
of-response was not related to the stimulus conditions. What does
this mean? The author did not comment. The results, however,
suggested an interesting hypothesis: Sociometric choices are based

on motivational manifestations rather than the residuals of instrumental learning. Conventional assessment of multivariate results gives little consideration to variates associated with null findings; only results associated with rejection of the null hypothesis are assimilated into the literature.

Similar admonitions apply to the situation in which multivariate studies yield uniform results across measures. Sometimes such configurations may derive from spurious correlations (e.g., when frequency measures and density measures are used in the same analysis). Once such artifacts are ruled out, though, "consistent" results tell us that the experiment has had a wider range of behavioral effects than could be documented with the use of a single variate. Manipulations affecting *both* latencies and rate-of-response do not mean the same thing as manipulations affecting one but not the other. It is one thing to urge that investigators use multivariate research designs; it is another to draw sensitive conclusions from multivariate results.

SOCIAL ACTS: TO SPLIT OR NOT TO SPLIT?

Whatever the central issue in observational research, every investigator depends heavily on the selection of an appropriate system for classifying behavior. As Gellert (1955) observed, no classification system can be completely satisfactory "...since, by the very process of classification, violence must be done to the essential continuousness, and to the great complexity of human behavior." Use of "specimen records" and videotape recordings minimize selectivity by assuring the continuous, non-categorical recording of the entire behavior stream and situation of the child (see Wright, 1960). Every experienced observer knows, however, that physical and psychological constraints make certain that the final record will be selective.

Everyone who has ever written on the subject is agreed that classification systems must serve the research issue(s) at hand. What does this mean? That investigators should use valid classification systems? That classification systems must conform to armchair analyses of the natural world? Or be data-based? Considerable confusion surrounds this issue since investigators are notoriously unsystematic in rationalizing their choice of classification systems. Local traditions, rather than rational decisions, seem to determine whether the investigator will be a taxonomic "lumper" (i.e., who uses large, inclusive categories) or a taxonomic "splitter" (i.e., whose classification systems are based on smaller, less inclusive units). Factor analysis has shown that such molar constructs as attachment, aggression, altruism, sociability, and ascendance relate to molecular units in extremely complex ways. When tradition alone determines the classification system, then, the choice may or may not be appropriate.

Both naive theory (Heider, 1958) and the major personality theories are built around broad, molar constructs rather than narrow classes of social events. Attachment is a major theoretical

construct, not proximity-seeking; aggression elicits the consideration of research workers, not pushing and shoving; altruism subsumes
sharing; and achievement transcends grade-getting.

Underlying the use of broad, molar constructs is the notion of
functional equivalence--that distinctly different behaviors can
produce similar effects on the environment. Both following the
mother and talking to her relate to proximity-maintenance; both
striking another child and hurling insults can inflict pain and
suffering. Although morphologically dissimilar, insults and
physcial attack are thus equivalent in their environmental consequences. In this equivalence lies the basis for conceptually
linking the two social acts.

Functional equivalence seems to be a straightforward, uncompli-
cated idea. In a number of ways, though, it is a complex notion.
First, a social act rarely has only one function. Tugging at the
mother's skirts may secure her attention but simultaneously elicit
annoyance and aggression. Or, tugging at the mother's skirts may
secure positive attention in one situation but negative attention
in another. Given that most social acts have multiple effects on
the environment, it is not easy to establish the functional equivalence of different behaviors across time and across situations.
Second, short-term vicissitudes may determine that a child fusses
at his mother and clings to her on one occasion, while he calls to
her and shows his toys to get her attention on another. Third,
longer-term vicissitudes, associated with the processes of socialization, determine that seeking physical contact, following the
mother from place to place, and clinging to her skirts may characterize the attachment activities of an 18-month-old child while
intellectual or physical accomplishments may be used to obtain
praise and attention when this same child reaches the age of six.
Other transformations, across situation and across time, occur
in later childhood, adolescence, and adulthood. Constructs like
attachment thus cover a wide range of social acts, patterned in a
manner that varies widely from child to child, from situation to
situation, and from time to time. To use such constraints, then,
it must be assumed that extraordinarily diverse actions share common
functions.

Few investigators have bothered to demonstrate functional equivalence empirically. In a series of early studies, the term
dependency was used to subsume: a) clinging or seeking affection
from teachers, clinging or seeking affection from children, seeking
attention or approval from teachers, and seeking attention or
approval from children (Heathers, 1955); b) touching or holding,
being near, securing positive attention, securing reassurance,
comfort, or consolation, and securing negative attention (Sears,
Whiting, Nowlis, & Sears, 1953); c) seeking physical contact, seeking to be near, seeking reassurance, seeking positive attention,
seeking help, and seeking negative attention (Mann, 1959); d)
attention-seeking, questions, comments, glances, paintings, praise-
seeking, help-seeking, permission-seeking, and time-in-session
(Gewirtz, 1956). The inclusion of such diverse elements in these
studies was based on a clear logic: each element relates *a priori*
to securing contact with other individuals and/or nurturance from

them. But was the functional equivalence of these elements established empirically? Next to nothing was known prior to these
studies about interrelations among individual differences in these
social acts and/or their instrumental value.

Both the studies cited and more recent investigations show
that these measures actually define a diffuse domain. First, intercorrelations are near-zero (cf. Mann, 1959; Sears, Whiting, Nowlis,
& Sears, 1953). Certain measures are significantly intercorrelated
owing to the sequential nature of the social activity. For example,
Gewirtz (1956) reported positive correlations among measures of
attention-seeking, questions, and comments, but these three elements occurred in sequence during the observation session thus
assuring that they would be significantly interrelated. Second,
factor analytic studies reveal a diverse domain. Gewirtz (1956)
reported the existence of two distinct dimensions of attention-
seeking in one observational study: a) active, direct verbal
attempts to gain or maintain the attention of the adult; and b)
nonverbal, passive actions used by children when there exists conflict about more direct means of gaining attention. The findings
even suggest that one of these components (active attention-seeking)
may be two-dimensional.

Circumstances have not been much better in observational studies
of infant attachment. In one series of investigations (Stayton &
Ainsworth, 1973; Coates, Anderson, & Hartup, 1972; Maccoby & Feldman, 1972), the evidence for consistency across situations and
across behaviors varied widely from measure to measure and from
study to study. Substantial intercorrelations among some attachment
behaviors were sometimes noted (e.g., between touching and proximity-seeking) but these derived, again, from the behavioral sequences in which the social acts were embedded rather than from
co-variation among independent social events. (E.g., Children must
be close to their mothers in order to touch them.) The failure
to discover substantial intercorrelations among the various attachment behaviors may stem from the use of unreliable measures and
small samples (cf. Masters & Wellman, 1974), but it is not likely
that functional equivalence can ever be demonstrated via intercorrelations among such environmentally labile activities as looking
at the mother, vocalizing to her, touching her, crying in her
absence, and clinging during reunion. Wide variations exist in
the contingencies associated with these social acts from the
earliest months of life; such variations are almost certain to
produce extensive individual differences in the organization of
the child's social activity with respect to the mother (Bowlby,
1969; Weisberg, 1963).

Disagreement remains concerning the best way to conceptualize
the relation bewteen molecular and molar structures. No one seriously argues that proximity-seeking (as measured by following the
mother about the house) is irrelevant to the construct of attachment even though individual differences may be minimally correlated
with individual differences in other theoretically-relevant behaviors.
Sroufe and Waters (1977) have argued that investigators ought to take
an organizational approach in classifying attachment activity.

Accordingly, focus needs to be shifted from the presence or absence of designated molecular units to the presence or absence of behavioral "organizations" measuring the security or insecurity of the child's tie to the mother. Stable individual differences were observed by these investigators when molar measures were used that simultaneously stressed: a) proximity-seeking; b) avoidance and resistance during reunion; and c) failure to cease crying during reunion. Qualities of attachment to the mother assessed in this manner at 18 months of age were also found to predict successful problem-solving at 24 months of age (Matas, 1977) and effectance in peer relations at 3 years (Waters, Wippman, & Sroufe, 1978). It is interesting to note that, in this instance, the organizational assessment of infant attachment was parametrically heterogeneous: frequencies, latencies, and intensities were used at many different levels of analysis to derive the single molar measure for classifying mother-child relations in terms of the "security" of attachment.

Another method for determining the relation between molar and molecular structures is to search for commonalities across theoretically-related social acts in their elicitors, terminating conditions, and developmental progressions. Masters and Wellman (1974) pointed out that certain sequences of events evoke a concordant series of behavior changes from many individuals even though individual differences in the magnitude of these changes may not be correlated. Thus, high concordance was observed to occur across infants in behavior changes from a preseparation to a postseparation session constructed by Coates, Anderson, and Hartup (1972): most subjects increased visual regard of the mother, touching her, proximity-seeking, and crying, even though individual differences in frequency scores were not highly correlated. Maccoby and Feldman (1972) also reported increases in crying and decreases in manipulative play from preseparation to postseparation, and Ainsworth and Wittig (1969) reported that the incidence of crying prior to separation from the mother was lower than its incidence in other situations-- including reunion with the mother after separation. Additional commonalities were observed in the children's behavior toward the mother in the presence of a stranger. Maccoby and Feldman (1972), for example, found increases in crying and proximity-seeking along with decreases in manipulative play and distance-attention bids. Altogether, these commonalities describe a broad, central orientation in social relations earmarked by: a) distress at separation from the mother, and b) the use of the mother as a "secure base" in the presence of a fear-evoking stimulus. Whether such commonalities were produced by integrated socialization pressues or whether they reflect common motive states cannot be asserted. But, at a descriptive level, the commonalities define concordance in mother-child relations that justify the use of a molar construct (i.e., attachment).

Developmental commonalities can also be used to connect molecular and molar structures in social behavior. Maccoby and Feldman (1972) observed one group of children at 2, 2 1/2, and 3 years of age. The following were the major results: a) in the presence of the mother, manipulative play and the use of distance-

attention bids were directly related to chronological age while
crying and proximity-seeking were inversely related to this variable; b) in the absence of the mother, manipulative play was directly related to age and crying was inversely related to age; c) in
the presence of a stranger, manipulative play was directly related
to age while crying and proximity-seeking were inversely related
to the age variable. Considered separately, these associations do
not reveal much about molar structures in social activity. Taken
together, the age changes suggest concordant progressions wherein
proximal set-goals permit the child to explore more widely in the
presence of the mother with increasing age. Although individual
differences are not highly intercorrelated in these data, coherence
in the behavior system is suggested by the commonalities existing
in the developmental changes.

Most investigators use a combination of deductive reasoning
and empirical observation to select theoretically-relevant social
acts to be considered in commonality analysis. Bowlby's (1969)
list of "attachment behaviors" (e.g., sucking, smiling, crying,
vocalizing, clinging, and following) was constructed in this
manner, and several commonality analyses of infant attachment have
been based on it (Masters & Wellman, 1974; Smith, 1977). Alternatively, the investigator can select social acts as theoretically-
relevant by more inductive means. Beginning with a large, heterogeneous and undifferentiated set of acts, factor analytic methods
can then be used to demonstrate equivalencies among them. Certain
ethologists (e.g., Blurton Jones, 1972) have argued that inductive
methods of this kind are superior to deductive methods. Factor
analysis, however, is only inductive when the original correlation
matrices are based on large numbers of undifferentiated measures.
A matrix that includes only items pre-selected on the basis of
guesses about functional equivalence will yield a deductively-
derived structure rather than an inductively-derived one.

Most commonly, categorical systems are selected deductively.
In the case of aggression, both hitting and derogation will be
observed on the grounds that each produces injury or damage.
In the case of attachment, both clinging to the mother in her
presence and crying in her absence will be observed since each may
bring about contact between mother and child. The investigator
thus builds-in a connection between molecular and molar structures
a priori. Whether these connections stem from formal theory or
naive notions about the organization of social activity is not
important. Empirical verification of the connections must occur,
however, because a priori assumptions about functional equivalence
may be wildly mistaken.

No ethogram exists to elucidate the manner in which social
activity is organized across various levels of analysis. "Lumpers"
remain convinced that essential nuances are neglected when social
relations are described reductionistically. "Splitters" remain
convinced that the conditions under which molecular elements appear
and disappear within integrated behavior systems (e.g., attachment
or aggression) can be understood only through differentiated measurement. We contend, however, that this very "integration" of molecular

units into more generalized behavior systems is the occurrence that necessitates simultaneous study at different levels of analysis. To the extent that ontogenesis involves either integration or hierarchization in social activity, molecular and molar structures must eventually be linked together within a single data base.

Contemporary technologies, including video-tape apparatus, portable devices for data recording, and computer software, are available to assist in the simultaneous examination of social activity at different levels. Fitzpatrick (1977a; 1977b) has invented an efficient multiple event sampling device (ELOG) with online capacity for storing both simultaneous and successive events, including the durations and densities of social acts as well as their frequencies. Software (BEHAVE) is available to give a cumulative and continuous data stream over a large number of variables along with their sequential properties.

In one demonstration series, we examined the relation between dominance structures (Level I) and various modes of communication (Level II) occurring in sibling interaction. Dominance was used as a molar construct to describe interchanges in which one child tried to change the behavior of the other--specifically, by *calling attention, making negative demands,* or *attempting to take objects* (toys). Communication was coded in terms of *visual attention, vocalizing, manipulation of objects, locomotion,* and *physical contact.* Sequential analysis of the response densities revealed the following behavioral clusters: a) *Call attention*--both visual attention and object manipulation were directed principally at the child's own acts before, during, and after these incidents; verbalization was common during these acts; locomotion was minimal. b) *Negative demands*--object manipulation was common both before and after such acts, increasing during the act; visual attention was directed at the other child during the act and object manipulation was likely to be dyadic rather than monadic; speech densities were relatively low. c) *Attempts to take object*--interaction resembled "negative demands" except that visual attention to the other child accompanied the act even more consistently; speech densities during the act were lower.

Whether these sequences characterize the dominance interactions of other children is not known. But the data fragments suggest that visual attention is embedded in dominance interaction in ways not suggested by theories linking attention structures and dominance hierarchies (Abramovitch, 1975). Multiple levels of analysis also can be used to examine developmental changes in dominance activity, continuities and change in individual differences, and situational constraints on such interaction. It is increasingly clear, for example, that toys play a fundamental role in early dominance interactions. To understand their value as social stimuli requires simultaneous examination of commonalities at both molecular and molar levels (see Eckerman, in press).

Comment

Insufficient attention has been given to the linkage between

molecular and molar structures in social activity. Examination of
molecular units is compatible with the study of broad configurations.
Molecular elements may be studied in relation to molar constructs
without making the assumption that the smaller unit is an "index"
of the larger one. Indeed, the outcomes (functions) of broad
classes of social activity should be studied more often with
morphological structures simultaneously under analysis.

SOCIAL RELATIONS: TO SPLIT OR NOT TO SPLIT?

Although the term "social interaction" is used extensively in
the observational literature, most studies are centered on the
actions of individuals who are engaged in social interaction, not
on social interactions *per se*. (For example, attachments are nearly
always conceptualized as characteristics of the child, not as features of the child's interactions with the parent.) Sometimes, the
essential elements contained in an interactive event can be extracted
by combining monadic units, either across individuals or in sequential
analysis (cf. Sears, 1951). But, many times, the systemic features
of social interaction require examination of the total ebb and flow
of social activity occurring over time--"... by looking at the social
system and not at the individual roles" (Bales, 1950).
According to Hinde (1976), social relationships can be classified in terms of: a) the content of the interaction; b) the diversity of the interaction (i.e., whether relationships are marked by
single or multiple content); c) the quality of the interaction;
d) degree of reciprocity (symmetry) in constrast to complementarity
(asymmetry); e) the frequency and patterning of the interaction;
and f) the degree of intimacy. Children's social relations are
rarely classified in more than one of two ways; usually, the classification is based on interactional content. Thus, the infant-
caretaker relationship is described in terms of the affective and
motoric events occurring between the infant and an adult (Maccoby
& Feldman, 1972) or the characteristic organization of these events
(Ainsworth, 1972; Sroufe & Waters, 1977). By and large, interactional diversity, reciprocity and intimacy are used to classify
social relations more frequently by clinical psychologists and
psychiatrists (cf. Sullivan, 1973) than by developmental psychologists.
Each dimension used in describing social relationships can be
applied to multiple levels. Interactional content, for example,
can be used to classify relationships in broad, functional terms
(e.g., caretaker-child relationships and spouse relationships).
Within these classes, sub-classes can be identified (e.g., basic
caretaking interactions; teaching/learning interactions; play
interactions). And, within each of these sub-classes, more specific interactions can be isolated (e.g., feeding, toileting, and
comforting; direct tuition, imitation, and means-ends connections;
rough-and-tumble interactions and organized games). Finally, within
these interactions, classifications can be based on specific
communication modes. For example, teaching/learning interactions

can be studied according to the occurrence of verbal elaborations, repetitions, or the discriminate use of rewards and punishment. By simultaneous classification of social relations across different levels of analysis, basic communication processes, their development, and the broader functions of the relationships themselves can be understood better.

Observers have scarcely begun the task of describing social relations in multi-dimensional terms at multiple levels of analysis. Much of the required methodology is available, but an enormous task remains. Multiple analysis is indispensible, however, to the understanding of social relationships in both ontogenetic and evolutionary perspective.

CONCLUSION

It has been argued that observational research would benefit from the use of a broader range of assessment parameters than traditionally employed. Whether one's intentions are to study social acts or social relations, the use of multiple levels of analysis should be encouraged. Such strategies are needed in numerous investigations--including studies of individual differences, studies of the processes of socialization, and studies of social activity in situational context.

ACKNOWLEDGEMENT

Financial support in the preparation of this essay was provided by grant No. HD PO1 5027, to the Institute of Child Development, University of Minnesota.

REFERENCES

Abramovitch, R. S. The relation of attention and proximity to dominance in pre-school children. Unpublished doctoral dissertation, University of Minnesota, 1975.

Ainsworth, M. D. S., & Wittig, B. A. Attachment and exploratory behavior of one-year-olds in a strange situation. In B. M. Foss (Ed.), *Determinants of infant behavior* (Vol. 4). London: Methuen, 1969.

Ainsworth, M. D. S. Attachment and dependency: A comparison. In J. L. Gewirtz (Ed.), *Attachment and dependency*. New York: Wiley, 1972.

Arrington, R. E. Interrelations in the behavior of young children. *Child Development Monographs*, 1932, No. 8.

Bales, R. F. *Interaction process analysis: A method for the study of small groups*. Cambridge: Addison-Wesley, 1950.

Blurton Jones, N. Categories of child-child interaction. In N. Blurton Jones (Ed.), *Ethological studies of child behaviour*. Cambridge: The University Press, 1972.

Brady-Smith, J. E., Newcomb, A. F., & Hartup, W. W. Friendship and
    incentive conditions as determinants of children's social
    problem-solving. Paper presented at the Meeting of the Ameri-
    can Psychological Association, Toronto, August, 1978.
Bowlby, J. *Attachment*. New York: Basic Books, 1969.
Coates, B., Anderson, E. P., & Hartup, W. W. Interrelations in
    the attachment behavior of human infants. *Developmental
    Psychology*, 1972, *6*, 218-230.
Dawe, H. C. Analysis of two hundred quarrels of preschool children.
    Child Development, 1934, *5*, 139-157.
Eckerman, C. O. The human infant in social interaction. In R. B.
    Cairns (Ed.), *Social interaction: Methods, analysis, and
    illustrations*. Hillsdale, N.J.: Erlbaum, in press.
Ekman, P., Liebert, R. M., Friesen, W. V., Harrison, R., Zlatchin,
    C., Malmstrom, E. J., & Baron, R. A. Facial expressions of
    emotion while watching televised violence as predictors of
    subsequent aggression. In G. A. Comstock, E. A. Rubinstein,
    & J. P. Murray (Eds.), *Television and social behavior* (Vol. 5).
    Washington: U.S. Department of Health, Education, and Welfare,
    1972.
Fitzpatrick, L. J. Automated data collection for observed events.
    Behavior Research Methods and Instrumentation, 1977, *9*, 447-
    451. (a)
Fitzpatrick, L. J. BEHAVE: An automated data analysis system for
    observed events. *Behavior Research Methods and Instrumentation*,
    1977, *9*, 452-455. (b)
Foot, H. C., Chapman, A. J., & Smith, J. R. Friendship and social
    responsiveness in boys and girls. *Journal of Personality and
    Social Psychology*, 1977, *35*, 401-411.
Gellert, E. Systematic observation: A method in child study.
    Harvard Educational Review, 1955, *25*, 179-195.
Gewirtz, J. L. A factor analysis of some attention-seeking behaviors
    of young children. *Child Development*, 1956, *27*, 17-36.
Goodenough, F. L. *Anger in young children*. Minneapolis: University
    of Minnesota Press, 1931.
Hartup, W. W. Social learning, social interaction, and social
    development. In P. J. Elich (Ed.), *Fourth Western symposium
    on learning: Social learning*. Bellingham, Wash.: Western
    Washington State College, 1973.
Hartup, W. W. Aggression in childhood: Developmental perspectives.
    American Psychologist, 1974, *29*, 336-341.
Hartup, W. W., Moore, S. G., & Sager, G. O. Avoidance of inappropri-
    ate sex-typing by young children. *Journal of Consulting Psycho-
    logy*, 1963, *27*, 467-473.
Heathers, G. Emotional dependence and independence in nursery school
    play. *Journal of Genetic Psychology*, 1955, *87*, 37-57.
Heider, F. *The psychology of interpersonal relations*. New York:
    Wiley, 1958.
Hetherington, E. M. The effects of familial variables on sex typing,
    on parent-child similarity, and on imitation in children. In
    J. P. Hill (Ed.), *Minnesota symposia on child psychology* (Vol.
    1). Minneapolis: University of Minnesota Press, 1967.

Hinde, R. A.   On describing relationships.   *Journal of Child Psychology and Psychiatry*, 1976, *17*, 1-19.

Horowitz, F. D.   Incentive value of social stimuli for preschool children.   *Child Development*, 1962, *33*, 111-116.

Hutt, S. J., & Hutt, C.   *Direct observation and measurement of behavior*.   Springfield, Ill.:   C. S. Thomas, 1970.

Jack, L. M.   An experimental study of ascendant behavior in preschool children.   *University of Iowa Studies in Child Welfare*, 1934, *9*, No. 3.

Jersild, A. T., & Markey, F. V.   Conflicts between preschool children.   *Child Development Monographs*, 1935, No. 21.

Kobasigawa, A.   Observation of failure in another person as a determinant of amplitude and speed of a simple motor response.   *Journal of Personality and Social Psychology*, 1965, *1*, 626-630.

Levin, H., Baldwin, A. L., Gallwey, M., & Paivio, A.   Audience stress, personality, and speech.   *Journal of Abnormal and Social Psychology*, 1960, *61*, 469-473.

Liebert, R. M., & Baron, R. A.   Short-term effects of televised aggression on children's aggressive behavior.   In J. P. Murray, E. A. Rubinstein, & G. A. Comstock (Eds.), *Television and social behavior* (Vol. 2).   Washington: U.S. Department of Health, Education and Welfare, 1972.

Lippitt, R., & White, R. K.   An experimental study of leadership and group life.   In R. G. Barker, J. S. Kounin, & H. F. Wright (Eds.), *Child behavior and development*.   New York: McGraw-Hill, 1943.

Maccoby, E. E., & Feldman, S. S.   Mother-attachment and stranger-reactions in the third year of life.   *Monographs of the Society for Research in Child Development*, 1972, *31* (Whole No. 146).

Mann, N.   Dependency in relation to maternal attitudes.   Unpublished master's thesis, State University of Iowa, 1959.

Masters, J. C., Barden, R. C., & Ford, M. E.   Affective states and learning.   Unpublished manuscript, University of Minnesota, 1978.

Masters, J. C., & Wellman, H.   The study of human infant attachment: A procedural critique.   *Psychological Bulletin*, 1974, *81*, 218-237.

Matas, L.   The mother-child relationship and the development of competence during the second year of life.   Unpublished doctoral dissertation, University of Minnesota, 1977.

McGrew, W. C.   *An ethological study of children's behavior*.   New York: Academic Press, 1972.

Mischel, W.   *Personality and assessment*.   New York: Wiley, 1968.

Morgan, G. A., & Ricciuti, H. N.   Infants' responses to strangers during the first year.   In B. M. Foss (Ed.), *Determinants of infant behavior* (Vol. 4).   London: Methuen, 1969.

Murphy, L. B.   *Social behavior and child personality: Some roots of sympathy*.   New York: Columbia University Press, 1937.

Oster, H., & Ekman, P.   Facial behavior in child development.   In W. A. Collins (Ed.), *Minnesota symposia on child psychology* (Vol. 11).   Hillsdale, N.J.:   Erlbaum, in press.

Parke, R. D.   Interactional designs.   In R. B. Cairns (Ed.),
    Social interaction: Methods, analysis, and illustrations.
    Hillsdale, N.J.:   Erlbaum, in press.
Parten, M. B.   Social participation among preschool children.
    Journal of Abnormal and Social Psychology, 1932, *27,* 243-269.
Patterson, G. R.   A performance theory for coercive family inter-
    action.   In R. B. Cairns (Ed.), *Social interaction: Methods,
    analysis, and illustrations.*   Hillsdale, N.J.:   Erlbaum, in
    press.
Patterson, G. R., Littman, R. A., & Bricker, W.   Assertive behavior
    in children: A step toward a theory of aggression.   *Monographs
    of the Society for Research in Child Development,* 1967, *32*
    (Whole No. 113).
Rheingold, H. L., & Eckerman, C. O.   The infant's free entry into
    a new environment.   *Journal of Experimental Child Psychology,*
    1969, *8,* 271-283.
Rheingold, H. L., & Eckerman, C. O.   Some proposals for unifying
    the study of social development.   In M. Lewis & L. A. Rosenblum
    (Eds.), *Friendship and peer relations.*   New York: Wiley, 1975.
Sackett, G. P.   *Observing behavior* (Vol. 2).   Baltimore: University
    Park Press, 1978.
Sears, R. R.   A theoretical framework for personality and social
    behavior.   *American Psychologist,* 1951, *6,* 476-483.
Sears, R. R., Whiting, J. W. M., Nowlis, V., & Sears, P. S.   Some
    child rearing antecedents of dependency and aggression in young
    children.   *Genetic Psychology Monographs,* 1953, *47,* 135-144.
Smith, L., & Martinsen, H.   The behavior of young children in a
    strange situation.   *Scandinavian Journal of Psychology,* 1977,
    18, 43-52.
Sroufe, L. A., & Waters, E.   Attachment as an organizational
    construct.   *Child Development,* 1977, *48,* 1184-1199.
Stayton, D. J., & Ainsworth, M. D. S.   Individual differences in
    infant responses to brief separations as related to other
    infant and maternal behaviors.   *Developmental Psychology,* 1973,
    9, 226-235.
Sullivan, H. S.   *The interpersonal theory of psychiatry.*   New York:
    Norton, 1953.
Walters, R. H., & Brown, M.   A test of the high-magnitude theory of
    aggression.   *Journal of Experimental Child Psychology,* 1964, *1,*
    376-387.
Walters, R. H., Leat, M., & Mezei, L.   Response inhibition and dis-
    inhibition through empathetic learning.   *Canadian Journal of
    Psychology,* 1963, *17,* 235-243.
Walters, R. H., & Parke, R. D.   Influence of the response consequences
    to a social model on resistance to deviation.   *Journal of
    Experimental Child Psychology,* 1964, *1,* 269-280.
Walters, R. H., Parke, R. D., & Cane, V. A.   Timing of punishment and
    the observation of consequences to others as determinants of
    response inhibition.   *Journal of Experimental Child Psychology,*
    1965, *2,* 10-30.
Waters, E., Wippman, J., & Sroufe, L. A.   Attachment, positive
    affect and competence.   Unpublished manuscript, University of
    Minnesota, 1978.

Weisberg, P. Social and nonsocial conditioning of infant vocalizations. *Child Development,* 1963, *34,* 377-388.

Woodworth, R. S., & Schlossberg, H. *Experimental psychology.* New York: Holt, Rinehart, and Winston, 1954.

Wright, H. F. Observational child study. In P. H. Mussen (Ed.), *Handbook of research methods in child development.* New York: Wiley, 1960.

3.
Analysis of face-to-face interaction in infant-adult dyads

HEIDELISE ALS, EDWARD TRONICK, & T. BERRY BRAZELTON

Every researcher's theoretical framework influences his/her choice of methodology and methodology determines to a large extent the theoretical questions s/he can answer. Our model of early human development is based on the notion of complex differentiation and sequential reintegration of the organism's systems of functioning within the adaptive matrix of social interaction with adult conspecifics. For instance, the healthy term newborn is structured in such a way that it elicits from the adult caregiver the stimulation and organization it needs in order to maintain current functional homeostasis. The infant becomes increasingly skilled in the achievement and maintenance of this functional homeostasis. This allows it to attend to and incorporate important stimuli from the environment or to actively defend itself from them by shutting them out. Its ability to reach its own homeostasis, in turn, provides the infant with the necessary base and the flexibility to facilitate the emergence of the next level of organization. The provision of organization which takes place in continuous adaptation to and feedback from the environment potentiates the newborn's increasing differentiation. This differentiation comes from an internalized recognition of the infant's capacity to reach out for and to shut off social stimuli. It, in turn, results in growing complexity of the interactional channels and structures, thus increasing the opportunities for the individual system's differentiation. Given such a flexible system the infant's individuality is continuously fitted to and shaped by that of the adult. Our model is that of a feedback system of increasing expansion and potentiation of the developing organism embedded in and catalyzed by the interaction with his conspecifics (see also Brazelton, Tronick, & Als, 1977; Tronick & Brazelton, 1977).

33

The limits of this process of differentiation and expansion are set by the genetic endowment of the organism. The concretization of his unique development is influenced by the "opportunities" presented by the environment in the organism/environment transaction realized. The critical features of these transactions are the appropriateness of the structure of stimulation from the interaction and the appropriateness of timing of stimulation.

Goal of Research

The goal of our research is to identify situations which allow us to assess the structure of the current organization of the developing organism and to identify the ingredients of the organism-environment transaction. We hope to articulate the 1) levels of organization, 2) the degree of differentiation and 3) the unique characteristics of system regulation. These three aspects, the level of organization, the degree of differentiation, and the unique style of regulation are general aspects of functioning.

Strategy

The issue is to cull from a broad-based knowledge of the organism's spectrum of functioning the essence of newly emerging skills and capacities at each level in order to identify the current "developmental agendum" the organism is negotiating. The next task is to then devise situations appropriate to systematically elicit these newly emerging skills and, thus, see the current structure and limits of the organism's functioning.

Target Organism

We are focusing on the behavioral organization of the young infant in the first few months of life in the context of the caregiver-infant interaction in order to assess its newly emerging organizational capacities. The first item on a newborn's agenda is control over the physiological system, particularly breathing, heartrate, and temperature control. For preterm and at-risk full-term newborns this control is more difficult to achieve than it is for healthy full-term newborns. While control over these basic physiological demands is being achieved, the newborn begins to establish organization and differentiation of the motor system, affecting the range, smoothness and complexity of movement. The next major agendum is achieving a stable organization of its states of consciousness. The goals of this differentiation are to have all six states from deep sleep to intense crying available to the infant and to have transitions between states carried out more smoothly. Achieving control over transitions between states demands an integration of the control over the physiological and motoric systems and the states of consciousness. The adult caretaker can play the role of organizer (Sander, 1977) and can begin to expand certain states, e.g., the quiet, alert state, as well as the duration and quality of sleep states. In addition, the caregiver can help regulate the transitions between states for the infant.

As the state organization becomes differentiated and begins to be regulated, usually in the course of the first month, the next newly emerging expansion is that of the increasing differentiation of the alert state. The infant's social capacities begin to unfold. Its ability to communicate becomes increasingly sophisticated. The repertoire of facial expressions and their use, the range and use of vocalizations, cries, gestures, and postures in interaction with a social partner begins to expand. On the basis of well-modulated state organization it can negotiate this new range and regulation of social interaction skills.

METHODOLOGY

We have designed a face-to-face interaction paradigm in the laboratory to serve as an opportunity to maximize the display of social interaction skills between adult and infant. The infant is seated semi-upright in an infant seat. The mother is instructed to "play" with the infant without picking it up. The face-to-face situation in the laboratory is a stressful situation in that it provides no functional goals other than a situation for intense interaction. In that way it forces both partners to use any skills and resources they have to engage one another within a mutually satisfying cyclical interchange, but foremost it demands the newly emergent capacities of the well-developed infant in the first few months of life.

In this situation the infant has to 1) control its posture, sitting in an upright position in an infant seat, 2) maintain an alert state, 3) control its motor arousal, 4) control the autonomic demands this engenders, 5) process complex social information, and 6) simultaneously enact its own goals for the interaction. This situation, then, taps the important organization systems available to the very young infant (Brazelton, Tronick, Adamson, Als, & Wise, 1975).

Age of Infant

We have found that a 3-minute face-to-face session with healthy infants up to 5 months of age produces a typical sequence of engagement, acceleration of attention by each partner, a period of reciprocal play and cyclical attention, followed by deceleration of attention (Tronick, Als, & Brazelton, 1977; Tronick, Als, & Adamson, 1978). This then has become the target sequence for our analysis of reciprocity.

Sample

The core sample on which the analysis systems were developed consists of 12 healthy mothers and their normal full-term infants. All infants had been delivered at the Boston Hospital for Women. Recruitment of mothers occurred during the lying-in period. Mothers

were told that we were interested in the development of the social
capacities of infants during the first 6 months of infancy. Infants
were brought to the laboratory as soon as the mother felt comfortable
in taking her infant out. This varied from 11 to 28 days. All the
infants were seen at least once before they were 1-month-old and at
weekly time intervals through the 2nd month. Visits were 2 to 3
weeks apart from the 3rd through the 6th months. All infants missed
occasional sessions but at least 8 sessions were recorded for each
infant. Immediately after videotaping in the laboratory, we watched
the tape of that session with the mother and discussed how the
infant behaved. Our contacts with the mothers were relaxed, and
we felt that we and they were involved in a mutually shared project.

Use of Videotape

We have chosen videotape as our recording technique since it
makes the sequence immediately and repeatedly available for play-
back. We use a split-screen, two-camera system which allows us
to see simultaneously infant and caregiver in full-face view. The
passage of real time is visualized by a digital timer exact to a
100th of a second and displayed on the image. The recorded tape
can be played back at real time speed, slowed to 1/7th of real
time, or displayed frame by frame. This allows us to analyze a
sequence repeatedly and as slowly as is necessary (Brazelton
et al., 1975).

Systems of Analysis

The task of the process of interaction analysis, as we see it,
contains several steps. Figure 1 gives an overview of our approach.
We are using essentially two tracks of analysis which feed each
other, one a qualitative, descriptive track, and one a quantitative
track. These dual tracks provide checks for each other at each
step. The first step is that of data reduction. The form of data
reduction on the qualitative track is the narrative. It uses
elaborate prose to describe in 30-second by 30-second segments
what one sees happening for each partner in the attempt to capture
the flow of the interaction. On the quantitative track data reduction consists of the development of a quantifiable unit system which
we call the microbehavioral component specification. The first step
in achieving this microbehavioral system is a fine-grained segmentation of the observed behavior into definable units of behavior.
Then descriptors are developed, catalogued, and classified. A
discrete code number is assigned to each descriptor. A time period
is found which is appropriate to the units of behavior decided upon,
that is, the time period should be such that one whole behavioral
unit, but only one, can occur within the allotted time span. Thus,
the data are reduced on the one hand into prose, on the other hand
into coded micro units of behavior.
    On the basis of these data reductions, three major hypotheses
have been generated: 1) We can quantify second-by-second the
affective level of each partner; 2) we can quantify the regulation

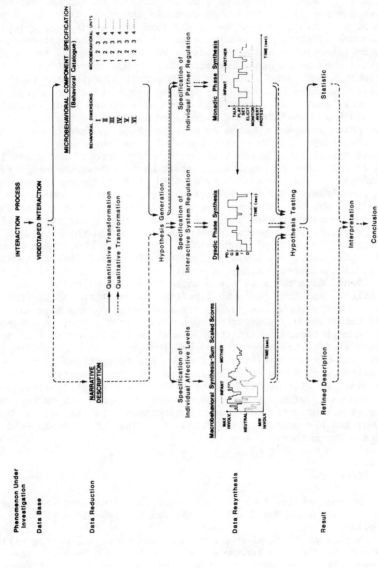

FIGURE 1. Model of Levels of Interaction Process Analysis.

of the interactive system as a whole; 3) we can quantify the regulation of each partner within the interactive system. We have developed three quantified systems of data resynthesis in order to be able
to test these hypotheses: 1) the Macrobehavioral Sum Scaled Scores,
2) the Dyadic Phases, and 3) the Monadic Phases, each leading to
a specific quantitative display of the data which can be used to
answer particular questions. The result can then either be in the
form of a statistic or can be in the form of a refined description.
Either one of them, the statistic or the refined description, can
then be interpreted and a conclusion reached in regards to the
original phenomenon under investigation. Thus, several alternate
or simultaneous paths of analysis are possible, depending on the
specific question at hand. For instance, one could choose a
completely qualitative path, indicated by a broken line in Figure
1. This would lead from the videotaped interaction via a narrative
description to dyadic phases or monadic phases scored in real time
from the videotape. From either one of those one could obtain a
refined description, which then could be interpreted and a conclusion drawn. Another possibility would be to choose the completely
quantitative path, indicated by a solid line in Figure 1, and go
from the videotaped interaction to microbehavioral components
specification, to either macrobehavioral scaled sum scores or to
dyadic or monadic phases and from either one of those to a statistic
appropriate to the hypothesis being tested, which then could be
interpreted and a conclusion reached. There are many other alternate paths, e.g., one could go from the videotaped interaction to
the microbehavioral components specification (a quantitative transformation), from there to the monadic phases (a quantitative transformation), and from there to a refined description (a qualitative
transformation). Or one could, for instance, go from the videotaped interaction via descriptors scored directly from the videotape in real time (a qualitative transformation) to monadic phases
(a quantitative transformation), and from there to a statistic (a
quantitative transformation). Some of the transitions of this system
are better worked out at this time than others. Some are not yet
possible. We will explain on the basis of two sample interactions
the components of these analyses systems and their respective functions as we currently see them. Interaction I is that of an 80-day-
old boy and his mother; interaction II is that of an 86-day-old
girl and her mother.

DATA REDUCTION

The qualitative form of data reduction first leads to a *narrative description*. The first interaction (80-day-old boy) is described
as follows:
The infant is looking off to the side where the mother will
come in. He lies completely quiet, back in his baby seat, face
serious, cheeks droopy, mouth half open, corners down, but there is
an expectant look in his eyes as if he were waiting. His face and
hands are reaching out in the same direction. As his mother comes

in, saying, "Hello", in a high-pitched, gentle voice, he follows
her with his head and eyes and she approaches him. His body builds
up with tension, his face and eyes open up with a real greeting
which ends with a smile. His mouth opens wide and his whole body
orients toward her. He subsides, mouthes his tongue twice, his
smile dies and he looks down briefly, while she continues to talk
in an increasingly eliciting voice. During this, his voice and
face are still, but all parts of his body except his face and eyes
point toward her. After he looks down, she reaches for and begins
to move his hips and legs in a gentle, containing movement. He
looks up again, smiles widely, narrows his eyes, brings one hand
up to his mouth, grunting, vocalizing, and begins to cycle his arms
and legs out toward her. With this increasing activity, she begins
to grin more widely, to talk more loudly and with higher-pitched
accents, accentuating his vocalizations with hers and his activity
with her movements of his legs. The grunting vocalizations and
smiles, as well as the cycling activity of his arms and legs come
and go in bursts--making up small cycles of movement and attention
toward her. She contains his hips with her hands as if to contain
the peaks of his excitement (30 seconds).

Meanwhile, with her voice and her face, as well as with her
hands, she both subsides with and accentuates his behavior with
her own. He looks down again, gets sober at 40 seconds, makes a
pouting face. She looks down at his feet at this point, then comes
back to look into his face as he returns to look up at her. She
lets go of his legs, and they draw up towards his body. He bursts
out with a broad smile and a staccato-like vocalization for three
repetitions (60 seconds). Each time, his face broadens and mouth
opens wide, his legs and arms thrust out toward her. She seems to
get caught up in his bursts, and smiles broadly, her voice getting
brighter, too. After each burst, he subsides to a serious face,
limbs quiet, and her quieting response follows his.

At 70 seconds, he subsides completely, and looks down at his
feet with a darkly serious face. She gets very still, her face becomes serious, her voice slows down and almost stops, the pitch becomes low. Her mouth is drawn down, reflecting his serious mouth.
After three seconds, he begins to brighten again into a wide, tonguing
smile. This time, he is more self-contained, holding back on the
movement of his extremities and his excitement. She responds immediately cocks her head coyly, smiles gently and her voice gently begins
to build up again. He builds up to two more staccato vocalizations
with smiles and jerky, cycling movements of his legs out toward her.
She contains his hips, and this time her voice doesn't build up to
a peak of excitement with him. She looks down after 6 seconds to pick
up his arms with her hands as if to keep control over his build-up.
He follows her downward look about 10 seconds later by looking down,
too. His movements subside and his face becomes serious. She is
quietly serious also, at 90 seconds.

He sneezes, she responds with a staccato "God bless you!" and
a brighter face, head nodding toward him. She begins to talk more
insistently as he looks serious, studying her face. He finally
brightens to a smile, and with it, she throws back her head to smile

broadly and excitedly. After this broad smile, they both subside,
he continues to look at her seriously and quietly. She talks
seriously to him, holding his buttocks and legs between her hands
(120 seconds). At prolonged intervals, he gives her two rather
brief, tentative but encouraging smiles. After each, he returns
to a quiet serious face, his body entirely motionless. She smiles
to his smiles, but doesn't get more insistent and continues to
talk quietly. At 135 seconds, he looks down at his feet, then comes
back to her with a longer smile--tongue showing at his lips. His
legs also cycle out toward her. She looks down when he does, moves
his legs more rapidly and her voice builds up. His smile decreases
after 5 seconds and he looks away again (150 seconds). Then, they
begin another period of serious looks, alternating with brief smiles
in short cycles. She builds up with each of his cues, pumping his
legs, smiling and vocalizing more herself, building up to a final
peak. Each partner produces wide smiles, her voice becomes high-
pitched, her hands pump his legs together. He subsides first to
look down and serious. She loses her broad smile, gets up to leave,
letting his legs go. At this he looks beseechingly up into her
face, his mouth turns down, his eyebrows arch, his legs and arms
quiet, and he follows her with his eyes and head as she moves
away...(180 seconds).

The second interaction (86-day-old girl) would read as follows:
The infant is leaning to one side in the chair, head forward,
trunk slumped sideways, arms out to the sides, as the mother comes
in with a high-pitched "Hi Jane. You're falling over." The infant
bobs her head, peripherally watching the mother, staying suspended
to the side. As the mother bends way down to catch the infant's
eye, continuously talking in a fast stream of high-pitched vocalizations, the infant stills, head suspended and body slumped to the
side; looking past the mother. The mother taps the infant's belly
with extended finger, flailing out her right arm. The mother,
continuing to talk, now in a more low-keyed and disappointed tone,
moves the infant's trunk back in the seat, one hand on the infant's
trunk, one hand on the infant's face, pushing her head back as if
to force her to look at the mother. The infant widens her eyes and
with half open mouth briefly glances at the mother, bobbing her head
forward again. As the mother lets go of her face, the infant instantly slumps sideways, head suspended and eyes averted down. The
mother moves sideways repeatedly to catch her line of vision. The
infant shuts her out actively (30 seconds), swiping with her arm and
looking to the side. As the mother moves back a little, the infant
quickly shoots a glance towards her then averts her eyes again,
simultaneously throwing out her arm.

The mother attempts to orient the infant again by tapping Jane's
trunk pointedly with her finger. The infant bobs her head and then
looks up seriously with large, dark eyes and a half pout. The mother
pushes the baby all the way back in the seat, but she jerks herself
forward again and bobs two more times only to resume her former unavailable position, her head directed down, eyes cast downward. The
mother's voice is serious now as she repeats several times: "Will
you look at me?" She grasps the infant's hands and the infant bobs

sideways with her whole body, watching alternately both the mother's hands (60 seconds). The mother continues to hold her hands and produce a stream of insistent words; she leans very close into the infant in an effort to get through to her. As the infant looks up, the mother sits back a little and instantly the infant looks down again bobbing trunk and head. The mother pushes her back and then she replaces one hand on the infant's trunk, other hand on her face, attempting to push her head (90 seconds) in order to catch her eye. "You just don't want to have anything to do with old mom."

In a renewed sally of enthusiasm, she addresses the infant with a broad smile: "Hey, you want to do this? Huh?" She takes hold of the infant's legs and cycles them. The infant again looks down at the mother's hands on her feet and catches her balance with her arm. The mother catches the infant's hand and moves the infant's trunk back in the infant seat. The mother's face lights up as the infant almost looks at her. But then the infant falls forward again the instant the mother lets go of her hands. The mother complains, "You just won't sit up" (120 seconds) and adjusts the infant's trunk sideways. Another attempt at moving her head back fails. She grabs both the infant's hands again and moves her back. The infant *very* briefly looks at her, then bobs forward again. The mother now leans in very closely, holds both her hands and begins to blow in the infant's face. The infant glances at her, leans forward as if trying to avoid the blow, glances again and finally relaxes her trunk, gives in, and for the first time in the interaction, sits back and looks at the mother. The infant smiles. The mother stops the blowing; still leaning very close to the infant, holding both her hands, she laughs: "I just didn't want to be ignored." The infant opens her mouth widely, smiling broadly. The mother reciprocates in broad smiles and soft talking, then repeats the successful blowing game (150 seconds). The infant sobers and then brightens up again, attempting to withdraw her hand from her mother's grip. After 10 seconds the infant's smile wanes, she opens her mouth and tongues, eyes just below the mother's face. She yawns briefly, pulls her arm away and curls out her lower lip, looking just past the mother. Then she lets herself fall forward again, bobbing her head. The mother moves her back by pushing on both her arms. The infant lets herself slump from side to side, always just missing eye contact with the mother, looking at the mother's hands and rooting to her touch. She bobs forward again to the mother's questioning and urging, "Hey."

As the mother leaves, pushing her with one hand back in the seat (180 seconds), the infant straightens up her trunk and head, raises her eyebrows, makes an "ooo" mouth and visually follows the mother out of the alcove.

These two narratives capture the differences in affective ambience and degree of mutual organization of the interactions. They can serve as a gross validation check for the data resynthesis systems applied to these interactions later on. The general validation question would be "Do the quantification systems capture those dimensions of the interaction as they are intended and do they highlight or at least preserve the overall organization and affective

ambience of the interaction?" In other words, is the interaction
as described in the narrative recognizable in the other quantification and data resynthesis systems?

The quantitative form of data reduction used is *Microbehavioral
Component Specification (Behavioral Catalogue)*: Essentially this
is a behavioral taxonomy which we have constructed. Our goal has
been to identify definable units of behavior which can be articulated
in reliable descriptors, to classify them, to catalogue them and to
assign a discrete code to each descriptor. We look at the two
partners separately in order to arrive at a comprehensive micro-
catalogue. Figure 2 shows the behavioral modalities chosen for
categorizing behavioral units. These modalities are assumed to
carry most message content in the interaction. Table 1 shows the
descriptors in each behavioral category grouped by behavioral
dimensions.

EXPRESSIVE MODALITIES
SCORED PER SECOND

INFANT	ADULT
FACIAL EXPRESSION	FACIAL EXPRESSION
VOCALIZATION	VOCALIZATION
EYE DIRECTION	EYE DIRECTION
HEAD POSITION	HEAD POSITION
BODY POSITION	BODY POSITION
	SPECIFIC HAND
	MOVEMENTS

FIGURE 2.   Expressive Modalities of Interaction.

TABLE 1.   DESCRIPTORS IN EACH BEHAVIORAL CATEGORY
OF THE MICRO ANALYSIS SYSTEM

INFANT

I.   *Type of Vocalization:*   1. none; 2. isolated sound; 3. grunt;
4. coo; 5. cry; 6. fuss; 7. laugh.

II.   *Direction of Visual Attention:*

1.   *Direction of Gaze:*   1. towards mother's face; 2. away
from mother's face; 3. following mother's face; 4. part
side, nose level; 5. part side, nose down; 6. part side,
nose up; 7. complete side, nose level; 8. complete side,
nose down; 9. complete side, nose up.

2.   *Head Orientation:*   1. towards, nose level; 2. towards,
nose down; 3. towards, nose up; 4. part side, nose level;
5. part side, nose down; 6. part side, nose up; 7. complete
side, nose level; 8. complete side, nose down; 9. complete
side, nose up.

3.   *Left/Right Modifier of Head Position:*   1. infant's left;
2. infant's right.

4.   *Blinks and Specific Eye Movements:*   1. blink; 2. eyes
crossed; 3. away and focused on specifiable object (such
as chair side) which is not used by mother as part of
interaction; 4. eyes shifted markedly to side relative
to axis of nose.

III.   *Facial Expression:*

1.   *Position of Infant's Cheeks* (examples only):   1. neutral,
relaxed position; 2. elongated, hollow; 3. raised upward
and puffed.

2.   *Eyebrow Position* (examples only):   1. neutral resting
position; 2. rounded with elevation in center; 3. flashing -
rapid up and down.

3.   *Mouth Position* (examples only):   1. neutral resting
position; 2. slightly opened without tension; 3. broad
smile; 4. yawn-open.

4.   *Eye Width:*   1. neutral; 2. wide; 3. narrow; 4. closed.

5.   *Tongue Placement:*   1. not exposed; 2. tongue exposed but
not extended beyond lips; 3. tongue exposed and extended
beyond lips.

TABLE 1 (continued)

---

6. *Specific Facial Expressions:* 1. cry face; 2. grimace;
3. pout; 4. wary/sober; 5. lidding; 6. yawn; 7. neutral;
8. sneeze; 9. softening; 10. brightening; 11. simple smile;
12. coo face; 13. broad smile.

IV. *Body Position and Movement:* 1. leaning forward and doubled
over; 2. body turned off to one side; 3. arching; 4. leaning
back; 5. slumped to one side; 6. neutral; 7. position being
changed by mother; 8. moving up in vertical plane; 9. upright
with head raised off cushion or neck extended and trunk
elongated; 10. leaning forward with back straight.

V. *Limb Movements:*

1. *Size of Limb Movement:* 1. none; 2. small; 3. medium;
4. large.

2. *Number of Limbs in Movement:* 1. none; 2. 1 limb; 3. 2
limbs; 4. 3 limbs; 5. 4 limbs; 6. only arms seen because
of maternal position - 1 moving; 7. as in 6. - 2 moving.

3. *Place of Movement:* 1. none; 2. midline; 3. between midline and shoulders; 4. side.

4. *Specific Arm and Hand Gestures:* 1. eye rubbing; 2. hand
to mouth; 3. swiping; 4. digit fidgits; 5. hands held
together at midline; 6. all four limbs extended forward.

5. *Specific Leg Gestures:* 1. kicking; 2. startle.

[*Miscellaneous Descriptors* (examples only): 1. cough; 2. bowel
movement; 3. hiccoughing.]

ADULT

I. *Type of Vocalization:* 1. abrupt, angry shout; 2. stern adult
narrative with tension evident; 3. rapid tense high-pitched
vocalizations which sound upset or exhorting; 4. too long
cessation of talking; 5. almost inaudible sounds such as
whisper; 6. adult narrative; 7. narration with some evidence
of "infantized" modification but no burst-pause pattern; 8.
rhythmic sounds with little internal modulation such as clicks
or sequences of "hi-hi-hi"; 9. burst-pause talking (labelled
type 1, 2 or 3 depending on characteristics specified in
text); 10. single bursts in rapid succession which have wide
pitch range; 11. burst of sound that "peaks"; 12. singing.

TABLE 1 (continued)

II.   *Direction of Visual Attention:* 1. towards infant's face; 2.
      towards infant's body; 3. away from infant but related to
      interaction; 4. away from infant and not related to interaction.

III. *Facial Expression:* 1. angry; 2. frown; 3. serious,"sad" or
      sober; 4. lidded; 5. neutral; 6. bright; 7. animated bright;
      8. simple smile; 9. imitative play face; 10. kisses; 11.
      exaggerated play face; 12. broad, full smile; 13. "Oooo"
      face.

IV.   *Body Position and Movements:* 1. turns body full side away;
      2. sits back and still; 3. slumping; 4. neutral - slight
      forward; 5. sideway shifts without curvature of back; 6.
      slight rocking forward and back; 7. large sideway shifts with
      back curvature so head is in infant's line of vision; 8.
      medium close forward; 9. extremely close forward; 10. large
      shift forward and back.

V.   *Hand Movement:* 1. abrupt handling of infant involving large
      shift in infant position; 2. sudden abrupt contact that does
      not entail changing infant position; 3. jerky jiggling of
      infant's limbs; 4. rough pounding on infant's body; 5. rough
      pulling of infant to sit; 6. hands not in contact with infant
      but are exposed, unrelated to interaction; 7. no movement or
      use of hands; 8. gently containing infant's body or limbs;
      9. light tapping or stroking on infant's body; 10. small
      adjustments of infant's garments; 11. gentle cycling of
      infant's limbs; 12. gradually pull-to-sit; 13. tapping or
      lightly stroking infant's face; 14. intense tickling; 15.
      intensely stroking baby's face; 16. large strokes of infant's
      body.

VI.   *Head Movement and Position:* 1. towards, nose level; 2. towards,
      nose down; 3. towards, nose up; 4. part side, nose level; 5.
      part side, nose down; 6. part side, nose up; 7. complete side,
      nose level; 8. complete side, nuzzling; 13. cocking.

[*Miscellaneous Descriptors* (examples only): 1. getting up to
leave alcove; 2. attending to a second person; 3. coughing.]

Coding

     In order to code the categorical description, a descriptor
from each category is selected by two observers who review the
interaction by watching the videotape repeatedly at normal speed

and at 1/7th of the natural speed. As proficiency in coding increases, more than one category can be scored during a single run
of the tape. In any case, the focus is always limited to either
the infant's behavior or the parent's behavior.

One observer operates the videotape deck, stopping the machine
and turning it off whenever a change in the category being coded
is observed. After discussing the change, the other observer enters
the appropriate code onto a data sheet which has one or two vertical
columns reserved for each category and a horizontal line for each
second of elapsed time. If necessary, the tape is reviewed a
second, and a third time, until an adequate descriptor is agreed
upon and coded.

It is important to vary the speed of observation while coding.
Slow motion permits careful detailed observation but it may also
produce distortions which will only be recognized when the interaction is viewed at normal speed. This is particularly true for
vocalizations which at 1/7th normal speed are skewed beyond recognition, as well as specific actions such as yawns and swipes which
are differentiated from similar behaviors, wide mouth and nonspeci-
fic large arm movement, by transformations over time as well as by
subtle variations in configuration.

Each second of the interaction is scored. The code assigned
describes the behavior for the whole second interval not for single
frames separated by a 1-second interval. This distinction is
important since the information contained in single frames may cause
a misrepresentation of the display contained across a second. A
facial expression, a hand gesture, a vocalization, are all dynamic
displays which take time to occur. Without temporal information,
the beginning of a smile might appear to be a grimace, a rapid
eyebrow raise might be missed or might be described as a prolonged
raise, or a series of blinks might be observed as eye closure.

We have attempted to record behavioral units in shorter time
intervals, such as 1/3rd second, but such fine-grained descriptions
rarely yielded more than redundant information using the level of
descriptors in this system. Procedural rules guide the selection
of descriptors in those instances when more than one descriptor
might be applicable because the behavior changed more than once
during a second or because the change occurred during the 1-second
interval. The code which retains the *most* information about the
change of display is selected. For example, if the infant shifts
its head from "towards and level" to "towards and up" during a
second, the behavior is coded as "towards and up", except when the
shift occurred during the last moments of the second *and* the new
position was maintained during the next second. If it was not maintained, it would be coded in order to retain the information that
such a shift occurred, even though it was not displayed for an
entire second. When a display occurs during a transitional point,
the "end points" of the change are coded. Thus, if the infant's
head crosses the midline when moving from "partside right" to
"partside left", only these latter codes are used. Or if the
infant grimaces slightly during a transition from a neutral facial
expression to a broad smile, the grimace is not described, for it

is not the predominant display. These examples illustrate a basic point about the coding procedure: the objective of categorical description is to retain information about an interactor's communicative displays. The system must be utilized with flexibility within a general matrix of nonarbitrary procedural rules--a flexibility within a general matrix of repeated and careful observation.

Reliability in the sense of repeated agreement among observers at the same time and over time is high and can be maintained. Scoring is always done with two observers. If they do not agree initially, the tape is reviewed until conflicts are resolved. The absolute percent agreement of different observers on the same tape was found to vary between .87 and 1.00 within our unit. Observers trained by us have obtained interrater reliability coefficients varying between .73 and .94.

Resynthesis

The microbehavioral component specification provides the analyzed behavioral element base for resynthesis attempts--the articulated building blocks or behavior ingredients of the interaction. After breaking down the overall flow of behavioral interaction and displays into these small units the key question is how to recombine the units to reconstruct the dynamic whole. One could, for instance, apply statistics such as frequency analyses, conditional probability techniques, factor or cluster analytic techniques to the data obtained with the microbehavioral system. In such cases, one would be seeking the statistical procedures to identify relationships among the components of interaction. We are reluctant to rely on such statistical procedures, however, because we are more interested in identifying the structure of interaction than simple contingencies in interaction. We believe that identification of structures of interaction comes from conceptual insights into the organization of interaction, which then can be evaluated by organizing the behavioral components in keeping with the insight and testing its adequacy. It is therefore our conviction that conceptual resynthesis attempts are superior to analyzing via statistical techniques, since the units of behavior we arrive at are not mechanically, but dynamically, interactive. It seems more appropriate to test *a priori* conceptual recombinations which attempt to reflect aspects of these dynamics with the behavior units arrived at, than to expect a better grasp on the dynamics of mechanistic recombination. Conceptual recombination is an effort to articulate our intuitions about the interrelationship of behavioral components.

The first step in the resynthesis process, then, is to generate specific hypotheses, which then guide the particular strategy of combining and displaying the behavioral components identified with the microbehavioral analysis. We have, thus far, developed three major hypotheses to guide our resynthesis attempts:

1. The microbehavioral components can be organized in such a way that *quantification* of each partner's *affective level* during the interaction is possible. This hypothesis has led to the

macrobehavior sum scaled scores.

2. The microbehavioral components can be organized in such a way that *regulation of the interactive system* as a whole can be quantified. This hypothesis has led to the *dyadic phases*.

3. The microbehavioral components can be arranged in such a way that the *regulation of the individual partners* within the interactive system can be quantified. This has led to the *monadic phases*.

Quantification of affective level: Macrobehavioral sum scaled scores. In this system the behaviors of each partner are scaled second-by-second along an affective involvement continuum from least involved to most involved. This scaling system uses five behavioral dimensions identified for the infant: 1. vocalization, 2. attention, 3. facial expression, 4. body position, and 5. body movement; six dimensions are identified for the adult: 1. vocalization, 2. attention, 3. facial expression, 4. body position, 5. head position, and 6. body movement. Each dimension is scored on a nine-point scale, from negative involvement, withdrawal, or refusal on the low extreme of the spectrum (score of 1) through neutral (score of 5) to high involvement--intense, positive affect, and total engagement (score of 9) on the high extreme of the spectrum.

Each point on each dimension, called a *macroscore*, is behaviorally defined in terms of specific microscores and their combinations derived from the microscoring system. For instance, the macrodimension of infant attention is defined by the microscore categories: *overall direction of eyes, specific eye direction, head orientation* and *head position.* The lowest macroscore for attention, reflecting avoidance, is "1" and is defined as *profile complete: eyes away.* It is made up of the following microscores, *eyes:* away (micro 2), *head:* either complete side and level (micro 7), complete side and down (micro 8), or complete side and up (micro 9), *head orientation:* either left (micro 1) or right (micro 2); and *specific eye direction:* either not applicable (micro 6) or eyes directed to more extreme away than head (micro 1). The highest macroscore for attention, reflecting concentrated gazing is "9" and is also defined by overall direction of eyes, specific eye direction, head orientation and head position, and duration for which a particular configuration is maintained.

Table 2 gives examples of infant and mother behavioral descriptors assigned to the end and midranks of each scale. The rank assignments are made on the basis of consensual judgment. The scoring manual for Adult-Infant Interaction in Appendix A contains the microscores and their translation into macroscores. Since the value of five is the neutral point, the flow of acceleration and deceleration from second to second, either for each dimension separately, or for the sum of all five or six macroscores can be graphed. This yields a quantitative picture of the overall buildup of an interaction and of the relative buildup within each dimension. The mother's curve can then be superimposed on that of the infant, using "neutrality" as the axis. This can be used to identify periods of synchrony and asynchrony by calculating correlation

TABLE 2. SCALES FOR INFANT AND MOTHER BEHAVIORAL MODALITIES

Scale Name	Negative Extreme (1)	Neutral Point (5)	Positive Extreme (9)

Infant vocalization	*crying*	no defined neutral
		
		rank 4 = no sound or
		     isolated grunt
		rank 6 = isolated non-
		     specific sound
			gurgling and laughs

Infant direction of visual attention	*prolonged look away* with head complete side and eyes directed away	*interrupted looking* with a glance of 30 to 10 seconds duration and head either towards or part side	*concentrating on mother* with a towards look of 10 or more seconds with head aligned towards
Infant facial expression	*cry face* with eyes narrow or closed, mouth opened with tongue exposed, contraction of eye orbits, eyebrows oblique	*neutral expression* with eyes normal width, mouth slightly open or lightly closed, no tension evidenced in cheeks, eye orbits or brows	*broad smile* with mouth opened in broad smile, cheeks elevated, eyes neutral to closed, eyebrows flattened
Infant body position and movement	*leaning forward and doubled over*, head either down by legs or off to one side with only crown exposed to mother	*neutral and relaxed* with body resting in upright position against molded cushions in chair body vertical axis in midline	*leaning forward with back straight* with 45° angle between legs and trunk

49

TABLE 2 (continued)

Scale Name	Negative Extreme (1)	Neutral Point (5)	Positive Extreme (9)
Infant limb movement	very large sustained movement of limbs (see text)	*no or little self-generated movement with at most one or two limbs moving in small arcs for less than 3 seconds*	*very large sustained movements of limbs (see text)*
Mother vocalization	abrupt angry shout	little or *no vocalization for a relatively brief (less than 10 second) period or narration with some evidence of "baby talk" adjustment but with no sustained rhythmic pattern*	*burst of sound that seems to "peak" over the rest of burst-pause pattern must be a major shift of modulation and pitch*
Mother (hand) movements	abrupt handling of infant involving a sudden large shift in his body position	no movement or display of hands	intense movements on infant body or face with sustained emphatic rapid rhythm, e.g., stroking of face; tickling
Mother facial expression	angry face with eyebrows oblique and drawn downward, lips tense and extended laterally	*bright face with eyes normal width, mouth neutral, eyebrows neutral, cheeks elevated, little movement or animation of facial features*	*fully animated face with maximal display of at least one facial feature, e.g., broad full smile, "superlook" imitation of infant's face, "cooo" face*

TABLE 2 (continued)

Scale Name	Negative Extreme (1)	Neutral Point (5)	Positive Extreme (9)
Mother direction of visual attention	*gaze directed completely away from infant for more than six seconds*	*away glances of less than 3 seconds directed completely off infant's face or body*	no defined positive extreme rank 7 = looking at infant for 7 or more seconds
Mother head movement and position	*not visible to infant*	*frontal (towards) infant with no movement*	*nuzzling infant with head touching infant*
Mother body position and movement	*not visible to infant*	*neutral sitting posture with trunk leaning slightly forward and still*	*movement forward and resulting posture of trunk leaning forward and head very close*

coefficients between individual macroscores or macro sum scores
across, let's say, a 10-second period. In this way, the average
amplitude of an interaction can be visualized and measured. Which
partner leads and which partner follows or holds off can be assessed.
A synchrony and dissynchrony can be attributed to the partner who
failed to pick up on the other's leads; we can identify periods
which seem to us to be relatively successful and what sequences
lead to deceleration.

Figure 3 shows the two interactions described above narra-
tively, scored in scaled macroscores. The horizontal axis is time.
The vertical axis is the sum of the scaled macroscores per second.
For the infant there are 4 categories (facial expression, visual
attention, body position and vocalization) which have ranged from
1 to 9. The category "Movement" has a range from 0 to 4. If the
infant's facial expression is more positive than neutral, then the
movement score of 0 to 4 is added. If the infant's facial expression is more negative than neutral than the movement score is

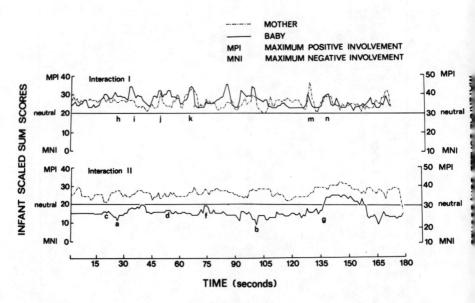

FIGURE 3.   Scaled Macro Sum Scores for Two Interactions.

subtracting. Thus an infant's neutral macro sum score is 20 [4
(number of dimensions) times 5 (neutral point on each dimension) +
0 (movement score at neutral)]. The macro sum score showing
maximum positive involvement is 40 [4 (number of dimensions) x 9
(highest scale point on each dimension); 36 + 4 (highest scores for
movement) with + sign = 40]. The macro sum score showing *maximum
negative involvement* is 0 [4 (number of dimensions) x 1 (lowest
scale point on each dimension) = 4; 4 - 4 (highest score for movement) with - sign = 0].

For the adult there are 6 categories (vocalization, hand movement, facial expression, visual attention, head position, and body
position) with ranges from 1-9. Thus, the adult's neutral point is
30; a maximum positive involvement scores is 54; a maximum negative
involvement score is 6 (Tronick, et al., 1977a).

The advantage of the specificity of these curves is the reten-
tion of detail about both partners. Interaction I shows the relative mutual involvement amplitude of both partners and the repeated
instances of moving in the same direction, affectively decelerating and,

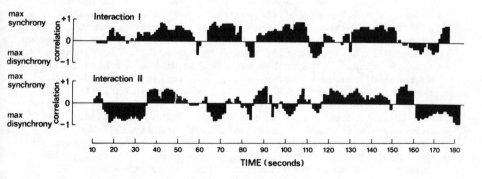

FIGURE 4.   Running Correlations of Macro Sum Scores for Two
Interactions.

accelerating. Interaction II shows the prolonged efforts of the
mother attempting to bring the infant into mutual cycling and the
success finally towards the end of the sequence. Figure 4 shows
running correlations across 10 seconds between the mother's and
infant's scaled sum scores. Each bar is the correlation of 10
seconds of scaled scores for infant and mother. The correlation
moves in 1-second jumps. Thus the first correlation is for
seconds 1-10, the second for seconds 2-11, the third for 3-12,
and so on. A high positive correlation reflects maximum synchrony
in the interaction, and a high negative correlation represents
maximum dissynchrony.

These graphs, thus, exemplify the high degree of synchrony
of both partners in interaction I, while the graph for interaction
II shows the much more prolonged periods of dissynchrony. This
resynthesis system thus permits quantification of the level of
affective involvement of the interactive partners (Tronick, et
al., 1977a).

*Quantification of the regulation of the interactive system:
Dyadic phases.* The second hypothesis guiding another resynthesis
attempt says that it is possible to organize the microbehavioral
components in such a way that the regulation of the interactive
system as a whole can be quantified. The method of resynthesis
developed to this end is that of the *dyadic phases.* This method
is also discussed by Tronick, et al. (1978). The dyadic phases
are defined by sets of clusters of behaviors of *both* partners,
therefore called *dyadic* phases.

There are five recognizable phases each representing a different "dyadic" state of the partner's mutual attentional and
affective involvement. Figure 5 shows a schematic presentation
of the phases. Typically an interaction begins with an *initiation
phase* (I). This is usually marked by the adult's bid for attention
from the infant. The mother may come in with a heightened facial
expression, raised eyebrows, shiny, glistening eyes; and with
rapid high-pitched "Hi! Hi!" tells the infant essentially: "I'm
here. I have come to play with you. Look at me! Play with me!"
Usually, she does not touch the infant during this phase. The
baby may sit far back in its seat, look tentatively at her with
slightly lidded eyes. It may remain still in order to ensure a
more prolonged and intensified approach from her. Finally, the
infant begins to respond and the *mutual orientation phase* (M)
begins. The infant, while looking at the mother, may vocalize,
brighten, raise its eyebrows, straighten its body, soften its
cheeks, and even cycle its arms and legs toward her. It seems to
be letting her know: "All right! I'm ready for you." The
mother at this point may begin to relax and become more modulated
and softer. When both partners are synchronous and there is less
staccato in movement and voice, she may touch the infant. They
may begin to exchange *greetings* (G), which are heightened reciprocal facial displays and vocalizations, one partner acknowledging
the response of the other. Peaks alternating between the partners
are being accentuated by "ooh" faces and smiles. This is the phase
of taking turns in build-up displays. Then gradually the partners

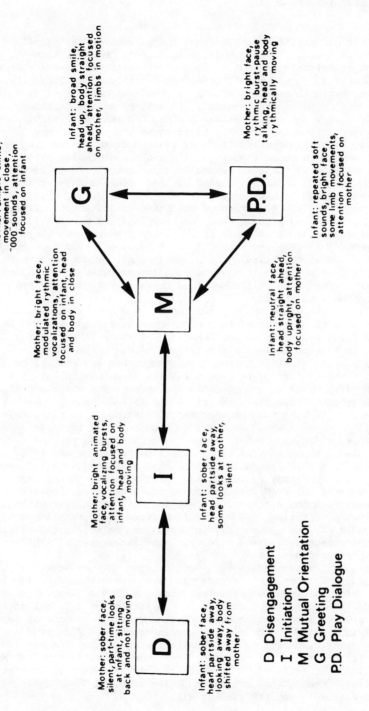

Mother: simple smile, movement in close, "000 sounds, attention focused on infant

Infant: broad smile, head up, body straight ahead, attention focused on mother, limbs in motion

Mother: bright face, rythmic burst-pause talking, head and body rythmically moving

Mother: bright face, modulated rythmic vocalizations, attention focused on infant, head and body in close

Infant: repeated soft sounds, bright face, some limb movements, attention focused on mother

Infant: neutral face, head straight ahead, body upright, attention focused on mother

Mother: bright animated face, vocalizing bursts, attention focused on infant, head and body moving

Infant: sober face, head partside away, some looks at mother, silent

Mother: sober face, silent, part-time looks at infant, sitting back and not moving

Infant: sober face, head partside away, looking away, body shifted away from mother

G
P.D.
M
I
D

D Disengagement
I Initiation
M Mutual Orientation
G Greeting
P.D. Play Dialogue

FIGURE 5. Model of Dyadic Phases.

may press one another on to a simultaneous peak of reciprocal,
heightened emotion, the *play dialogue* (P.D.). Both partners
attempt to maintain each other in this climactic state for a prolonged period. Eyes, voice, face, bodily closeness all oscillate
in synchrony with each other in a cyclical homeostatic curve ebbing
and flowing with repeated periods of build-up and relaxation.
Finally one or the other partner has reached the limit of his/her
capacity to maintain this heightened state. The infant may
suddenly avert its eyes, dull down, lose tonus in extremities or
trunk, and begin to move more jerkily and disjointedly. Its
vocalizations may become stressed or even fussy. It may turn his
head to the side in order to shut out the mother's face, or it
may sneeze, yawn or hiccough.

The mother may lose some of the initial excitement and vivacity
of the play dialogue and become stereotypical and repetitive in
her interactions. This leads to a deceleration and eventual *dis-*
engagement (D). She may gradually dull down, and tend to curb the
build-up and slowly bring it to disengagement, or she may overload
the infant by pressing it towards even faster build-up exceeding
its capacities which will often lead to an abrupt deceleration and
disengagement on its part.

In scoring these phases from the microbehavioral units, sets
of clusters of behavior of *both* partners are used and scoring is
recorded for second-by-second behavior. Certain behaviors can
substitute for other behaviors; for instance, in the initiation
phase, if the infant is turned away, the mother may attempt to
orient it by tapping *or* by urgent talking *or* by moving into its
line of vision, *or* by a combination of these. But there are also
necessary conditions that have to be met in each phase: that is,
initiation requires that one partner is attempting to elicit his or
her orientation. *Mutual orientation* requires that both partners
calmly orient to each other. *Greeting* requires one partner's
heightened acknowledgement of the other partner's orientation.
Play dialogue (P.D.) requires both partners to display simultaneous
heightened, animated, synchronous cycling with one another and
Disengagement (D) requires that one or both partners direct attention away from the other partner, without either partner attempting
to elicit orientation. We are still refining the translation manual
for dyadic scoring. These dyadic phases can be scored directly
from the videotape in real time with good interrater reliability
for experienced scorers.

Figure 6 shows the two interaction examples now scored with
the dyadic phase system. *Interaction I* starts with a greeting and
moves mainly between mutual orientation and play dialogue. Only
towards the end of the 3 minutes is play dialogue no longer achieved.
There are few intermittent brief disengagements, which might be re-
organizing pauses in the flow of the interaction. *Interaction II,*
on the other hand, starts with initiation and cycles for more than
2 minutes between initiation and disengagement, until finally, mutual
orientation is achieved. The partners quickly return to initiation
and disengagement, then achieve a 30-second build-up to greeting.
Play dialogue is not achieved at all.

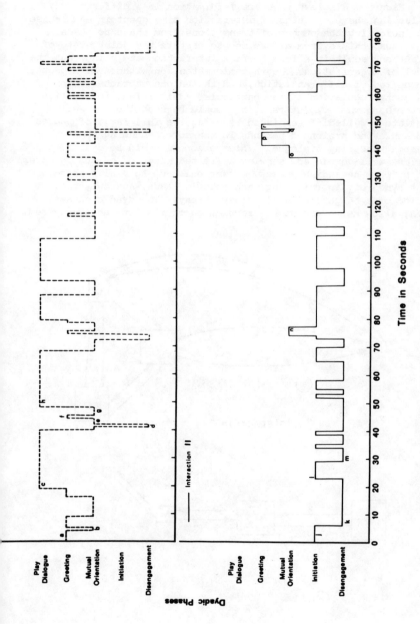

FIGURE 6. Dyadic Phase Scoring of Two Interactions (a).

57

Figure 7 displays the same information in a different way, reflecting the proportion of interaction time spent in each phase and indicating the number of transitions from phase to phase.

Thus, this system allows one to capture the joint state of infant and adult in a face-to-face interaction and brings out the level of organization, the rhythmic attention-withdrawal aspects, the degree of differentiation, and the unique characteristics of the joint regulation of the particular adult-infant interactive system as a whole. *Interaction I* could be described as well-modulated, well-differentiated, showing the full range of phases and achieving prolonged periods in the more demanding phases, greeting and play dialogue. *Interaction II* could be described as less well-developed, showing a limited range of phases, greater use of less demanding phases, slower build-up to a high phase, less synchrony in following each other's leads, and only one period of a heightened cycle of synchrony. The dyadic phases, then, allow us to depict the regulation of the interactive system.

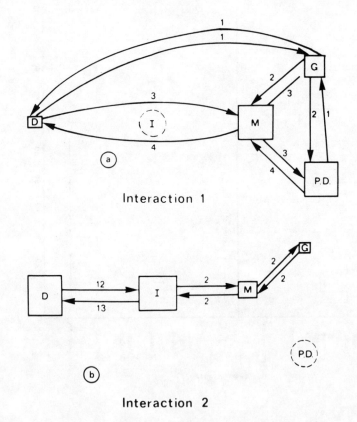

Interaction 1

Interaction 2

FIGURE 7. Dyadic Phase Scoring of Two Interactions (b).

Quantification of individual partner regulation: Monadic phases. A third hypothesis, guiding yet another attempt at re-synthesis of the data, states that the microbehavioral units can be combined in such a way that the regulation of each partner separately within the interactive system can be quantified. The resynthesis system developed to do this is referred to as the *monadic phase system.* This system is discussed more fully by Tronick, et al. (1977 and in press). A catalogue of systematic rules is used in order to score each partner's displays. Appendix B contains the manual with the combination rules for the 5 microbehavior scores for body, head, face, voice, and eyes for infant and adult separately, which are combined to yield one score per second per partner for the overall display.

These scores are thought to capture the overall expressive display of the combination of expressive behavioral modalities of each partner separately. Figure 8 shows the process of monadic phase construction. For each second an overall "monadic phase" is assigned on the basis of rules governing expressive scores derived from the *micro*system. For a behavioral display such as the following:

1	6	1	5	1
face	voice	*eye*	*head*	body
crying	whimper	extreme	part-side	doubled over
		away	down	

the "monadic phase" *protest* would be assigned. The monadic phases are designed to capture the range from least involvement via neutral to maximal involvement.

Figure 9 shows the interrelationship of inferred affective level, engagement, and message content of the scaled monadic phases.

Figure 10 shows a video image example of such monadic phases. It has to be kept in mind that such an example is only a static display, while a score in the system is actually based on behavior displayed during a second.

After developing this detailed system with its recombination rules, we are exploring scoring monadic phases second-by-second directly off the videotape. The original microscores will provide the reliability check. We are planning to eventually develop a manual for direct scoring of monadic phases. It is becoming apparent that the training process for direct scoring is facilitated by training in the microscoring process.

Figures 11 and 12 show the *monadic phases scoring* system applied to the two sample interactions. The infant in interaction I shows repeated buildups to the phases "talk", the most demanding in terms of integrating posture, heightened affect, and vocalization. In the course of the 3 minutes, the infant's peaks diminish somewhat. The mother starts very high, pulling the infant up repeatedly, follows his lead several times, and towards the end of the action diminishes with him, before a final build-up on her part.

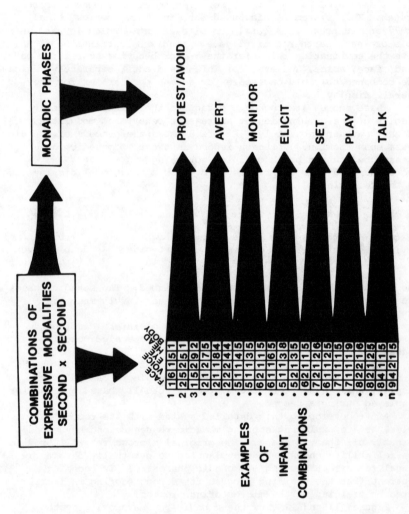

FIGURE 8. Model for Monadic Phase Construction.

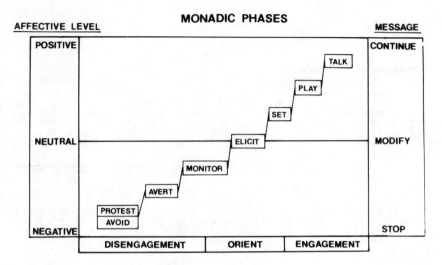

FIGURE 9.   Model of Inter-relationship of Constructs Underlying
the Monadic Phases.

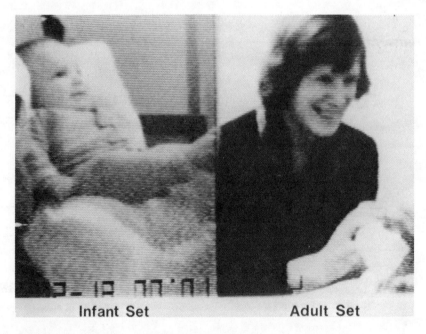

FIGURE 10.   Example of Monadic Phase Displays.

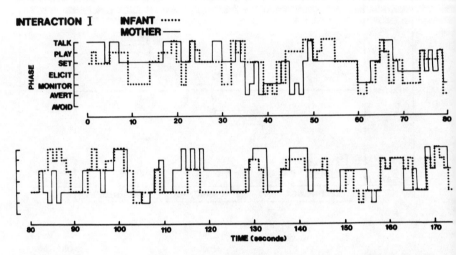

FIGURE 11.   Monadic Phase Scoring of Infant and Mother (Interaction I)

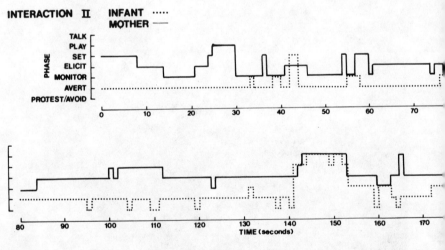

FIGURE 12.   Monadic Phase Scoring of Infant and Mother (Interaction I

In contrast, the infant in interaction II is averted much of the time. Then the infant very briefly achieves set, then averts again, even protests, and only eventually achieves a playing period.
The mother shows repeated efforts to bring the infant to higher phases, until eventually they achieve their joint buildup. Thus, the monadic scoring captures the contrast between interaction I and II.

SUMMARY

We have developed various levels of analysis and resynthesis of behaviors of adults and infants in interaction with each other in our structured 3-minute laboratory situation. Each system is geared to answer a specific question of regulation. Once the data are resynthesized in a specific way, such as with the macrobehavioral sum scaled scores, the dyadic phases or the monadic phases, the hypothesis which led to the development of the synthesis method can be tested. For instance, we have applied the macrobehavioral resynthesis method to answer the question of who leads and who follows in an interaction (Tronick & Brazelton, 1977). We have applied the dyadic and monadic phase scoring system to the question of differentiating mothers, fathers, and strangers in interaction with an infant (Brazelton, Yogman, Als, & Tronick, 1977). We have applied the monadic scoring system to document the process of development of organization of a blind infant and her mother (Als, Tronick, & Brazelton, 1977a), to assess the common components of regulation within the interactive matrix in a well infant and in a damaged infant (Als, Tronick, & Brazelton, 1977b), to differentiate the contributions of parents and of strangers to the interaction process (Dixon, Yogman, Tronick, & Brazelton, 1977), and to document the unique features of a different cultural expectation for the interaction (Keefer, Dixon, Tronick, & Brazelton, 1977). Thus far the results of our hypothesis testing are mainly in the form of refined descriptions. The next step is the derivation of quantitative parameters and the development of statistical procedures appropriate to such questions.

ACKNOWLEDGEMENTS

We would like to thank Dr. Lauren Adamson for her substantial contribution to the early development of our work. This work was supported by grant 3122 from the Grant Foundation.

REFERENCES

Als, H., Tronick, E., & Brazelton, T. B. The achievement of affective reciprocity and the beginnings of the development of autonomy: The study of a blind infant. Paper presented at the Meeting of the Society for Research in Child Development, New Orleans, 1977a.

Als, H., Tronick, E., & Brazelton, T. B.   Social interaction and
the development of organization in a well and in a damaged
infant. Unpublished manuscript, 1977b. (Available from H.
Als, Ph.D., Child Development Unit, Children's Hospital Medical
Center, Boston, MA., 92115.)

Brazelton, T. B., Tronick, E., Adamson, L., Als, H., & Wise, S.
Early mother-infant reciprocity. In M. A. Hofer (Ed.), *Parent-
infant interaction.* London: Ciba, 1975. pp. 137-154.

Brazelton, T. B., Tronick, E., & Als, H.   Early development of
neonatal and infant behavior. In J. Tanner & F. Faulkner (Eds.),
Human growth: A comprehensive treatise. New York: Plenum
Press, in press.

Brazelton, T. B., Yogman, M., Als, H., & Tronick, E.   Mother-
father-infant interaction. Paper presented at the Biennial
Conference of the International Society for the Study of
Behavioral Development, Pavia, Italy, 1977.

Dixon, S., Yogman, M., Tronick, E., & Brazelton, T. B.   A comparison of infant interaction with strangers and parents. Paper
presented at the Meetings of the Society for Research in
Child Development, New Orleans, 1977.

Keefer, C., Dixon, S., Tronick, E., & Brazelton, T. B.   A cross-
cultural study of face-to-face interaction: Gusii infants
and mothers. Paper presented at the Meetings of the Society
for Research in Child Development, New Orleans, 1977.

Sander, L. W.   The regulation of exchange in the infant-caretaker
system and some aspects of the context-content relationship.
In M. Lewis & L. A. Rosenblum (Eds.), *Interaction, conversation and the development of language.* New York: Wiley, 1977,
pp. 137-156.

Tronick, E., Als, H., & Adamson, L.   Structure of early face-to-
face communicative interactions. In M. Bullowa (Ed.),
Before speech: The beginnings of human communication.
Cambridge, England: Cambridge University Press, 1978, in press.

Tronick, E., Als, H., & Brazelton, T. B.   Mutuality in mother-
infant interaction. *Journal of Communication,* 1977, *7,*
74-79.

Tronick, E., Als, H., & Brazelton, T. B.   Monadic phases: A
structural descriptive analysis of infant-mother face-to-face
interaction. *Child Development,* in press.

Tronick, E., & Brazelton, T. B.   The joint regulation of infant-
adult interaction. *Journal of Cybernetics and Information
Science,* 1977, in press.

Yogman, M. W., Tronick, E., Dixon, S., Als, H., & Brazelton, T. B.
The goals and structure of face-to-face interaction between
infants and fathers. Paper presented at the Meetings of the
Society for Research in Child Development, New Orleans, 1977.

APPENDIX A: MICROBEHAVIORAL AND MACROBEHAVIORAL SCORING SYSTEM
               AND MANUAL

BABY

Baby Vocalization

   Micro: 1=none; 2=isolated sounds; 3=deep grunts; 4=coo; 5=cry;
6=whimper/fuss; 7=laugh.
   Macro: 1=Crying (micro 5 for 3 or more seconds or micro 5 for
3 or more times in 9 seconds with no silence 5 or more seconds); 2=
Protesting (5 for 3 or less seconds, not in string); 3=Whimpering
or fussing (micro 6); 4=None (micro 1); Grunts (micro 3); 6=Isolated
Sounds (micro 2, not fitting criteria for 8); 7=Coo (micro 4, not
fitting criteria for 8); 8=Repeated sounds or string of sounds
(micro 2 and/or micro 4 for 3 or more seconds of micro 2 and/or
micro 4 3 or more times in 9 seconds with no silence of five or
more seconds); 9=Gurgles and laughs (micro 7 or micro 7 more than
3 times in 9 seconds with no silence for 5 or more seconds; if a
micro 2 or 4 occurs within time span for string of laughs, this 2
or 4 and surrounding silences are coded 8).

Baby Attention

   Micro: Direction of Eyes: 1=towards; 2=away; 3=following;
4=looking at mother's "hands as toys".
   Micro: Specific Eyes: 0=not applicable; 1=eyes are directed
to more extreme away than head; 2=eyes are directed more towards
center than head; 3=away and looking at specifiable object.
   Micro: L/R modifier of head: 0=not applicabe; 1=our left;
2=our right.
   Micro: Head position: 1=towards; nose level; 2=towards, nose
down; 3=towards, nose up; 4=part side, level; 5=part side, down;
6=part side, up; 7=complete side, level; 8=complete side, down;
9=complete side, up.
   Macro: Attention: 1 = *Profile complete: eyes away - Avoidance.*
Eyes are micro 2; head is in position 7, 3 or 9. 2 = *Away:
Possible peripheral monitoring.* Eyes are 2 for greater or equal
to 10 seconds, head is in positions 1,2,3,4,5,6. 3 = *Very brief
looks with prolonged looks away.* a) Brief glance towards: a
micro 1 for 2 or less seconds within a look away (micro 2) for ten
or more seconds; b) Sweep: micro 2 for 10 or more seconds with the
head turning from side to side, 4,5,6,7,8,9; c) Complete side looking. A micro 1 for less than 10 seconds with the head in position
7,8,9. 4 = *Sober looking:* a) Oscillating: a look towards (1) of
two or less alternating with a look away (2) of two or less
seconds, repeated two or more times; head can be in 1,2,3,4,5,6;
b) Checking: a look (1) for 2 or less seconds and a look away
(2) for between 3 and 9 seconds duration. 5 = *Interrupted looking:*
a) Back-forth: a look for from between 3 and 9 seconds and a look
away of between 3 and 9 seconds with head in 1,2,3,4,5,6; b) Toward
look: a look (1) of between 3 and 9 seconds and looks away for 2

or less seconds with head in 1,2,3,4,5,6; c) Isolated look: look
(1) for between 3 and 9 seconds. 6 = See 7.; 6 is scored for looks
away (2) which are part of pattern described in 7. 7 = *Looking with
Chin Tuck:* a) Gaze with look away: looking (1) for 10 or more
seconds and a look away for between 3 and 9 seconds--this look
away is coded a 6; head is in position 2 or 5 for three or more
seconds; b) Gaze with away glance: looking (1) for ten or more
seconds and a look away for two or less seconds--this look away
is coded a 6; head is in position 2 or 5 for three or more seconds;
c) Chin tuck gaze: Looking (1) for ten or more seconds with head
in 2 or 5; d) Hand as toy look (micro 4) for any duration and with
head in any position.

Baby Movement

   Micro: 1=Large, 3 or 4 limbs; 2=Large, 1 or 2 limbs; 3=Medium,
3 or 4 limbs; 4=Medium, 1 or 2 limbs; 5=Small, 3 or 4 limbs; 6=
Small, 1 or 2 limbs; 7=None; 8=Mother moving baby's limbs.
   Macro: To derive the macro movement score, there are two steps.
First, the micro score should be translated into a score which
takes into account the duration of individual movements: 0=No
movement (micro 7); Mother moving infant's limbs (micro 8) or Small
movement of 1 or 2 limbs for less than 3 seconds (micro 6). 1=
Small movement of one or two limbs for 3 or more seconds (micro 6);
small movement of 3 or 4 limbs, for any duration (micro 5); or
Medium movement of 1 or 2 limbs for less than 3 seconds (micro 4).
2=Medium movement of 3 or 4 limbs for less than 3 seconds (micro 3)
or medium movement of 1 or 2 limbs for 3 or more seconds (micro 4).
3=Large movement of 1 or 2 limbs for less than 3 seconds (micro 2);
Large movement of 3 or 4 limbs for less than three seconds (micro 1);
or Medium movement of 3 or 4 limbs for three or more seconds (micro
3). 4=Large movement of 1 or 2 limbs for three or more seconds
(micro 2); Large movement of 3 or 4 limbs for three or more
seconds (micro 1); or a combination of micro 1 and 2 for 3 or more
seconds.
   Second; if the macro face score is 1, 2, or 3: multiply the
derived movement score by -1. If the macro face score is 4, 5, or
6: multiply the derived movement score by +1/2. If the macro
face score is 7, 8, or 9: multiply the derived movement score by
+1.

Miscellaneous Infant Micro Scores

   Blinks: 1=blink; 0=not applicable.
   Specific Hands: 00=not applicable; 01="Sams"; 02=digit fidgits;
03=eye wipe; 04=hand to mouth; 05=swipes; 06=four limb extension;
07=face shield with hand or arm; 08=self body caress; 09=handling
object such as toy.
   Specific Feet: 0=not applicable; 1=kick; 2=startle.
   Assorted: 0=not applicable; 1=sneeze; 2=coughs; 3=bowel movement; 4=tongue exposed slightly between lips; 5=full tonguing.

Baby Facial Expression

   Micro-Cheeks: 1=normal; 2=elongated hollow; 3=raised up.
   Micro-Orbits: 1=neutral; 2=maximum exposure of lids; 3=some
lower, no upper.
   Micro-Eyebrows: 1=neutral; 2=rounded; 3=up at center; 4=down
at center; 5=wrinkled; 6=wrinkled, farrowed, flattened; 7=flash,
raise.
   Micro-Mouth: 01=neutral closed; 02=corners up, slight open
or closed; 03=elongated, corners up, open mouth; 04=elongated,
corners up, wide open mouth; 05=protruded, open or closed, lip
curled down; 06=asymmetrical open mouth, corners down; 07=contracted
and closed; 08=open, rounded forward; 09=yawn.
   Macro-Facial Expressions: 1-1=Cry face; 2-1=Grimace; 2-2=Pout;
3-1=Wary/sober; 3-2=Frown; 4-1=Lidded; 4-2=Yawn; 5-1=Neutral; 5-2=
Sneeze; 6-1=Softening; 6-2=Bright; 7-1=Simple smile; 8-1=Coo face;
9-1=Broad smile; 9-2=Orgiastic smile.

Baby Body Position

   Macro: 1-1=Leaning forward and doubled over; 1-2=Body turned
completely to one side; 2-1=Arching or leaning very far back; 4-1=
Slumped and/or off to one side; 5-1=Neutral; 5-2=Adjusted by mother;
5-3=Hip jerk forward; 6-1=Movement up in the vertical plane; 8-1=
Body vertical with neck extended, trunk elongated and/or head off
back rest; 9-1=Leaning forward with straight back.

MOTHER

Mother Vocalization

   Underlying Conceptualization.   The goal is to code each vocalization based on its qualitative characteristics. The negative extreme
of the scale is used for vocalizations which are very loud, adult-like
in modulation, emphasis and rhythm. The positive extreme is utilized
for vocal patterns which are highly "infantized" in emphasis, modulation, and pitch and which are loud enough to become a focus of the
mother's activity at that point in the interaction. It is not possible
to categorize all the possible vocal patterns. Thus, for each scale
point one or more specific patterns are described and then an additional category is specified to be used for vocalizations not specified but determined to fit in that scale point.
   It is suggested that the first step in determining the appropriate
scores be to listen to the tape to determine the points at which the
patterns *change*. Additional runs can then be used to mark exactly when
these changes occur and to determine the actual score for each time
period.

Macro Vocalization

   1-1=Abrupt, angry shout. A loud and sudden startling vocalization; 1-2=Nonspecified pattern fitting the quality of 1-1; 2-1=Stern

adult narrative in which the volume is appropriate to adult interchange. Tension is evident in the voice. The vocalization may
involve addressing a real or imaginary adult in the situation;
2-2=Nonspecified pattern fitting the quality of 2; 3-1=Stern talking
as in 2-1 but without the extreme tension and harshness; 3-2=Rapid,
tense vocalization with a medium to high pitch range. May sound
upset or exhorting rather than stern; 3-3=Nonspecified vocalization
which has "3" quality; 4-1=A long cessation of vocalization which
is judged to be "too long" within the context of the interaction;
4-2=Almost inaudible sounds which lack modulation, such as whisper-
ing; 4-3=A soft adult narrative which lacks systematic changes in
modulation, pauses and emphasis. Not stern or tense; 4-4=Nonspeci-
fied vocalization consistant with quality of other category 4 patterns; 5-1=Little vocalization - soft neutral talking which has
long pauses but which does not have cessations in the stream of
vocalizations as in 4-1; 5-2=Narrative which fits the characteristics of 4-3 but which has some modification which makes it sound
more like "baby talk." The changes in vocalization to baby talk are
not however rhythmic in pause pattern or in emphasis and the modulation is muted; 5-3=Nonspecified vocalization pattern which is consistent with the quality of a "5"; 5-4=Whisper with modulated burst-
pause pattern; 6-1=Sounds that are rhythmic but have little internal
modulation and have only short pauses, such as clicks or "hi-hi-hi;"
6-2=Baby talk burst-pause talking but with little emphasis or modulation. Soft; 6-3=Nonspecified pattern "6"; 7-1=Burst-pause talking
of medium volume, emphasis and modulation. Pauses are of moderate
duration and are responsive to infant vocalizations; 7-2=Nonspeci-
fied "7" patterns; 8-1=Burst-pause talking which is highly modulated
and which is responsive to infant vocalizations. Much emphasis
during burst, often with drawing out of sound at the end of each
burst. Volume is variable but remains medium to loud; 8-2=Single
bursts in succession which have same modulation with variation in
pitch internal to each burst; 8-3=Nonspecified "8" patterns;
9-1=Bursts of sound as in 8-2 that seem to "peak" much change in
modulation with high emphasis; 9-2=Nonspecified "9" pattern.
     When the nonspecified pattern code is used, the actual vocali-
zation pattern should be described and, if it appears again, should
be specified as a defined pattern with its own categorical code within
the scale point.

Mother Hands

     As in the maternal vocalization scale, the individual scale
points each represent a particular quality of hand movement and not
specific actions per se. When possible, the actions in each scale
point are specified. If you see one which is not, decide on the
appropriate scale point and create a new categorical description.
     Macro: 1=Abrupt handling of baby which involves a large shift
in baby's position: 1-1=Sudden adjustment of body position; 2=
Sudden abrupt contact which is intrusive but does not entail changing
infant's position: 2-1=Single hand or finger poke; 2-2=Abrupt wipe
of face; 3=Rough, jerky, rhythmic movement of infant: 3-1=Jerky

jiggling of baby's limb(s); 3-2=Rough pouncing on infant's body;
3-3=Rough pulling to sit; 4=Hands not in contact with baby but
mother is moving them nervously without relating to infant: 4-1=
Mother rubbing eyes, adjusting her own hair, etc.; 4-2=Mother tapping
side of chair, etc., "noncommunicably"; 5=No movement or use of
hands (5-1); 6=Mother using hands to contain baby or to gently adjust: 6-1=Gentle containment of infant's body or limbs without
movement; 6-2=Nonabrupt adjustment of baby's body or head to midline; 7=Small movements which contact infant's body or limbs - light,
rhythmic or repetitive: 7-1=Light tapping or small stroking or
cycling of limbs or body; 7-2=Gentle "picking" or "grooming" movements on body; 7-3=Slight adjustment which is not of whole body or
head; 8=Gentle medium sized movements, rhythmic, emphasis is moderate: 8-1=Gentle medium to large cycling of infant's limbs; 8-2=
Gentle pull to sit; 8-3=Tapping or lightly stroking baby's face;
8-4=Emphatic but gentle stroking of baby's body; 9=Intensive movements of baby - emphatic, fast, but not poking or abrupt: 9-1=
Intense tickling; 9-2=Stroking baby's face with intensity; 9-3=Large,
full body stroking.

Mother Facial Expression

   Macro: 1-1=Angry face; 2-1=Full frown; 3-1=Serious, sad or sober;
3-2=Lidded; 4-1=Neutral flat; 5-1=Bright; 6-1=Animated bright; 7-1=
Simple smile; 7-2=Play face of low intensity; 7-3=Purse-lipped kiss;
8-1=Smile of moderate intensity; 8-2=Play face of moderate intensity;
9-1=Broad, full smile; 9-2="Superlook" playface; 9-3="ooooo" face.

Mother Attention

   Micro Attention: 1=Towards baby's face; 2=Look away from face,
but on baby's body; 3=Looking away from baby but related to interaction (e.g., looking at toy used in playing with infant); 4=Looking
away from baby, not related to interaction.
   Macro Attention: 1=Complete looking away (Micro 3 or 4 for more
than 6 seconds); 2=Interrupted looking away from baby (Micro 3 and
4 for between 3 and 6 seconds with micro 1 or 2 for two or less
seconds); 3=Away, looking on baby's body (Micro 2 for more than 6
seconds); 4=Interrupted (part-time) looking at baby (Micro 1 for
between 3 and 6 seconds and micro 2 for between 3 and 6 seconds);
5=Away glances off baby (Micro 1 for between 3 and 6 seconds with
micro 3 or 4 for two or less seconds); a series of alternating
glances (micro 1 for two or less seconds alternating with micro 3
or 4 for two or less seconds occurring more than once); 6=Away
glances on baby (Micro 1 for between 3 and 6 seconds with a micro
2 for 2 or less seconds; *or* Micro 1 for more than 6 seconds with a
micro 2 of 2 or less seconds. In this case, score the micro 1s
7 and score the 2s, 6.); 7=Completely sustained looking towards
(Micro 1 for more than 6 seconds). Note: Macro scale points 8 and
9 are not used.

Mother Head Position

Micro Head Position: 01=Towards and level; 02=Towards and down; 03=Towards and up; 04=Part side, level; 05=Part side, down; 06=Part side, up; 07=Complete side, level; 08=Complete side, down; 09=Complete side, up; 10=Positions 01, 02, 03, 04, 05, and 06 with small nodding or shaking of head; 11=Positions 01, 02, 03, 04, 05, and 06 with medium size to large nodding, shaking or cocking, not sustained; 12=Thrusting head forward towards baby with neck extension; 13=Nuzzling baby with head; 14=Gone; 15=Cocked head position in 01, 02, 03, 04, 05, or 06 head; 16="Cock-thrust" - micro 12 with head tilted.

Macro Head Position: 1=Gone (micro 14); 2=Side, profile face (micro 07, 08, or 09); 3=Part side, sustained (micro 04, 05, or 06, for three or more seconds); 4=Part side, not sustained (micro 04, 05, or 06 for 2 or less seconds); 5=Frontal, still (micro 01, 02, or 03); 6=Frontal with small nodding, shaking or cocking (micro 10 or 15); 7=Shaking, nodding or cocking (micro 11); 8=Thrusting (micro 12 or micro 16); 9=Nuzzling (micro 13).

Mother Body Positon

Macro: 1-1=Going away from alcove; 1-2=Turns full body to side; 3-1=Sitting back and still; 4-1=Slumping near neutral; 5-1= Neutral, slight forward lean; 5-2=Sitting down on chair; 6-1=Large sideway shifting without curving body; 6-2=Slight rocking forward and back; 7-1=Large sideway shifts into line of vision with curving of body; 7-2=Medium lean forward; 8-1=Large forward and back rocking; 9-1=Movement forward, close to baby and sustained.

APPENDIX B: MONADIC PHASE SCORING MANUAL

The manual provides definitions for the monadic phases based
on the micro-temporal (second x second, modality x modality) level
of analysis.   This manual is designed to be used in conjunction with
the microscoring manual in Appendix A.   The numbers in parentheses
refer to microscores in the microscoring manul.   * indicates that
a behavior is sufficient for the assignment of the corresponding
monadic phase.   ⌐‾‾‾⌐ indicates that a behavior precludes the
assignment of the corresponding monadic phase.

TABLE 1. INFANT MONADIC PHASES

BODY	HEAD	FACE	VOICE	EYES
Protest: A strong negative affective expression that also involves attempts to orient away from the partner.				
Lean (1-1)*				
Side (1-2)*				
Arch (2-1)*		Cry (1-1)*		
			Cry (5)*	
			Cry (6)	
	Sideways (7,8,9)	Grimace (2-1)		Away (2)
Slump (4-1)		Grimace (2-1)		Away (2)
Adjust (5-2)		Grimace (2-1)		
Aversion: Negative affect expression including a partial or complete turning away from the partner.				
	Sideways (7,8,9)			
	Towards/Up (3)	Neutral (5-1)		Away (2)
	Part side/Up (6)	Neutral (5-1)		
Monitor: Affect can be relative negative to somewhat positive while orientation is primarily toward the partner.				
		Grimace (2-1)		
		Pout (2-2)		
		Wary (3-1)		
		Frown (3-2)		
		Lidded (4-1)		

72

Table 1 (continued)

BODY	HEAD	FACE	VOICE	EYES
	Toward/Down (2)	Neutral (5-1)		
	Part side/Down (5)	Bright (6-2)		
		Bright (6-2)		

Set: Affect is neutral to somewhat positive while orientation is generally toward the partner in a position already set for the more positive states.

	Part side/Down (5)	Bright (6-2)		
	Toward/Down (2)	Bright (6-2)		
	Toward/Up (3)	Neutral (5-1)		
	Part side/Up (6)	Neutral (5-1)		

Play: Affect is positive and orientation is fully toward the partner.

		Sim. Smile (7-1)	Single (2)*	
		Coo (8-1)	Single (2)*	
		Bd. Smile (9-1)	Single (2)*	
		Orgiastic (9-2)	Single (2)*	
			Laugh (7)*	

Talk: Affect is positive and orientation is fully toward the partner and some vocalization occurs.

		Sim. Smile (7-1)	Single (2)	
		Coo (8-1)	Single (2)	
		Bd. Smile (9-1)	Single (2)	
		Orgiastic (9-2)	Single (2)	
			Coo (4)*	

73

TABLE 2. ADULT MONADIC PHASES

BODY	HEAD	FACE	VOICE	HANDS	EYES
Avoid: A strong negative affective expression that involves attempts to orient away from the partner.					
Leave (1-1)*	Sideways (7,8,9)*	Angry (1-1)*	Shout (1-1)		Away (4)
Away (1-2)*					Away (4)
					Away (4)
					Away (4)
					Away (4)
Back (3-1)		Frown (2-1)			Away (4)
Slump (4-1)		Serious (3-1)			Away (4)
		Lidded (3-2)			Away (4)
			Adult (2-1)		
			Stern (3-1)		
			Pause (4-1)		
Avert: Negative affective expression including a partial or complete turning away from the partner.					
					Away (4)
			Adult (2-1)		
			Tense (3-1)		
		Frown (2-1)	None (4)		Body (2)
		Serious (3-1)	None (4)		Body (2)
		Lidded (3-2)	None (4)		Body (2)
		Neutral (4-1)			Body (2)

74

Table 2 (continued)

BODY	HEAD	FACE	VOICE	HANDS	EYES
Monitor: Affective expression is somewhat negative but orientation is primarily toward the partner.					
		Bright (6)	Low (4)		
		Frown (2-1)			
		Serous (3-1)			
		Lidded (3-2)	None (5)		
		Neutral (4-1)	Burst Pause (6)		
		Neutral (4-1)	Burst Pause (7)		
		Bright (5)	Burst Pause (6)		
		Bright (5)	None (5)		
		Bright (5)	Low (4)		
Elicit: Affect may vary widely but actions are performed to produce orientation (monitoring) by the infant.					
Line of Vision (7-1)*		Neutral (4-1)	Neutral (4-1)		
Sideways (6-1)*			Exhort (3)*		
				Abrupt (1)	Away (4)
				Sudden (2)	Away (4)
				Rough (3)	Away (4)
				Adjust (6-2)	Away (4)
Medium Close (7-2) or Close (9-1)	Thrust (12) Nuzzle (13) Cocked (15) Thrust-Cock (16)	Bright (5-1) or more negative			

Table 2 (continued)

BODY	HEAD	FACE	VOICE	HANDS	EYES

Set: Affect is neutral to positive while orientation is generally toward the partner in a position already set for the more positive states.

BODY	HEAD	FACE	VOICE	HANDS	EYES
		Bright (5)	Burst Pause (7)		
		A. Bright (6-1)	Narrative (5)		
		A. Bright (6-1)	Low B.P. (6)		
		A. Bright (6-1)	Burst Pause (7)		
		Sim. Smile (7-1)	Low (4)		
		Sim. Smile (7-1)	Narrative (5)		
		Sim. Smile (7-1)	Low B.P. (6)		

Play: Affect is positive and orientation is fully toward the partner.

BODY	HEAD	FACE	VOICE	HANDS	EYES
For./Back (8-1)					
Medium Close (7-2)	Thrust (12)	A. Bright (6-1)			
or	Nuzzle (13)	Sim. Smile (7)			
Close (9-1)	Cocked (15)	Smiles (8)			
	Thrust-Cock (16)	Coo (9)	Burst (9-1)*		

Talk: Affect is positive and orientation is fully toward the infant and "infantalized" voclizations occur.

BODY	HEAD	FACE	VOICE	HANDS	EYES
		Simple Smile (7)	Hi B.P. (8)*		
			Burst Pause (7)*		

4.
Interactive patterns
as units of behavior

GERALD R. PATTERSON & DENNIS MOORE

The determination or selection of meaningful units of behavior
is a recurring problem in observational studies of human interaction.
This process generally begins with the selection of behaviors to be
observed via a structured observation format. Although there are no
systematic guidelines for selecting specific study or target events
from all possible behaviors, specific research goals may aid in nar-
rowing the potential field. A closely related decision concerns the
degree of detail with which behavior is coded. Investigators vary
widely along this molar/molecular dimension. For example, in sampling the interactions of preschool children, one investigator may
focus upon such molecular behaviors as "arm cocked above head--threat
gesture." Others might sample more molar units, such as "push",
"hit", and "kick", or the still more molar "physical aggression."
Each strategy has its own set of utilities and liabilities, which we
have only begun to understand (Altman, 1965).
    Careful consideration of current knowledge about the population
to be studied, research questions of interest, and the degree of analytic detail required of the data should provide a starting point
from which to produce a behavior recording system which has heuristic
value. The first steps in structuring an observational strategy have
an obvious, and enormous, impact on the results of all future research
that utilizes the system. This is because the specific structure of
the system and the form in which the events are recorded place rigid
limitations on the types of questions that can be answered and the
kinds of analyses which can be conducted. Given the construction of
an observational system with a priori face validity, the next step
is to demonstrate that data can be recorded in a reliable fashion.
However, even after an observational system has been shown to have
acceptable levels of interrater and temporal reliability, it must
still satisfy the critical requirement of functional validity. As
used here, the term "validity" refers to the degree to which the observed units of behavior produce data which answer questions about
ongoing social interactions.

77

The individual behavioral events within an observational system, taken one at a time, may or may not produce useful information. Any given event is embedded within an ongoing interaction. To understand an event, it will be necessary to specify how it relates to this ongoing interaction. How does one decide which events are important? How is one to conceptualize the relation between ongoing interaction and a particular behavioral event? Each investigator has his/her own articles of faith as to what is important and what is not, and each has his/her own mode of analysis. The latter may range from factor analysis to simple descriptions of behavior frequencies.

The purpose of this chapter is to describe the sequence of analyses followed at the Oregon Social Learning Center (OSLC). The data for the analyses were from families of aggressive, conduct problem children observed in their homes. We employed several complex filters when looking at interactional processes. One filter consisted of some amalgamation of social learning principles and hypotheses from coercion theory (Patterson, 1978). Another filter involved a search for interactional "units". Three kinds of units were examined. One consisted of relations between what a child did at t_1 and what s/he did at t_2. Another, and more interesting, unit consisted of the relation between what the child did at t_1 and what another family member did at t_2. The third unit was characterized by more extended interactions which were repeated frequently. These extended units were labelled as interactive patterns. The findings presented are admittedly preliminary, but sufficient to give some information as to the general utility of the various approaches to the problem.

FUNCTIONAL UNITS: THE EARLY STUDIES

The data used for our initial studies in this area were collected using the Family Interaction Coding System (FICS) (Patterson, Ray, Shaw, & Cobb, 1969; Reid, 1978). This observational code was constructed to sample a range of behavioral events, with the major focus on aversive behaviors. Fourteen of the 29 behavior categories are classed as aversive; the remainder are prosocial behaviors or activities. The FICS samples behavior every 6 seconds, and records those behaviors and reactions to them in sequential order. Several studies examining the reliability of the FICS show: (1) overall entry by entry agreement is consistently about 75% (Reid, 1978); (2) overall observer agreement for the aversive categories is 85% (Taplin & Reid, 1977).

Comparisons between known groups of aggressive and normal children in home settings have shown that aggressive children display significantly higher rates of those behaviors classed as aversive than do normal children (e.g., Patterson, 1976). Results of sequential analyses indicated that the display of the same aversive behaviors were reacted to differently by the families of the two groups of youngsters. Both normal and aggressive children were regularly punished for engaging in aversive behavior, but, whereas punishment was often effective in terminating those behaviors in normal children, aggressive children continued to display the same aversive behaviors, even though they continued to be punished (Kopfstein, 1972; Patterson, 1976; Snyder, 1977). It appeared from these studies that aversive behaviors were functionally different for aggressive and normal children. These analyses also suggested that the behavioral differences were not solely a function of differences in children, but may also have been the result of different interactive processes in the two groups of families.

An important question raised by these data is the extent to which aversive behavior by children is affected by the reactions of others. Obviously, a simple rule of thumb, (e.g., that punishment used by parents of an aggressive child appears to accelerate child aversive behaviors), will not provide enough information to determine the probability of immediate and subsequent displays of aversive behavior by any given child. It appears that rather than studying simple one-step dyadic units (child behavior → parent behavior), it may be necessary to examine longer chains of parent-child behaviors for a fuller understanding of child aggression.

Therefore, our first step in constructing larger interactional units from molecular behavioral events was to create classes of child behavior. Not all children in the above study demonstrated precisely the same aversive behaviors, and some behaviors occurred too infrequently for individual analysis. We attempted to group aversive child behaviors into classes which appeared to serve the same function (Patterson & Cobb, 1973). This was done by computing the conditional probabilities for child aversive behaviors, given the occurrence of specific antecedent behaviors by others with whom the child interacted. Antecedent behaviors which increased the likelihood of aversive events were calculated for each of the 14 coercive behaviors.[1] Child aversive behaviors sharing the same antecedent networks were grouped into classes. On this basis, the study by Patterson and Cobb (1973) identified two such classes of aversive child behaviors: *Hostility*, child aversive behaviors that followed specific antecedents by mothers and older sisters; and *Social Aggression*, which included behaviors preceded by specific antecedents from younger siblings.

These two classes differed not only in terms of which family members were involved, but in other respects as well. Family members punished 32% of the *Hostile* child behaviors and 49% of *Social Aggressive* child behaviors (Patterson, 1976). Given that a *Hostile* behavior displayed by a child was punished by another family member, there was an increase in the likelihood that hostile behavior by the child would immediately recur or persist. This effect was labeled "punishment acceleration." In contrast, the punishment acceleration effect was observed to be minimal for the *Social Aggression* class. These results suggest that the aggressive behavior of children may be structured in relatively complex behavior patterns. Thus, aggressive "units" of child behavior may be sequentially ordered, both as a function of the

---

1. A series of studies reviewed in Patterson (1977, 1978) demonstrated experimentally that controlling events do, in fact, control behavior. A series of $N = 1$ studies were carried out employing ABA reversal design to demonstrate causal status for a number of controlling antecedents.

agents involved with the child's aggressive behavior, the specific consequences for that behavior, and the effect upon the next response.

These simple analyses were useful in describing dyadic interchanges. They demonstrated that antecedent and consequent events dispensed by another person may influence the pattern of certain child behaviors. However, it may also be the case that the child's own behaviors serve as instigators of behaviors that follow. Comparisons of conditional probabilities to base rate values, as cited above, do not take this possibility into account and may lead one to overestimate the significance of the behavior of the other person. Support for the assumption that the child's previous response determines, to some degree, his or her subsequent responses has been reported by Patterson (1976). He showed that children's aversive behavior tends to occur in "bursts" which are followed, presumably, by relative quietude. A more complete empirical description of an interactive interchange should account for variance in a child's behavioral sequences affected by (a) individual differences in the child, (b) child-agent interaction, and (c) child-setting interaction.

In order to carry these analyses further, it was necessary to revise our observational system. The 6-second sampling format used in the FICS tends to produce artificial segmentation of behaviors. In this sytem, the behavioral entries recorded may or may not represent behavioral onset (e.g., they may represent continuing behavior instead of a series of discontinuous behaviors). The resultant sequential ordering of events may inflate both the frequencies and conditional probabilities obtained. This was not considered a major problem for the above analyses. The need for greater precision for the conduct of complex interactive analyses, however, required that the observational format be modified. The following sections describe the changes in the observational system and the initial results of interactive pattern analyses using data collected by that system.

A FURTHER SEARCH FOR STRUCTURE

The Family Interaction Coding System (FICS) (Reid, 1978) was revised to permit greater accuracy in the sequential recording of behavior. This revision (Moore, Forgatch, Mukai, & Toobert, 1977) changed the recording and scoring formats to provide accurate measures of the onset and duration of target behaviors, while retaining the majority of the original behavior categories. Instead of scoring behavioral epsidoes every 6 seconds, behavior was recorded on magnetic tape using a standard set of categories, at the point in time at which it began. The data from the tapes were transcribed in such a way that the sequence of behavioral interactions could be preserved, as well as the starting and end points of each interaction and the durations of each individual behavior. The resultant data sheets provided sequenti ordering of events from multiple interactants over a representative time frame. As stated previously, frequency of behavior, the onset, the duration, sequential order of interactions, and combinations of these measures can be derived from protocol sheets.

With the revised observation system, it was hoped that patterns

or structures of child aversive behaviors could be identified and
that these patterns could be predicted and understood by reference
to the child's own response sequences and by reference to the pattern
or structure of his/her interactions with other family members. The
overriding hypothesis which guided this work was that aggressive
children engage in aversive behavior in a nonrandom fashion. Following from a social learning point of view, it was hypothesized that
children employ aversive behaviors and strategies to manipulate their
social environments to attain positive payoffs. If these hypotheses
were essentially correct, and if the observational system were adequate, then it should be possible to measure and find both (1)
systematic patterns of child aversive responding and (2) predictable
impacts of these patterns on the immediate social environment. No
assumptions were made regarding whether or not the use of such behavioral patterns requires conscious awareness by the interactants.
Instead, such patterns might be comparable to the "social games"
described by Berne (1964) and Harris (1969), in which certain patterns
of behavior are assumed to lead to predictable outcomes without the
awareness of such patterns by the interactants involved. It was not
hypothesized that patterns of aggressive child interactions are invariant; it was simply hypothesized that probabilistic statements
could be made about the patterns of such interactions.

The term "coercion hypothesis" has been coined to describe the
present program to studies (Patterson, 1978). These investigations
have been designed to examine the possibility that aversive behaviors
produce regular and predictable patterns in social interaction. We
feel that aversive behaviors are systematically employed, to some
extent, by all children to produce desired outcomes in their social
relationships. We have also assumed that in the present context,
these hypotheses would contribute to our understanding of the various
interactional units.

In the first attempt to use the new code system to examine these
issues, over 60 hours of observational data were collected in the home
of one family, which consisted of two parents, a 6-year-old daughter,
Tina, and a 3-year-old son. Tina was described by her parents and
by project staff as a highly coercive child whose behavior was pro-
blematic in both home and school settings. An early analysis of
portions of these data (Moore & Patterson, 1977) demonstrated dramatic differences in Tina's behavior, depending upon whether the
father was present or absent during home observations. The analyses
described here are based on only 14 hours of observational data, during
which the family was absent. This was done in the hopes of providing
a homogeneous setting in which to examine the behavior patterns of
interest.

Is Coercive Behavior Serially Dependent?

Initial inspection and analyses of observational data collected
in Tina's home focused upon her aversive responses. Casual inspection
of the data showed that her aversive behavior was not evenly distributed across observational sessions. Instead, it tended to fluctuate
between periods of high and low density. Figure 1 provides an illustration of these fluctuations from a portion of a typical 2-hour observation segment.

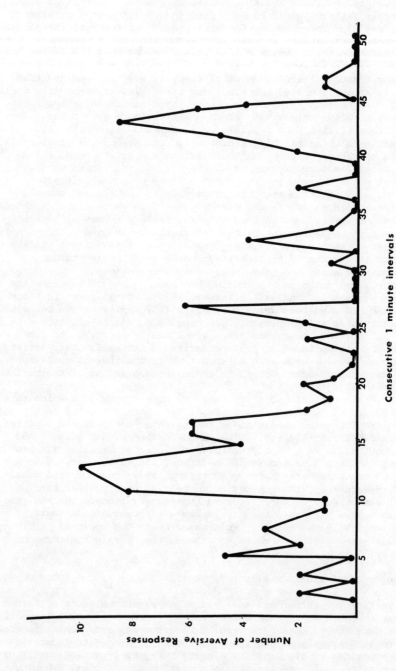

FIGURE 1. Fluctuations in Tina's Aversive Responses.

The observational data suggested that Tina's aversive behaviors fluctuated in an orderly fashion, i.e., they seemed to recur every 25 minutes. To test for the stability of the regularity, auto-correlations for lags 1 through 30 were computed using 1-minute intervals. Analysis of the 2-hour segment displayed in Figure 1 resulted in significant correlations at Lag 1 ($r = +.53$; $df = 86$; $p < .01$), Lag 12 ($r = -.25$; $df = 75$; $p < .05$), and Lag 27 ($r = +.25$; $df = 60$; $p < .05$). The results suggest that the behaviors may have been cyclic in nature, but the data were insufficient for a proper test of the hypothesis.

These fluctuations in the output of aversive behaviors are not surprising. Obviously, Tina could not emit six aversive behaviors per minute indefinitely. However, the fact that the fluctuations tended to be cyclical in nature seems quite interesting, although no explanations for this outcome can be offered at present.

Examination of Tina's aversive behaviors showed that they tended to occur in bursts, followed by periods of neutral or prosocial behavior. As the density of her aversive responses increased, the time period between bursts seemed to decrease. It seemed, then, that the bursts, themselves, would be a likely area to search next for structure in social interaction. The most frequent bursts or chains were thus identified and grouped according to the type of aversive behavior which initiated them. Tina's behavior "Complain" was the most common initiation for one coercive chain; "Argue" was the next most frequent event for initiating extended coercive inter-changes. Most interchanges initiated in this manner were with her mother. A third coercive interchange occurred with her brother, initiated by "Physical Negative" (hitting or shoving). These chains of behavior were then analyzed for patterned responding using sequential lag analyses as described by Sackett (1978).

We included in the present analyses only those chains that were preceded by at least 15 seconds of neutral or prosocial behavior by Tina. For each chain, Tina's behaviors were listed in sequential order from her 1st through 8th behavior. A conditional probability was calculated for each behavior occurring at Lags 1 through 8.[2] These values were then compared to the base rate values for each behavior. The base rate values were derived from an analysis of all of the observation data collected while her father was absent and were corrected by subtracting from the numerator and denominator those events involved in calculating the conditional probabilities.

Results of these analyses are summarized in Table 1. The first column gives the overall base rate values for each of the target behaviors (e.g., hitting comprised about 1.9% of Tina's observed behavior). Proceeding across the table, probabilities are given

---

2.   The decision to stop at 8 was almost entirely arbitrary. Sackett (1978) typically seems to run his analyses to Lag 15. It was thought that for the present purposes the additional labor involved would not be cost-effective. The reason for this is that in the later stages some cross-lag analyses require geometric increases in data as one moves from one lag to another. In view of this, we assumed that the cross-lag analyses would probably only move through the first 2 lags.

Table 1.   THREE PATTERNS FROM TINA'S INTERACTION WITH MOTHER AND BROT[

Position in chain / Behavior initiating the chain	Overall Base Rate (BR)	Lag 1			Lag 2			Lag 3		Lag 4	
		Rj[1]	p[2]	z[3]	Rj	p	z	p	z	p	
Physical Negative (PN) N=35	.019	PN	.103	3.64 ***	PN	.179	7.69 ***	.135	5.84 ***	.111	5
Argue (AR) N=61	.079	AR	.258	5.23 ***							
Complain (CP) N=90	.070	CP	.19	4.46 ***	CP	.15	3.60 ***	.13	2.80 **	.15	4
	.160	PL	.26	2.59 *							

Position in chain / Behavior initiating the chain	Overall base rate (BR)	Lag 5			Lag 6		Lag 7		Lag 8	
		Rj	p	z	p	z	p	z	p	
Physical Negative (PN) N=35	.019	PN	.139	7.26 ***	.062	2.89 **	.061	3.03 **	.152	2
Complain (CP) N=90	.070	CP	.12	3.05 ***	.12	3.05 **	.09	2.42 *	.11	3

[1] Tina's behavior at each lag position.
[2] Probability of Rj at each lag position.
[3] Binomial Z test comparing difference between conditional and correcte[d] base rate probability.

   * $p < .05$
  ** $p < .01$
*** $p < .001$

for the same behavior repeated at each subsequent position or lag
on the chain, then the Z score is given for the statistical difference between the observed and base rate probabilities at each
lag. The only exception is shown at Lag 1 for the behavior "Complain".
Although the probability that Tina's complaining at Lag 1 was .19,
the probability that she would engage in play at this position in
the chain was also high (.26), so that fact is noted in the table.
The binomial Z is a test recommended by Sackett (1978) as a means
for testing the significance of the increase of a conditional over
a base rate value.[3]

The data presented in Table 1 suggest that once Tina began to
complain, that same behavior had a chance higher than base rate
(10 times as likely) of occurring again at each of the next eight
junctures. This once-begun-likely-to-reappear phenomenon was also
observed for arguing and hitting. In effect, the occurrence of any
one of the three behaviors was likely to initiate an interactional
ripple effect. It is *not* the case, of course, that each time Tina
complained, hit, or argued, she would run through seven more like
behaviors in sequence.

The protocols were then examined to determine the actual frequency with which these behaviors occurred as adjacent events in a
sequence, e.g., Complain, Complain or Hit, Hit, Hit. These adjacent
occurrences were labeled patterned sequences.

Table 2 summarizes descriptive data relating to the patterns
for Tina's complaining, arguing, and hitting. As can be seen, most
of the patterns consisted of just two consecutive, like behaviors.
However, it is of considerable interest that approximately one-third
of all three types of behaviors comprised pattern sequences.

It was hypothesized that these patterns would most likely occur
during intervals characterized by a high density of Tina's coercive behavior. To evaluate this possibility, the frequency of
child aversive behaviors was tabulated for each 5-minute interval,
as well as the frequency for each pattern sequence. As expected,
the analysis supported the hypothesis that sequential patterns of
aversive behavior are most likely to occur during intervals of
high density aversive behavior ($r = .79$; $df = 155$; $p < .001$). Although some relationship between density and sequence is to be
expected by chance alone, the magnitude of the observed correlation
is large and suggests that further study of such patterns might
facilitate an understanding of bursts of aggressive behavior.

Interactive Analyses: Within Patterned Sequences

The sequential lag analyses presented in the previous section
suggest that some type of interactive "structure" might exist out to

---

3. When the base rate values for a target behavior were less than
.10, only Z values significant at better than the .01 level were
included in the table. Following Sackett's rule partially compen-
sates for the problems raised by low base rate events.

TABLE 2.   SOME DESCRIPTIVE DATA FOR THREE OF TINA'S PATTERNS

Content of Patterns	Frequency				Total % in patterns
	Individual events	Two component patterns	Three component patterns	Four or more components	
Complain	267	25 (18.7%)	12 (13.5%)	7 (10.5%)	42.7%
Argue	211	25 (23.4%)	7 (9.9%)	1 (1.9%)	35.2%
Physical Negative	87	7 (16.1%)	4 (13.8%)	1 (4.6%)	34.5%

as many as eight sequential responses for "Complain", seven for
"Physical Negative", and two for "Argue" events. We therefore
attempted to identify the relative contributions of both the
sequential behaviors of the child and the behaviors of the persons
with whom the child interacted. Because we had most data on chains
initiated by Tina's "Complain", it was selected as the focus for
this cross-lag analysis. The first step was to tabulate the mother's
reactions at each point in the sequence. The mother's behavior was
tabulated in terms of her reactions to occurrences of Tina's "Complai
This decision resulted in very small samples of events entering the
analyses at any particular cross lag. This limitation of data made
it impossible to interpret the results of cross-lag analyses beyond
position 4 (Lag 3). Figure 2 summarizes the results of the cross-
lag analysis. At Lag 1, the most likely mother-dispensed antecedent
for "Complain" was "Talk"; for Lag 2, the most likely mother antecedent was "Disapproval"; and at Lag 3, it was mother "Complain".

   While tentative, the findings are of interest in suggesting that
both mother and daughter may be contributing to a kind of patterned
dyadic interactional unit. We assume that sequential-lag and cross-
lag analyses of this kind may be useful in determining whether or
not patterned structures exist in various types of dyadic interchange. In effect, sequential-lag analyses may identify which parts
of dyadic interchanges should be examined more closely.

   Because of the way the data were prepared for the cross-lag
analyses, only tentative support is given to the hypothesis that
both interactants influence the progression of "patterned" chains.
In the analyses, the only fixed variables in each of the sequences
was Tina's initial "Complain". Thus, between Tina's initial "Complai
and a subsequent "Complain" (e.g., at Lag 2), she could have displayed
an actual sequence such as Initial Complain → Play → Complain. Therefore, it is not clear that any of the mother's reactions to "Complain"
really affected later occurrences of "Complain". For this reason, a
series of molecular functional analyses were carried out in an attempt
to identify behaviors by the mother which altered the base rate probability for Tina emitting consecutive "Complaints". In other words,

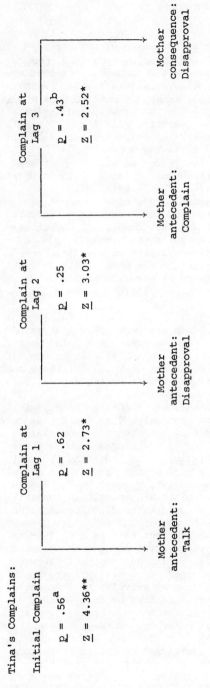

Tina's Complains:

Initial Complain

$\underline{p}$ = .56[a]

$\underline{Z}$ = 4.36**

Mother
antecedent:
Talk

Complain at
Lag 1

$\underline{p}$ = .62

$\underline{Z}$ = 2.73*

Mother
antecedent:
Disapproval

Complain at
Lag 2

$\underline{p}$ = .25

$\underline{Z}$ = 3.03*

Mother
antecedent:
Complain

Complain at
Lag 3

$\underline{p}$ = .43[b]

$\underline{Z}$ = 2.52*

Mother
consequence:
Disapproval

[a]Given that a Complain did occur at Lag 1, the probability was .56 that Mother Talk was the antecedent. The $\underline{Z}$ compares this conditional to the corrected base rate for Mother Talk.

[b]Given that a Complain did occur at Lag 3, the probability was .43 that Mother Disapproval would follow it immediately.

* $\underline{p}$ < .05

** $\underline{p}$ < .01

*** $\underline{p}$ < .001

FIGURE 2: Cross-lagged analyses: Mother's reactions to Tina's "Complain".

87

were certain behaviors emitted by mother which were associated with her demonstrating a pattern of CP, CP, CP rather than CP, non-CP, non-

Studies cited earlier in this chapter had suggested that aversive consequences to aggressive child behavior were associated with immediate increases in the performance rates. Tina's "Complain" chains were analyzed for those effects. As in the previous analysis, all of Tina's four behavior sequences, beginning with Tina CP, were identified. Next, each interactive mother behavior was tabulated prior to, at various points during, and following a pattern.

Tina's first "Complain", in the sequences studied, produced significant changes in the base rate probabilities of the mother's ongoing behavior. If one considers mother's talking to be a reinforcing event and mother's disapproval and use of commands as punishing events, then interesting findings emerge from the first functional analysis. Following the first "Complain", mother was significantly less likely to use direct Alpha commands ($p = .053$; $Z = -5.70$; $p < .01$), and somewhat less likely to use Disapprove ($p = .144$; $Z = -1.19$; n.s.). The mother was more likely to Talk" ($p = .303$; $Z = 2.19$; $p < .05$). In other words, these results are consistent with the idea that Tina's complaining may be maintained by positive reinforcement.

Two-Unit Patterns. The probability of a second "Complain" immediately following Tina's first "Complain" was .33. Analyses of mother-dispensed antecedents for these two-unit "Complain" patterns produced no significant findings. These negative results suggest that the mother-dispensed events which actually control these patterns might be found in the reactions of the mother during and following patterns.

The subsequent overall hypothesis was that Tina's complaining sequences maximized the likelihood that her mother would reciprocate with prosocial reactions. Analysis of the mother's prosocial responses suggested that she tended to give a single such response and then shift to independent behavior, or to providing Tina with negative reactions. The probability of mother providing a second prosocial behavior to Tina, given a first, was only .18. Two possibilities concerning Tina's complain sequences were investigated. First, a complain sequence could be used to increase the likelihood of continuing her mother's prosocial behavior, given that it had started; this arrangement might best be described as positive reinforcement (neutral or prosocial antecedent by mother → Complain by Tina → mother prosocial). The second possibility was that Complain might be used to terminate an aversive intrusion by her mother, getting her to switch from an aversive to a prosocial behavior. This second possibility would best be described as negative reinforcement: aversive intrusion by mother → Complain pattern by Tina → mother prosocial behavior. These two possibilities were examined separately.

Mother's reaction to Tina's individual "Complain" behaviors (97 isolated events) suggested strongly that Tina's complaining significantly increased the probability that the mother would subsequently react positively towards her. Forty-five percent of the reactions by mother to these "Complains" were prosocial. This was

significantly higher than the mother's base rate probability for
prosocial behavior ($Z = 4.95$; $df = 96$; $p < .01$). Even single
instances of "Complain" by Tina served to ensure mother's prosocial
reactions.

If Tina ran off two "Complains" in a row, the mother reacted
by providing positive consequences 67% of the time. This again
produced a significant increase over the base rate likelihood of
mother prosocial behavior ($Z = 4.55$; $p < .01$). There was an
apparent increase in efficiency for these two-unit chains in pro-
ducing mother-positive behavior over that which obtained for single
complaint events. This increase, however, was only of borderline
significance ($Z = 1.71$; $df = 14$; $p < .06$, one-tailed test).

These results provide modest support for the idea that the
function of Tina's "Complains" was to keep prosocial interaction
going with her mother. If one could demonstrate that prosocial
behaviors dispensed by the mother were reinforcers for Tina, then
it could be said that her patterns of coercive responses maximized
reinforcement. At one level, this poses a paradox. How can it be
that *aversive* child behaviors, in isolation or in patterns, produce
positive reinforcement? While counter-intuitive, the relationship
is the same as one described in the 1920's by a careful clinical
observer, Alfred Adler (1964), and more recently by social learning
theorists as well.

The mother, over the course of the observations, was quite abra-
sive in her interactions with Tina. In fact, 68% of her interactions
with her daughter were aversive; this included such events as Argue,
Disapprove, Complain, Hit, Command, Ignore, Request, and Noninteract.
As shown in Table 3, given that Tina complained, this base rate of
.68 was reduced to .49 ($Z = 4.01$; $df = 48$, $p < .01$). Given that Tina

TABLE 3.   SOME FUNCTIONAL RELATIONS FOR TINA'S COMPLAIN PATTERNS

Antecedents	Aversive Maintenance Events For:			Positive Outcomes:		
	Two Unit	Three Unit	Four or More Units	Two Unit	Three Unit	Four Unit
Positive antecedent	33%	75%[a] (3/4)	100% (2/2)	67%	100%[b] (2/2)	100% (2/2)
Aversive antecedent	75%	88% (8/9)	100% (5/5)	44%	44% (4/9)	69% (3/5)

[a]Refers to the limited number of events entering into the calculations.

[b]Some of the consequences could not be coded for these patterns, e.g.,
the session ended.

ran off two "Complains" in a row, the probability of the mother be-
having aversively toward her was only slightly reduced (.44). It
should be noted that on the majority of occasions (70%), the mother
provided not only an aversive *antecedent* for Tina's first "Complain",
but at least one or more aversive behaviors during her complaint
pattern. It is assumed that reactions occurring *during* the pattern
are critical in determining the duration of the pattern. In effect,
maintenance reactions may be major determinants of pattern length
and, indirectly, of bursts as well. The data strongly suggest that
Tina's first "Complain" was often not effective in removing the
mother's aversive intrusion, but produced another aversive intrusion
as well. This in turn was followed by a second "Complain" by Tina
which finally produced a positive response from mother, i.e., an
exemplar of negative reinforcement for complain patterns.

It appears that the type of input from mother (i.e., aversive
or nonaversive) during the execution of an aversive pattern determined whether it would be continued or terminated. The relationship
seemed to vary as a function of which reinforcement mechanism was
involved. Given that mother talking was an antecedent for Tina's
first "Complain", then the second "Complain" tended to produce a
positive maintenance event for mother's talking and another positive
consequence. These two-unit patterns maximized positive outcomes.
If the pattern was one of negative reinforcement, the second "Complain"
seemed necessary as a means of turning off the noxious intrusion by
the mother, which also tended to persist as maintenance events.
Going on to the second "Complain" in the pattern doubled the likelihood of a positive outcome.

Three or More Unit Patterns. Of the 44 instances of two consecutive "Complains" by Tina, 43% extended to even longer patterns.
An analysis of the antecedents for these longer patterns produced
nonsignificant outcomes.

There was only a small number (six) of longer "Complain" chains
with positive antecedents (cf. Table 3). For this reason, the
trends must be interpreted with extreme caution. In general, these
patterns worked very well. They tended to produce a positive outcome. However, the price for the outcome also seemed high, in that
they were accompanied by aversive maintenance events. The most
that can be said is that longer patterns seemed to perpetuate the
interaction, but at a cost. There were 14 longer patterns with
aversive antecedents. For almost all of them, there were one or
more aversive maintenance events. It seemed likely that if Tina
had stopped after her first CP, she would have received an aversive
antecedent plus an aversive consequence. However, going on to a
third or fourth CP appeared to produce a more favorable outcome.
It is hypothesized that the function of these longer patterns was to
terminate persistent aversive intrusions.

These speculations were based upon a limited sample of events
from a single response for one dyad. This is hardly a satisfying
state of affairs. For this reason, it was decided to examine briefly
the functional relations characterizing the "Physical Negative" (PN)
pattern, in that all of these patterns involved the younger brother.
This would introduce a new dyad and a new response. Given two

adjacent "Hits", then the likelihood of going on to yet another was .42. Every one of the longer patterns was associated with aversive maintenance reactions by the brother ("Hit", "Yell") and/or the mother ("Disapprove"). As might be expected, the larger the number of aversive maintenance events, the longer the PN pattern. The Fisher exact chi square for this association was significant at .04. This correlation is suggestive but hardly convincing. In future studies it will be necessary to carry out experimental manipulations to demonstrate that introducing aversive maintenance events does indeed produce longer chains. For the present, however, this small amount of data suggests, again, that for Tina, one function of extended patterns may have been to cope with unwelcome noxious reactions from family members. As noted earlier, the other function for one pattern may have been to extend positive social interactions.

Reliability of Observers

As noted by methodologists (e.g., Hartmann, 1977), the choice of which measure of reliability to use depends upon the task at hand. In the present instance, the fact that observers tend to agree in their total scores from a session protocol is of little import. In the present context, as suggested by John Reid (personal communication), the more appropriate question concerns the agreement in estimating various functional relationships, e.g., $p(CP1/CP1)$.

Two-and-one-half hours of data were available from the father absent condition, during which time both observers were present. The focal point for many of the analyses was Tina's "Complaint" pattern. Therefore, it was selected as the basis from which to examine observer agreement. Two functional units, which were thought to occur with a frequency sufficient for analysis, were examined. These were the probability of a second CP, given the first CP, and the probability of a third, given the second CP (see Table 4).

Hartmann (1977) has suggested that the Pearson product moment correlation is the most appropriate means for expressing agreement. In the present instance, this could be done by calculating each of the several dozen functional relations separately for each observer's data. At this time such reliability analyses are in progress. This

TABLE 4.   OBSERVER AGREEMENT FOR TWO FUNCTIONAL UNITS

Observers	$p(CP_2/CP_1)$	$p(CP_3/CP_1)$
A	.14	.03
B	.12	.04

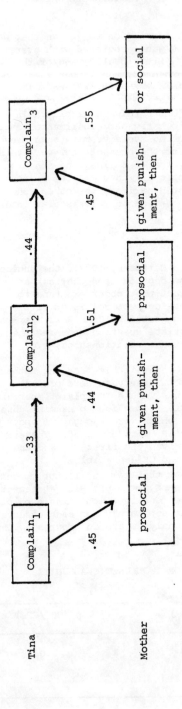

FIGURE 3. An interactive pattern for Tina and mother.

model is certainly to be recommended, and it will be followed in future studies.

An Interactive Pattern

A repetitive interactive pattern is analogous to the games described by Harris (1969) and Berne (1964). The next behavioral event relates probabilistically to the prior behaviors of both persons. In the present context, Tina's behavior at t_3, correlates with her own behavior at t_2, and this in turn with her behavior at t_1. These serial dependencies may describe an autistic-like continuity in Tina's behavior such that her behavior is run off regardless of the reactions of the mother. Figure 3 summarizes the information available for the interactive pattern relating to Tina's Complain. The probability is quite high (.33) that given one Complain, she will move on to a second. Given the second Complain, there is an even higher probability she will continue on to a third. However, this apparent continuity may be viewed in part as a reaction to the mediating reactions of the mother. Given that the mother reacts in a prosocial fashion to Tina's first Complain, there was a very good chance that Tina would *not* proceed to the second Complain. If, on the other hand, the mother responded aversively, there was a .44 chance of her going on to the second Complain. A similar set of outcomes held for her second Complain. In the pattern, each person is reacting to the other, i.e., a mutually determined transaction.

Given more data, it would be possible to construct separate interactive antecedents. As noted earlier, the conditional values resulting from separate analyses would be considerably higher than those found in Figure 3. But, as it stands, even the patterns for the combined data (positive and negative antecedents) seem to describe a means of maximizing positive reactions from a family member who was typically either aversive or nonreactive. As the data in the lower right illustrate, the mother tended not to continue prosocial interactions, i.e., the probability of proceeding to a second prosocial behavior given the first was only .18. The mother did, however, tend to continue being aversive, given that she had made an aversive initiation to Tina.

In one sense the mother was quite predictable, i.e., given she was aversive, she would likely continue being aversive. Given that she was being prosocial with Tina, however, the best bet was that she would not continue to be so. One might think of this interactive pattern as a child's technique for minimizing uncertainty in dyadic interactions.

DISCUSSION

The analyses presented in this chapter represent our most recent attempts to empirically describe family interaction. As mentioned earlier, the results and interpretations are far from conclusive. The data from Tina and her family are only partially analyzed, and data from two additional families are awaiting analysis to replicate the approach. Within these constraints, the results still revealed interesting trends.

Most prominent was the fact that analysis of behavior on both molar and molecular levels showed nonrandom ordering of events. Tina seemed to display regularity in her high-rate "bursts" of aversive behavior. She appeared to structure her use of specific aversive behaviors, and she altered this structure at various choice points dependent upon input from her environment. The use of the structured patterns was associated with increased positive payoff from the environment, providing evidence of their functional nature.

Writers such as Kantor (1959) and Sherif (1967) have long held the study of interactional process to be a focal point for psychology. However, the problem then, as now, concerns the means by which one investigates this process. Given an interest in social interaction as it occurs *in vivo*, the most likely outcome is that of being overwhelmed by its complexity. In this report, the approach taken to circumvent some of this complexity consisted of applying a series of progressively finer filters. The first of these filters focused attention on aversive behavior from an aggressive child. The child's behavior was sampled only from a single, very homogeneous setting within the home. The analysis then proceeded to chunk behavior into large dyadic (and commensurately smaller samples) of events. The complexity of social interaction was made manageable, and patterns seemed to emerge.

When we first encountered Sackett's paper describing sequential lag analyses, it seemed that it might be used as a first phase in such an analysis. As used here, the first step in its application remains intuitive. It requires a lucky guess on the part of an investigator as to just what it is about a dyadic interaction that is interesting. Examination of the raw interaction protocols should highlight some repetitive interactional sequences. At that point, a judicious application of the sequential lag analysis seems to answer the question of whether or not there is some kind of structure actually extant.

Given a series of significant findings for one or both members of a dyad, one suspects that some kind of structure exists. Sequential lag analysis, however, does not tell one what the structure is. For example, one might ask whether the structure is mediated by the behavior of the other person. If so, what are the behaviors of the other which keep it going on and lead to its termination? These questions are thought to constitute a second stage in the search. Our proposed functional analysis format seems an efficient way to set about this second stage. The problem here lies in the enormous amounts of data required.

The data presented in this report demonstrated that coercive behaviors were distributed in a nonrandom fashion. There was, in fact, a suspicion that these variations might be systematic, i.e., regular cycles with a period interval of 25 to 30 minutes. The sequential lag analyses identified three patterns of coercive behaviors for the child: a "Complain", an "Argue", and a "Physical Negative" pattern. Most of these patterns consisted of adjacent events lasting for two or three patterns. Membership in a pattern accounted for a substantial amount of occurrences for each of the three responses. The data showed that the patterns were most likely to occur during intervals characterized by high density coercive interchanges.

It was hypothesized that each of the patterns had some special utility. One pattern, "Tina Complain", was examined. The pattern served two functions. The data suggested that, given a positive behavior by mother, the pattern was associated with an increased likelihood of the mother's continuing her prosocial interaction. When the mother was being aversive, Tina's "Complain" pattern tended to turn off the attack.

This methodological study offers modest support for the idea of a two-phase approach to the empirical analyses of social interaction. As it stands, the obvious flaws in this approach stem from the questions of limited data and its generality. The interactive patterns and the method used to derive them may apply only to one family, or a highly restricted population of families. Our strategy now is to replicate and to progressively increase the complexity of intearction, applying better and better analytic tools each step of the way.

ACKNOWLEDGEMENTS

This research was supported by MH 29757-01 provided by the National Institute of Mental Health, Section on Crime and Delinquency. The Oregon Social Learning Center in Eugene, Oregon is an affiliate of the Wright Institute, Berkeley, California. The writers gratefully acknowledge the dedicated cadre--Susan Conti, Marion Forgatch, John McDonald, Leona Mukai, Deborah Toobert, and Katie Whalen--who organized and hand-tabulated the immense amount of interaction data necessary for the study. We are particularly indebted to John McDonald for his insightful contribution to several aspects of the data analyses, and to John Reid for his extensive rewriting of an earlier draft of the manuscript.

REFERENCES

Adler, A. *Social interest: A challenge to mankind.* New York: Capricorn Books, 1964.

Altman, S. Sociobiology of rhesus monkeys. II. Stochastics of social communication. *Journal of Theoretical Biology,* 1965, 8, 490-522.

Berne, E. *Games people play.* New York: Grove Press, 1964.

Harris, T. *I'm ok, you're ok.* New York: Harper and Row, 1969.

Hartmann, D. P. Considerations in the choice of inter-observer reliability estimates. *Journal of Applied Behavior Analysis,* 1977, in press.

Kantor, J. R. *Inter-behavioral psychology.* Granville, Ohio: Principia Press, 1959.

Kopfstein, D. The effects of accelerating and decelerating

consequences on the social behavior of trainable retarded children. *Child Development,* 1972, *43,* 800-809.

Moore, D. R., Forgatch, M. S., Mukai, L., & Toobert, D. Family interactional coding system. Unpublished manuscript, Oregon Social Learning Center, 1977. This code is a revision and extension of the earlier 1969 code system developed by the Social Learning Project (see Patterson et al., 1969).

Moore, D. R., & Patterson, G. R. Behavior structure in deviant family systems. Paper presented at the meeting of the American Psychological Association, San Francisco, August, 1977.

Patterson, G. R. The aggressive child: Victim and architect of a coercive system. In L. A. Hamerlynch, L. C. Handy, & E. J. Mash (Eds.), *Behavior modification and families. I. Theory and research.* New York: Brunner/Mazell, 1976.

Patterson, G. R. Naturalistic observations in clinical assessment. *Journal of Abnormal Child Psychology,* 1977, *5,* 309-322.

Patterson, G. R. A performance theory for coercive family interactions. In R. Cairns (Ed.), *Social interactions: Methods, analysis, and illustrations.* Chicago: University of Chicago Press, 1978, in press.

Patterson, G. R., & Cobb, J. A. Stimulus control for classes of noxious responses. In J. F. Knutson (Ed.), *The control of aggression: Implications from basic research.* Chicago: Aldine, 1973.

Patterson, G. R., Ray, R. S., Shaw, D. A., & Cobb, J. A. Manual for coding of family interactions, 1969 revision. (See NAPS Document #01234 for 33 pages of material. Order from ASIS/NAPS, c/o Microfiche Publications, 440 South Park Avenue, New York, New York 10016.)

Reid, J. B. (Ed.) *A social learning approach to family interaction (Vol. 2). A manual for coding family interactions.* Eugene, Oregon: Castalia, 1978.

Sackett, G. P. The lag sequential analysis of contingency and cyclicity in behavioral interaction research. In J. Osofsky (Ed.), *Handbook of infant development.* New York: Wiley, 1978, in press.

Sherif, M. *Social interaction: Process and products.* Chicago: Aldine, 1967.

Snyder, J. J. A reinforcement analysis of interaction and problem and nonproblem children. *Journal of Abnormal Psychology,* 1977, *86,* 528-535.

Taplin, P., & Reid, J. B. Changes in parent consequences as a function of family intervention. *Journal of Consulting and Clinical Psychology,* 1977, *45,* 973-981.

5.
Describing behavior:
The ethologists' perspective

NICHOLAS G. BLURTON JONES & ROBERT H. WOODSON

A basic step in the objective study of relationships is to
describe "who does what to whom". From this starting point one
can proceed to elaborations of the analyses described by Hinde
(1976). But there is an even more basic step: deciding how the
"what" in "who does what to whom" is described. One of the
characteristics of early ethological studies of animals and people
was the composition of "behavior catalogues": lists of items of
behavior defined in terms of their constituent motor patterns. The
status which these items and lists were supposed to hold was never
made very explicit. In this chapter our main aim is to discuss
these behavior catalogues and the methodological and practical
considerations involved in their design and use.

In the past, ethological behavior catalogues were regarded
as anything from a convenient way of describing the data that were
gathered, to some absolute (or potentially absolute) representation
of the way the animal's behavior was organized. The concept of
the "fixed action pattern" had much to do with this latter view.
The animal's behavioral repertoire was held to consist of a number
of relatively inflexible, possibly innate, behavior patterns,
organized by CNS structures or pathways. The most interesting
question about behavior was thought to be: Which patterns were
performed when? In retrospect, one can see that at that stage of
the development of the study of behavior (regardless of the theoretical connotations of the concept of the fixed action pattern)
it was of immense (if temporary) heuristic value to believe that
behavior could be split into a number of relatively fixed motor
patterns. They could be described anatomically, without the
description being dependent on any interpretation, one could tell
whether the patterns were performed or not, and consequently, one
could count and record their occurrence without interpretation.
The interpretation of behavior could thus become a topic for

97

scientific study and not simply comprise circular elaborations of concepts already built into one's raw data. It was also assumed that the descriptions were useful in enabling us to discover the causes and consequences of behavior. It still comes as a surprise to find people saying "Yes, these descriptions are all very fine but do they get at anything *meaningful* (or psychologically significant) about behavior?" This is, like all unexpected questions, very fundamental. It relates to absolutely basic aspects of one's approach to the study of behavior. We discuss several aspects of this question in this chapter.

When some ethologists (for instance Grant, 1969; McGrew, 1972; Blurton Jones, 1967, 1972) began to look at human behavior, they probably began with the common expectation that the flexibility of behavior would be so great as to prohibit the use of this descriptive approach. It was thus a welcome surprise to find motor patterns that could be observed repeatedly. This was such a surprise, and so enhanced the possibility of an objective study of behavior, that a good deal of effort was devoted to lengthy and detailed description (e.g., Grant, 1969; Blurton Jones, 1971), and to simple investigations of the way in which observable behaviors fit together in nature (Blurton Jones, 1967, 1972). Probably none of us gave any thought to the other connotations of the early concept of "fixed action pattern". We were clearly not arguing that the observation of repeatedly recognizable movements implies much about their physiology or development. It is also obvious now that we stopped far short of analyzing the more complex ways in which the observables were organized into functioning systems (cf. Hinde & Hinde, 1976; Waters, 1978).

It quickly became evident that while the behavior catalogues that were produced (largely independently) bore very close resemblances to each other, there were also sizable differences. The same is true of Rhesus monkey behavior catalogues (Reynolds, 1976). Obviously, the behavior catalogues were not tapping some absolute description, even though the authors seemed to use the same criteria for determining which items from which list were "better". During 1973 and 1974, the authors, together with J.S. Chisholm and M. F. Hall, worked on a catalogue of behaviors to record in observational studies of mother-infant interaction in five different cultures. During this exercise some of the criteria employed in composing such lists became clearer. A shortened version of this catalogue, used in our current study in London, is included as an Appendix to illustrate some of the issues that we discuss.

CONSTRUCTING A CATALOGUE

In our description of items and in our choice of items to describe, we attempt to exploit our intuitive interpretation but to remove interpretation from the definitions. We believe that intuitive interpretation is a supremely valuable source of ideas but is no substitute for science or objectivity. In holding this belief we are taking a stand on some fundamental and long-standing issues in

Univarsitas
BIBLIOTHECA
Ottaviensis

the study of human behavior.[1] We believe that the categorizations
and concepts that people hold about their behavior are not complete
or accurate descriptions or explanations of what causes who to do
what to whom. In this we agree with psychoanalysts (among others),
and are at odds with ethnomethodologists, and some social anthropologists.

Building-In Distinctions to Test

One salient aspect of our catalogue construction was the
maximization of the opportunity to test motivational interpretations.
Thus we debated whether to distinguish different ways in which an
adult "leads" a child ("ways", and "flavor" and the use of adjectives
and adverbs are, we find, cues to incompleteness of description).
We felt that if an adult "leads" a child to holding it hand-in-
hand, preceding, concurrent and subsequent behavior will tend to
differ from that which accompanies "leading" where the adult holds
the child's forearm or upper arm. Parents and child-watchers will
share our suspicion that the latter involves more "compulsion" or
"control" than the former. We felt that to record both forms of
"lead" as equivalent would tend to obscure potentially interesting
differences between situations, individuals, ages, cultures, etc.
Indeed, we have no evidence of anything similarity between the two
forms of "lead" but we need to give ourselves the chance to collect
evidence about the similarities and the distinctions between the
meaning of the two patterns of "lead".[2] The fact that different
languages categorize behavior differently does not impugn the
validity of the behavior catalogues or the categories employed.
We are not concerned in these studies with the way people think
about their behavior (the "emic" approach): we are interested in
the way in which it can be observed that they behave (the "etic"
approach: Harris, 1968). Psychology has repeatedly confused these
approaches in its ambition to use behavior to study the "psyche".
Both are valid and important, but to confuse the two is fatal.
The desire to examine the "meaning" of patterns (such as the
two forms of "lead"), also influences the content of our behavior
catalogue. By "meaning" we imply the most observable features of
the preceding, contemporary and subsequent behavior of parent and
child, and some observable features of the situation. Thus we

---

1. Somehow these issues have died, or nearly died, much more
quietly in the study of animal behavior, which probably says more
about the emotional difficulties of studying our own species than
about real differences between people and animals.

2. That we use the same verb in English is no guarantee that all
languages confuse these patterns. Navajo (Chisholm, personal
communication) for example, has so many distinct verbs that the
definitions in behavior catalogues would be much briefer if written
in Navajo.

ensured that our catalogue included behavior seen during "disputes"
or in requests by the child to find something or stay near the
parent. Again, the choice of the items in the catalogue is totally
subjective. The descriptions are not, and the aim is to enable us
to test our subjective impressions: Is leading by the hand less
likely to follow fretting, stamping by the child, taking/removing
objects, or smacking by parent, than leading by the arm is?

The investigator's interest will always influence the composition of his/her catalogue. The need to keep one's catalogue short
counteracts the desire to test intuitive distinctions and may result
in catalogues that bear little similarity. We suggest, however,
that investigators interested in the same general topics, who used
the same criteria as us, will probably derive very similar lists,
whereas differences will arise when their intuitions differ.
Researchers from different cultures might start with somewhat
different catalogues. We have to argue that they would nonetheless
end up with similar catalogues and interpretations if they observed
the same populations of subjects. To this extent we are arguing
that behavior catalogues have a subjective origin but an objective
content and application.

Adverbs and "Flavor"

Strangers to the ethological approach may be concerned that
describing and recording the individual observable items of which
behavior is composed will cause us to lose the "meaning" or "flavor"
of the behavior. Yet one of our primary aims is to allow ourselves
to test the possibility that we may be wrong about what we think
behavior means. No test will be possible if we fail to describe
everything that gives us impressions about the meaning of the behavior. Whenever we find ourselves wishing to qualify a description
with an adverb or an adjective, it is clear that there is something
we have failed to describe.

What Do We Gain By The "Discovery" of a New Motor Pattern or Gesture?

The description of a "hitherto" undescribed behavior is pleasing
not because it adds to the collection but because it shows us what
it is about someone's behavior that determines our impressions about
it. Tinbergen and Tinbergen (1972) described a "slow blink" that
sometimes appears when a child looks at an adult. This is one of
the previously undescribed observables that gives us impressions
about the "way" the child is looking at a stranger. Marvin and
Mossler (1976) described the facial components of "coy" behavior by
a child. In doing so, they explained why some smiles "look" coy and
some do not. They told us what made us interpret the behavior as
"coy". As a result, we can describe what we see and put our interpretations to the test: Do smile and gaze avert combinations occur
in different situations than smile and gaze combinations and so on?
The description of what we are seeing allows us to avoid the
circularity of everyday interpretation and test the usefulness of
our categorizations for summarizing the real-world performance of
behavior.

The description of hitherto unnoticed motor patterns not only increases our ability to test interpretations, but also increases our ability to examine behavior with more subtlety. Most ethological analyses are too crude (we would defend them by saying that one has to start somewhere, sometime, and that simple measures and questions may tell us a lot), and ethologists must strive to make operational (and therefore testable) the more complex of our everyday ideas about behavior. But in addition we must be prepared to go beyond these. There is no reason to believe that everyday life gives us a perfect understanding of behavior: if we believe that it does we ought to cease all behavioral research immediately. The development of an extensive and detailed list of observable aspects of human behavior permits us to examine a realistically wide range of combinations and arrangements of behaviors into functioning systems whose nature and complexity may be impossible to label with everyday concepts or the theoretical entities derived from them.

Items That Describe The Situation

Our current observational research involves English working and middle class primiparous families, seen either in the home or a laboratory setting. In these settings, we would not expect much variation in the immediate physical environment of interaction (e.g., size of room, furniture, etc.). Working with isolated nuclear families such as these, we would also not anticipate a large number of "extra" people with whom the child could interact. Accordingly, the present catalogue does not extensively sample either of these type of information. In our cross-cultural work, however, the situation was much more varied and the catalogue we used reflected this. By recording the number and status of people observed with the child it was possible to examine the influence of these parameters. Chisholm (1978), for example, demonstrated differences in Navajo mother-infant interaction related to whether the infant lived in an extended family camp or an isolated, neolocal family. Similarly, we considered the presence or absence of furniture a potential influence on observed interaction. Physical contact with a mother seated on a chair or bench requires lifting by the mother. If she is on the ground, however, most toddlers can easily climb onto mother's lap and indeed obtain her nipple almost unassisted (Ainsworth, 1967). The catalogue used reflected this consideration.

We record distance and positions, such as those observed in physical contact with mother, because we expect them to influence interactions. In our current research, we find that maternal responses to child vocalizations are very much more frequent if the child is less than 4 feet from mother in a group situation. Similarly we record whether the infant has its eyes closed, partly because opening the eyes influences mothers, and also because an infant with eyes closed is receiving different stimuli than an infant with its eyes open. This could influence the sequence of behavioral events that occur.

*Behavior That Seems Causally Insignificant But Leads
to Responses From Others*

Some items are included not because we are curious about their
causation but because they have a big effect on the behavior of
other people. Coughing or burping do not excite questions about
motivation but they do evoke responses from adults (which can lead
to "socially motivated" coughing). We record coughs, chokes and
burps because the individual variation in maternal response may
be interesting if they were not recorded. Furthermore, certain
episodes of maternal behavior would be inexplicable and liable to
subsequent classification as "initiations" of interaction rather
than as maternal behaviors contingent on offspring behavior.

*Include Behavior If It Seems Important Even If We Fail
to Define It Well*

We are extremely dissatisfied with our description and categories of adult speech. Nonetheless it seems essential to make
some distinctions between categories that one expects to occur in
response to different things and lead to different outcomes. We
are especially dissatisfied with our failure to discriminate the
grammatical aspects of commands and prohibitions from the paralinguistic. We suspect that observers use the paralinguistic
criteria more than the grammatical. It would be better if we
could be clear about which they are trying to us.

Frequency of Occurrence

There is little point in attempting to record behavior that
will occur so rarely that quantitative analysis will be impossible.
This explains why many items were omitted from the catalogue for
our latest study. On the other hand, one consideration works against
omitting rare items. The item may be of special interest to the
investigator or it may tell us something highly important about the
actor. An example is our item "no hold" when the child is on the
mother's lap but she neither has an arm round it nor a hand on it.
This looks so bizarre that one feels impelled to record it in case
any subject can be characterized by this behavior.

Number of Items in the Catalogue

It is said that the more items observers have to record the
less reliable they are. Our impression is that anything that breaks
the observers "flow" (such as trying to ignore an obvious event or
trying to classify an event into an uncomfortable wastebasket category
is much more disruptive.
  Practice considerations (for example, the number of keys on
a recording device) could restrict the number of items one can record.
Given the rapid development of flexible but inexpensive recording
systems these restrictions need not be severe. Of course, the
fewer items there are, the easier it is to learn a particular catalogue

Further, a catalogue that is designed to cover a wide age range is
actually a series of catalogues. At any one time an observer only
needs to know the items relevant for the age-group s/he is observing.
A relatively large number of items is made necessary by the basic
considerations of the approach described in other sections. It is
most important to assure the possibility of testing assumptions
about social behavior.

Reliability and Validity

We have not claimed or demonstrated that ethological descriptions are any more reliable than other recording systems. We doubt
that they are but find this of minor importance. Most of our
discussion has concerned the validity of behavioral descriptions.
We claim that our way of describing behavior allows one to test more
basic assumptions than others and we regard this as a more useful
feature than validity as usually defined. "Face validity" refers
simply to the extent to which a method reflects one's preconceptions.
"Construct validity" is often no better. If one validates a measure
by assessing its ability to discriminate two groups, for instance,
one is merely demonstrating its association with whatever criteria
were used to discriminate the groups. The new measure may be no
more valid than the previous criteria, which may be very poor
indeed! Any such validation technique merely defines the new
measure as partly redundant - if it measures something already
measured, why have a new measure? To regard this kind of validation as important leads inevitably into a fossilized psychology in
which any escape from the areas currently investigated is fore-
closed. There is no absolute validity to any measure in science.
Psychology's obsession with validity and reliability has arisen
from its confusion of etic and emic questions, from the consequent
attempt to cloak primarily subjective concepts in a false aura of
objectivity, and from the isolation of large areas of psychology
from practical questions.
    Reliability has some practical importance, but it is not
evidence of the validity of a measure. Traditionally one hopes
that high reliability implies freedom from biased recording. But
high reliability is always demonstrated by observers whose training
involves the development of shared biases. Reliability matters very
much when teams of observers split subjects between them in a study
(e.g., when one wants to compare results of two different observers
on two different cultures, or when one wants to combine the data of
a team of observers to intercorrelate measures on their whole sample).
In this context the correlation coefficients usually computed as
measures of reliability are of little value. What matters is
whether there is a difference in the central tendency of the scores
of the different observers. If one observer records two items at a
higher rate than another observer this will tend to produce a
correlation between these items that is purely artifactual and will
also obscure genuine patterns of variation. Unfortunately, it is
not possible to allocate subjects to observers randomly with respect
to all the relevant variables until after you have measured these

variables. This means that one may treat the data of one observer
as a replication of another's or (more economically) treat observer
as an independent variable in one's experimental design. Cheyne
(personal communication) has defended and applied this approach in
an (equal cell sizes) analysis of variance design in his study of
smiling (Cheyne, 1976). We have used the same approach, treating
observer as a dummy independent variable in multiple regressions.
The advantage here is that differences in the observer's recording
can be "controlled" by making observer the first independent variable
in the analyses. One loses one degree of freedom for each observer
but gains from the number of additional subjects the observer can
record. Blurton Jones, Ferreira, Farquhar and Macdonald (in preparation) examined correlations between maternal behavior and language
test scores within the data of each of three observers and found
significant correlations in the same direction in each case and in
the same direction as in the total sample. The levels of recording
by each observer did not differ significantly. They then proceeded
with more detailed analyses using the combined data.

There are circumstances in which this technique cannot be used--
for example, when one observer collects the data on one culture and
another on another culture. Comparison of correlations within each
sample is safe but comparisons of absolute frequencies or durations
of behavior are not possible. Obviously one cannot be complacent
about the reliability of observations. It is unlikely that the
reliability testing carried out before and after the field work
gives us a secure basis for comparing simple frequencies of behavior
across cultures. One needs to specify the extent of error and variation in conclusions that can arise from different levels of reliability. For one thing it might give us a yardstick by which to judge
failure and success in replication studies.

CONCLUSIONS

The criteria that are employed in constructing "behavior
catalogues" cluster around two main issues: one practical set
(number of items, reliability, rarity, situation defining) and one
set deriving from a very basic methodological stance, firmly within
the etic approach (i.e., building in the opportunity to test
categorizations and classifications, searching for new, undescribed
patterns which show us what we are seeing when we get impressions
about behavior, aiming to remove adverbs, separating reliability
and validity).

Ethologists have probably been wrong in claiming that their
observational studies are purely inductive. Ethologists have many,
many hypotheses in mind when they plan their observations and their
behavior catalogues. They certainly refuse to include "dependent
variables" whose coherence and unidimensionality has not been
tested. In the study of social and emotional behavior, no motivationa
category has seemed to be a worthwhile dependent variable for an
ethologist to use initially. Even "attachment", a concept greatly
influenced by ethology, has still not been described clearly. Is

it a causal, functional or a descriptive category? Is it a concept
that is intended to label some aspects of the data or is it a
concept that is destined to endure until the "right measures" have
been found? But let us turn the tables on ourselves and return to
an issue raised in the introduction: Are the items in our catalogues
psychologically meaningful? How do we relate our data to other
people's ideas about behavior?

   One can demonstrate whether the behavior items are meaningful
in the sense that they reflect a distinctive set of antecedent
situations or behaviors, or of consequent behaviors or responses
or events. We are not particularly interested in whether our data
are meaningful to the subjects themselves. The behavior items are
likely to occur in combinations and patterns that are highly meaningful in our terms: that is, in close association with observable
antecedents and consequences. It is our aim to discover such
patterns. They may or may not coincide with everyday or pre-
existing concepts. Thus Lewis and Weinraub (1974) discriminate
proximal and distant attachment behaviors, maintaining the use of
the label "attachment" for both even though they demonstrated only
differences between the occurrence of the two sets of behavior.
Blurton Jones and Leach (1972) described the same clusters of
behavior but demonstrated that only one cluster (proximity behaviors
like touching, crying on separation, and "arms up") showed any
"preferences" for mother (often claimed to be one of the characteristics of attachment). They saw no grounds for calling the non-specific
cluster (talking, proffering and receiving objects, smiling)
attàchment behaviors. Data from a recent study (Blurton Jones,
Ferreira, Farquhar and Macdonald, in preparation) show the same
clusterings in another sample at ages 39, 21 and 15 months. Again
it is the talking-proffering cluster that is directed to other
adults as well as mother. As yet further analyses have given no
grounds to suggest that factors influencing one cluster also
influence the other, as surely is implied by treating them as part
of the same behavioral system. Thus we regard the interpretation
given by Lamb (1977) to his data on childrens' interaction with
mother and father to be significantly superior to Lewis and Weinraub's
formulation. It is, of course, clear that our analysis of this
behavior requires the separate recording of proximity, touch, arms
up, crying, proffering, talking, smiling and would not have been
reached by recording categories such as "attachment behaviors",
"attention seeking", etc. We can see no defense for putting
concepts above the data but we can also see that the simplest analyses
of the data may not be adequate. It is thus correct that theoretical
categories should die with a struggle and that we should examine
very complicated organizations of behavior items (see also Waters,
1978). Given that behavior is likely to be organized into evolu-
tionarily adaptive systems there is little reason to expect simple
clustering in time to be the ultimate, or even a particularly
important, aspect of behavioral organization. And there is
probably even less reason to expect behavioral organization to
correspond either to everyday categories, or motivational or trait
theories.

REFERENCES

Ainsworth, M. D. S. *Infancy in Uganda: Infant care and the growth of love*. Baltimore: Johns Hopkins University Press, 1967.

Blurton Jones, N. G. An ethological study of some aspects of social behavior of children in nursery school. In D. Morris (Ed.), *Primate ethology*. London: Weidenfeld and Nicolson, 1967.

Blurton Jones, N. G. Criteria for use in describing facial expressions of children. *Human Biology*, 1971, *43*, 365-413.

Blurton Jones, N. G., & Leach, G. M. Behavior of children and their mothers at separation and greeting. In N. G. Blurton Jones (Ed.), *Ethological studies of child behavior*. Cambridge: Cambridge University Press, 1972.

Cheyne, J. A. Development of forms and functions of smiling in preschoolers. *Child Development*, 1976, *47*, 820-823.

Chisholm, J. A. Navajo infancy. Unpublished doctoral dissertation, Rutgers University, 1978.

Grant, E. C. Human facial expression. *Man*, 1969, *4*, 525-536.

Harris, M. *The rise of anthropological theory: A history of theories of culture*. New York: Crowell, 1968.

Hinde, R. A. On describing relationships. *Journal of Child Psychology and Psychiatry*, 1976, *17*, 1-20.

Hinde, R. A., & Hinde, J. S. Towards understanding relationships. In P. P. G. Bateson and R. A. Hinde (Eds.), *Growing points in ethology*. Cambridge: Cambridge University Press, 1976.

Lamb, M. E. Father-infant and mother-infant interaction in the first year of life. *Child Development*, 1977, *48*, 167-181.

Lewis, M. & Weinraub, M. Sex of parent x sex of child: Socio-emotional development. In R. Richart, R. Friedman, & R. Vande Wiele (Eds.), *Sex difference in behavior*. New York: Wiley, 1974.

Marvin, R. S., & Mossler, D. G. A methological paradigm for describing and analyzing complex non-verbal expressions: Coy expressions in preschool children. *Representative Research in Social Psychology*, 1976, *7*, 133-139.

McGrew, W. C. *An ethological study of childrens' behavior*. New York: Academic Press, 1972.

Reynolds, V. The origin of a behavioral vocabulary: The case of the Rhesus monkey. *Journal for the Theory of Social Behavior*, 1976, *6*, 105-142.

Tinbergen, E. A., & Tinbergen, N. Early childhood autism - an ethological approach. *Zietschrif Tierpsychologie*, 1972, *10*, 1-53.

Waters, E. Traits, relationships and behavioral systems: The attachment construct and the organization of behavior and development. Unpublished manuscript, University of British Columbia, 1978.

APPENDIX: BEHAVIOR CATALOGUE

This behavior catalogue is currently in use in our longitu-
dinal study of the social development of working and middle class
children in London. It is designed for the first phase of the
observational work on children under the age of twelve months.
Accordingly, items will be added as the children increase in age
and the range and characteristics of their behavior change. The
catalogue is a revised version of an earlier one used in studies
in which the observer did pencil-and-paper recording. In our
current research we have adapted the behavior 'organ' devised
by R. Dawkins at Oxford University and, concurrently, changed
some aspects of the catalogue to exploit the potential available
in and counter the problems arising from the use of automated
recording devices.

ak - touch, hand on. S's hand contacts for a time any part of R
   with no or only very small non-rhythmical irregular movements.

al - lead, guide. In lead, S takes R by the hand, wrist or arm,
   and proceeds in front of R. Each locomotes under his own
   power and neither provides impetus to the other. In guide,
   S places his hand on the back of R and may walk slightly
   behind.

am - hand on breast/bottle. Appropriate during feeding situations
   when either a) B rests his hand on the breast or bottle with
   or without rhythmic grasping or sustained clinging or b) M
   keeps her hand on her breast such that the nipple is rendered
   more accessible to B.

ap - proffer. S holds out an object towards R. The object is
   held below an imaginary line between shoulders of S and R
   (thus excluding S holding the object above his head). Not
   applicable when the proffered object is food (vis *DP* - proffer
   food object).

ar - receive. S extends arm and takes in his hand the object
   proffered by R. The arm is not flexed until R has released
   his grip, though R may not have a grip but merely have the
   object resting in his palm. If R does not release his grip,
   on the object and/or flexes his arm while still holding it,
   and S continues to try and get the object from R, S's behavior
   is not *ar* (receive) but *bv* (take). Not applicable when the
   proffered object is food (viz *DR* - receive food object).

as - crash. S may or may not be locomoting, but loses control of
   his posture and falls forwards, backwards or to one side.
   Some part of S's body will thus contact the floor, furniture,
   some object or other person, or a combination of these. S may
   or may not reach out with his hands and arms to cushion the
   fall or stop it by reaching out to catch hold of an object or

person. Includes cases in which it is not clear whether the
child sits suddenly or simply falls. Crash is assumed to be
accidental and when it appears that the child attempts to
charge deliberately (i.e., takes aim beforehand) this is
called *charge* and scored as *at* (attack/charge).

at - *attack*. The various modes of attack are as follows:
  hit: A forceful contact on R by hand of S. Includes beat,
  and punch i.e., attack events in which it is the fist
  rather than the open hand which makes contact with R. To be
  described as "forceful", a movement must be quick, beginning
  from the elbow and/or shoulder of R, be accompanied by locomotion towards R and/or bending of trunk towards R, and involve
  a movement of the wrist and/or forearm starting at least 6"
  from R's body (a slow pressure on R or a brief contact from
  less than 6" score as *bl* (push) and *gx* (pat respectively - not
  as *at*). Each hit is scored.
  object beat: Same as above, except that S brings object into
  contact with R. If object is long and thin (e.g., a stick),
  lever action may make smaller movements of arm into fully-
  fledged *attack*. In some cases, score *at* when tip of object
  travels 6" or more.
  smack-slap: Same as hit, except that hand is open and contact
  is made with open palm or back of hand. Also includes repeated
  smacking or slapping of children by mothers, each slap being
  scored as one *at*.
  kick: S brings his foot, usually the distal end into contact
  with R. The movement is quick and forceful, and the foot
  travels 6" or more towards R. A kick never comes from ankle
  movements alone - it always involves movement of the knee and/or
  hip.
  pinch: The child places its fingers on the body of another
  person and squeezes the flesh tightly.
  pull hair: S grasps R's hair and pulls sharply or steadily,
  sometimes also with a twisting movement.
  throw at: Criteria by which this can be distinguished from
  aw (throw to) not certain. May be that in *throw at* movement
  is overarm and accompanied by frown and fixation, *throw to*
  more usually underarm and not accompanied by frown, but more
  probably by playface/smile(s).
  poke: The fully-extended fingers are brought forcefully against
  R in the same direction as they are pointing. The movement is
  quick and forceful, comes from a distance of more than 6", and
  is from the elbow and/or shoulder rather than the wrist.
  shake: S grasps R with one or both hands, usually by the
  shoulders or upper arm, and by rapid extension and flexion of
  his arms, causes R to move back and forth rapidly.
  shove: A sharp or sudden push. S's arms or hands are extended
  against R (with or without a grip) and a quick and forceful
  extension of the arms (with or without a lunging movement forwards) propels R away from S, often, but not necessarily causing
  R to stumble and possibly fall. The fact that the force against

R is applied in one or a few quick bursts rather than as a
steady maintained pressure distinguishes shove from *bl* (push).
charge: As in shove, except that beforehand S takes aim at R
and locomotes steadily towards him, either by walking or running
or on a bike.

aw - *throw to, project towards.* S causes an object to move towards
R by motion of his arms or legs. The object may be thrown
overarm or underarm or kicked with the foot through the air,
or projected along the ground (as when one individual rolls a
toy train to another).

ax - *impart motion.* Refers specifically to interactions in which R
is on a pram, bike, swing, slide, etc. S pushes or pulls on
part of R's body, with or without a grip, or on the object
which is supporting R's weight. Thus mother may push child
who is seated on a swing, or push a bike on which the child is
seated.

az - *place object.* S puts an object onto a surface in front of R
so that it is in direct view of R.

bl - *push/pull.* S imparts motion to all or part of R (e.g., his
arm) by exerting a slow and steady force against him, usually
with one or both arms in which case force is usually exerted
upon open palms directed against R. S grasps part of R and
imparts motion to R by exerting a slow and steady force towards
himself.

bm - *remove object from mouth.* S takes an object directly from R's
mouth. Not to be confused with removing the nipple from B's
mouth during a feed (oz) or taking away from R an object which
R is not mouthing or sucking. The objects implied in this
category may be toys, fingers, toes, or food objects outside
of feed situations (i.e., snacks and tidbits).

bp - *point.* A gesture of very constant form in which one finger
(most often the index finger) and usually also the thumb are
extended towards a near or distant object with the palm directed
downwards or rotated slightly inwards towards the body and the
remaining fingers loosely curled towards the palm. Excluded
from point are gestures in which two, three or more fingers
are extended. Typically, in pointing towards a distant
object, the arm is also raised and extended, so that arm and
index finger form a straight line from the shoulder. In
pointing at a nearby object, the arm position is more variable
and the index finger may touch the object being indicated.
One point is scored each time the arm is raised or extended
with extension of the index finger, and only if the pointing
position is abandoned and then renewed is a second point recorded. Small tapping movements of the index finger made
during pointing are not counted separately.

br - restrain. S prevents motion of R against R's active resistance, judged by his movements or the inclination of his body. As a result of S's action, R is forced to remain stationary. *NB*: if R does move as a result of action of S, this is *bl* (push/ pull).

bt - bounce, toss. S holds R erect by his arms or trunk and moves him up and down such that except for the points of support, there is no body contact between S and R. Simply holding R in the air is *hp* (support, hold up) and *bt* requires at least two cycles up and down.

bv - take, try take. S attempts to remove an object from the grasp of R. S may or may not succeed in wholly gaining possession of the object and, because of R's maintaining his grasp on the object, a tug-of-war may result.

bx - hug. A transitory behavior defined by its dynamics. S encloses R or part of R (e.g., a leg) with both arms or more rarely with only one and exerts sudden strong pressure towards his own ventral surface, thereby pulling R and S together. The hands are not usually gripped or clasped by S around R but may be. S is usually slightly inclined from the waist towards R, but may or may not be supporting R's weight or providing balance. It is diagnostic for *hq* that the squeezing movement is brief.

ck - cough, choke, hiccough, burp. The distinctive sound of gas or air being brought up from the stomach. Convulsive expulsion of air or matter, or an attempt to dislodge it, or to "scratch" an irritation in the throat. Accompanied by distinctive sounds, but less often choking or gagging may be silent. When silent it seems to be more accompanied by relatively violent movements of the head, shoulders and upper body, often with head forward and down and hands at throat or mouth. Usually there is a distinctive facial expression as well.

cl - cling, grip. S's hands and fingers are flexed, enclosing part of R's body or clothing.

cr - defecate, urinate. Use only in situations where it is possible to see that feces or urine are being eliminated.

cs - side-on orientation. The lateral side of S's trunk faces the ventral side of R's trunk.

ct - face-on orientation. The ventral side of S's trunk faces the ventral side of R's trunk.

cw - away orientation. The dorsal side of S's trunk faces the ventral side of R's trunk.

cx - trunk contact. S's trunk contact is wholly or nearly wholly in direct contact with R's trunk. Used during contact or very close proximity situations.

cz - *no trunk contact*. S's trunk is not in contact with R's trunk during contact situations.

dk - *avoid feed*. S closes its mouth, averts its face and/or twists its body or pushes away from food offered directly into its mouth by any means. Includes cases in which child actively pushes away the proffered breast, bottle, spoon, etc.

dl - *sit, squat, kneel, lie*. S is not standing (see *dt* stand) and *ds*(support stand), and his weight is predominantly supported by a surface such as the ground or a raised platform or a chair.

dp - *proffer food object*. The motor patterns in this category are the same as those described for *ap* (proffer). The two categories are distinct, however, inasmuch as this category involves offering to R's hand a food object such as candy, biscuits, bits of fruit and a cup with liquid (including water). Not to be confused with *ov* (snack-to-mouth), *ow* (object to mouth) or *ox* (start micro-feed).

dr - *receive food object*. Motor patterns involved in this category are the same as those described for *ar* (receive). The distinction between the two categories is that this one involves food object(s). Not to be confused with *ov* (object to mouth), *ow* (snack to mouth), and *ox* (start micro-feed).

ds - *supported stand*. S is upright and, for the most part, supporting his weight. However, to maintain balance, S has his hand(s) contacting some surface. This surface may be a wall, an edge of furniture or a person. Distinguish this category from *fl* (lean) by noting, first, S's trunk is upright, perpendicular to the floor and, second, there is no or very little trunk contact with the supporting surface.

dm - *stand unsupported*. S is motionless and upright with his weight supported by his legs and feet.

dt - S is more than 10 feet away from but in sight of R.

dv - S is between 6 and 10 feet from R.

dw - S is between 3 and 6 feet from R.

dx - S is less than 3 feet from but not in contact with R.

dz - S is in contact with but is not being held by R.

cv - *out of sight of observer*. S is no longer in observer's visual field.

ek - kiss. S's closed and/or pursed mouth (i.e., lips rather than teeth) or any part of his face including the chin contact some part of the other person.

el - look. Visual behavior in which it is evident from the position of S's eyes and/or facial disc that his gaze is directed to some person or towards some action he is performing, probably with his hands.

ev - inspect. S's gaze is focussed on his own manipulation of some part of R's person or clothing, usually the skin surface or hair. Very similar to non-human primate grooming. Usually accompanied by neutral or "concentrating" facial expression (furrowed brows, lips together?).

es - smile. All expressions of the face in which the brows are not noticably drawn together in a frown and mouth corners are retracted and raised so that an imaginery line connecting them would fall nearer the upper than the lower lip. The mouth may be open or closed and the upper and/or lower teeth may or may not be exposed. Half smiles count as smiles, but when a laughing sound accompanies a smile or "playface" the smile and the sound together score as *ul* (laugh).

ez - eyes closed. S's eyes are not open and the face is relaxed i.e., not crying.

fk - rock. S moves or is caused to move rhythmically back and forth. When S rocks himself, he may sway from the waist either backwards and forwards or more rarely from side to side, or move his whole weight alternately from one foot to the other, usually with body held stiffly and arms slightly out. Alternatively, rocking motion may be passively imparted to R by S via movements of S's legs, arms or trunk, as when a mother rocks her baby by moving him to and fro in her arms, or by holding him against her swaying trunk or by "jiggling" him on her knee. This category should be distinguished from *ik* (jumps), *fx* (adjust posture), *bt* (bounce, toss), and *hk* (adjust hold).

fl - lean. S's weight is primarily supported by his feet or buttocks (i.e., he may be standing or sitting), but part of his weight is supported by a surface by virtue of the fact that his hips and/or part of his upper torso are inclined against that surface. The supporting surface may be a person or an object.

fm - climb object. S climbs on to or off of an object, *not* a person (viz *gw* - climb person), starting from the floor or some other surface. The four limbs are alternately extended and flexed, resulting in approximately vertical gross body movements. The legs usually push while the arms pull. This category covers

any attempt to get onto the object whether or not B succeeds
in that attempt.

fr - *fret*. Non-rhythmic nasal or strangulated sounds associated with
pucker face and of varying duration. The pitch of the sound may
differ with the age of the child. May be lower in neonates and
infants and higher in toddlers and young children.

ft - *stamp-flap, tantrum*. S stamps or kicks his feet on the floor or
in the air with violent waving or flapping of the arms. This
may often be accompanied by shaking of the head, red face and tears.

fw - *head wag, nod*. Slow repeated rhythmical up and down or side to
side movements of the head. Includes head nod and head shake for
"yes" and "no".

fx - *adjust position/posture*. S moves limb or limbs and/or trunk from
one previously held position to a different position or posture,
which is also held. Alternatively, S almost immediately resumes
the position held before the movement (in which case *fx* has the
meaning of fidget). Note that this category is distinct from *hk*
(adjust hold) in that S is responsible for the change in posture.

gk - *suck object*. An object is placed between the lips and tongue and
then licked or sucked or bitten. This category excludes objects
involved in the feeding situation (e.g., bottles, spoons, breasts)
but includes pacifiers and parts of people other than R.

gl - *suck self*. Motor patterns here are identical to those described
for *gk* (suck object) but this category refers exclusively to
parts of S's body (e.g., digits, toes, etc.) being sucked by S.

gm - *arms up*. S extends one or both arms towards R, holding them more
or less parallel with the hands not in contact either with one
another, or with R. Not to be confused with *gt* (reach object).

gp - *mild physical stimulation*. S makes small movements of his
fingers or hand on part of R's body. Includes patting, rubbing,
"fiddling" and caressing. "Fiddling" consists of often absent-
minded seeming manipulations of child's fingers, feet, etc.
Rubbing is the circular or back and forth movement of S's hand
held palm down and more or less flat on part of R. Patting is S
bringing hand, usually the palm, in contact with R from a distance
of less than 6" with movement of the wrist only, or only the
smallest movements of the elbow (this distinguishes *gp* from *gx*
(vigorous patting). Patting and rubbing are characteristically
rhythmical, and of small amplitude. "Fiddling" is not usually
very rhythmical and can include mild or low amplitude tickling
(distinct from *gz* - tickle). *gp* also includes mild poking and
tapping, which are distinguished from *at* (attack) by the small
amplitude of the movement and/or the presence of rhythmicity.

gr - *London burping procedure*. A specific burping or winding procedure taught in London hospitals. The baby is leaned forwards and supported by the neck, chest or mandible with one hand, and patted or rubbed on the back with the other.

gs - *stimulate to suck*. S moves finger or nipple of breast or bottle around R's lips or to and fro or backwards and forwards inside his mouth. (Requires more than one movement to qualify as *gs*). Alternatively, S makes repeated small movements of his finger(s) on the central side of R's cheek. Usually occurs in a feeding context, but may be done without feeding to test whether a baby is hungry.

gt - *reach to object*. Motor patterns similar to those involved in *gm* except that the arm(s) tend to extend forward rather than upward. Further, this category is meant to cover those instances in which S's reach is directed towards an object, whether the object is located on some surface or is in the possession of another person.

gv - *get off, get down*. S maneuvers himself from a position in which his weight is fully supported by another person into a position in which his weight is fully or almost fully supported on the floor or some other surface. Does not include unsuccessful attempts to get off or get down, which should be scored *fx* (change position/posture).

gw - *get on/climb person*. S climbs on to a person, starting from the floor or some other surface. The four limbs are alternately extended and flexed, resulting in approximately vertical gross body movements. The legs usually push while the arms pull. This code refers to any attempt to get onto a person whether or not the child succeeds in its attempt.

gx - *vigorous physical stimulation*. S makes repeated, rhythmical contact with R's body with an amplitude of movement of more than 6 inches from R's body surface. This will involve movements originating from S's elbow or shoulder but not from the wrist alone. Rhythmicity distinguishes *gx* from single slaps or beats in *at* (attack).

gz - *tickle*. Large, sudden or rapid movements of the hand on a part of R's body. More specifically, the fingers are placed on R's body and then wiggled and squeezed with R's flesh or clothes between the fingers.

hk - *adjust hold*. S is holding R, supporting his entire weight, and alters the orientation and/or trunk contact aspect(s) of the hold. This adjusting need not be 'permanent' so that the trunk contact and orientation conditions return to what they were immediately prior to the *hk*. Note that S can *hk* with or without *fx* (adjust position/posture) and vice versa.

hl - *pick up.* R is on an object or surface or is being held by
  another person and S lifts R from that object, surface or
  person. In the case of R being held by another person, *hl* is
  distinct from *hr* (receive hand-over) in that R is not 'proffered'
  to S by that other person prior to the pick up.

hm - *put down on object.* S is holding R and places R on an object
  such as a slide, walker or playhorse. Distinct from *hs*
  (confined put down) in the sense that the object onto which R
  is placed is not a 'maintenance' object (e.g., crib, pram,
  playpen, changing table) but a 'play' object.

hp - *support hold.* There is no trunk contact and S supports part
  or all of R's weight with her two hands. R may be sitting or
  standing on S's knees or lap, or sitting or standing on the
  floor. If S supports all of R's weight, she merely raises him
  for a period and replaces him on the same spot, still without
  trunk contact. (If more than one repetition of such an event
  occurs, score as *bt* (bounce toss)).

hr - *receive hand over.* R is being held by another person and that
  person 'proffers' R to S and S 'receives' R into physical
  contact.

hs - *confined put down.* S places R onto or into an area or object
  such that R's subsequent ability to move away from that place
  is limited by physical barriers (e.g., playpen walls) or
  minimal surface area (e.g., table tops used for diaper changes).

hv - *free put down.* S places R onto a supporting surface in such
  a position that R's subsequent ability to move away from that
  position is unimpaired by physical barriers or limited surface
  area.

hw - *hand over.* S is holding R and 'proffers' R to another person.

hx - *pick up/down.* S, in one or very few motions, picks up and puts
  down R. The effect of this maneuver is to transfer R to
  another position but leave him in the same free/confined/on
  object condition.

hz - *no hold.* R is sitting on S's lap in any position and S is not
  providing R with any balance support with her arms or hands.
  There may be or may not be trunk contact, and S may touch R
  lightly with her fingers (e.g., by "fiddling" with his hand)
  but not in such a way as to provide support.

ik - *jump.* S is standing on a surface or is being held by a person
  and by means of rapidly alternating bending and straightening
  of the knees moves his trunk up and down in a fairly vertical
  plane. S's feet might or might not leave the ground.

il - locomote. S moves a distance of 1 ft or more by means including, walking, crawling, running, skipping, riding a bicycle or sliding down a slide. Used only when observer is unable to diagnose the movement as *ip* (approach), *iv* (leave), or *iw* (follow).

im - support walk. Upright locomotion in which balance support and/or impetus is derived from either a surface or a person. This category can occur in two modes: a) active - here S supports himself in upright locomotion through hand but *not* trunk contact with a surface or person. In this active mode it is S himself who provides the impetus. b) passive - here S both supports, through hand contact, and provides the greater share of the impetus to R while R is engaged in upright locomotion.

ip - approach. S moves by any means directly toward R, thus reducing the distance between them. If approach to a specific other person is not clear until S has locomoted near enough to tell, score *il* (locomote) or *im* (support walk) until it is clear, and then score *ip* (approach).

is - pass. S locomotes by any means on a path that is neither toward or away from R, but passes in front or to one side or behind R. Distinct from *ip* (approach) and *iv* (leave).

iv - leave. S moves by any means directly away from R.

iw - follow. S is facing towards R and R is facing away from S. Both are locomoting in the same direction, but the distance between them remains roughly constant. If S stops and R continues moving towards him, score *ip* (approach).

ix - go out of sight. S by any means moves out of R's visual range.

iz - come into sight. S by any means moves into R's visual range, having previously been out of R's sight.

ok - drink. S takes in fluid from a container which he either holds himself or is propped. Not applicable to taking fluid from a bottle during a feeding.

ol - manipulate on person. Any manipulation of objects (including animals) in which the object rests on part of another person, usually the lap.

om - demonstrate. S manipulates an object in front of R, having firs behaved towards R in such a way as to direct his attention to the object. This may be by look, speak, point, touch, etc. whic should all be recorded separately. The object may be held or placed on the floor or some other surface.

op - *manipulate*. Any handling of objects not covered by other categories, but excluding small "fumbling" movements of an object while the attention is directed elsewhere.

or - *manipulate same object*. Motor patterns as for *op* (manipulate) but limited to objects which have been received (*ar*), taken (*bv*), or placed (*az*).

os - *adjust*. Covers motor patterns involved in everyday caretaking activities (e.g., diaper changes, nose wipes, etc.), but which are of a limited duration. (Extensive caretaking periods will be handled with condition codes.)

ot - *eat*. S feeds himself by putting food into his own mouth.

ov - *object to mouth*. S places a non-nutritive object *directly* into R's mouth.

ow - *food to mouth*. Outside of a feeding situation, S places a food object or a container holding a nutritive fluid (including water) *directly* into R's mouth.

ox - *on nipple*. Category covering the start of a micro-feeding period. S's actions result in the introduction of the teat or bottle into the mouth. In a feeding, either M or B could be 'responsible' for the nipple actually going into B's mouth so that either person could score as S.

ox - *off nipple*. S is the person whose actions are 'responsible' for the nipple leaving B's mouth at the end of the micro-feeding period, as in *ox*. Again, either M or B could take the role of S. Note, however, that *oz* would follow *ox* only after the *ox* lead to at least a 'neutral' period of B on the nipple. In those instances wher the immediate response to *ox* is avoiding the nipple, *dk* (avoid feed) is the appropriate category.

uk - *call*. Verbalizations of a kind which indicate to R that he should approach or take notice of S.

ul - *laugh*. Open-mouthed smile with audible vocalization employing rapid or staccato expulsions of breath. This is a laugh. Squeal is a loud high-pitched vocalization of only gradually-changing frequency (either up or down), with sudden cessation.

um - *command*. Meaningful verbalizations employing the grammatical imperative without softening qualification of "please" or its equivalents. e.g., "Come here" or "Go away," but not "Come here will you, darling, please?" or "Please go away."

up - *playnoise*. A "blanket" term used to cover a range of non-verbal noises which imitate trains, sirens, cars, animals, etc: onomatopoeic vocalizations.

ur - *warn, threaten punishment.* A verbalization which seems designed to prevent R from carrying out a behavior he is starting. Could usefully be confined to threats of unpleasant consequences (e.g., physical punishment) for R if he persists in his action. Distinct from *um* (command, prohibit) and *uz* (criticize).

us - *scream.* Intense, high-pitched, non-rhythmical and long vocalization associated with strenuous expiration of breath and almost silent inhalation.

ut - *talk.* Meaningful verbalizations delivered in a conversational tone of voice, exclusive of those categorized as *uk, ux, uz, um,* or *ur.* Young children's vocalizations are scored as *ut* (talk) if, for the observer, the vocalization is a meaningful verbalization. Utterances which sound like conversation but are incomprehensible to an observer speaking the same language, score *uv* (unspecified vocalizations).

uv - *vocalize.* For children, noises other than *uw* (cry), *up* (imitative playnoises), *us* (scream), *ul* (laugh) and those which the observer cannot recognize as meaningful verbalizations (*ut*). For adults, all of the above, plus exclamations (ooh! aah!) and non-verbal acknowledgements (mm-mm).

uw - *cry.* Repeated, rhythmic vocalizations associated with pucker face, and except in neonates, tears. Rhythmicity is the criterion for distinguishing *uw* from *fr* (fret) and *us* (scream).

ux - *sing, hum, chant.* Stylized and rhythmic patterns of sound made up of vocalizations which may or may not be meaningful verbalizations or onomatopoeic.

uz - *criticizes.* Meaningful verbalization derogatory to R. Distinct from *um* (command, prohibit).

6.
Levels of analysis for interactive data collected on monkeys living in complex social groups

STEPHEN J. SUOMI

Observational scoring of behavior has become an increasingly complex enterprise in recent years. Objective standards of scientific acceptability have become more strict--no longer are anecdotal reports or diary accounts routinely accepted as credible scientific evidence of ongoing behavior patterns. Different types of scoring systems have proliferated and become acceptable. Heated arguments concerning the "correctness" of different operational definitions of similar behavior patterns are not as common as they were a decade ago. Moreover, striking technical advances have been made in data acquisition and storage systems, and new statistical procedures have been developed to provide more powerful analytical tools than were previously available. Investigators are no longer limited to paper and pencil approaches to the collection of observational data, or consigned to tedious hours of transcribing audio tapes of moment-by-moment descriptions of ongoing events. Instead, they may choose among many different types of accepted scoring systems, time sampling procedures, modes of recording observations, and data analysis techniques. Perhaps as a result of these advances, some investigators have become more willing to study interactions among members of complex social groups, rather than limiting their observations to isolated individuals or dyads.

The increases in sophistication of both observational scoring techniques and the social settings in which they have been employed have not occurred without some new difficulties arising. In particular, investigators who possess advanced data acquisition system often find themselves collecting more data from complex social groups than they can possibly analyze without overwhelming their ability to comprehend the results. This necessitates decisions regarding selective analysis of only a portion of the entire data set. These decisions regarding *what* to analyze often become more difficult than decisions concerning *how* to analyze the data that are finally

119

selected. Moreover, even after interactive data have been collected, reduced, and analyzed, these investigators often discover that their results are exceedingly difficult to communicate to colleagues. Perhaps this is one reason why published accounts of such complicated observational analyses have been scant in the literature to date.

This chapter addresses the problem of deciding what level(s) of analysis is (are) appropriate for specific studies of social interactions that utilize observational scoring techniques on complex social groups. The advantages and limitations of various levels of analysis for such interactions will be detailed. Throughout the chapter, "level of analysis" will refer to the degree of detail concerning an interaction that is provided by a given set of data. For example, observational data collected on a focal subject interacting with members of its social group might be limited to frequency counts of the subject's behaviors that fall into predefined categories. A more detailed level of analysis of the same individual engaging in the same interactions might include information regarding the identity of the targets of the focal subject's behaviors. An even more detailed level of analysis might involve unraveling the actual sequences of behaviors between the subject and its interaction partner(s). On the other hand, a "higher" level of analysis might ignore specific behavior patterns displayed by the subject and instead characterize its interactions as "friendly", "playful", or "hostile".

In order to simplify comparisons among different levels of analysis, certain assumptions will be made about the nature of the observational data under consideration. Specifically, discussion will be limited to cases where (a) focal subjects can be identified and their behaviors monitored over observational sessions of "standard" (e.g., 15-minute) time periods, (b) the investigator is able to define an exhaustive set of behavioral categories for both the focal subject and any individual with whom it might interact during the course of an observational session (see Sackett, 1978a, for a detailed specification of exhaustive category systems), and (c) the investigator has the capability to record and preserve the sequence of behavioral occurrences, as defined by his or her scoring system, during each session. Consideration of the relative efficacy of different types of time sampling procedures (e.g., absolute frequencies, absolute durations, modified frequencies, point samples, or termination rates) will not be discussed in this chapter; detailed comparisons of time sampling can be found in Gottman (1978), Bakeman (1978), and Sackett (1978a).

SUBJECT CATEGORY PROFILES AND PARTNER PROFILES

The level of analysis of observational data that has appeared most often in the psychological literature is that of subject *category profiles*. At this level, categories of behaviors are operationally defined, and some index of their incidence is collected for each subject. If the categories are so defined as to be exhaustive, they can be expressed as relative proportions of total subject activity, presenting an individualized "behavioral profile" for the subject.

These profiles are typically compared between groups of subjects, between individual subjects, and even between different measurements on the same individual. One common analytic technique has involved subjecting each category's scores to an analysis of variance, with subsequent tests indicating which means differed from each other for which categories (e.g., Suomi & Harlow, 1972; Sackett, Holm, & Ruppenthal, 1976). Nonparametric techniques such as Mann-Whitney tests can also be used with profile scores (see Suomi, 1974). Multivariate analyses could also be applied to such data (see Lamb, 1977).

Generally speaking, category profile scores represent a level of analysis that is quantitatively sound without being conceptually overwhelming. This level of analysis has proven to be of sharp enough focus to have enabled investigators of rhesus monkey behavior to differentiate individuals on the basis of age, sex, rearing history, and social test setting, as well as numerous acute experimental manipulations. Category profile scores have been used with similar discriminative success in many other areas of inquiry.

Nevertheless, category profile scores represent a relatively gross level of analysis. Such scores tell us nothing about the distribution of a subject's activities toward various members of its social group. This is, of course, not a problem when subjects are tested under conditions of individual housing or as part of a dyad. When more than one other individual are present in the test situation, however, information regarding the identity of the subject's partner in any given interaction is not available. Moreover, this level of analysis totally ignores the behaviors of the other individuals in the test environment, resulting in severe limitations on the interpretation of detectable differences between sets of profile scores (cf. Lewis & Rosenblum, 1974).

An alternative to category profiles that provides a roughly equivalent level of analysis involves identification of the relative proportions of a subject's total activities that are directed toward each individual in its immediate social environment. This *partner profile* approach enables an investigator to determine with whom a subject spends most of its time within complex social groupings, but it does not enable the investigator to determine *how* the subject spends its time with each available social partner. Nevertheless, this approach has enjoyed considerable use in anthropology and ethology, although comparative and developmental psychologists have not employed it as frequently as they have employed category profile analyses. It shares many of the disadvantages of the category profile approach, especially with respect to providing information about the specific activities of a subject's interactive partners.

CATEGORY PROFILES FOR DIFFERENT SOCIAL PARTNERS

Many of the problems inherent both in partner profile and in category profile approaches largely disappear if one utilizes a slightly finer level of analysis. At this finer level, the relative proportion of time the subject spends in interactions with every social partner is determined, but in addition, separate category profiles are calculated for the subject's interactions with each of those partners. Thus, the investigator obtains specific levels of behaviors encompassed by each category for activities directed toward each social partner. Data collected at this level of analysis can be compared not only internally, i.e., a comparison between the category profiles of behaviors directed by the subject toward each partner, but also between different situations or ages for the same subject. For example, Hansen (1966) used such an approach to differentiate the activities that mother-peer-reared (or surrogate-peer-reared) rhesus monkeys directed toward mothers (or surrogates) from those directed toward peers or toward other adult females in the group. Lamb (1977) has also used this approach to demonstrate that in certain settings human infants interact quite differently with their fathers than they do with their mothers. More detailed and precise comparisons can be made between different individuals or groups of individuals at this level of analysis. Such comparisons have been employed by Suomi (1978) and by Golopol (1977) in studies of the various social relationships that male and female rhesus infants develop with different monkeys in their social groups in different environmental settings.

Determination of category profiles for different social partners can be quite effective for identifying the behavioral differences which characterize the different social relationships that individuals form in various settings. Unfortunately, the results of such analyses can become exceedingly complicated when a scoring system containing many categories is employed and/or there are many individuals with whom the subject interacts. Indeed, in such cases "standard" statistical analyses of the differences between these various behavioral profiles may well yield too many "significant" findings to be easily described (or comprehended) within a single presentation. However, when one has an exhaustive scoring system and samples subject interactions with all other members of the subject's social group, *it might not be necessary* to analyze all the data collected in order to answer specific research questions. For example, many studies of macaque social development (e.g., Hinde & Spencer-Booth, 1967; Ruppenthal, Harlow, Eisele, Harlow, & Suomi, 1974; Hinde & White, 1974) have focused primarily on a single social relationship formed by the subjects under observation, even though data on other relationships involving these subjects were also available.

Of course, investigators do not always have concrete *a priori* reasons for limiting the extent of their data analysis. Consider a case in which a new social group containing 10 individuals is formed, and the behaviors directed by each individual toward each other group member are recorded using an observational scoring system that has a total of 10 behavioral categories. A complete category profile analysis for all possible social relationships would involve making comparisons among 90 different profiles, each

with 10 different elements. How should an investigator faced with
such an extensive data base begin his or her analysis? What portion
of the data base should provide the initial focus of analysis for
this level of interactive data?

Useful answers to such questions can often be found in the results of preliminary analyses performed on the same data base but
at a higher level of analysis. If one has an exhaustive category
scoring system and is sampling all possible social relationships in
the group, then, for each subject in the group, it is possible to
sum scores for each category across all the subject's partners in
the group, or to sum across all categories the behaviors directed
toward each partner in the group. In other words, from the original
data base one can *derive* either overall category profiles or overall
partner profiles for each subject in the group. Such a scoring
system is said to be hierarchical, in that measures obtained at one
level of analysis can be combined in such a way to yield data
appropriate for a higher level of analysis. Because analytical
comparisons performed at the level of overall category or partner
profiles typically yield results that are not conceptually overwhelming, such results can serve as useful guides for subsequent
analysis performed at the finer level of actual data collection.
Specifically, choices as to where to begin analysis at this finer
level can be made on the basis of proportion of total variance
accounted for either by different categories of behavior or by
different social targets.

For example, in the above data set it might be found that 85%
of a subject's interactions were directed toward 3 of the 9 other
individuals in the social group. An investigator might well begin
his or her analysis of category profiles for various partners by
focussing upon these 3 particular partners. Alternately, if the
results of an overall category profile anlaysis indicated that 85%
of a subject's scores across all partners fell into 3 of the 10
categories sampled, it would seem prudent to focus initial analysis
at the individual profile level on those 3 categories. In any case,
hierarchical scoring systems enable an investigator to perform such
selective analyses.

One limitation of the use of these profiles for analyzing a
subject's different social relationships with various partners is
that little or no information regarding the contributions to the
interactions made by these partners can be obtained directly. One
way to circumvent this problem is to collect concurrent observational data on individuals with whom the focal subject is interacting. The distributions of the partners' behaviors directed toward
the focal subject can be compared with the focal subject's own
category profiles. When repeated samples of such profiles are
available, inferences regarding the effects of the partners' behaviors
can be tested. For example, Hinde and Atkinson (1970) described
a basis for formulating hypotheses concerning "responsibility" in
social interactions between rhesus monkey mothers and infants.
Using data collected on mother-infant pairs in which not only the
focal infants' behaviors were recorded but also the activities of
their mothers, Hinde and White (1974) were able to show close

agreement between their empirical findings and Hinde and Atkinson's predictions that assigned differential responsibility between mother and infant for specific changes in levels of various interactive measures.

Yet, because such data ignore temporal relationships between the behaviors of the focal subject and those of its particular interaction partner, assessment of any immediate effect of a given behavior pattern by one individual on the activity of its inter-action partner cannot be made at this level of analysis. Instead, such temporal relationships must become the focus for an even finer level of analysis, that of specific sequences of behaviors which constitute the interactions themselves. The next section describes characteristics of such sequential analyses.

SEQUENTIAL LEVEL OF ANALYSES

The modes of data collection, analysis, and interpretation presented thus far have all involved a certain degree of summarizing individual occurrences of behavior patterns over standard observation periods. A more precise procedure involves recording each behavior pattern *as it occurs within* the period of observation. This procedure provides a running account, or "play-by-play record"; it preserves the order of behavioral events that transpire during the observation period. "Order" or "sequence" can be expressed either in terms of behavioral events, e.g., behavior C follows behavior B which follows behavior A, or in terms of small intervals of time, e.g., 1-second units. A more complete description of these two approaches is provided by Sackett (1974) and by Gottman and Bakeman (this volume).

Many formal treatments of sequential analysis of behavioral activity have been restricted to consideration of the order of occurrence of behaviors displayed by a single focal individual; behaviors directed toward the focal subject by other individuals are not included among the components that make up the various sequences under analysis. One frequently-cited example has been the stochastic analyses of behavioral sequences developed by Altmann (1965) to identify consistent patterns of behavioral elements displayed by individual rhesus monkeys. Indeed, such an approach has been common among ethologists seeking to analyze "fixed action" or "modal action patterns" in terms of microbehavioral components and sequences (Barlow, 1975). Dawkins (1976) has even developed some hierarchical models that are based on the concept that there may exist relatively standard *sequences of sequences,* wherein the order of the higher-level sequences tends to be independent of the order of elements which consitute the lower-level sequences that make up the base of the hierarchy. The mathematic characteristics of such models become very complex very rapidly as the hierarchies are expanded.

The degree of complexity presented by a sequential approach to observational study of behavior is increased even more when one turns to social interactions. If one faithfully records the sequence of behavioral changes that constitute an interactive bout, interpretation of sequences can be made in terms of behavior patterns, exchanges between participants, or more likely, both. Even in social interactions involving only dyads, "simple" calculations of base rates and conditional probabilities for elements in the sequences become a complicated task.

Yet, despite the added problems inherent in the collection, analysis, and interpretation of sequential interactional data, this level of analysis has received increasing attention in recent years. This is because sequential data can be used to describe patterns of interaction as they occur in real time, providing a basis for identifying the actual behavioral units employed by the participants in the interaction. Moreover, sequential data can provide an empirical basis for calculating sequential dependencies within streams of interactive behavior. Such dependencies can be used to form hypotheses regarding causal relations among behavioral components displayed by each individual involved in the interaction.

It should be pointed out that inferences about causality are not as easy or straightforward to develop from sequential data as might be initially expected. A common view is that sequential analyses of interactions enable an investigator to infer causality if they show that behavior B is significantly more likely than chance to occur if the immediately preceding behavior was A. The inference is that behavior A by one individual *causes* behavior B by a second individual, i.e., B is a "reaction" to the occurrence of A. Unfortunately, life is not that simple. There are a number of reasons why knowledge that P(B/A) > P(B) in an interaction setting is insufficient evidence for the inference that A *caused* B.

First, several alternative explanations exist for the finding that P(B/A) > P(B). It may be that B was not caused by A, but instead that B *and* A were both caused by an event that preceded them, with the subject displaying A simply having a shorter latency to react than the subject displaying B. Alternatively, the individual exhibiting B may have actually "signalled" the first subject to display A via a means not apparent to the observer, so that in fact the "true" causal relation between the two individuals' activities would be reversed. In neither case would the simple attribution of causality from A to B be appropriate, given only that P(B/A) > P(B).

A parallel issue involves the degree to which an observer's ability to predict the occurrence of behavior B is improved by knowledge that behavior A was the immediately preceding behavior. In information theory terms, the degree of improvement, or *decrease in uncertainty,* over base-rate estimation of B which is provided by knowledge that A was immediately antecedent can be represented as:

$$\frac{P(B/A)}{P(B)} \ ,$$

i.e., the ratio of the conditional probability of B given A to the base-rate probability of B. If this ratio is greater than 1.0, its magnitude will represent the degree to which B is *more* likely to occur following A than would be expected by chance. If the ratio is less than 1.0, the magnitude of its reciprocal will represent the degree to which B occurs *less* often following A than would be expected by chance. Thus, the ratio (or its reciprocal) provides an index of the reduction in uncertainty regarding one's ability to estimate when B will occur that is provided by behavior A's appearance. In this example, A could be one behavior in Subject #1's repertoire and B could be a different behavior in Subject #2's repertoire, #1 and 2 being interaction partners.

According to Bayes Theorem, the conditional probability of B given A can be represented as

$$P(B/A) = \frac{P(B) \ P(A/B)}{P(A)}$$

(See Goude, 1978 for a discussion of Bayes' Theorem in this context). If this equation is divided on both sides by the expression P(B), one then obtains the equation

$$\frac{P(B/A)}{P(B)} = \frac{P(A/B)}{P(A)}$$

Now, I have already stated that

$$\frac{P(B/A)}{P(B)}$$

represents the improvement in prediction (decrease in uncertainty) of B provided by knowledge that A occurred. But what is the meaning of the expression

$$\frac{P(A/B)}{P(A)} \ ?$$

In fact, it should be apparent that

$$\frac{P(A/B)}{P(A)}$$

represents the degree of improvement in identification of the antecedent A through knowledge that the immediately consequent behavior was B. P(A/B) is the conditional probability that an individual has initiated behavior A, given that the social target responded with behavior B.

$$\frac{P(A/B)}{P(A)}$$

thus reflects the extent to which one is better able to identify an individual's behavior by knowing what the result was, in terms of target animal's immediate response.

This second equation therefore implies that the improvement in prediction of a behavior that one obtains if the antecedent of the

behavior is known *is exactly equal to* the improvement in prediction
of that antecedent activity that is provided by knowledge of its
immediate consequence. What this means is that an observer gains
exactly as much reduction in uncertainty about one individual's
behavioral initiate from knowledge of the target individual's
response as the reduction in uncertainty that the observer can
gain about the target's behavior from knowledge of the type of
stimulus that allegedly "triggered" the target's response. This
is true even if the repertoires from which A and B were selected
are different, and it is true even if $P(A) \neq P(B)$ and $P(A/B) \neq$
$P(B/A)$.

    To put these facts into a real-life behavioral example, assume
that the unconditional probability that an adult male rhesus monkey
will display a threat within any 5-second period is .07. However,
also assume that if an infant female directs a play bout at the
adult male, the conditional probability of seeing a threat from
the adult male within 5 seconds of the female's play initiate is
.84. Thus, our ability to predict the occurrence of the adult
male threat within any 5-second period is increased by a factor of
12, i.e.,

$$\frac{P(B/A)}{P(B)} = \frac{.84}{.07} = 12,$$

if we know that the immediately preceding behavior was a play
initiate by a female infant. However, our ability to guess when a
female infant initiated a play bout will *also* increase by a factor
of 12, if we know that within 5 seconds of the behavior in question,
an adult male threatened this infant. This is true even if the base
rate of play by the adult female, $P(A)$, is markedly different from
the base rate of threat by the adult male, $P(B)$, and corresondingly,
the two conditional probabilities, $P(A/B)$ and $P(B/A)$, are also
quite different. In the present example, the actual value for
$P(A)$ might be .02, with $P(A/B)$ thus equal to .24. We therefore
can obtain the same gain in information about the adult male's
threat from knowledge of the infant's play initiate as we can
obtain about the infant's play from knowledge of the adult male's
threat.

    A different way to employ sequential interactive data as descrip-
tive or model-fitting tools centers on the analysis of sequences of
more than one lag (either in events or in time units). Most traditional contingency analysis (e.g., Bakeman, 1978) can become
exceedingly complicated at even short lags, so that comprehension,
let along interpretation, of such analyses becomes a formidable
task. However, an elegant alternative to contingency analysis exists
for such sequential data; it is the time series lag analysis procedure
described by Sackett (1974). Still, interpretation of the results
of such analyses often present problems. This is because our
ability to evaluate the statistical departure from "chance" of auto-
and cross-correlations at various lags is not matched by our ability
to interpret the meaning of the statistical test results, especially
when longer lags are involved. One needs to specify predictions

concerning lag data outcomes by which testable hypotheses that are
more specific than "does it differ from chance" can be subjected to
scrutiny. The problem is to express theoretical predictions in
terms of expected lag analysis outcomes.

One intriguing solution to this problem is provided by Sackett
(1978b). Sackett asks the question "what should true interactions
look like, in terms of sequences of behavior?" One way to answer
the question is to develop various "models" of interactive sequences
and then test the goodness of fit of an empirical data set with the
models' predictions. The simplest model might be, "all behaviors
by A and B are equally likely to occur," i.e., a model of totally
random distribution of behaviors. Such a model would rarely
describe an interaction of interest. A second model might be "all
behaviors of A are autocorrelated, i.e., $P(A_T) = f(A_{T-M})$, and all
behaviors of B are autocorrelated, i.e., $P(B_T) = f(B_{T-N})$." Such
a model implies that A and B both have cyclicity, but their cycles
are independent and thus any "interaction" between them is entirely
coincidental. A third model might be that the behaviors of A are
autocorrelated, but the behaviors of B are conditionally dependent
upon A, i.e., $P(B_T) = f(A_{T-X})$.

An empirical example for this last model can be found in demand
feeding of an infant by its mother. Here, the mother may be responding to "feeding cues" displayed by the infant when it becomes hungry.
If the probability that the infant will emit such cues is a predictable function of the time since the infant's previous feeding session,
it will also be a function of the time since the infant emitted the
cues that resulted in the previous feeding. Thus, the probability
that the mother will initiate feeding can be described in terms of
the occurrence of the infant's "feeding cues", which is, in turn,
autocorrelated with the previous display of "feeding cue" behavior
by the infant. Additional examples of interaction models can
readily be developed. Each model can be tested with respect to
goodness of fit with a body of interactive data, using either nonparametric tests involving chi square distributions or multiple
regression techniques.

Such an approach has interesting possibilities. For example,
an investigator interested in the development of interactions between
members of a newly formed pair might employ such an analysis to
identify the basis for predictable changes in the form of interaction. Kummer (1971) reported data of this form in describing the
formation of new groups of captive baboons. On the other hand, the
approach also can be used to study the development of interactions
among newborns, in order to trace qualitative changes in the observed
patterns of sequences. We are currently using such an approach to
describe the differential development of various social relationships
by rhesus monkey infants.

HIGHER LEVEL ANALYSES

As indicated in the above paragraphs, interactive data that
preserve sequences can yield a basis for testing sophisticated models

of encounters between individuals. With the aid of high speed data
reduction and analysis routines, investigators can collect, store,
and digest enormous amounts of such interactive data (see chapters
by Simpson and Stephenson in this volume). Moreover, there now
exist powerful statistical tools to analyze these complex data.
Yet, there have been relatively few published accounts that actually
examined such sequential interactions in detail. This may be in
large part due to the undeniable fact that such data tend to be
exceedingly complex and tedious to digest.

Shunning the difficult details of sequential analysis of interactive data, some investigators have advocated alternative approaches
to study of such interactions. For example, Mason (1978) has
recently questioned the validity of "counting and classifying behavioral events." Instead, he has opted for classification by
outcomes of behavioral interactions, e.g., determination of winners
and losers, as well as description of structural characteristics of
the interactions, such as length or number of participants involved
in each bout (see also Anderson & Mason, 1974). Internal analyses
of interaction sequences are otherwise ignored in this scheme.
Thus, quality and outcome of interactions are stressed, rather
than contents.

Hinde has also recently (1976a, 1976b, 1977) advocated examination of interactions at more global levels of analysis than those
at which the data are originally collected. He sets forth a model
in which interactions, as described at the data collection level,
are abstracted to identify *relationships* between individuals.
Relationships are described not only in terms of content and diversity of the component interactions, but also with respect to reciprocity, power, quality, cognitive level, and penetration. Characteristics of relationships, in turn, are abstracted to identify
social structures. Changes at each of these various levels of
analysis are hypothesized to occur over different time scales.

Such an approach to study of relationships and social structure
is considerably more manageable than are most interactive analyses,
at least in terms of taxing one's conceptual capabilities. For
example, theorizing becomes much easier if one does not have to try
to comprehend interactions involving four or five variables. Nevertheless, the empirical validity of such theorizing is only as good
as its links to the original data. If the abstractions from these
data are such that accurate summaries of a new set of data cannot
be obtained from predictions based on the abstractions, the empirical
validity would be questionable.

It is not conceptually difficult to develop an empirical basis
for abstracting interactive data to higher levels of analysis, such
as that of relationships. For example, descriptions of outcome of
interactions, a measure suggested by Mason (1978), might be obtained
directly from sequential interactive data by examining only the last
2 or 3 elements of each sequence of behaviors or interactive bouts
involving the individuals in question. Such "end" elements would
certainly provide information regarding outcome without necessitating
examination of each and every element in each and every sequence involving these individuals. Similarly, the qualities of relationships

described by Hinde (1976a, 1976b)--for example, "control" and
"power"--can be readily abstracted from sequential data, as
described earlier. Other characteristics of interactions could be
abstracted from the raw data as well. For example, an investigator studying the development of interactions by infants might
abstract the duration of each bout with peers, in terms of number
of behavioral exchanges, in order to have a developmentally sensitive index of quality of interactions by these young participants.

In each of the above examples, the higher-level analyses had
their basis in sequential inneractive data. Each higher-level
measure was derived directly from these data. Thus, in any specific
instance a higher-level measure could be operationally defined by
actual recorded sequences of individual behaviors. This, of course,
is not true of all "higher-level" measures. For example, many
rating systems require observers to make decisions regarding some
"quality" of an individual's interactions as a basis for coding.
This is in contrast to a system that records the behaviors first
and then derives the ratings from the behavioral sequences.

There can be little question that observational systems
employing ratings have had a long and largely successful history
in the social sciences. Over the years the sophistication of ratings systems has increased substantially, so that now it is possible
to employ approaches, such as Q-sort techniques, that can produce
data whose distributions are highly similar across different ages
of subjects and in different situations. Block (1971), to cite a
prominent example, has employed such rating systems to generate and
analyze data that demonstrate remarkable consistency and continuity
of personality traits for individuals over period of years, even
decades, often encompassing large changes in physical and social
surroundings for some subjects. Moreover, the raters who provided
data for many of these individuals were not highly trained
laboratory assistants, but individuals whose primary exposure and
interests in the subjects were independent of the study itself
(e.g., parents, teachers, and peers). Those raters, of course,
did not base their evaluations of the subjects on the results of
statistical tests performed on frequency, duration, and sequences
of behaviors emitted by subjects when in the presence of the
observers. Rather, the ratings were based on the subjective
evaluations of the raters, with guidelines (e.g., scales) provided
by the experimenters. Demonstrations of the validity and reliability of such data can be impressive (see Block, 1971 for
numerous examples).

When ratings are obtained in such a fashion, however, information about specific behavior patterns that provided the original
basis for the ratings is not preserved. There exist a number of
circumstances where such loss of information may be disastrous
(Cairns, 1977). This is especially true for many developmental
studies. Here, some aspects of the subjects' behavioral repertoires usually change during the time between birth and maturity.
If one employs a ratings system that produces data with highly
similar distributions at each age, the rating system will be insensi-

tive to any age-related changes in the behavioral basis for the rating scales. Such a system may well yield high consistencies for individuals over repeated measures (Block, 1971), but it cannot describe the behavioral details for maintaining such a consistency. This will likely be a fundamental omission in studies where direct behavioral intervention is part of the experimental protocol.

For example, consider a study where the primary intent is to examine the play behavior of rhesus monkeys during the first 2 years of life. It is certainly possible to develop a rating system whereby each individual studied can reliably be assigned a position on a scale of "proficiency at play" each time it was sampled. Such a rating system might well yield data indicating that infants who were most proficient at play in their social peer group at 2 months, tended to be highest in play proficiency upon reaching the age of 2 years. These data, however, would by themselves produce little or no information concerning how the criteria for "play proficiency" had changed over this time period. Proficiency at 2 months might well be reflected by the number of interactive exchanges with a partner, at 4 months by the range of different behavior patterns that constituted a play bout, at 8 months by the number of different participants the individual engaged in its play, at 15 months by the degree to which the individual changed its repertoire as a function of the identity of its partner(s), and at 24 months by its success in enlisting "allies" in aggressive rough-and-tumble play bouts involving several participants. The ratings would themselves be insensitive to this information. They would be largely useless for consideration of specific manipulations that might be used at specific ages to elevate rankings of certain individuals in the group. On the other hand, if the ratings had been derived from behavioral scores instead of the raters' immediate evaluations, the behavioral basis for any given rating at any given age could be disclosed whenever desired, simply by analyzing the behavioral scores at the level of the actual sequences observed. Stevenson-Hinde and Zunz (1978) have, in fact, already developed one such behaviorally based rating system for young rhesus monkeys.

The point to be made is that while higher-level analyses of interactions may prove to be much more amenable for theory development and conceptualization than are complicated sequential analyses of behavioral components of the interactions, the former measures may be inadequate for detailed study of many problems of behavioral development. However, this problem can be largely eliminated if the ratings have themselves been derived from interactive data, i.e., if the observational scoring system is hierarchical in nature. It is not necessary to perform *all* the analyses of such data at the level of individual sequences of behaviors. Instead, the raw data can be initially used only to derive the ratings data; only after the ratings have been examined and analyzed need one return to the original interactive data with more specific questions that could be answered by focussing only on small portions of the total interactive record.

CONCLUSION

This chapter has examined the characteristics of interactive data collected and interpreted at various levels of analysis. Certain generalities about different levels can be pointed out at this point. It should be apparent that an investigator's evaluation of any given interaction can be highly dependent on the level utilized. Clearly, as one moves to finer and finer levels, progressively more detailed information about patterns of interactions is obtained. On the other hand, such information may become so extensive that overall patterns or trends may be lost in the details. Thus, interactive data examined at grosser levels of analysis are usually less tedious to interpret.

Given that different levels of analysis can yield different sorts of findings, how should the prospective investigator determine at which level to collect any given set of interactive data? In the past, there existed few useful guidelines and no universally acceptable solutions. However, the technological advances that have recently been made in data acquisition and storage systems (see chapters by Simpson and Stephenson) now provide investigators with an attractive option. Specifically, one can design an observational scoring system that is hierarchical in nature, in that data at higher levels of analysis can be derived from the scores that are originally collected at a finer level. When one collects observational data using such a hierarchical scoring system, the raw data will set the lower limit for possible levels of analysis. Any higher level can be utilized with such a data base, since data points appropriate for the higher level can be derived from the raw data. Thus, an investigator possessing such data can choose the level of analysis to suit his or her desired conceptual complexity. Moreover, s/he can refocus the analysis to yield a more sensitive view of the data or, alternatively, take a more general perspective with respect to the original level of analysis, depending on the outcome of that analysis.

For example, Suomi (1977) has presented an analysis of data collected on adult male rhesus monkeys, living in artificial laboratory "nuclear families", in which the focus of the analysis was shifted to progressively smaller units of behavior. It was found that at the grossest levels of analysis, adult males appeared to be inactive and insensitive to changes in their social environment that were associated with major shifts in the activity patterns of their adult female and infant cagemates. On the other hand, analyses performed at the partner profile level revealed that adult males were clearly differentiating their behaviors toward infants on the basis of the infants' sex and blood relation to the adult males' mates. Contingency analyses performed at the level of individual interactive sequences involving adult males and various classes of partners revealed that most of the variance at the partner profile level of analysis could be attributed to a relatively small number of behavioral sequences between the adult male and each class of infant partner. Thus, for this data set, markedly different conclusions could be drawn, depending on the level of analysis chosen.

Findings such as these should remind us that there exists no one "optimal" level of analysis, nor one most "appropriate" set of dependent variables for observational data in general. Instead, choice of level of analysis must be dictated by the specific research question under consideration. Collection of data that are amenable to analysis at several levels enables the investigator at the very least to ask a wider range of such questions. Considering the present extent of our knowledge about interactions within complex social groupings, that in itself represents no small gain.

ACKNOWLEDGEMENTS

Some of the research described in this chapter was supported by USPHS grants #MH-11894 and RR-0167 from the National Institute of Mental Health and from the National Institute of Health, respectively, as well as by funds provided by the Grant Foundation and by the Graduate School of the University of Wisconsin-Madison. I wish to express my gratitude to Dr. Michael E. Lamb for his comments on an earlier version of the chapter.

REFERENCES

Altmann, S. A.   Sociobiology of rhesus monkeys. II: Stochastics of social communication. *Journal of Theoretical Biology,* 1965, *8,* 490-522.

Anderson, C. O., & Mason, W. A.   Early experience and complexity of social organization in groups of young rhesus monkeys (*Macara mulatta*). *Journal of Comparative and Physiological Psychology,* 1974, *87,* 681-690.

Bakeman, R.   Untangling streams of behavior: Sequential analyses of observational data. In G. P. Sackett (Ed.), *Observing behavior: Data collection and analysis methods (Vol. 2).* Baltimore: University Park Press, 1978.

Barlow, G. W.   Modal action patterns. In T. A. Sebeok (Ed.), *How animals communicate.* Bloomington, Ind.: Indiana University Press, 1977. Pp. 94-125.

Block, J.   *Lives through time.* Berkeley, Ca.: Bancroft Books, 1971.

Cairns, R. B.   Beyond social attachments: The dynamics of interactional development. In T. Alloway, P. Pliner, & L. Krames (Eds.), *Attachment behavior.* New York: Plenum Press, 1977.

Dawkins, R.   Hierarchical organization: A candidate principle for ethology. In P. P. G. Bateson & R. A. Hinde (Eds.), *Growing points in ethology.* New York: Cambridge University Press, 1976.

Golopol, L.   Social behavior patterns of rhesus monkeys reared in a nuclear family versus monkeys reared in an open pen. Unpublished honors thesis, University of Wisconsin-Madison, 1977.

Gottman, J.   Nonsequential data analysis techniques in observational research. In G. P. Sackett (Ed.), *Observing behavior: Data collection and analysis methods (Vol. 2).* Baltimore: University Park Press, 1978.

Goude, G. Psychobiological aspects of the function of probability
    judgments. In K. Immelmann, G. Barlow, M. Main, & L. Petrinovich
    (Eds.), *Early development in animals and man.* New York:
    Cambridge University Press, in press.
Hansen, E. W. The development of maternal and infant behavior in
    the rhesus monkey. *Behaviour,* 1966, *27,* 107-149.
Hinde, R. A. On describing relationships. *Journal of Child
    Psychology and Psychiatry,* 1976a, *17,* 1-19.
Hinde, R. A.   Interactions, relationships, and social structure.
    Man, 1976b, *11,* 1-17.
Hinde, R. A.   On assessing the bases of partner preferences.
    Behaviour, 1977, *62,* 1-9.
Hinde, R. A., & Atkinson, S. Assessing the roles of social partners
    in maintaining mutual proximity, as exemplified by mother-
    infant relations in rhesus monkeys. *Animal Behaviour,* 1970,
    18, 169-176.
Hinde, R. A., & Spencer-Booth, Y. The behavior of socially-living
    monkeys in their first two and a half years. *Animal Behaviour,*
    1967, *15,* 169-196.
Hinde, R. A., & White, L. E. Dynamics of a relationship: Rhesus
    monkey mother-infant ventro-ventro contact. *Journal of Compara-
    tive and Physiological Psychology,* 1974, *86,* 8-23.
Kummer, H. *Primate societies: Group techniques of ecological
    adaptation.* Chicago: Aldine-Atherton, 1971.
Lamb, M. E. Father-infant and mother-infant interaction in the first
    year of life. *Child Development,* 1977, *48,* 167-181.
Lewis, M., & Rosenblum, L. A. *The effect of the infant on its
    caregiver.* New York: Wiley, 1974.
Mason, W. A. Social ontogeny. In J. G. Vandenberg & P. Marler
    (Eds.), *Social behavior and communication.* New York: Plenum,
    1978, in press.
Ruppenthal, G. C., Harlow, M. K., Eisele, C. D., Harlow, H. F., &
    Suomi, S. J. Development of peer interactions of monkeys reared
    in a nuclear-family environment. *Child Development,* 1974, *45,*
    670-682.
Sackett, G. P. A nonparametric lag sequential analysis for studying
    dependency among responses in observational scoring systems.
    Paper presented at the Western Psychological Association meeting,
    San Francisco, 1974.
Sackett, G. P. Measurement in observational research. In G. P.
    Sackett (Ed.), *Observing behavior: Data collection and analysis
    methods (Vol. 2).* Baltimore: University Park Press, 1978a.
Sackett, G. P. A paradigm for determining characteristics of
    interactions using lag sequential analyses. Paper presented at
    the Zentrum fur interdisciplinare Forshung, University of
    Bielefeld, West Germany, 1978b.
Sackett, G. P., Holm, R., & Ruppenthal, G. C. Social isolation
    rearing: Species differences in behavior of macaque monkeys.
    Developmental Psychology, 1976, *12,* 283-288.
Stevenson-Hinde, J., & Zunz, M. Subjective assessment of individual
    rhesus monkeys. *Primates,* 1978, in press.

Suomi, S. J.   Social interactions of monkeys raised in a nuclear
      family environment versus monkeys raised with mothers and
      peers.   *Primates,* 1974, *15,* 311-320.
Suomi, S. J.   Adult male-infant interactions among monkeys living
      in nuclear families.   *Child Development,* 1977, *48,* 1255-1270.
Suomi, S. J.   Differential development of various social relation-
      ships by rhesus monkey infants.   In M. Lewis & L. A. Rosen-
      blum (Eds.), *The social network of the developing infant.*
      New York: Plenum, 1978, in press.
Suomi, S. J., & Harlow, H. F.   Social rehabilitation of isolate-
      reared monkeys.   *Developmental Psychology,* 1972, *6,* 487-496.

7.
Problems of recording behavioral data by keyboard

MICHAEL J. A. SIMPSON

I. INTRODUCTION

This chapter describes and evaluates a recording system that we have used to study the interactions between rhesus monkey infants and their mothers living in social groups throughout the infants' first 2 1/2 years of life. Where possible, examples are used to make general points about problems of recording behavioral data.

Our system uses 40-channel event-recorders, operated by observers who press keys corresponding to specific channels. The system is computer-compatible (White, 1971), and the data collected through it are stored on DEC LINCTAPE and analyzed by a PDP 12 computer. Check sheets are also used to provide background data about the social interactions of the 8 to 12 members of each of our six social groups. Because the primary aim in this chapter is to illustrate the problems of evaluating a recording system, neither the hardware of the system (described by White, 1971), nor the machine code and FORTRAN programming supporting the system (mainly of interest to the users of PDP 12 computers, which are becoming obsolete), will be discussed.

Any recording system must obviously be judged with reference to its specific aims. Our aims in studying the above group-living mother-infant pairs have included:

1. Providing information on infants and mothers comparable to that collected on check sheets by Hinde and his colleagues (e.g., Hinde & Spencer-Booth, 1967; Hinde, 1973). For example, we continue to count "rejections" (e.g., Hinde & Spencer-Booth, 1967; White & Hinde, 1975, p. 528).
2. Preserving information about the timing and sequences of maternal and infant actions. For example, what events follow within 5 seconds of an infant making contact with its mother?
3. Making possible studies that would enable us to characterize relationships between different mother-infant pairs

137

(e.g., Hinde & Simpson, 1975). For example, do mother-
infant pairs differ in how well mother and infant coor-
dinate the timing of their approaching and leaving one
another?

4. Recording data in a single "pass", in a form requiring
   minimum further editing. At the outset of our present
   study in 1972, we thought that any editing system would
   likely be exceedingly cumbersome, and we thus decided to
   accept a certain number of errors as inevitable "noise".
   Those errors noticed during recording were identified so
   that we could correct our computer printouts as they were
   produced. Moreover, we always checked a printout of the
   sequence of approaches, contacts, and leaves, to eliminate "illogical" sequences (such as "infant leaves, infant
   approaches, mother approaches," when approach or leave
   are so defined that only one partner can be responsible).
   Systems working at finer levels of detail (see Discussion
   of this chapter) require that video or film records be
   viewed repeatedly, because the detailed information can
   only be obtained from the video-tapes over several viewings. Such systems also demand an editing facility for
   correcting mistakes made in working from video-tapes.

The first three aims outlined above can be achieved more effectively if the data collected are reliable. It was therefore
important for us to use behavioral measures on which individual
subjects differed consistently from each other. As Kraemer and
Korner (1976) have pointed out, one may fail to find individual
consistency in 12-week-old rhesus monkey infants because the
behavior of the infants is inconsistent from day to day in that
week, or because the observers are inconsistent in recording their
behavior, or for both reasons. Indices of the observers' consistency or reliability seem easy to obtain, but studies of individual
differences also require assessments of the subjects' consistency.

Of course, the reliability with which a particular measure
separates our subjects is not our only reason for preferring it.
Of overriding importance is the relevance of the measure to the
problem at hand (Hinde & Herrmann, 1977). For example, observers
can uniformly agree about the length of time rhesus monkey infants
spend near their mothers, but at certain ages such proximity scores
might reflect the prevailing weather conditions rather than any
aspect of the infants' relationships with their mothers.

It could be argued that if our measures prove to be "valid" in
the sense of being relevant in an interesting and effective way to
our study problem (see Anastasi, 1968, for a discussion of "validity" and "reliability") we need not be concerned about the details
of reliability. To find, for example, that some measure of infant
social play at 12 weeks allows us to predict some measure of social
competence at 1 year, is enough in itself, provided that the entire
study can be replicated. In short, nothing succeeds like success.

Unfortunately, a time-consuming study such as the present one
could require another 5 years to repeat. More important than this
practical difficulty is the empirical finding that, in general,

behavioral studies do not achieve the wholesale "successes" cari-
catured above. It is often the case that a measure of behavior at
one age allows one to predict behavior at a later age with only
moderate success. In such cases, one would want to ensure that
such a result did not merely reflect unreliable observation techniques. Moreover, one might wish to test the reliability in recording each of the various measures in advance, so that one could
eliminate any that proved clearly unreliable.

Although reliability can be studied empirically, as I shall
show (see also Dunbar, 1976; Simpson & Simpson, 1977), one can
often predict some of the sources of error. First, different study
programs, or different observers within the same program, may be
operating according to different definitions of a particular behavioral category. In the case of play, this could be because it
is impossible to make a workable definition of play that is both
rigorous and explicit (see L. E. White, 1977a, 1977b, and below).
Section III of this chapter considers the kinds of scoring difficulty arising out of the use of various kinds of behavioral categorization, together with different kinds of recording procedure.
In section IV, I examine the reliability of successive days' counts
of play episodes initiated by 12-week-old rhesus monkey infants,
and then in section V, I attempt to estimate how much of the day-
to-day error in scores can be attributable to observer error, In
section VI,I then examine the natural history of observers in a
situation where two observers have watched the same mother and
infant. In section VII, Discussion, the uses of single indices of
reliability are criticized, and certain pitfalls of our keyboard
system are outlined.

II. THE OBSERVATIONAL SYSTEM

Recording Systems Utilized

The WRATS keyboards used in the present study (White, 1971)
have 39 keys, excluding the title-data key. The system records
presses and releases of each key to 0.10 seconds, so that information about sequences is preserved, as long as successive key
changes are more than 0.10 seconds apart. Keys that "stick down"
can be used for recording states (e.g., near mother) or activities
with duration. To release them, such "duration" or "D-keys" must
be pressed again. While set, they are lit up, to remind the user.
"Instantaneous" or "I-keys" record duration for only as long as
the user holds them down.

By using keys in combination, a user can increase the number
of categories recorded. Our experience suggests that observers
manage comfortably when they have to record new events as often as
once every 3 seconds, so long as the events have clear-cut onsets
and offsets, and so long as there are few enough keys (about 25)
to be used without moving the hands more than about 3cm. Additional keys should represent behavioral categories that tend to occur
infrequently or that tend to occur at separate times from the main

set of categories. For example, in a system for recording the infant's interaction with its mother, additional keys concerned with its interaction with others while it is away from its mother's side (and not interacting with mother), can easily be managed.

We have used our WRATS keyboards in two main ways:

1. To follow the details of not only what mother and infant did to each other, but also (in less detail) what the infant did to its inanimate surroundings and cohabitants (the Mother-Infant, or M-I keyboard);

2. To cover the interactions between the infant and the other animals in its social group, with the infant as the focal animal (the Social, or SOC keyboard).

For some infants, such "social" data were recorded in their early weeks (SE in Table 1). In addition, we sampled interactions involving *all* members of each group, using a Pen Data check sheet (PD in Table 1).

Schedule of Observation

The M-I keyboard was used in weeks 2, 4, 6, 8, 10, 12, and 16 for 22 infants, and only on weeks 4, 8, 12, and 16 for most of the remaining 11. For most infants the SOC system replaced the M-I system after 16 weeks and was used for data collection in weeks 20, 24, 28, 36, 44, and 52, and then at every half year up to 2 1/2 years. Every month, each of the 6 social groups in which the infants were living also provided at least 6 hours of Pen Data. Each week of keyboard watching on a particular infant was done on three separate mornings, in 2-hour watches.

Categories Recorded

Table 1 lists the categories of behavior recorded and shows which system was used for each category. The listing is not exhaustive. Where categories have been derived to correspond with those already used in published studies, the studies are noted. More complete definitions of the other categories will appear in later reports.

The categories in Table 1 have been classified as Instantaneous (I), Duration (D), or Multi-Component-Through-Time (MCT) in order to distinguish those that present common problems for scoring and analysis. Instantaneous (I) acts include hitting and making an approach, where to approach is to cross a boundary line 60cm from the partner being approached. Of course, such acts usually take more than an instant for the observer to recognize, but in practice the instant at which they occur can be defined relatively easily. States with duration (D) are those which last for some finite time, like being in proximity. D states usually have instantaneous starts (e.g. "infant approaches") and ends (e.g., "mother leaves"). Being alone, however, has a "Multi-Component-Through-Time" start: an individual's alone key is pressed only after he has been more than 60cm from another monkey for at least 5 seconds. Its definition depends on *More than one Component through Time*, i.e., a lapse of 5 seconds in addition. "Play" is another example of a MCT activity. The qualities

TABLE 1. BEHAVIORAL CATEGORIES RECORDED

Category		Lit	MI	SOC	SE	PD
Approach (across 60cm distance)	I	√	√	√	NM	-
Leave (across 60cm distance)	I	√	√	√	NM	-
Make contact with any body part (not brief hits)	I	√	√	√	-	-
Break contact with any body part (not brief hits)	I	√	√	√	-	-
Hit, bite, or shove	I	√	√	√	√	√
Passively prevent nipple contact	MCT	√	√	√	√	-
Mother restrains infant	MCT	√	√	-	√	-
Mother pulls nipple up out of infant's mouth	MCT	-	√	-	-	-
Beckon	I	-	√	-	-	-
Mother carries infant to another	I	-	-	-	√	-
Mother carries infant from another	I	-	-	-	√	-
Groom	D	√	√	-	-	-
Groom onset only	D	√	√	√	√	√
Initiation of contact or play	I	√	√	√	√	√
Infant whoos	I	√	√	√	√	-
Infant squeaks	I	√	√	√	√	√
Infant jerks	I	-	√	√	√	-
Mother jerks	I	-	√	√	√	-
Infant has tantrum	I	√	-	-	-	√
Infant enters a new box	I	√	√	√	√	-
Bounce	I	-	-	√	√	-
On mother's back	I	-	√	-	-	-
Cuddle (with others only)	I	-	-	√	√	-
Mount	I	√	-	√	√	√
Present	I	√	-	√	√	√
Threaten	I	-	-	√	√	√
Fear grin	I	-	-	-	-	√
Remark key	I	-	√	√	√	-
Infant out of sight	D	-	√	√	√	-
On nipple	D	-	√	√	√	-
Ventro-ventral	D	√	√	√	-	-
Nonventro-ventral	D	-	√	√	-	-
Any kind of contact	D	-	-	-	√	√
Any kind of contact with O	D	-	√	-	-	√
Near	D	√	√	√	√	-
Mother's arm around infant	D	√	√	√	√	-
Play	MCT	√	√	√	√	√
Infant alone	MCT	-	√	√	√	-
Infant feeds	MCT	√	√	√	√	-
Infant fiddles	MCT	√	√	√	√	-
Locomotor play by infant or display	MCT	√	√	√	√	-
Displays only	MCT	-	-	-	-	√
Displace	MCT	√	-	-	-	√
Avoid	MCT	√	-	-	-	√
Chase	MCT	√	-	-	-	√
Attack	MCT	√	-	-	-	√
Solicit support	MCT	-	-	-	-	√
Pace	MCT	-	-	-	-	√

Note: Categories included in: Hinde, Rowell, & Spencer-Booth (1964),
       Hinde & Spencer-Booth (1967), Hinde & White (1974), and Ruppenthal
       et al. (1974).

of "animation" (e.g., definition in Ruppenthal, Harlow, Eisele,
Harlow, & Suomi, 1974), and "playfulness" depend on the combination
of a number of activities occurring in a sequence that can only
show certain properties as it occurs (see White, 1977b; Loizos,
1967). "Play", and also various kinds of "rejection", are considered further in section III.

Some MCT activities can be constructed from detailed sequential
records of their components. In making our keyboard records of
rejections comparable with check-sheet records, we were forced to
do this (see section III). The category "Rest" (not in Table 1),
defined as a period of 700 seconds or more in proximity with mother, is an example of a MCT activity that can be used only when records have already been running for at least 700 seconds. Because
700 seconds is a particular time in a range of possible times, the
meaningfulness of taking that time is not self-evident in quite
the way that the meaningfulness of the category "play" might be.
However, it can be shown that bouts of continuous proximity to
mother of at least 700 seconds are distinct in other respects as
well as durations from shorter bouts.

Methods for Ascribing Initiative

To assign responsibility for changes in proximity to mother,
the Mother-Infant keyboard had four I keys (infant approaches,
mother approaches, infant leaves, and mother leaves) and one D key
(proximity). The keyboard was constructed so that when one of the
approach keys was pressed, the proximity key was automatically set
also, and not released until one of the leave keys was pressed.
The Social keyboard systems dealt with the focal infant's proximity
to named others, as well as to the mother. Responsibility for the
focal infant's approach was recorded by holding the approach key
down long enough to both press and release the key naming the partner who had been approached. Whenever a particular partner approached that focal infant, the key corresponding to the partner would be
pressed and held down long enough for the approach key to be both
pressed and released. In general, pressing an "animal name key"
while the "behavior key" was already down meant that the focal
infant initiated the activity, and pressing a "behavior" key when
the "animal name key" was already down meant that the named partner
was responsible for the activity. This convention gave us a good
compromise between ease of programming for decoding the records and
economy of keys ("punctuation" keys were not needed to separate the
actions being recorded). To the surprise of all who learn the system
the convention is quickly learned.

The Mother-Infant had too few keys left over to deal with social
activities with others by name. Instead, there was a key for "infant initiates" and one for "other initiates", and these were used
in conjunction with "hit", "play", and "any kind of contact with
other".

Contact with mother, in both the Mother-Infant and in the Social
system, used "make contact" and "break contact" keys, analogous to
the approach and leave keys in the M-I system. But the state of

contact was not automatically set by pressing a "make" key; the user had to specify the kind of contact made by pressing a D key for "ventro-ventral contact", or another for "nonventro-ventral contact", and the user also had to release the contact key(s) before pressing a "break" key.

III. HOW DIFFERENT RECORDING SYSTEMS CAN AFFECT THE SCORES OF BEHAVIORAL CATEGORIES WITH DIFFERENT KINDS OF DEFINITION

In using a recording system that was intended to make our data as comparable as possible to those collected by check sheets (Hinde & Spencer-Booth, 1976; Hinde, 1973), we have been forced to consider how behavioral categories and scoring systems interact to produce scores. I do not believe that data collected by event-recorders are somehow closer to the "truth" than data collected by paper-and-pencil methods, although in some ways event recorder data can be more complete. For example, if the keyboard operators can touch-type, they will not need to look away from the animals often and they will be less likely to miss events. Moreover, our keyboard system can record the order and timing of events with a "temporal resolution" much greater than that which could be achieved with pencil-and-paper methods. In general, using a keyboard is a relatively effortless way of preserving detailed information about timing (see also section VI).

However, increasing the temporal resolution of one's data does not necessarily increase their validity for a particular study. To paraphrase Rosenblum (1978), if a threat a day by an alpha male suffices to keep the beta male at bay, then in a study of alpha's relationship with the others it may be enough to know that he threatens the beta male during a particular day. Additional detail, such as how often he threatens, may not improve our predictions about other aspects of the relationship between alpha and beta. In each hour of our check-sheet data on events in each social group ("Pen Data", see Table 1), each pair of animals concerned could either score a "1" or a "0" for each defined action. Thus Penny would score once in an hour for threatening Elaine whether she threatened Elaine once or more than once. In that sense the scoring system can be said to be "one-zero" (Altmann, 1974). Therefore, whenever we devise scoring systems that provide more detail, the possibility always remains that the additional detail is irrelevant to the problem being studied. In the remainder of this section, such questions of relevance or validity are not raised.

Before considering various scoring systems in relation to each other, it is important to point out three special problems of one-zero sampling, the basis for our check-sheet data. First, information about frequencies of instantaneous (I) events is lost (e.g., Altmann, 1974). In other words, the number of half minutes in which an infant was near its mother does not necessarily reflect the frequency of proximity bouts. Second, when working with durations of states (D events), it is important to remember that one-zero scores of the proportions of intervals in which some state occurs are unlikely to reflect accurately the proportion of time the animal spent in that state. The proportion is usually exaggerated (e.g., Altmann, 1974;

Simpson & Simpson, 1977), and the factor by which the proportion is exaggerated can only be calculated if the occurrence and nonoccurrence of the state under study is generated by a Markov process (Cane, personal communication; Simpson & Simpson, 1977), and if the number of occurrences of that state is already known (a frequency count impossible with one-zero scoring alone). Finally, one-zero scoring systems add more to the variance of a measure of the occurrence of a state than do most other systems (Cane, personal communication; see Figures in Simpson & Simpson, 1977), although rare events of short duration can be missed altogether by scan sampling. These difficulties peculiar to one-zero scoring systems have attracted attention because they are reasonably obvious and because the systems hold out the promise (perhaps illusory, see Simpson & Simpson, 1977) of quantification.

Table 2 compares four scoring methods, including one-zero check-sheet scoring (1-0 CS) already referred to. The table summarizes the interconvertibility of scores of I, D, and MCT behaviors collected by the four methods. A Scan check sheet (Scan CS) is one divided by lines which represent the instants at which the animal being scored is scanned, such as the 30th, 60th, 90th, 120th ... seconds of a session in which the scans are made "on" every half minute. Scan scores are meaningful only for enduring states like proximity (see Table 2). Frequency records (Freq) are simply counts of occurrences. A check sheet can, of course, be designed for recording the frequency of occurrence of I events, as well as for making one-zero samples of D states (e.g., Hinde, 1973).

The cells of Table 2 provide information about the prospects for score comparisons for each type of behavior. Thus for D behaviors, the "*" shared by one-zero check sheets and the event recorder indicates that comparisons between the scores, while possible, raise problems because one-zero scores do not reflect durations directly (above). For this reason, scan scores also share a "*" with one-zero scores. In contrast, scan scores and event recorder scores share a "√" for durations, because the former reflect the latter in a simple way, and, if the scanning interval is short relative to the bout-lengths and gap-lengths of the state being scanned, they do so accurately (Simpson & Simpson, 1977).

In Table 2, MCT behaviors are shown as posing problems for all possible comparisons between the different scoring systems. MCT actions are those that observers must watch for a certain amount of time before they can decide that the actions have occurred, for the observers must recognize a combination of elements that cannot occur simultaneously. Thus, "approach-withdrawal play" might be recognized by a combination of elements, like chasing and fleeing, which would not otherwise occur in rapid succession in one interaction. In the absence of other cues, observers must wait until the same animal has both approached and withdrawn from its partner before they can score "play". The reliance of definitions of play on adjectives like "animated" (e.g., Ruppenthal et al., 1974) underscores the same point: "animation" can be seen only in sequences with finite durations. Sade's (1973) static line drawings of the twisted and fluid postures of playing rhesus monkeys seem to contradict this point.

TABLE 2.   COMPARABILITY OF SCAN CHECK SHEET, ONE-ZERO CHECK SHEET,
FREQUENCY COUNT AND KEYBOARD EVENT-RECORDER SCORES OF
ACTIONS WHICH ARE INSTANTANEOUS (I), DURATION (D), OR
MULTI-COMPONENT THROUGH TIME (MCT)

Type of Behavior	Method of Recording			
	Scan CS	1-0 CS	Freq (CS or ER)	ER
(I) e.g., approach hit	n.a.d.	(a)	√	√
(D) e.g., proximity	√*	*	n.a.d.	√*
(MCT) e.g., rejection	n.a.d.	*	*	*
e.g., play	*(b)	*	*	*

Note: For each line the conventions link scores as follows:
√ - scores directly comparable for the recording methods
(e.g., if observers using a scan check sheet and an event
recorder with duration keys both record proximity, their
records should agree within one or two scanning intervals.
* - scores comparable, but problems arise (e.g., one-zero
check sheet scores both exaggerate and increase the variance
of duration scores made by scan check sheets or event-recorders;
other examples in text).
n.a.d. - not applicable by definition of the behavioral
category and the scoring method (e.g., "instantaneous" hits
cannot occur on the instant when the stopwatch shows the
half minute).
(a) - see text.
(b) - bouts of play with finite duration could be scored
with difficulty by scan methods.

But "fluid" implies a quality of movement, which must be inferred
from the drawings.
Difficulties in recognizing "rejections" are also instructive.
In the check-sheet scoring of Hinde and Spencer-Booth (1967), what
is rejected is an attempt.   Rejections are scored "*when* he or she
tries to get on the nipple or ventrally".   According to a pedantic
view, the italicized words are contradictory; the trying takes
time to recognize, so that the record cannot be made "when" the
trying starts', only some time later.
Compared with the 30-second time lines of most check sheets,
these observer "recognition times" are unrealistically short, and
it is almost always easy to make the "one-zero" decision: "Has
there or has there not been one or more episodes of rejection or
play in the past half minute?"   Scan check sheets, which force
the observer to decide whether a tantrum, or an episode of play,
or rejection was occurring at this instant would sometimes provide
difficulty.

The same problem becomes much more apparent when a keyboard event-recorder is used. A system which records time continuously seems to demand that the observer be temporally accurate in making time-consuming decisions like "has this infant begun to play?". Meanwhile, other events (such as, "infant approaches or leaves its mother", "infant is hit by its sister") continue to occur, and these must also be recorded in correct sequence relative to the bouts of play and rejection. This situation would clearly be intolerable for the overly conscientious observer. In addition to not employing such observers, we use the following partial solutions. First, we do not attempt to analyze the durations of bouts of play. Second, in deciding on the occurrence of a new bout of play we use such criteria as: "new activity recorded since play was last recorded", "distinct pause in play", and "focal infant has initiated play with a new partner."

Our methods of "converting" event-recorder events into "rejections" comparable to those scored on check sheets illustrates how the components of relatively "molecular" events can be recombined, after recording, to produce higher-order categories. After the recordings had been made, R_1s (Table 3) were reconstructed by the computer from occasions when mother had broken contact with her infant within 5 seconds of the infant making contact with her. R_3s (Table 3) used the 5-second criterion in the same way. Of course a mechanically applied criterion of precisely 5 seconds is arbitrary, but we found that many rejecting mothers usually moved away within 5 seconds if they were going to move away at all. "Passive prevents" (R_2) by the mother were quick and clear enough to be scored as such with the keyboard event-recorder.

Given the nature of our solutions to the problems of recording MCT-type behaviors with the keyboard, we do not expect perfect interobserver reliability, and I would not be surprised if keyboard users disagreed considerably about the frequencies of play bouts, which depend on the observers' ideas of what consitutues a new bout for an individual. These ideas can never in practice be made fully explicit, and different observers may work with different implicit criteria, whether or not they succeed in recording comparable overall frequencies.

Thus, there exists some basis for suggesting that a keyboard event-recording system may not necessarily enable observers to produce reliable scores of MCT activities, like play or rejections. Sections IV and V examine the reliability of play scores actually produced by the present study.

IV.   THE RELIABILITY OF PLAY SCORES FOR 32 12-WEEK-OLD INFANTS

Our recording timetable has enabled us to assess the consistency of infant scores from 2-hour record to 2-hour record. At any one age, e.g., 12 weeks, three 2-hour records are made, and Kendall's coefficient of concordance (W) (Siegel, 1956) can be used to assess the consistency with which the scores can be ranked. One measure of an infant's tendency to play socially is the total

TABLE 3.   DEFINITIONS FOR CHECK-SHEET AND EVENT-RECORDER
                     SCORES OF REJECTIONS

Rejection	Check Sheet	Event-Recorder
R_1	Mother moves out of contact when infant attempts to make contact with her nipple or ventrum	Any contact broken by mother within 5 seconds of a conact made by the infant
R_2	Mother passively prevents infant's access to her nipple or ventrum, e.g., by interposing her arm turning her body	As check-sheet def., includes passive prevents by mother against an infant already in contact with mother's body
R_3	Mother hits, bites or pushes her infant when it attempts to get to her nipple or ventrum	Hit, bite or shove within 5 seconds of a contact made by infant

Note: In both systems, total rejections (R) = the sum $R_1 + R_2 + R_3$.
            In the check-sheet system, an R_1 can also be an occasion
            when mother moves away from the infant who is attempting to
            reach her nipple, *before* the infant even touches her.

number of play bouts or episodes which he initiates in a 2-hour
session. For the consistency with which the 32 infants could be
ranked in their first, second, and third 2-hour watches, W was
calculated at .526, and this degree of consistency was statistically significant at $p < .02$.
      Such a relatively low level of reliability could reflect both
unreliable observers and unreliable infants, whose play scores
were being affected, for example, by day-to-day variations in conditions, like weather or intragroup aggression. Section V attempts
to assess the contributions of observers to this degree of error,
and shows how estimates of observers' consistency are affected by
the populations of scores being considered.

V.   A POST HOC STUDY OF ERROR INTRODUCED BY OBSERVERS

      Throughout the first 16 weeks of their lives, the play of 32
infants was recorded both by the MI keyboard system and social
keyboard system. On 47 mornings two observers, one using each
system, watched the same infant throughout the same 2-hour period.

TABLE 4.   MEASURES OF THE CONSISTENCY OF TWO OBSERVERS IN SCORING
THE BEHAVIOR OF THE SAME ANIMAL DURING THE SAME 2-HOUR
OBSERVATION PERIOD ON THAT ANIMAL (SAME DAY RECORDS, OR
SDR); AND THE CONSISTENCY OF 2-HOUR OBSERVATIONS ON THE
SAME ANIMAL ON DIFFERENT DAYS (DIFFERENT DAY RECORDS,
OR DDR).   DIFFERENT DAY RECORDS CAN BE MADE BY EITHER
DIFFERENT OBSERVERS, OR THE SAME ONE.

	rS		MEDIAN DIF BETW RECORDS		MEDIAN SCORE BY SOC SYSTEM*		N†	
	SDR	DDR	SDR	DDR	SDR	DDR	SDR	DDR
Infant initiates social play per 2 hours	.57	.20	3.0	8.0	2.5	9.5	29	46
Partners to the infant init. soc. play/2 hours	.85	.22	4.0	10.0	8.5	9.0	29	47
Infant approaches mother per 2 hours	.97	.60	3.0	17.0	12.5	33.0	42	55

Note: *see text.
        †Occasions when both observers (SDR) or both records (DDR)
        recorded zeroes are excluded, so Ns differ according to
        behavior scored.   In general, records from 2-week-old
        infants had some approaches to mother, but no social plays.

These "Same Day" ("SDR") records (Table 4) were ranked, so that
the rank of the MI records could be compared with the rank of the
equivalent SOC records for each infant-day.   The Spearman rank-
order correlation coefficient (rS) was used to assess the agreement
between the observers (Table 4).   At present, we are ignoring the
possibility that the two methods of recording may have introduced
different kinds of bias.

Rank-order correlation coefficients are crude indices of
agreement (Cane, personal communication) and, as we shall see,
are unlikely to be widely generalizable from one assessment of
reliability to other situations.   A formal study of interobserver,
interrecord, and residual variance could form a more viable starting point for such extrapolations.   Unfortunately, the raw play
scores were so far from being normally distributed that they dis-
couraged us from making such a study.

We were able to assess the error introduced *both* by observers'
and infants' day-to-day variation in behavior, using the same infants.   There were 66 occasions on which the same infant was

observed by the two recording systems on different days of the same week. For example, Klyde might have been watched with the MI system on Monday, Wednesday, and Thursday, and with the SOC system on Tuesday, Friday, and Saturday. He would thus have given us 3 pairs, the first being Monday MI with Tuesday SOC. There were 66 such instances where the same infant was observed by the two systems on different days, called "Different Day Records", or "DDR" in Table 4. From these analyses are excluded all pairs where zero play was scored with both systems. Most of the 2-week-old infants did not play socially.

Table 4 shows that the observers' consistency in scoring play initiated by the infant was poor by current standards (rS was .57) (cf. Ruppenthal et al., 1974, Patterson, 1977), although the observers agreed better about rankings of play received ($rS = .85$), and they performed quite well in scoring the infants' approaches to their mothers. This finding suggests that observers can agree consistently when the categories are simple.

Inspection of Table 4 shows that the median differences between observers' scores were approximately the same for all three behaviors. Observers did not differ more when scoring episodes of play initiated by the infant, for which the rS was so low. However, Table 4 also shows that the sizes of the scores themselves differed according to whether they were of play episodes initiated or play episodes received. For example, with a median of 2.5, half the scores of play episodes initiated must have been 0s, 1s, and 2s, while a median of 8.5, for play episodes received, reflects larger scores and suggests a greater range of scores. In other words, variation from score to score was almost certainly greater for play received than for play initiated. (For the infants' approaches to their mothers, an even greater range of scores was possible).

In any study of interobserver consistency, a Spearman rank-order correlation coefficient depends on the degree of observer error relative to score difference. In general, an rS can be decreased because the differences between the scores decrease relative to the errors introduced by observers, or because the observers' errors increase, or for both reasons. It follows that, in the absence of information about the sizes of differences between scores, rSs can tell us little about interobserver reliability.

The previous section provided an estimate of the reliability with which 12-week-old infants' play scores were ranked through three 2-hour watches. From the Kendall W of .526, the average Spearman rank-order correlation coefficient expected between any two of those watches (rS_{AV}) can be calculated (Siegel, 1956). This rS_{AV} is .29--considerably less than the .57 for the rS for interobserver agreement calculated earlier.

Table 4 also contains the rSs for comparisons between Different Day Records, matched as described above in this section. When between-record variance is added to between-observer variance, rS becomes .20. One conclusion that can be drawn is that the low rS_{AV} of .29 for the 12-week-old infants is probably not due entirely to low interobserver reliability; when the different observers work from the same record, rS improves considerably.

Before concluding that observers and monkey infants together make play scores too unreliable to be useful, we should add that our data analyses used our data by weeks, rather than by 2-hour records. Combining the "Same Day Records" of this section into threes, to make scores for the weeks of data, brings the rSs for interobserver agreement to .81 and .90, for play initiated and received by the infant, respectively. Doing the same for "Different Day Records" produced rSs of .80 and .78. The object of this section, however, is not so much to proclaim our reliability in scoring play as to raise questions about the uses of single indices of reliability.

VI. THE NATURAL HISTORY OF RECORDING WITH THE MOTHER-INFANT
     KEYBOARD SYSTEM

Our keyboard system was introduced to facilitate the accurate recording of durations of events, and of the order in which they occurred relative to each other. The following analyses compare the performance of two observers in recording certain kinds of temporal data and illustrate ways in which we have checked the observers' reliability.

The observers were located in separate blinds. Both were 7m away from the same mother and infant who were part of a social group of 10 individuals. During a 2-hour (7200 seconds) recording session, the first observer recorded 4545 seconds near mother, and the second, 4579 seconds. The difference between the observers, of 34 seconds, would be serious if the infant and mother had been together only once, and if the difference had represented a delay of one of the observers in recording the departure of the infant. In fact, the infant was near its mother 26 times, and 18 of the "near" bouts could be matched in the two records. (More could not be matched, because the observers were working from slightly different angles. As a result, one observer sometimes recorded the infant as out of sight, and then stopped recording, whereas the other could still see the infant and continued to record.)

The median difference between bouts recorded by the two observers was 1.6 seconds (irrespective of sign), and the maximum error was 7.0 seconds. The Spearman rank-order correlation coefficient of .99 for the agreement between the observers adds only the information that most of the different bouts must have differed from the others by at least 1.6 seconds.

If the observers agreed on the duration of half the bouts of time to within 2 seconds, it is likely that they were agreeing about the occurrences of the onsets and offsets of these bouts in real time.

However, the observers may not have agreed about who (mother or infant) was initiating or terminating their bouts of proximity by approaching or leaving, respectively. There were 46 occasions when both observers saw the beginning and/or end of the same bout of proximity between mother and infant, and on 4 of these the observers disagreed about whether mother or infant made the move.

Responsibility for contact between mother and infant was recorded
in the same way, and on the 53 occasions when both observers saw
the same contact change, there were 5 disagreements about whether
the mother or the infant was responsible. Together with the timing analysis, this "responsibility" analysis was reassuring, in
that reasonable agreement in recording the timing and nature of
such simple events could be obtained while the observers were also
dealing with all the other MI keyboard events (Table 1). For a
more sophisticated example of comparing observers' records of
complex events, see Patterson (1977).

In contrast to such encouraging results, it was found that
one observer recorded a total of 10 "whoo" calls, while another
only 2. In general, "whoo" calls are difficult to locate or even
hear, especially when the wind blows through the trees. Note that
a difference of 8 in two scores made in a single 2-hour record
might not alone be alarming in comparison to the median differences
of 3 or 4 in the third column of Table 4, but such a difference
does point out potential difficulties concerning measures involving
"whoo" calls.

The observers differed even more in their totals for play:
one scored 51 and the other 35. Nevertheless, the two observers'
rankings of play through the successive 300 seconds of the record
agreed reasonably well (rS = .85). While one observer was apparently more ready to see "new" bouts of play and was thus "biased",
both agreed reasonably about when, during the record, the infant
was playing most often. The discussion in section III has already
led us to expect overall biases in scoring play.

VII. DISCUSSION

First I want to consider some general problems that arise
when one attempts to assess the performances of recording systems.
Then, in the spirit of this volume, I shall examine the special
limitations of a keyboard event-recording system.

Successful replication of a study as a whole is perhaps the
only convincing test of its reliability. In certain long-term
studies such as the present one, where the same animals are observed or tested repeatedly in approximately the same conditions,
the reliability of parts of the study can be assessed as the
study progresses (e.g., section IV). If we fail to get reliable
data from parts of a study, or if we fail to replicate whole
studies, we may then want to examine our procedure more closely.
In particular, we may want to check not only our observers' performances but also whether irrelevant variations in the animals' conditions are making their performances vary from record to record.
A pilot study might be designed to make such checks in advance,
so that we can avoid wasting time, observers' attention, and keyboard keys on unreliable measures.

I attempted in section IV to isolate the contribution of observer error. Here, the Spearman rank-order correlation coefficient (rS) was used, so that I could compare the error arising

in the two different conditions: same animal, same day, different observers; and same animal, different day, same or different
observers. A simple index of reliability can inform us about
how well observers can discriminate among the individual members
of a particular set of animals' performances, on a particular
behavioral score, in a particular situation. But, by itself the
index cannot tell us whether the observers are agreeing successfully because they agree closely about the scores, or because
the animals' scores differ from each other so much that observer
error does not matter (section IV, and see also section V's contrast between proximity and play scores). Like any other performance measure, a reliability measure reflects many processes.
In particular, such a measure summarizes the result of a comparison between two sets of scores, each of which is the result of
complex, situation- and subject-dependent processes.

It follows that reliability measures cannot be extrapolated
from isolated test situations to real situations, unless we know
enough about the populations of scores in both test and "real"
situations to be sure that the distributions of the animals'
scores are similar in the two situations. I showed in section IV
that this is often not the case.

In examining the populations of scores, as well as the observer errors, one is moving away from unitary measures of reliability towards the "natural history" of what observers do. For
example, they may differ by more than 1.6 seconds about half the
bouts of proximity that they record, and they may show considerable bias in recording the frequency of play bouts. In considering "real-life" uses of a measure, like length of proximity
bout, it is necessary to know whether the different bouts usually
differ from each other by tenths of seconds, seconds, or tens of
seconds, before the reliability of the "real life" observations
can be judged.

Some difficulties with scoring systems can be deduced *a
priori*, given information about the nature of the scoring systems
and the behavioral categories scored. However, most of us are
wise in these ways only after making the empirical studies already referred to. Of special interest are those behavioral categories that take the observer time to recognize, because the categories take time to occur. Such categories raise problems for
someone operating a system that demands that decisions about behavioral occurrences be up-to-the-second. The observer must face
the conflict between making a relatively uninformed guess about
the occurrence soon, or delaying long enough to make a more in-
formed judgment. The tasks of distinguishing separate bouts in
play episodes, and therefore counting bouts (sections II and V),
and of recording the onsets of events involving goal-directed
activities (as when a mother rejects an infant's *attempt to* ...
section II) can be especially difficult.

A keyboard recording system imposes a "digital" or "on-off"
description onto the data being recorded. The most easily, and
therefore most usually, recorded behaviors are those defined so
that their onsets are clear-cut. For rhesus monkey infants, an

approach defined as crossing a 60cm line around mother is usually
easy to record, because infants seldom linger at this distance;
they are already in the act of moving towards. In contrast, activities that start gradually, as when a courting male and female
Japanese macaque gradually subside into contact with each other,
or moments at which individuals cross arbitrarily fixed boundaries,
like the distinction between facing and broadside, can be very
difficult to record when first viewing the behavior sequence in
question.

Often, one needs to run over the sequence several times, and
for this a video-recording or film-editing system becomes necessary. One's system of writing the data down from the film needs
very flexible editing facilities, not usually provided by an event-
recording system (but cf. Stephenson, this volume). In dealing
with activities which become recognizable only as they unfold
through time, the advantages of being able to view repeatedly
become very evident.

Of greater interest are the conceptual problems arising when
a recording system, like a keyboard system, imposes a digital pattern on the data. The emphasis of a study using a keyboard event-
recorder is all too easily shifted away from the following themes.
First there is the question of the "reality" of the division of
complex categories into bouts. Whose reality? Observers may
come to agree quite well about when they think beginnings of play
bouts occur in the stream of behavior. But do the subjects of
the study analyze the stream of events in the same way as the observer, and could different subjects even be doing such an analysis in different ways (cf. Simpson, 1976)? Rosenblum (1978) has
also considered this and related problems in greater depth.

Second, keyboard recording systems may oversimplify the exercise of assigning responsibility or initiative for situations (like
proximity) to the interacting animals being observed. For example,
Stephenson has shown a video sequence of courting Japanese macaques
which included two episodes in which the male and female spent time
sitting near each other. In the first episode, the approach, in
the sense of crossing an arm's reach distance, was assigned to the
male because he was moving when that distance was closed. A manageable keyboard system for handling macaque courtship in real time
might have to restrict itself to "approach" and "leave", in the
boundary-crossing sense already defined, with some additional categories for vocalizations, orientations, gestures, and the actions
of other animals. Working from video-tape, however, allows an
investigator to go further. In terms of the more difficult category of "moving nearer", the above episode began with the male
moving nearer to the female in two stages (the second taking him
across the above-mentioned boundary), then the female made the
final move towards the male, before the male left. If we consider
the relative orientations of the male and female we find that the
male turned his back after his first approach, contradicting a
simpleminded view of the apparent intention of his approach. After
his second approach, he faced the female briefly, then turned his
side and sat down. The female then moved nearer and turned her

back. By now, it is not clear who is most responsible for
proximity in this episode.

Third, influences from one partner to another in an interaction may be oversimplified. When the above Japanese macaque
sequence was examined step-by-step on a TV monitor, three aspects
of it were striking. First, the five key presses on the original
keyboard recording representing the females' actions, and the
seven for the male's, intermeshed in a smooth sequence, except
at one point. The "smoothness" was like that of two dancers; it
seemed difficult to isolate obvious points at which one partner
"pushed" the other into its next action. Moreover, the one
exception in this well-oiled sequence came after the second vocalization recorded for the female. It seemed that the male made
his approach "at once" after it. Finally, the contrast between
this one immediate "effect" of the female on the male, and the
mutual coordination of their other activities was striking. For
example, in the second sequence in which the two animals were together, the only "pushing" step in the interaction was the moment
when the male, in sitting down near the female, also turned so
that his side rather than back was towards her. She flinched
away immediately, before the couple gradually subsided into contact.

Two reactions to this account are possible, First, we can
admit that mutual coordination and timing are possible, and for
this reason we should not always expect to find that one partner
has to be pushing the other at every stage in a sequence. Second,
however, we may have failed to recognize an intricate sequence of
such pushes, because our observations were crude and/or misdirected.
These responses are compatible, though the second suggests the
easier line of research: continue to search for second-by-second
influences from partner to partner (e.g., Stephenson, this volume).
For present purposes, it is important to note that only when the
same behavioral sequence is recorded by more than one method (keyboard recording in real time, and repeated viewings of the video
sequence) do such questions of emphasis become especially obvious.

Two themes already mentioned, "whose reality does this set
of criteria for the onset of an action represent?" and "to what
extent is an interaction a matter of one partner acting, and the
other reacting, second-by-second?", come together as follows. If
we fail to identify who is responsible for the onset of a play
session, for example, it could be that the onsets of play bouts
being set down by us are events which are uninteresting to our
playing subjects. Clearly, in devising our categories, we should
pay as much attention as we can to the ways in which our subjects
respond to social events, as Rosenblum (1978) emphasizes.

VIII. CONCLUSION

It can be difficult to assess a recording system because of
the problems of generalizing widely from particular indices of reliability allied to a particular situation. Reliability indices

are usually unitary measures of complex processes occurring when observations are made, and they are most valuable when tailored to narrowly defined problems. Relatively naturalistic studies of our observation procedures, combined with deductions from *a priori* guesses about the properties of our behavior categories and recording systems, can sometimes help us to understand why particular recording systems do not work well with particular kinds of behavioral categories.

Keyboard event recording systems, by requiring the user to make precise decisions about times of onsets and offsets of events, can provide special difficulties. The data are all too easily put into a digital form which may not necessarily reflect "reality" with which our subjects are dealing. Moreover, analyses of such data can lead us to make unduly simple decisions about who is responsible for beginning interactions when neither partner in fact may be responsible, or when both may be cooperating.

ACKNOWLEDGMENTS

This work was supported by the Medical Research Council. I am grateful to Donna Anderson, Sylvia Howe, Jeannette Hanby-Bygott, Milbrey Leighton-Shapiro, Marion Leslie, Anne Simpson, Ann Weisler, and Lilyan White for their help with the observations, and for discussion of the issues raised here.
Roger Scarlett and Ted Harrison have continued to improve and support the WRATS system, and this study would not have been possible without them. I thank Robert Hinde and Pat Bateson for their helpful criticisms of this paper.

REFERENCES

Altmann, J. Observational study of behaviour: Sampling methods. *Behaviour,* 1974, *49,* 337-367.
Anastasi, A. *Psychological testing.* New York: MacMillan, 1968.
Dunbar, R. I. M. Some aspects of research design and their implications in the observational study of behaviour. *Behaviour,* 1976, *58,* 78-98.
Hinde, R. A. On the design of check-sheets. *Primates,* 1973, *14,* 393-406.
Hinde, R. A., & Herrmann, J. Frequencies, durations, derived measures and their correlations in studying dyadic and triadic relationships. In H. R. Schaffer (Ed.), *Studies in mother-infant interaction.* New York: Academic Press, 1977.
Hinde, R. A., Rowell, T. E., & Spencer-Booth Y. Behaviour of socially living rhesus monkeys in their first six months. *Proceedings of the Zoological Society of London,* 1964, *143,* 609-649.

Hinde, R. A., & Simpson, M. J. A.   Qualities of mother-infant
    relationships in monkeys. *The parent-infant relationship.*
    Ciba Foundation Symposium 33 (new series). Amsterdam:
    Elsevier, 1975.
Hinde, R. A., & Spencer-Booth, Y.   The behaviour of socially
    living rhesus monkeys in their first two and a half years.
    Animal Behaviour, 1967, *15,* 169-196.
Hinde, R. A., & White, L. E.   Dynamics of a relationship:
    Rhesus mother-infant ventro-ventral contact. *Journal of
    Comparative and Physiological Psychology,* 1974, *86,* 8-23.
Kraemer, H. C., & Korner, F. A.   Statistical alternatives in
    assessing reliability, consistency, and individual dif-
    ferences for quantitative measures: Application to be-
    havioral measures of neonates. *Psychological Bulletin,*
    1976, *83,* 914-921.
Loizos, C.   Play behaviour in higher primates: A review.   In
    D. Morris (Ed.), *Primate ethology.* London: Weidenfeld
    and Nicholson, 1967.
Patterson, G. R.   Accelerating stimuli for two classes of
    coercive behaviors. *Journal of Abnormal Child Psychology,*
    1977, in press.
Rosenblum, L. A.   The creation of a behavioral taxonomy.   In
    G. P. Sackett (Ed.), *Observing behavior,* (Vol. 2).
    Baltimore: University Park Press, 1978.
Ruppenthal, G. C., Harlow, M. K., Eisele, C. D., Harlow, H. F.,
    & Suomi, S. J.   Development of peer interactions in monkeys
    reared in a nuclear family environment. *Child Development,*
    1974, *45,* 670-682.
Sade, D. A.   An ethogram for rhesus monkeys: I. Antithetical
    contrasts in posture and movement. *American Journal of
    Physical Anthropology,* 1973, *38,* 537-542.
Siegel, S.   *Nonparametric statistics.* New York: McGraw-Hill,
    1956.
Simpson, M. J. A.   The study of animal play.   In P. P. G.
    Bateson & R. A. Hinde (Eds.), *Growing points in ethology.*
    Cambridge, Eng.: Cambridge University Press, 1976.
Simpson, M. J. A., & Simpson, A. E.   One-zero and scan methods
    for sampling behaviour. *Animal Behaviour,* 1977, *25,* 726-731.
White, L. E.   Play in animals.   In B. Tizard & D. Harvey (Eds.),
    The biology of play: Clinics in developmental medicine,
    No. 62. London: Heinemann, 1977a.
White, L. E.   The nature of social play and its role in the
    development of the rhesus monkey. Unpublished doctoral
    dissertation, Cambridge University, 1977b.
White, L. E., & Hinde, R. A.   Some factors affecting mother-
    infant relations in rhesus monkeys. *Animal Behaviour,* 1975,
    23, 527-542.
White, R. E. C.   WRATS: Computer-compatible system for auto-
    matically recording and transcribing behavioural data.
    Behaviour, 1971, *40,* 135-161.

8.
PLEXYN:
A computer-compatible grammar
for coding complex
social interactions

GORDON R. STEPHENSON

Primates pose problems for those of us who wish to record and
analyze their behavior. Their social behavior is especially subtle
and sequentially complex, and the pace often pushes observers to
the limits of their capacities to record what they see. Recording
the incidence, duration, coincidence and sequence of primate interactions in even the simplest social setting of the pair is an ex-
hausting task. When there are more than two subjects, observers
can be overwhelmed. Cine film or video tape, of course, can record
almost all that the observers can see, and sometimes more, but
these are expensive means and, ultimately, the cine or video record
must be re-recorded in categorical form for analysis.

This paper describes a set of empirically derived methods
that ease the observer's burden when categorically recording complex
social interactions among primates. The methods were developed in
the course of studies on rhesus, Japanese and stumptail macaques
(Stephenson, 1967, 1973; Stephenson, Goldfoot & Essock-Vitale, 1978),
and in collaboration with colleagues studying humans (Lamb, 1978a,
1978b; Lozoff & Brittenham, 1977; Wolf, Breslau & Novack, 1978).
The methods include keyboard entry and computer transcription of
grammatically structured strings of characters that are used as
codes to describe the observations. The defining properties of
the codes reduce redundancy in the entries and direct the flow of
control in Program PLEXYN, a grammar processing program that veri-
fies, completes and reformats the record for subsequent data analysis
programs. The overall strategy of the methods is to minimize the
observer's task at the moment any observation is made by allowing
him/her to concentrate on what s/he sees at the moment s/he sees
it rather than requiring recall of what s/he has already seen, and
by minimizing the number of descriptive elements that must be entered in real time to completely describe what s/he saw. Tactics
pertaining to this strategy have been developed at both the recording

and the coding levels of data acquisition and will be presented accordingly.

TACTICS AT THE RECORDING LEVEL

Tactics that minimize the observer's task during recording will be considered in terms of the keyboard, the conventions, and the grammatical structures for entering observations.

Keyboard

Electronic keyboards for data entry offer many advantages over the more traditional methods of recording observations. Voice notes on magnetic tape or ink pen tracings on moving paper can record entries in real time, but both techniques entail tedious and time consuming transcription before analysis. Other methods compromise temporal aspects of the record; checklists or clocks and counters lose sequence information and handwritten notes tend to lag unevenly behind the action. By letting his/her "fingers do the talking", so to speak, in a touch-type manner on a electronic keyboard, the observer can avoid the losses that otherwise occur in the course of frequent shifts from action to notebook and back, and s/he will have his/her data in computer-compatible form for analysis without the cost of keypunching that all other methods incur.

The keyboard that was used in the studies from which the methods here derive was originally designed as the field portable terminal of a computer based system for recording the "Senders, Signals, and Receivers" (SSR) in primate communication events (Stephenson, Smith, & Roberts, 1975). Current SSR System keyboards and applications have been described in detail elsewhere (Stephenson & Roberts, 1977) and will only be outlined here.

Observations are entered on the keyboard as grammatically structured strings of characters. The character set includes 0 - 9, A - Z, and +, -, /, *, !, =, $, @, %, blank, and "segment", which can be either < or >. The physical arrangement of these 48 characters is depicted in Figure 1. Their arrangement follows from their grammatical functions. For example, characters 0 - 9 are arranged as a numeric pad for rapid entry of double digit names. Characters A - Y are organized into a 5 by 5 grid that can be used as a reference grid for locations of subjects as well as to code behaviors observed. To facilitate their use in error correction, the ? and the Z are offset from the other characters at the bottom of the array. The position and function relations of the remaining characters will become apparent in the following text.

Data entered on the keyboard are recorded on one track of a stereo tape recorder operating at 1 7/8 ips (inches per second). The parallel track is usually used to record complementary voice notes or subject vocalizations. Some time later, the tape is played back into a mini-computer at 15 ips; 1 hour of data is transcribed and timed to the nearest .05 seconds in 7 1/2 minutes. After

FIGURE 1. The physical arrangement of the standard character set on an SSR System model 7B keyboard.

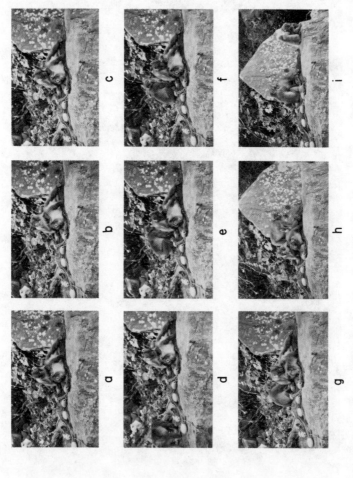

FIGURE 2. A grooming sequence among central males at Koshina, Kyushu, Japan. The second ranking male approaches and sits behind the fifth ranking male, who is grooming the fourth ranking male. The second ranking male then leaves, walks on and over the fourth ranking male, and moves away about 4 feet, where he sits down. A juvenile male approaches, sits in front of the second ranking male, and grooms his back intermittently.

transcription, the record can be printed and stored on disk or computer tape for subsequent analysis.

An example of a standard SSR System transcript is presented in Figure 3. The character strings in the "ENTRY" column are the observer's descriptions of the action depicted in the series of pictures in Figure 2. The integer in the "FRAME" column before each string is the number of twentieths of a second between the entry of the very first character in the record and the entry of the character that starts the particular string. In this way, the frame value represents the relative time of each string to the nearest .05 seconds. The clock time in the "TIME" column before each frame was computed from the time statement (line 4 in Figure 3). This string, !Tnnnn, where n is a digit, was entered by the observer as part of the header information before the first data segment. The clock time when the string was entered was encoded in the numeric substring as hour and minute. The frame value of this string relates keyboard time to original clock time. This relationship is used to compute the clock time of every string in the record.

Conventions

Several conventions are followed in forming the character strings that describe observed events. The characters +, -, /, *, !, and "segment" are software defined to function as carriage control characters; whenever they appear in the data, a new line is started in the transcript. The conventions for using these line starters are as follows. A + is used to start entries that indicate the occurrence of a momentary event or the onset of a continuous event. A - is used to start entries that indicate the termination of a continuous event. Lines that begin with a / are treated as comments and, while they remain in the transcript, they are ignored by data processing programs. An * is used to indicate that the event described in this entry occurred at the same time as the event described in the immediately preceding entry. Such simultaneous entries are treated as though they were + entries. To indicate a simultaneous entry that is not a + entry, the * is followed immediately by an @, which in turn, is followed by the appropriate line starter. This sequence of characters will assign the frame of the previous line to the line following the *@ (see line 26 in Figure 3 and line 27 in Figure 4). The ! is used to start special data lines like the time statement, the date line, the observer identification line, etc. The "segment" character is used to delimit portions of data within a record, such as the subsets of data from a series of focal subjects in a continuous observation session. The beginning and the end of a segment are identified by < and > respectively.

The tactic of starting entries with line starters instead of ending them with an "enter" key enhances the temporal accuracy with which behavioral events are recorded. Behavioral events either begin (occur) or end, which is a 1 bit decision. The search for the + or the - is a simple task. The more difficult task of keying

```
 1: 1PART1, KOSHIMA MALE GROOM #24
 2:        TIME           FRAME ENTRY
 3:      11:03:43.2          1 !D690127
 4:    *11:04:00.0        337 !T1104
 5:      11:04:03.7        411 <
 6:      11:04:05.8        452 +13L12
 7:      11:04:12.8        593 /%
 8:      11:04:13.7        611 +13A21
 9:      11:04:22.3        782 +13LF21
10:      11:04:28.6        909 +12G1?%
11:      11:04:32.7        991 +21%RH G%IN13%LF$6I=35%3@NR1%S
12:      11:05:07.8       1693 +13LK%5
13:      11:05:13.6       1810 +21LK%5
14:      11:05:22.0       1977 +21LK13%LF
15:      11:05:27.6       2090 +12W=1
16:      11:05:32.4       2185 *
17:      11:05:34.6       2230 +2?12SB21
18:      11:05:38.0       2298 *12LK21%B
19:      11:05:52.1       2579 /12 21$5=13%2 ED
20:      11:06:09.8       2932 +13IZEC
21:      11:06:18.8       3113 -?
22:      11:06:31.4       3364 +12 21 13$1 6I=135%3
23:      11:06:43.3       3602 +12W$=3
24:      11:06:46.6       3670 +12W013
25:      11:06:53.3       3803 *13LK12
26:      11:06:56.8       3872 *21?@
27:      11:06:59.2       3921 -21G
28:      11:07:02.0       3977 +12S@NR1$=3@NR2
29:      11:07:13.4       4205 +12Z3$=4
30:      11:07:19.3       4322 +21CH SF 13
31:      11:07:27.7       4491 +21 13$4I=14%1
32:      11:07:44.0       4816 *21G13%H%F
33:      11:07:54.2       5021 +13 12$5=43%1
34:      11:08:08.0       5298 +80SF12
35:      11:08:13.6       5410 +80G12%B
36:      11:08:30.3       5742 +21 13 08 Z80 12$4I 4=1813%2=14
37:      11:09:13.8       6612 -80G
38:      11:09:17.0       6677 +=
39:      11:09:29.4       6925 -=
40:      11:09:32.5       6987 +12L
41:      11:09:36.7       7071 +80F12
42:      11:09:53.1       7399 / 21GC13
43:      11:10:02.3       7583 >END
```

FIGURE 3.   Raw SSR System transcript describing the action depicted in
    the panels in Figure 2. Line 12 corresponds to panel a, line 15
    to d, line 20 to g, and line 35 to i.

```
 1: 1PART1, KOSHIMA MALE GROOM #24
 2:  T FRAME  S A O   SOD DIS LOC S  A  O  L COMMENT OR RAW DATA
 3:  O     1 !                  D690127
 4:  O   337 !                  T1104
 5:  O   411 <
 6:  O   452 +13L 12
 7:  4   593 +13A 21+           NR1           S
 8:  O   782 +13LF21+353    50
 9:  O   909 +21G 13-          RH IN LF
10:  O  1693 +13LK                    5
11:  O  1810 +21LK                    5
12:  O  1977 +21LK13                 LF
13:  O  2090 +12W    1
14:  9  2185 *         IGNORED
15:  O  2230 +12SB21                         ENDS   13
16:  O  2230 -12W 00    140                  INSERT OFF
17:  1  2230 +12LK21              B
18:  9  2579 /                    12 21$5=13%2 ED
19:  O  2932 +13ECOO
20:  2  3364 .12  21 133   1
21:  2  3364 .12  13 153   150
22:  2  3364 .21  13 353    50
23:  O  3602 +12W 00 3                       ENDS   15
24:  O  3602 -12SB21    1372                 INSERT OFF
25:  O  3670 +12WO13
26:  1  3670 +13LK12
27:  1  3670 -21G 13    2761                 ENDS    9
28:  O  3977 +12S 00 3          NR2          ENDS   23
29:  O  3977 -12W 00    375                  INSERT OFF
30:  9  4205 +   5    SUB SYN 12Z3$=4
31:  2  4322 +21CH13
32:  2  4322 +21SF13
33:  O  4491 .21  13 141    33
34:  1  4491 +21G 13                F
35:  O  5021 .13  12 431    5
36:  O  5298 +80SF12
37:  O  5410 +80G 12              B
38:  9  5742 +        BAD DIS 21 13 08 Z80 12$4I 4=1813%2=1413
39:  O  6612 -80G 12    1202                 ENDS   37
40:  8  6677 +80G 12
41:  8  6925 -80G 12    248                  ENDS   40
42:  O  6987 +12L 00                         ENDS   28
43:  O  6987 -12S 00    3010                 INSERT OFF
44:  O  7071 +80F 12
45:  O  7399 /                               21GC13
46:  O  7583 >                               END
47:  O  7583 \                               ERRS    3
```

FIGURE 4. Data from transcript in Figure 3 after being processed by
   Program PLEXYN. Corresponding lines in the two figures have
   common frame numbers. In the modifier fields, alphanumeric substrings are left justified and numeric substrings are right
   justified.

in the correct coding characters, each of which involves more than
a 5 bit decision, can then follow without affecting the accuracy of
temporally locating the start of the entry with respect to the
start of other entries. This is especially so when a record
includes both common and uncommon codes. Without line starters,
the entry of uncommon codes would lag with respect to the temporal
location of common codes simply because the observer has to think
a bit longer to recall the correct keying sequence.

Two other conventions that help the observer maintain temporal
accuracy at the line level of syntax are the rules for correcting
an erroneous line starter and for repetition of the effective
contents of the immediately preceding line. The effective contents
is the portion of the entry that remains after all within line
error corrections have been taken into account (see below). A
mistaken line starter can be corrected immediately by following
the line starter character with a %, and then restarting the line
with the correct line starter (see lines 7 and 8 in Figure 3). When
the % character represents the total effective contents of the line,
as it would after the last ? in a line, the above sequence of
characters will assign the frame of the erroneous line to the
corrected line that follows it.

Repetition of the effective contents of a line is indicated by
a similarly short sequence of characters, the line starter (+ or -,
but not *) followed by the = character. The sequence will repeat
the previous line's contents at the new time of the line starter
(see lines 37 through 39 in Figure 3 and lines 39 through 41 in
Figure 4).

A second set of conventions circumscribe the usage of characters within regular data lines (lines that start with +, -, or *).
The sender, signal, and receiver of the event are entered as the
subject, action and object of the line. Names of subjects and
objects are entered as two digit substrings. This convention
provides for ninety-eight different names (01 - 98). The name 00
is reserved for "not entered" (inserted by the grammar processor)
and the name 99 is reserved for "unknown" (entered by the observer).
Optionally, if the number of names needed is known to be less than
9, names can be defined as 1 digit substrings, with 0 as "not
entered" and 9 as "unknown". Mnemonic labels for the categorical
codes that describe the action are entered as substrings of one or
two of the alphabetic characters A - Y. This convention provides
for six hundred fifty different labels, which is almost certainly
many more than anyone would ever try to use. Following Zipf's (1935)
law, the most common categories are assigned the one character codes
whenever it is mnemonically convenient. To enhance error detect-
ability, the second letter of two letter labels is different from
the first whenever possible. The character Z is reserved for a
special form of error notation that facilitates in-line correction
of erroneous entries immediately after they are made (see section
on error correction below). The other characters have special
syntactic functions in the line. The ?, for example, is used to
direct the grammar processor to delete all characters back to but
not including the liner starter. The =, $, @, and % are used to

delimit alpha-numeric substrings that modify parts of the entry or
carry contextual information such as proxemic relations or the
location of the event in the study environment. The blank is used
to separate substrings when the sequence of characters would otherwise be ambiguous, e.g., between names in a multiple subject or
object and between behavior codes in a multiple action. None of
this second set of conventions applies in comment lines, and the
special data lines that begin with ! all have their own customized
rules, depending on the way header information is to be used in
the particular user's analysis programs. The character conventions
are summarized in Table 1.

Syntax

The sequence of substrings that describes an observed event
is prescribed by a grammar or set of syntactic rules. A complete
string includes a line starter and three phrases, which are
designated a) the event phrase, b) the proxemic phrase, and c)
the location phrase. The syntactic elements by phrase and in the
order in which they would usually appear in a fully descriptive
entry are a) subject, action and object, b) distance from subject
to object, subject orientation, object orientation, and direction
from subject to object, and c) location of the subject. The
subject, action, object and location can each be modified by a 1 - 3
character substring. For example, string 11 fully describes subject 21 grooming object 13

$$+21\%RH \; G\%IN13\%LF\$6I = 35\%3@NR1\%S \hspace{2cm} (11)$$

in Figure 2a. The event phrase indicates that subject 21, with his
right hand (21%RH), grooms in an intensive manner (G%IN) object
13's left flank (13%LF). The proxemic phrase ($6I=35%3) indicates
that the subject is about 6 inches from the object and oriented
about 45 degrees to the right of facing directly toward the observer, while the object is oriented about 45 degrees to the left of
facing directly toward the observer. The location phrase indicates
that the subject is at site "Net Rocks 1" (@NR1) and that it is
sunny (%S) there.

While it might take only 10 seconds or so to enter the 30
characters in string 11, in many instances, that would be too much
time; the observer would have missed the start of the next event.
On the other hand, it is not at all clear that any of this information can be omitted. While the order of who, does what, to whom,
where, reflects the hierarchy of information that is intuitively
if not otherwise imposed on the acquisition of data in studies of
primate communication, a semeiotical consideration of communication
events (Stephenson, 1973) indicates that the more contextual information of "where" with respect to one another (proxemics) as well as
"where" with respect to the physical environment (location) is
essential for, rather than merely incidental to, the proper analysis
of the event. To maximize the opportunities to record complete
descriptions of events observed, a tactic has been designed that

TABLE 1.   *CHARACTER CONVENTIONS FOR PLEXYN PROCESSOR*

Scope	Character(s)	Usage
segment		marks beginning (<) or end (>) of a data segment in the current record
line	+	starts line that describes the incidence of a momentary event or the onset of a continuous event
	-	starts line that terminates a continuous event
	*	starts a + or a - line that is simultaneous with the immediately preceding line
	/	starts a comment line; contents will be ignored by processor
	!	starts a line with special user information
	?	deletes all characters in line back to but not including the line starter; if ? is the last character, the line is discarded.
phrase	+,-,*	starts event phrase; precedes subject, or act subphrase
	$	starts proxemic phrase; precedes distance substring
	@	starts location phrase; precedes location substring
coding unit	mixed	incorporates a subphrase or a subphrase and its modifier
	Z	deletes the current partial or just completed coding unit
subphrase	=	precedes orientation index or indices
	%	after $, precedes direction index; after +, -, or *, precedes modifier substring of adjacent name or action label;

Table 1 (continued)

Scope	Character(s)	Usage
		after @, precedes modifier substring of location label
	1-8	index orientation after an = or direction after a % preceded by a $
	0-9	names subjects or objects as n-digit substrings in event phrase (n = 1 or 2)
	A-Y	labels action as a 1 - 2 letter substring in event phrase
	A-Y, 0-9	modifies name, action label or location label as a 1 to 3 character substring
	blank	separates names in multiple subject or object separates name modifier from following action label separates action labels in multiple act

facilitates the piecemeal collection of all the information on a catch-as-catch-can basis. To accommodate the incomplete entries that piecemeal collection entails, the grammar for structuring the character strings had to be made nonobligatory in a way that Program PLEXYN would be able to process the incomplete entries unambiguously. Nonobligatory means that none of the syntactic elements listed in the preceding paragraph is formally required in any entry. The elements that are required in an entry are specified by the values of the coding properties of the categorical codes that are used in the entry. Examples will be presented phrase by phrase after the logical basis for the catch-as-catch-can tactic is described.

Status Modules

The catch-as-catch-can tactic is implemented through the determination of status modules in the data record. The concept of status modules derives from the observation that, while events

often change in rapid succession, proxemic relations and locations
usually do not. Status modules assume that the information coded
in proxemic and location phrases will be used in data analysis as
status information on the spatial components of context in which
communication events occur rather than as events in and of themselves. Values for status variables in the analysis programs can
be updated as the coded observations on proxemics and locations are
encountered in the record. The scope of a coded observation's application to the analysis of events, however, need not be limited to
only those entries that originally coincided with or followed its
place in the record. Through definition of status module delimiters,
Program PLEXYN can change the place of a proxemic or location phrase
in the record from where it was actually entered to where it
logically should have been entered had the observer had enough
time to do so at the moment it was first observed. For example,
subject 13 may have left subject 12 and approached and lay in
front of subject 21 before 21 began to groom him (string 11 above).
The observer may have had time to code only

+13L12	(6)
+13A21	(8)
+13LF21	(9)

before grooming started. Not until then was there enough time to
enter a complete description of the event, the proxemics, and the
location. Through definition of the status module coding property
of category label A (approach) as a module delimiter for location
data, Program PLEXYN backspaces its output file and moves the
information in the location phrase (@NR1%5) from where it was
encountered during processing of the record (at string 11) to where
it belongs (at string 8). The general rule for status modules is
to backspace one string after another until a delimiter of the
appropriate type is found, move the information there, and then
return to the current string. Special notation in the output
indicates that this information was moved; the raw transcript can
always be consulted should uncertainties arise. Similarly, with
category LF (lie in front of) defined as a status module delimiter
for proxemic data, Program PLEXYN backspaces to move the information
in the proxemic phrase from string 11 to string 9. The observer's
limitations can thus be accommodated by foreknowledge of his/her
real time data problems, by appropriate evaluation of the coding
properties of the particular codes, and by phrasing his/her
observations as time permits.

Event Phrasing

The event phrase is the basic phrase in any entry and it must
be represented by at least a subject or an act. Grammatically, the
subject is the name (a two digit substring or, optionally, a one
digit substring) or series of names (alternating with blanks) that
immediately follows the line starter. The act is a substring of
one or two of the characters A - Y or a series of such substrings

(alternating with blanks) that immediately follows the subject.
Objects are grammatically defined as names that follow acts.
Since, through coding properties, an act can have an assumed subject, and/or an assumed object, an act by itself immediately after
the line starter can be a legitimate entry. A subject by itself,
however, is not legitimate. If a subject is not followed by an
act, it must be followed by an orientation or a location or both.
An entry of this alternate form is interpreted as a status change
at that point in the record and the retrospective search for an
appropriate status module delimiter is skipped. If a subject is
not followed by an act, orientation or location, the entry will
be tagged an error when it is grammatically processed by Program
PLEXYN.

Modification of a name or an act in the event phrase is indicated by the character % after the digits or letters followed by
the 1 - 3 character substring. Modifiers after names usually
function as nouns (e.g., 13's left flank). Modifiers after acts
function as adverbs (e.g., grooms intensively), and modifiers
after locations function as adjectives (e.g., sunny NR1).

Often there is too little time to enter modifiers for all
elements in the event phrases, or it may not be appropriate for
the particular problem being studied. The research interests
of the observer must dictate the degree of modification attempted.
PLEXYN only makes it possible. For example, if the observer
is interested in grooming, it would probably be desirable to
modify the object as to which part of its body is being groomed
(e.g., 13%LF). Other entries that describe acts upon the object,
like push (PS) or hit (HT), may not require object modification
for that observer's use of the data. Another alternative, when
the number of subjects is less than nine, is to code the subject
name with the ten's digit and the part of the body with the one's
digit. This relabeling technique can also be applied to the modification of acts. Instead of enhancing the specification of a
categorical code through modifiers, the subset of code that pertains to a kind of act may be expanded. For example, grooming in a
cursory manner (G%CU) or grooming in an intimate manner (G%IN) can
be expressed as GC or GI, respectively. The disadvantage of
labeling changes like these is that they expand the lexicon of
codes and slow the observer's response as s/he attempts to classify
the observed event into the proper category and enter it with the
proper label.

Proxemic Phrasing

The proxemic phrase is formally delimited by the $ character.
The substring of integers that immediately follows the $ is taken
as the distance between the subject and object. An "I" at the end
of the substring changes the units from feet to inches. (PLEXYN is
easily modified so that a "C" changes the units from meters to
centimeters.) If there is a distance substring, there must also
be an object, either entered or implied through the coding properties
of the act in the entry. The = character delimits the substring of

digits that index the orientations of all individuals named or
implied in the event phrase. The % character in a proxemic phrase
delimits the single digit substring that indexes the direction from
subject to object in space.

The indices of an individual's orientation and direction are
imposed from the observer's point of view by imagining a circle
centered on the individual with a radius extending outward every 45
degrees around the circle. The nearest 45 degrees is about the
best that one can do consistently in the course of following the
shifting proxemics of complex social interactions among primates.
Clockwise, from the observer's point of view, the radius that
points to 1:30 o'clock has an index value equal to 1, 3:00 o'clock
equals 2, 4:30 equals 3, 6:00 equals 4, 7:30 equals 5, 9:00 equals
6, 10:30 equals 7, and 12:00 equals 8. The index value 0 is
reserved for "not entered" or "unknown". The value 9 is reserved
as a marker for orientation errors detected by Program PLEXYN, e.g.,
when the number of orientation indices does not match the number
of individuals in the entry. Some of the character strings in
Figure 3 will serve to illustrate how proxemic variables are
assigned values by the observer.

As the scene opens in panel 2a, individual 13 is lying in front
of individual 21 and 21 is grooming 13's left flank. By convention,
the orientation of a lying, sitting or locomoting individual in the
horizontal plane is taken as anterior and normal to the transverse
axis at its shoulders. By convention, each individual's orientation
is entered in the ordinal position in which its name appears or is
implied in the string. In string 11, the orientation of subject 21
is encoded in the first digit after the = character and, from the
observer's plane of reference, has an index value of 3. The orientation of object 13 is encoded in the second digit and has an index
value of 5. By convention, the proxemic direction is taken from
subject to object. In string 11, the direction has an index value
of 3.

The simplicity of the proxemic indices in these entries belies
their subtlety in expressing the relative orientation and location
of individuals. For example, string 15 encoded the direction in
which subject 12 was walking in panel 2d. When the observer later
had an extra moment, s/he also entered string 19 (to be retrospectively edited into the data stream) to indicate the direction
from 12 to 21 and the distance between them. Since the proxemic
relation between 21 and 13 had been entered previously, after
editing the proxemic relation between 12 and 13 can be calculated
as about 5.5 feet apart and approximately parallel (13's 5 is 90
degrees from 21's 3, which is 90 degrees from 12's 1) but oriented
in opposite directions and on opposite sides of 21 (13 is to the
observer's right of 21, and 21 is to the observer's right of 12).
Such extrapolations of proxemic relations are possible because the
notation system is completely complementary. For example, after
entering the observations that subject 12 sat behind 21 and subject
13 closed his eyes, the observer had a chance to enter the proxemic
relations among all three males (string 22 re panel 2g). The order
of the individuals' names in string 22 follows from the observer's

attention to the action in the immediately

$$+12 \quad 21 \quad 13\$1 \quad 6I=135\%3 \qquad\qquad (22)$$

preceding panels where 12 was the prime actor and thus the subject
of most of the strings. If, instead, the observer had not come
upon the scene until after 12 had sat behind 21, s/he might have
entered string 22a.

$$+13 \quad 21 \quad 12\%6I \quad 1=531\%7 \qquad\qquad (22a)$$

Reconstruction of the scene from either of these strings will yield
the same proxemic relations among the individuals.

Given that the proxemic data ultimately refer to the spatial
relations among the study subjects, the system of notation here may
appear to be counter-intuitive. Indeed, the initial versions of the
indexing system had attempted to express proxemic relations in
relative rather than absolute terms, but the resulting code had
been too cumbersome to implement. The tactic of taking these values
from the observer's point of view has the powerful advantage that
the frame of reference for any entry in any context is constant
because it is in the observer's mind. Generally, the position of
the observer with respect to the observed is quite stable over the
course of an observation session, hence the values of the indices
can be related to the physical environment through special observer/
environment proxemic entries that describe the distance and direction from the observer's position to at least two reference points
in the study environment. Obvious features such as doors, windows,
rocks, bushes or trees are chosen for the reference points so that
they can later be located in a plan or map. Subsequent data processing programs use the observer/environment proxemic statements
(!@Pl$nn=n%n, where n is an appropriate digit and Pl equals point
1) to transpose the values of proxemic variables to the environmental
frame of reference. Values in the statement can be updated as the
observer's position changes in the course of taking data.

Several examples of the way in which the syntax and the proxemic
indexing system operate together to enhance specification of the
observer's description of ongoing events are evident in strings 12
through 22 above. In string 15, the orientation substring (=1)
indicates that subject 12 was walking in direction 1. As mentioned
above, the grammar is non-obligatory and in a simple entry like
string 15, not even the proxemic delimiter $ is required for Program
PLEXYN to process the sequence of substrings unambiguously. Similarly, the $ would not have been necessary in string 23. In both
cases, the value of the digit would be assigned to the orientation
variable in the uniform format produced by Program PLEXYN. During
data analysis, the value would be assigned to the variable for 12's
orientation status. On the other hand, while the proxemic notation
system was also used to determine the value of the modifier in string
13 in order to indicate in which direction 21 looked, the syntax of
the % character after an act assigns the value of the digit to the
act modifier variable rather than to the proxemic direction variable

(see line 12 of Figure 3 and line 10 of Figure 4).

Location Phrasing

The location phrase is formally delimited by the @ character. The label is a 1 - 3 character substring that describes the locations in a convenient way. In my studies of rhesus monkeys at the Vilas Park Breeding Research Facility of the Wisconsin Regional Primate Research Center, for example, I use the structural steel of the roof and the regularly spaced discontinuities in the floor surface (see Weisbard & Goy, 1976, Fig. 1) to determine the locations and their labels, e.g., section 12 of the floor (F12). Dr. Peter Wasser of Purdue University (personal communication, 1976) has suggested using the 5 by 5 grid of characters A - Y as a frame of reference for locations. By imposing this image on the study environment, and imposing the 3 by 3 grid of characters 1 - 9 on each cell of the 5 by 5 grid, the observer has a 225 cell mnemonic device for coding locations. This could be especially useful in the field situation, be it the living room in a human family's home or an unfamiliar place on the African plain.

The location can be modified in the usual way, with a 1 - 3 character substring delimited by a % character. For example, in string 11, it was noted that location NR1 was sunny (@NR1%S). This modification was found useful after it was noticed in preliminary studies of rhesus grooming behavior that, when the sun was bright during the winter months, intense grooming was more likely to occur in sunny areas of the large indoor-outdoor pen than in shadowy areas. Similarly, the location distribution of children's behavior on a playground may vary with the presence or absence of wet areas such as puddles after a rain. For continuity in subsequent analyses, it would be better to modify location labels based on a permanent reference system than to label the puddles themselves.

Error Correction

Complex coding schemes like the current one are likely to produce occasional errors in the course of recording observations. Errors perceived retrospectively, as when the observer recognizes that s/he has perseverated on a misidentification, are better corrected with a comment at the moment and manual editing after transcription. Most errors, however, are perceived immediately, just as they are being entered. To keep the amount of manual editing to a minimum, Program PLEXYN and the grammar for recording observations allow for several levels of immediate correction of the most common kinds of errors. From gross to refined, the three levels of immediate error correction are deletion, replacement and "zeroing".

Correction by deletion is indicated by entry of the ? character. Just after Program PLEXYN reads a new line of data from the input file, it scans the line for the last ? and begins grammar processing with the first character after the last ? or after the line starter (when there is no ? in the line). For example, in string 17 of

Figure 3, grammar processing would begin at the character 1 in 12's name after the last ?. All characters beween the ? and the line starter are ignored. Thus, the correct time of the entry is maintained. If the ? is the last character in the line, the whole string is ignored.

Correction by replacement is indicated by reentry of the relevant substring delimiters and characters. For example, in string 28 of Figure 3, NR2 replaces NR1. In string 36, the orientations 1813 are replaced by 1413. Program PLEXYN assigns values of variables as it grammatically processes the string from left to right. In the processing of string 28, the first @ directed the flow of program control in the syntax analysis section of Program PLEXYN to the location parser. After the location substring NR1 had been extracted, encoded in A format, and assigned as the value of LOC (the location variable), the $ directed the flow of control to the proxemic parser. After the proxemic information was extracted and assigned, the second @ directed the flow of control once again to the location parser, where the second location substring was extracted and assigned to the variable LOC, thus replacing the previously assigned value. In string 28, the second @ was necessary to redirect program control to the location parser. In string 36, a second $ was not necessary because control had already been directed to the proxemic parser and the second = was sufficient to lead to reassignment of new values for the orientation variables. Similarly, %F in string 32 would lead to replacement of the value H for the variable MOB (object modifier) by the value F rather than the value of the proxemic direction or some other modifier delimited by the %, because the processor was at the object section of syntax analysis when the % was encountered. As suggested by this example, the % is a more immediate delimiter than are the phrase delimiters @ and $.

Correction by "zeroing" is indicated by the entry of the Z character, which zeros the value of the current coding unit in the string. Coding units are character substrings bounded by appropriate syntactic delimiters. In the event phrases, for example, a coding unit is a name and its modifier or an action label and its modifier. The modifier is not obligatory, but if it is present, it is considered to be part of the name or action coding unit, as the case might be. In line 18 in Figure 3, the first name coding unit (12) is bounded by the line starter and the first letter of the action label. The action coding unit (LK) is bounded by the last digit of the preceding name and the first digit of the following name. The second name coding unit (21%B) is bounded by the last letter of the action label and the first trailing blank at the end of the line. Name coding units in a multiple subject like that in line 22 are separated by blanks. While the blank is a syntactic delimiter of the coding unit to its right, however, it does not function that way for the coding unit to its left. In line 22 of Figure 3, for example, the second name coding unit (21) is bounded on the left by the blank between 12 and 21, but on the right, it is bounded by the first digit of the third name. Similarly, the action coding unit (SF) in line 30 is bounded by a blank on the left and the first non-blank on the right.

The "zeroing" effect of a Z is similarly bounded by syntactic delimiters. For example, in string 20 the observer erroneously entered I to code "eyes closed", realized his/her error before completing the code, zeroed the I with a Z, and then entered the correct code EC. If the Z had been entered before the I, it would have zeroed the variable SUB (1) (first subject's name) instead of the variable ACT(1). In line 36, the erroneous name 08 was followed by the separator blank before the Z was entered, but since the next syntactic delimiter is after the Z, the 08 is the current coding unit and its contents will be zeroed. The coding unit convention gives the user one last chance to correct a name or an action label after entering the blank as a separator. When Program PLEXYN determines a syntactic error, like a categorical code of more than 2 characters, it scans ahead. If a new syntactic delimiter is encountered before either a Z or an appropriate replacement sequence, Program PLEXYN inserts an error message for that line in its output file.

Phrase Order

While the event phrase is assumed to be represented by characters at the beginning of the legitimate portion of the string, i.e., immediately after the last ? or the line starter, whichever is later in the line, the order of the proxemic and location phrases is not fixed. This is because the proxemic and location phrases have special delimiters, but the event phrase does not. In effect, the line starter is the leading delimiter of the event phrase. This tactic precludes the need for an extra character in the most common kind of string, and thereby saves time at entry. On the other hand, it also makes it difficult to correct an error in the event phrase once the observer has finished the phrase and has moved on to entering the proxemics or location. In practice, errors in names and action labels seem to be perceived more quickly than other errors and are nearly always correctable by "zeroing". Some perception of errors, like realizing that the subject's name is wrong after the categorical code for behavior has been entered, can only be accommodated by deletion with the ?. But a deletion at this point in the string is usually not too costly in terms of time. Errors later in the string, where the location and proxemic phrases are typically entered, would be more costly, hence the grammatical capacity to correct them by whole or partial replacement.

TACTICS AT THE CODING LEVEL

Tactics that minimize the observer's task at the coding level will be considered in terms of minimizing the number of names needed to describe the more common events and managing the onset and termination of events that have a measurable duration.

General Considerations

The coding tactics are incorporated into Program PLEXYN through values assigned to the 15 coding properties of each categorical action code. The properties represent general logical conditions for use of the codes. They are summarized in Table 2. The values of the properties direct the flow of control in Program PLEXYN as it checks the use of each code in the transcript against the rules of usage for the code that have been incorporated into the values of its properties. The effects of some of the values that the various properties can take are outlined below.

The value of the first coding property is the categorical code label itself, that is, the one or two character substring of letters A through Y that mnemonically labels the action. In Figure 3, for example, L is the label for leave, LF is for lie in front of, and LK is for look. In Program PLEXYN, this value is stored in the array variable KOD (K,N). The value of subscript K is the sequence number that was assigned to the code as the list of the user's codes was read in from a file at the beginning of the PLEXYN processing run. Reading the list rather than defining the codes in the corpus of the program facilities refinement of the code list by simple insertion or deletion before the next run. The second subscript, N, is the number of the coding property, e.g., for the categorical code look, KOD(K,1) = LK.

Program PLEXYN processes the raw transcript of entries at two levels. First, the analysis of syntax breaks out the subject, action, object, proxemic, and location components that are represented in the line. If the effective contents of the line do not pass the syntax analysis, a line with the entry type, current frame, line starter, character position in the string where the error was detected, 7-character error message, and the whole unprocessed string, is written into the output file in the standard syntax error format

(1X,I1,I6,1X,A1,2X,I2,2X,3A3,54A1).   syntax error

If the line passes syntax analysis, the components broken out are examined in terms of the rules of usage that are defined by the coding properties of the action code(s) in the entry. Usage analysis begins with a search of the list of action codes to find a match for the code(s) in the current entry. If none of the values of KOD(K,1) match the current code, a line with the entry type, current frame, line starter, 7-character error message, and the whole unprocessed string, is written into the output file in the standard usage error format

(1X,I1,I6,1X,A1,6X,3A3,54A1).   usage error

In this case, the error message would be BAD KOD. If the match is found, but the component representations do not meet the requirements of the coding properties of the current code, a line of output in the standard usage error format is produced. If all requirements are met, the entry type, current frame, line starter, subject, action, object, data movement sign, orientation of subject, orientation of object, direction from subject to object, distance from subject to object, 2-digit distance fraction, location, and the modifiers of subject, action, object and location, whether these variables were assigned values from the current entry or have their reinitialized values, are all written into the output file in the uniform data format

$$(1X,I1,I6,1X,A1,I2,A2,I2,4A1,A3,A2,5A3).$$ uniform data

Examples of output in the above formats can be found in Figure 4, which is a listing of PLEXYN's output file after it has processed the manuscript in Figure 3. The lines in the two figures can be compared by referring to their frames.

Properties That Minimize The Number Of Names

The second through sixth coding properties define the name requirements and restrictions of each action code. The second coding property, KOD(K,2), defines whether a subject and/or an object must accompany the action whenever it is used in an entry. For example, if KOD(K,2) = 1, the action code does not require any names, but if KOD(K,2) = 4, both subject and object names are required.

The third property, KOD(K,3), defines any restrictions on the identities of the subjects accompanying the action code. The list

TABLE 2.   CODING PROPERTIES FOR PLEXYN PROCESSOR

---

1. mnemonic coding label
2. subject/object requirements and restrictions
3. subject identity restrictions
4. default subject name
5. object identity restrictions
6. default object name
7. continuous, momentary, or momentarily continuous designation
8. additional components required for "match" to terminate
9. number of entries in which code is currently ongoing
10. reference number to subset of mutually exclusive codes, if any
11. incidence or onset terminates other codes by exclusion
12. general class terminator when minus entry
13. status module delimiter
14. local or user-defined special processing to be done
15. number of seconds within which property 14 applies

---

of restrictions follows the list of codes in the file and is read
into a table at the beginning of the PLEXYN run. The restrictions
are designed to enhance error detection. For example, in a study of
giving care to newborn humans at home, it is unlikely that baby
picks up (PU) anyone. In the rush of recording data, however, the
observer could accidently reverse the names in a string describing
father (named 2) picking up baby (named 3). If the user had
defined code PU's third coding property as greater than 0, Program
PLEXYN would use the value of KOD(K,3) as the index to the table
of subject restrictions, find that the name 3 was an illegal subject
for the index value of PU's third coding property, and produce a
usage error line with the message BAD SUB.

For those actions that do not require that a subject name
accompany them in the entry, KOD(K,4) can be defined as the default
name of the subject. For example, while father, older sibling and
other individuals may pick up baby, the most likely person to pick
up baby is mother (named 1). By defining the default subject of
PU in this study as mother, the entry +PU3 is enough to describe
mother pick up baby. Program PLEXYN will insert the default name
and produce the completed and uniformly formatted line in the output
file.

The fifth and sixth coding properties parallel the third and
fourth properties, but apply to the object instead of the subject.
KOD(K,5) defines any restrictions on the identities of objects
accompanying the action code. For those codes that do not require
that an object name accompany them, KOD(K,6) can define the default
name of the object. For the example above, the most likely object
of PU is baby. By defining the default object of PU as baby, the
entry + PU is enough to describe mother picking up baby. As above,
Program PLEXYN will yield a completed and uniformly formatted line.

The effect of declaring default names for the most likely
subject and object of an act is to decrease the number of characters
that would otherwise be needed to completely describe the event.
In the example above, two of four characters after the line starter
were not needed to completely describe the most common occurrence
of the action code PU. If the number of possible names required
that the names be two digits rather than one, the savings would have
been even greater than the fifty percent it was here. Over the
course of an hour of observations, the savings effected by taking
the most likely expectations into account through appropriate
default subject and object values can markedly enhance the observer's
attempts to keep up with the stream of action as it occurs.

Properties That Manage Continuous Categories

The seventh through twelfth coding properties facilitate
management of the onset and termination of continuous categories of
action. The value of the seventh property indicates whether the
category is continuous. When an action label with KOD(K,7) greater
than zero is encountered by Program PLEXYN, Subroutine ONGO is
called to check whether an event with this category has already been
entered into table KON. KON is a two dimensional array that stores

the line number, frame, subject, index K of the act, and object of all events that are currently on in the observation session. For example, when PLEXYN processes the action G in line 11 of Figure 3, KON is scanned to match for G's index K. If a match is not found, the above information describing the event is stored in KON, the line is written into the output file and processing moves on to the next event. If a match is found, the current and stored events must be compared in more detail to determine whether the current event, which consists of a subject and object as well as an action, is the same as the one in table KON. In the example, G is the label for groom. Since more than one subject monkey can groom a particular object monkey at any one moment, but one subject monkey can not groom more than one object monkey (i.e., it is so rare that an entry stating so is probably an error), the critical value for determining whether the current entry and the stored entry are the same is the name of the subject. In this example, if the names are the same, Program PLEXYN writes an error message into its output file, noting that the subject and action are "already on at line," with the line number in the output file where the event was onset. If the subjects are different, then, as above, the current line is stored in KON and written into the output file in the uniform format.

The critical values for matching the current event with those in table KON are indicated by the eighth coding property. If KOD(K,8) = 1, only one event of this category can be on at any one time. If KOD(K,8) = 2, the current entry must agree in both action and object before it matches an event in table KON. If KOD(K,8) = 4, the current entry must agree in subject, action and object to match one in table KON.

The ninth coding property is a dynamic one. Its value is initialized to zero and then incremented and decremented during the run to keep track of the number of events of this category that are currently on. If KOD(K,9) = 0, processing can be speeded up by skipping the search for a match in table KON.

An ongoing action can be terminated by an entry that indicates specific termination of the ongoing action, by entry of an action that is defined as mutually exclusive with the ongoing action, or by entry of a general terminator of the class to which the ongoing action belongs. An ongoing action is specifically terminated with a minus entry in which the - line starter is followed by an effective contents that fulfills the requirements of the ongoing action's eighth coding property. If no entry in table KON adequately matches the current entry, PLEXYN writes the unprocessed string and a message that notes that the entry was NOT ON into its output file in the usage error format. If an entry in KON adequately matches the current entry, the terminating line of entry type, current frame, line starter, subject, action, object, duration (number of sweeps from onset to termination) and line number in the output file at which the onset was entered, is written into the output file in the standard termination format

(1X,I1,I6,1X,A1,I2,A2,I2,1X,I6,18X,'ENDS',I5).   termination

The value of the tenth coding property is the class number to which the particular category belongs. A class consists of mutually exclusive categorical actions, i.e., actions that cannot be (or are extremely unlikely to be) performed by a particular subject at the same time. For example, a monkey does not self groom (SG) and groom (G) another at the same time. If these two codes are assigned to the same class, the onset of an event with one of them will terminate an event with the other, if the other is on and the match in table KON is complete as defined by the value of the eighth coding property of the action in table KON. If the match is complete, Program PLEXYN writes the current entry into its output file in the uniform format with an appended message noting that the current line ends a previous entry at its onset line number in the output file. That line of output is followed by the terminating entry in standard termination format, with an appended message noting that the off was inserted. The current entry is then stored in the place in table KON that was previously occupied by the event just terminated, except if the terminator code is defined as momentary, in which case the current event is not stored.

Exclusion can also be indicated by the value of the eleventh coding property. If KOD (K,11) > 0, program control is directed to a special list of codes that are terminated by the incidence or onset of the current code. The list of specifically excluded codes for each excluder code follows the list of subject and object restrictions in the file and is also read in at the beginning of the run. The codes in table KON are compared to the codes in the list of the current excluder. If no match is found, the current entry is written into the output file and, if continuous, stored in KON. If a match is found, the integer value of KOD(K,11) is used to further test whether the entry in KON should be terminated through mutual exclusion. If KOD(K,11) = 2, the requirements of the potentially terminated code's eighth property are ignored and all entries in KON with a code that matches one of the mutual exclusions of the current code (and with a subject that matches the current subject) are terminated. Similarly, if KOD(K,11) = 4, the eighth property's requirements are ignored and all entries in KON with a mutually excluded code and a subject or object that matches the subject of the current entry are terminated. For example, if one monkey has been grooming another and one of them leaves, the act of leaving logically terminates the act of grooming, regardless of whether it was the groomer or groomee that left. Knowing this, the user can define leaving as a mutual excluder of grooming and set the eleventh property of the categorical code leave to equal 4. Entry of + name L would then terminate any grooming event in which the subject named was groomer or groomee as well as recording the subject's current action of leaving. This capacity to define mutual exclusions and the conditions under which they operate aleviates much of the need to recall what has been entered and is currently ongoing. This in turn, allows the observer to concentrate on what s/he sees at the moment s/he sees it.

A positive value for KOD(K,11) does not always indicate that
there is a list of codes to match. Sometimes KOD(K,11) must be
given a value to specify some degree of override that the code has
over other members of its class of mutual exclusions. In such case,
a null string represents the code in the list of terminated codes.

The twelfth coding property also involves termination of ongoing events. In contrast to the tenth and eleventh properties,
however, which terminate ongoing actions when the current code is
part of a plus entry, the twelfth coding property operates as part
of a minus entry. If KOD(K,12) > 0, the code is a general class
terminator. The codes it can terminate are members of its class
or specified in a list of its mutual exclusions. Determination
of an adequate match is directed by the integer value of KOD(K,12)
in the same way that the value of the eleventh property determines
a match, through reference to the value of the potentially terminated code's eighth coding property. The general class terminator
is especially useful when mutually exclusive codes are likely to
change quickly from one to another within the class or set. When
the last of the series ends without being replaced by a mutually
exclusive event, the observer can specifically terminate the
event without specifically recalling which of the set is currently
on, by entering the appropriate name (if needed) and the label of
the general class terminator after the - line starter. If PLEXYN
finds a match for the current entry in table KON, the label of
the general class terminator is replaced by the label of the code
that matched, the line specifically terminating the event is written
into the output file, and the terminated event is deleted from
table KON. If no match is found, the unprocessed string will be
written into the output file with the message NOT ON in the usage
error format.

In brief review, when KOD(K,7) > 0, KOD(K,1) is the label for
a continous categorical code, and table KON is checked to see
whether the entry is already on. The requirements for an adequate
match in this check are indicated by the value of KOD(K,8). If the
effective contents of the current entry do not match any of the
entries already in KON, they are entered there as well as written
into the output file in the uniform data format. If the contents
are already in KON, the raw string and the error message are produced as output in the usage error format. The number of entries
in KON with KOD(K,1) as act is maintained and stored at KOD(K,9).
Entries already in table KON can be terminated specifically with
a minus entry or through mutual exclusion by another code in a plus
entry. A specific label can be used to terminate with a minus
entry, or, if KOD(K,12) > 0, a general class terminator label can
be used. If an appropriate match is found, the terminated contents
are produced as output in the termination format and the stored
contents are deleted from table KON. If a match is not found, the
raw string and an error message are produced in the usage error
format. Table KON is also checked when KOD(K,10) > 0 or KOD(K,11)
> 0, which respectively indicate that the current code mutually
excludes other members of its class or the codes in its list of
specific exclusions. In either case, if an adequate match is found,

the terminator line is output in the uniform data format with a note that it ends a previous entry. This line is followed by output of the terminating line in the termination format. If a match is not found, the current entry is simply written into the output file and stored in table KON.

If a categorical code is not continuous, it is either momentary or momentarily continuous. For a momentary category, KOD(K,7) = 0. The values of KOD(K,8) and KOD(K,9) of a momentary category are irrelevent and initialized to 0. A momentary code, however, can be mutually exclusive with the numbers of a class and/or a list of other codes, and it can also be a general class terminator. If KOD(K,11) > 0 or KOD(K,12) > 0, PLEXYN proceeds as described above for continuous codes, except that the current entry is not stored in table KON.

The last case, when KOD(K,7) < 0, is the case where a category is typically momentary or of short duration, but occasionally can be longer. If, on those occasions, the observed duration would be of special interest to the observer, then the code should be defined as momentarily continuous. For example, in Dr. Dennis Drotar's studies of caretaking by potentially abusive mothers at Case Western Reserve University School of Medicine, tickling is typically of short duration, but can become abusive when continued for a longer than normal time. Similarly, many of baby's bouts of verbal behavior are of short duration, but they can be extended. Because these categories are usually of short duration, defining them as continuous would result in adding an unnecessary complexity to the coding process. Defining them as momentary, on the other hand, would make it illegal to terminate an unusually long event. While the designation "momentarily continuous" sacrifices some of the error checking, it does allow PLEXYN to accommodate coding categories with these other attributes.

A momentarily continuous code is managed in much the same manner as a continuous code. Management of a minus entry is exactly the same, with a termination when a match is found in KON and an error message when it is not. If a match is found on a plus entry, however, instead of writing an error message that the entry is already on, the line number and frame of the stored entry are replaced by corresponding values from the current entry and the current entry is output in the uniform data format. If a match is not found, the current entry is entered into KON as well as output to the processed file. An analysis of infant verbal behavior provides a good example of the utility of this tactic. The set of codes describing baby's verbalization can be defined as momentarily continuous and mutually exclusive members of a class. As each of baby's verbal events is encountered by PLEXYN, the place in table KON where the last entry in this class was stored is updated with the values of the current entry. Knowing this during the observation session, the observer can mark the termination of an unusually long event of the class by a minus line with the general terminator label of the class. Since each was defined as mutually exclusive with the others in the class and their place in KON was always specifically updated during the PLEXYN processing run, the last that was entered will be specifically terminated by the general class terminator, the label of which is replaced by that in KON, and the correct duration will be computed for output in the standard termination format.

Status Module Delimiters

The value of the thirteenth coding property indicates whether a code is a status module delimiter. If KOD(K,13) = 1, the code delimits proxemic modules. If KOD(K,13) = 2, the code delimits location modules. If KOD(K,13) = 3, it acts as a module delimiter for either or both. During processing, the value of this property is examined for each label in the act field as the PLEXYN processor backspaces through its output file searching for the delimiter of the current status module.

Local or Special User-Defined Conditions

The fourteenth and fifteenth properties refer to special user-defined checks or changes that are performed by a user-structured subroutine called LOCAL. The integer value of KOD(K,14) > 0 directs program control to the appropriate part of the subroutine. In FORTRAN IV, this is done through a computed GO TO. The absolute integer value of KOD(K,15) > 0 is the number of seconds from the current event during which the local condition applies. The sign of the value is the temporal direction from the event in which the condition applies. One case where these properties have been used is to check whether a subject monkey is mounted on another when an intromission is scored for that subject. If not, a warning message would be produced as output in the comment field of the uniform data format.

SUMMARY

Tactics that ease the observer's burden at the moment observations are made have been combined into a set of syntactic rules and coding properties for touch-type entry of descriptive character strings on an electronic keyboard. The logic of the rules and the properties has been taken into account in the design of Program PLEXYN. This program is a complex syntax analyzer that permits the observer to enter partial strings with a minimum number of descriptive elements instead of requiring formally complete and properly formatted ones. PLEXYN draws on user-defined values of the coding properties to verify, complete and uniformly reformat the entries in the observer's record for subsequent data processing programs. Entries that do not meet the requirements of syntax or usage are labeled with an appropriate error message.

The syntax and coding properties of PLEXYN reflect the somewhat broken grammar of English language verbal descriptions of actions and interactions observed in real time. The syntax provides several levels of immediate error correction. The capacity for default subjects and objects permits much of the essentially redundant subject and object identification data to be shifted out of the data stream and into the values of coding properties from where they can be added to the record during PLEXYN processing. Management of the onset and termination of events that have duration is facilitated by means of mutual exclusions that have been declared through the values of other coding properties as well as by explicit termination statements. As the many examples suggest, the more developed the expectations an observer has about the creatures s/he observes, the more complete can be the code s/he uses to describe their behavior, and the less will be his/her burden as s/he records what s/he sees.

Program PLEXYN has been implemented in FORTRAN IV on a Harris 6024/5 computer operating under DOS with 28K words of core memory and a CDC 5-megabyte disk. It is in the process of being implemented in C on a PDP-11/20 computer operating under MINI-UNIX with 28K words of core memory and an RK05 disk. Program listings are available from the author.

REFERENCES

Lamb, M. E.   Infant social cognition and "second order" effects. *Infant Behavior and Development*, 1978, *1*, 1-10.   (a)
Lamb, M. E.   Interactions between 18-month-olds and their preschool-aged siblings.   *Child Development*, 1978, *49*, 51-59.   (b)
Lozoff, B., & Brittenham, G.   Field methods for the assessment of health and disease in pre-agricultural populations.   CIBA Foundation Symposium, 49 (New Series). Amsterdam: Elsevier, 1977.
Stephenson, G. R.   Cultural acquisition of a specific learned response among rhesus monkeys.   In D. Starck, R. Schneider, & H. J. Kuhn (Eds.), *Progress in primatology*. Stuttgart: Fischer, 1967.
Stephenson, G. R.   Testing for group-specific communication patterns in Japanese macaques.   In E. Menzel (Ed.), *Precultural primate behavior*. Basel: Karger, 1973.
Stephenson, G. R., Goldfoot, D. A., & Essock-Vitale, S. M.   PARSYN: A computer-compatible grammar for coding dyadic encounters. *Behavioral Research Methods and Instrumentation*, 1978, in press.
Stephenson, G. R., & Roberts, T. W.   The SSR System 7:   A general encoding system with computerized transcription.   *Behavioral Research Methods and Instrumentation*, 1977, *9*, 434-441.
Stephenson, G. R., Smith, D. P. B., & Roberts, T. W.   The SSR System: An open format event recording system with computerized transcription.   *Behavioral Research Methods and Instrumentation*, 1975, *8*, 259-277.
Weisbard, C., & Goy, R. W.   Effect of parturition and group composition on competitive drinking order in stumptail macaques *(Macaca arctoides)*.   *Folia Primatologica*, 1976, *25*, 95-121.
Wolf, G., Breslau, N., & Novack, A.   A behavioral validation of delegation in primary care teams.   Working paper #M-78-2, College of Industrial Management, Georgia Institute of Technology, Atlanta, Ga., 1978.

Zipf, G. K. *The psycho-biology of language: An introduction to dynamic philosophy*. Cambridge: The M.I.T. Press, 1965.

9.
The sequential analysis
of observational data

JOHN M. GOTTMAN & ROGER BAKEMAN

Recently, there has been a resurgence of interest in sequential analysis. In the late 1940s, classic papers by Shannon and Weaver (1948) proposed a method for quantifying the amount of information transmitted in a communication channel. Those papers led Miller and Frick (1949) to suggest information theory as a generally useful approach for studying response patterning in single organisms. Their work was generalized and popularized for psychologists by Attneave (1959) and for biologists by Quastler (1958). However, after the late 1950s these sequential procedures fell into general disuse by both psychologists and biologists (see Chatfield & Lemon, 1970; Slater, 1973).

The renewed interest in sequential analysis in the past decade has been stimulated by groups of scholars in diverse fields. For example, observational research in which some form of sequential analysis has been used has been conducted by developmental psychologists interested in bidirectional effects in caretaker-infant interaction (e.g., see Lewis & Rosenblum, 1974), primatologists interested in peer interaction (Rosenblum, Coe, & Bromley, 1975) and other social behavior (Altmann, 1965), educational and clinical psychologists interested in children's aggressive behavior in schools (McGrew, 1972; Raush, 1965) and in families (Patterson, 1974), human ethologists interested in children's nonverbal behavior (Blurton Jones, 1972) and in conversational patterns of talk and silence (Jaffe & Feldstein, 1970), clinical psychologists interested in marital interaction (Raush, Barry, Hertel, & Swain, 1974), and ethologists interested in the information conveyed by social signal and response systems across a variety of species (Wilson, 1976; Chatfield & Lemon, 1970).

The renewed interest in sequential techniques thus comes in part from increasing research activity on social interaction between organisms rather than from the study of response patterning

185

over time in one organism. In our experience, such research
increasingly requires the development of statistical techniques
for sequential analysis. Currently many researchers apply no
statistical techniques at all, and when statistical methods are
used they are neither applied consistently nor are they the most
powerful tools available. Some research questions may remain
unaddressed because researchers will not raise those questions
that they do not know how to approach. This state of affairs is
likely to keep crucial concepts of interaction at the level of
unquantifiable metaphors alluded to in discussion sections.

In addition to the interest generated by the study of social
interaction, an additional stimulus that has renewed interest
in sequential analysis has come from methodological investigations
of change in single units over time, particularly the use of time-
series analysis of the interrupted time-series experiment (Glass,
Willson, & Gottman, 1975; Gottman & Glass, in press). This work
on time series has also led to the search for methods to analyze
continuous data across systems within one subject or within one
dyad. However, a discussion of the application of time series
methods for sequential analysis to discrete time data with
continuous variables is beyond the scope of this chapter (see
Box & Jenkins, 1970).

The techniques discussed below primarily apply to the study
of an individual case, although many of the techniques result in
scores which can be summarized across cases. In most of the
examples presented here, the case will be a dyad. This reflects
our own and others' current concern with social interaction as
well as our belief that sequential techniques are especially suited
for the study of interaction.

In sum, this chapter reviews techniques for the sequential
analysis of categorical observational data, that is, data that are
discrete and represent an ongoing stream of behavior. Not
discussed here are problems of data encoding (what behaviors
should be encoded, what constitutes an appropriate behavioral
"unit") or data sampling (what organism should be observed, how
long should they be observed), but the techniques described here
do assume a continuous sampling strategy, one that encodes uninterrupted sequences of behavior. Because of the popularity of
what is usually termed "time-sampling" (Goodenough, 1928; for a
recent discussion of such "one-zero" sampling see Altmann, 1974),
this point requires some emphasis. It is quite common to record
the presence or absence of particular behaviors within successive
time intervals; such data may or may not be appropriate for
sequential analysis. The matter would appear to hinge on the
relationship between the time interval used and the minimum
duration for the behaviors under consideration. When the recording
interval is shorter than the minimum duration, then it seems
perfectly reasonable to regard the data as recorded continuously,
and to proceed with sequential analyses.

DATA TYPES

Because the type of data at hand affects choice of an analytic strategy, a brief typology of data types is presented here. It should be emphasized that this is a typology of data *representations,* not the behavior sampling strategies, and although the last two of the three discrete data types below are described as though behaviors had been time sampled, this is done mainly for ease of representation. (As will be demonstrated later, casting data that are continuously sampled to begin with into a time-sampled format facilitates many subsequent analyses.) Use of this typology, then, not only classifies most cases in the literature but suggests which analytic techniques might be appropriate for a given case.

Data appropriate for sequential analysis fall rather clearly into one of two general classes: discrete or continuous. Only the former are discussed here. The latter type results when the score for some continuous variable (like intensity, say) is recorded at each successive time interval. Such data, usually termed *time-series data,* are simply a string of scores and are often represented with a line graph.

Discrete sequential data can be subdivided in several ways, but three types occur most commonly in the literature. The first we will call *event sequence data* and results when the stream of behavior is encoded as a sequence of events or behaviors usually defined so as to be mutually exclusive and exhaustive. Such data are simply a string of codes or symbols. The second type we will term *timed event sequence data* and results with duration, and not just sequence, of events is recorded. Such data can also be represented as a string of codes, but each code would represent not only an event, but an event lasting for a given time interval. For example, imagine four behaviors coded 1, 2, 3, and 4. A behavior stream recorded as event sequence data might look like "24213" while the same stream recorded as timed-event sequence data might look like "224222111133."[1]

Other data types could be defined. For example, suppose we observe the following string of behaviors: Time 1: Mother holds infant, infant vocalizes, mother vocalizes; Time 2: Mother continues to hold infant, infant vocalizes, mother rocks infant, etc. We could consider each unique combination of codes as a new code as Altmann (1965) does, but this becomes unwieldy if more than a few behaviors are under consideration. Alternatively, such data can be represented as a sequence of sets of codes; each set then

---

1. Elsewhere RB has termed these Type I and Type III data respectively--see Bakeman & Dabbs, 1976; for further discussion of these issues, see Sackett, 1978.

represents behaviors occurring within a time interval. Such
timed-multiple-event sequence data can be analyzed in their own
right, but the purpose in describing this data type here is to
suggest how under some circumstances discrete could be transmuted
into continuous data. For example, we could assume that the
number of concurrent behaviors indicates activity or intensity of
a behavioral system (e.g., see Brazelton, Koslowski, & Main, 1974).
In this way discrete data can be transformed into continuous data.
Thus type of data usually, but not always, limits choice of an
analytic technique.

DESCRIBING DISCRETE SEQUENCES

Two facts impress us about the techniques discussed in this
section: their complete simplicity and their under-utilization by
researchers. All the techniques here rely on nothing more than
conditional probabilities in one guise or another. Three different
specific ways of assembling conditional probabilities to describe
discrete sequential data are detailed below.

Transitional Probabilities (lag 1)

Imagine that we observe two adults conversing (Jaffe &
Feldstein, 1970) or a mother and infant gazing (Stern, 1974; Jaffe,
Stern, & Peery, 1973) or a mother and infant vocalizing (Anderson,
Vietze, & Dokecki, in press) or a mother and infant engaging in
a "behavioral dialogue" consisting of communicative acts (Bakeman
& Brown, 1977). In all of the above cases, the interaction can
be represented as a sequence of discrete dyadic states; that is,
at each successive time interval either (a) both parties are
inactive or quiescent, (b) one is active (A talks, mother vocalizes,
or gazes, or engages in a communicative act), (c) the other is
active (B talks, infant vocalizes, etc.), or (d) both are active
(A and B both talk, mother and infant vocalize concurrently, etc.).
As an example, assume that we encoded dyadic state for 437
successive time intervals and that the raw frequencies were as
follows:

$$F = [\ 141 \quad 123 \quad 105 \quad 68\ ]$$

In this case, $f_3 = 105$ and is the number of times the dyad was
observed in state 3 (infant active). More interesting from a
sequential point of view is the lag-one transition frequency
matrix (rows = t, columns = $t+1$),

$$F = \begin{bmatrix} 98 & 21 & 14 & 7 \\ 21 & 84 & 6 & 12 \\ 14 & 6 & 60 & 25 \\ 7 & 12 & 25 & 24 \end{bmatrix}$$

In this case, $f_{34} = 25$ and is the number of times state 4 (co-acting) immediately followed state 3 (infant active). Note that with 437 observations there are 436 transitions.

Now, the above interaction can be described with a lag-one transition probability matrix,

$$P = \begin{bmatrix} .70 & .15 & .10 & .05 \\ .17 & .68 & .05 & .10 \\ .13 & .06 & .57 & .24 \\ .10 & .18 & .37 & .35 \end{bmatrix}$$

In the general case, P_{ij} is the probability that the dyad will make a transition from state i at time t to state j at time $t + 1$. For example, the dyad is observed 105 times in state 3 and 25 of those times state 4 followed, so

$$P_{34} = f_{34}/f_{3+} = .24.$$

Note that all rows must sum to one.

Transition probability matrices are often presented graphically as state transition diagrams (e.g., see Bakeman & Brown, 1977; Stern, 1974; for an introductory discussion see Kemeny, Snell, & Thompson, 1974). An example using the transitional probabilities given in the previous paragraph is presented in Figure 1. The circles represent the dyadic states, and the arrows

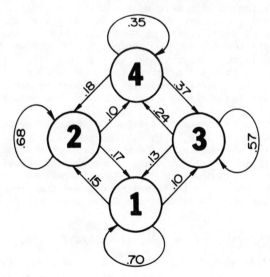

Figure 1. State transition diagram for a four-state system. The least probable transition from each state is not shown.

represent the transitional probabilities between them. For example, the probability of a transition from state 1 to state 2 is .15 and from state 1 to itself is .70. In order to keep the diagram uncluttered, the lowest transitional probability in each row was not drawn (in this case, these are the transitions between states 1 and 3 and between 2 and 4).

Transitional probabilities are descriptively interesting by themselves, but it also makes sense to ask, for example, if state 4 followed state 3 more often than chance would suggest. If the states are independent of each other, the probability of state 4 following state 3 should be no different from the probability of state 4 anywhere in the sequence, and so p_{34} (predicted) = p_4 = 68/437 = .16 and f_{34} (predicted) = $f_3 p_4$ = 105 x .16 = 17. Next, the difference between observed and predicted values could be guaged with a binomial test,

$$z = (x - NP) / \sqrt{NPQ}$$

$$= (f_{34} \text{ (observed)} - f_3 p_4) / \sqrt{f_3 p_4 (1 - p_4)}$$

$$= (25 - 17) / \sqrt{105 \times .16 \times .84} = 3.76.$$

As N increases beyong 25, the binomial distribution approximates a normal distribution and this approximation is rapidly asymptotic if P is close to 1/2 and slowly asymptotic when P is near 0 or 1. When P is near 0 or 1, Siegel (1956) suggested the rule of thumb that $NP(1 - P)$ must be at least 9 to use the normal approximation. Within these constraints the z-statistic above is approximately normally distributed with zero mean and unit variance, and hence we may cautiously conclude that if z exceeds $\pm$ 1.96 the difference between observed and expected probabilities has reached the .05 level of significance (see also Sackett, 1978). However, because dyadic states in successive time intervals (or simply successive dyadic states in the case of event sequence data) are likely not independent in the purest sense, it seems most conservative to treat the resulting z simply as an index or score and not to assign p-values to it.

This procedure can be used either with event sequence or with timed-event sequence data, although the two data types require slightly different computations for the predicted probability (P or p_4 in the example above). The above example assumed timed-event sequence data; because states may follow themselves, frequencies for all states appear in the denominator, and the predicted probability for state 4 after state 3 (or after any state for that matter) is

$$f_4 / (f_1 + f_2 + f_3 + f_4) = 68/437 = .16,$$

as noted above. However, with event sequence data, states may not follow themselves, the frequency for the previous state is omitted from the denominator, and the predicted probability for state 4 after state 3 is

$$f_4/(f_1 + f_2 + f_4) = 68/332 = .20.$$

Transition matrices are central to Markov models and very likely the reader has encountered such matrices in the context of a discussion that included the word "Markov." For that reason the reader may believe that the use of transitional probabilities implies Markov models. However, that is not the case. Lag sequential probabilities are a tool for *describing* the data. Markov models, on the other hand, are used as a data reduction device for *fitting* the observed lag sequential probabilities with a simpler mathematical assumption.

For example, we may find that a lag-one or first-order Markov model adequately estimates all the lag sequential probabilities (see, for example, Jaffe & Feldstein, 1970). The transition probability matrix after two lags can be *computed* from the data by calculating the frequency with which state *j* follows state *i*, not immediately but after some other state has occurred. If we *assume* a first-order Markov model then we can *estimate* the lag-two matrix by squaring the lag-one matrix, a result which follows from the Chapman-Kolmogorov equations (see Gottman, Markman, & Notarius, 1977). The matrix computed from the data can be compared to the matrix predicted from the first-order Markov model to test the adequacy of that model. Three common goodness-of-fit tests--the log-likelihood ratio test, the Pearson chi-square test, and the Freeman-Tukey test--are discussed and the asymptotic equivalence of the three proved by Bishop, Feinberg, and Holland (1975, pp. 513-516).

Measures derived from information theory provide yet another way to test the adequacy of a simple Markov model; this approach is discussed in a subsequent section below. In the next section, however, transitional probabilities are used simply as descriptive devices, as a way of summarizing data; nothing is assumed or implied about an underlying mathematical process.

Lagged Probability Profiles

A transitional probability is simply a lagged conditional probability, and if nothing to the contrary is stated, a lag of one is usually assumed. But transitional probabilities with lags greater than one can be computed, and often can be used to describe sequential data in simple and powerful ways. An especially useful device in this regard is the lagged probability profile: Probability is indicated on the ordinate while successive lags after some criterion behavior are represented on the abscissa; that is, the probabilities with which one behavior follows another criterion behavior at a lag of one, of two, of three, and so on, are computed and plotted. Note that the interpretation of such a probability profile depends in part on the type of data. For event sequence data, successive lags represent sequential event positions; while for timed-event sequence data, successive lags represent successive time intervals after the criterion behavior.[2]

For example, Hinde and Simpson (1975), who were concerned with assessing various qualities of the mother-infant relationship in rhesus monkeys, observed two infant-mother dyads first when the infants were 4 weeks and then again when they were 12 weeks of age. Three of the behaviors recorded were (a) infant joins mother, (b) infant leaves mother, and (c) mother leaves infant. The criterion behavior was infant joins mother. Two probability profiles were constructed, the first (dotted line) indicated the probability that the mother would leave the infant in the first time interval (lag 1, 0-5 sec), in the second (lag 2, 5-10 sec), etc., while the second profile (solid line) plotted the probability that the infant would leave the mother at successive lags (see Fig. 2). These graphs suggest in a quite compelling way that the behavior of Ari and her mother is not especially in harmony while that of Becky and her mother meshes quite well. Note that the profiles for Becky and her mother are quite parallel, especially at 12 weeks of age. This means that Becky's mother was less likely to leave Becky at precisely those times when Becky was also less likely to leave.

Lag Sequential Techniques

Often behavior appears quite "programmatic" in that chains or sequences of two, three, or more behaviors (like tip hat, nod, greet, leave) recur. But how can such common sequences be detected? One way would be to compute the observed probabilities for all the possible chains of various lengths (e.g., see Selleck & Bakeman, 1965; Bobbitt, Gourevitch, Miller, & Jensen, 1969; Bakeman & Brown, 1977); but, when more than five or six behaviors are encoded or when sequences of more than four or five behaviors are under consideration, this approach produces an intellectually staggering amount of information. For example, for 10 different codes and sequences of all lengths from 2 to 6, the number of unique sequences possible is

$$10^2 + 10^3 + 10^4 + 10^5 + 10^6 = 1,111,100.$$

A more flexible approach to sequential detection has been suggested by Sackett (1978). Imagine that we observed a young child and recorded the following four behaviors: take, hit, cry, and give. Each behavior in turn is designated the criterion behavior and the probabilities with which the other behaviors follow it at different lags are computed (see Table 1). If a behavior

---

2. Computer programs for lag sequential analysis of event sequential, timed-event sequential, and multiple-timed-event sequential data are available from Roger Bakeman, Department of Psychology, Georgia State University, Atlanta, Georgia 30303. See also Sackett, 1978.

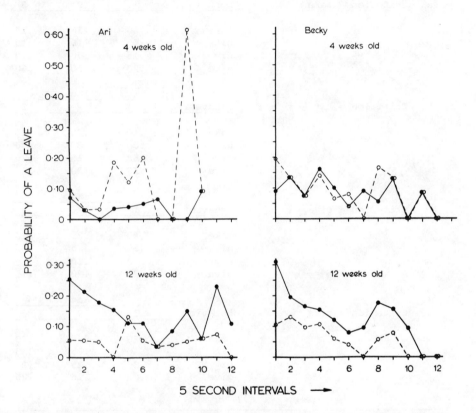

Figure 2.   Probabilities of visits initiated by infant being ended
by mother (open circles, dashed lines) and by infant (closed circles,
solid lines) when the visits have lasted between 0 and 5 sec, 5 and
10 sec (i.e., lasted into the second 5-sec interval), 10 and 15 sec,
and so on (from Hinde & Simpson, 1975).

TABLE 1:   LAG SEQUENTIAL PROBABILITIES: AN HYPOTHETICAL EXAMPLE

a. Criterion = take	behavior	lag 1	lag 2	lag 3
	take	.00	.10	.15
	hit	.65*	.10	.15
	cry	.15	.70*	.10
	give	.20	.10	.60*

b. Criterion = hit	behavior	lag 1	lag 2	lag 3
	take	.10	.35	.25
	hit	.00	.30	.30
	cry	.80*	.15	.20
	give	.10	.20	.25

c. Criterion = cry	behavior	lag 1	lag 2	lag 3
	take	.40	.25	.20
	hit	.35	.25	.35
	cry	.00	.30	.30
	give	.25	.20	.15

d. Criterion = give	behavior	lag 1	lag 2	lag 3
	take	.30	.25	.20
	hit	.40	.25	.25
	cry	.30	.25	.35
	give	.00	.25	.20

Note: These values are hypothetical. We have assumed that the
asterisked values have corresponding z-scores greater than 1.96.

is sequentially independent of the criterion, then its conditional
probabilities at various lags should be about the same as its simple
or unconditional probability. In this case, let us assume that each
of the four behaviors was observed about equally often. Any substantial deviation from .25 then indicates a deviation from the
expected value; as before, the extent of this deviation can be
gauged with a z-score.

Now, the conditional probabilities given in Table 1 indicate
which behavior was most likely at each lag after a particular

criterion behavior, and this information in turn suggests possible sequences. Consider, for example, only panel *a*. After a take (the criterion behavior), a hit was quite likely at lag 1, a cry at lag 2, and a give at lag 3. If we examined only this panel, we might conclude that the sequence take/hit/cry/give occured with some frequency. But this would be premature. We need to ask first if cry followed hit at lag 1 and if give followed hit at lag 2 and cry at lag 1. In fact, cry did follow hit at lag 1 (panel *b*), and so the take/hit/cry sequence is confirmed, but give was not especially likely either at lag 2 after hit (panel *b*) or at lag 1 after cry (panel *c*). We conclude that after a take there was either a hit/cry sequence or else a sequence of two random

TABLE 2:   *SELECTED LAG SEQUENTIAL PROBABILITIES OF DISTRESSED*
AND NONDISTRESSED COUPLES WHEN HUSBAND'S COMPLAINT
ABOUT A MARITAL PROBLEM IS THE CRITERION BEHAVIOR

Behavior	lag					
	1	2	3	4	5	6
Nondistressed couples[a]						
Wife complaint	.24	.13	.18	.16	.17	.18
Wife agreement	.30*	.05	.19*	.09	.15*	.11
Husband complaint	.00	.38*	.14	.26*	.17	.22
Husband agreement	.02	.11	.07	.07	.08	.07
z-score	9.77	10.31	5.11	3.57	2.38	--
Distressed couples[b]						
Wife complaint	.23*	.11	.17*	.14	.16	.12
Wife agreement	.16	.03	.08	.05	.06	.09
Husband complaint	.00	.33*	.15	.25*	.17	.20*
Husband agreement	.01	.07	.05	.06	.06	.07
z-score	3.90	9.11	2.50	5.02	--	2.10

Note: Twenty-four behaviors were coded, but the four selected here always included the highest z-score. At each lag, the behavior with the highest z-score is noted with an asterisk and that z-score is given.

[a]Number of frames = 2,546.

[b]Number of frames = 2,271.

behaviors followed by a give. Thus this approach lets us detect
sequences not only of the form "take/hit/cry" but also of the form
"take/x/x/give" in which "x" indicates that some behavior occurred,
but none predominantly.

A major advantage of the lag sequential method is exactly this
ability to detect sequences with random elements. For example,
imagine that cry was quite likely at lag 2 after take and that cry
was also somewhat likely at lag 1 after both hit and give, but that
no particular behavior dominated the lag 1 position after take. We
would conclude that although the take/hit/cry and take/give/cry
sequences both occurred, the dominant sequence was really take/
x/cry--that is, a cry frequently followed a take but only after
some intervening behavior.

An example may further clarify the Sackett lag sequential
method. Gottman, Markman, and Notarius (1977) coded the behavior
of distressed and nondistressed married couples. Table 2 shows the
transition probabilities for two behaviors of the husband and two
behaviors of the wife (actually 24 behaviors were coded). Most
discussions of a marital issue began with a complaint. For nondistressed couples we see that couples cycle through agreement
after a complaint, suggesting a sequence that we have called
"validation". Distressed couples, however, have a most probable
sequence of meeting a complaint with another complaint, which we
have called "cross-complaining". We also see that at lag 6 for
nondistressed couples the transition probabilities return to their
unconditional levels (all z-scores are negligible), suggesting that
the validation sequence ends after five lags.

DESCRIBING STRUCTURE IN DISCRETE SEQUENCES

In the previous section we were concerned with describing
order in behavior streams at the level of particular behaviors.
In this section we are concerned with describing the orderliness
of the stream as a whole. We ask: How predictable, on the
average, are behaviors, that is, do we enhance predictability
appreciably by knowing just the previous behavior, the previous
two behaviors, etc.? These questions can be addressed using
measures derived from information theory.

Basic Information Measures

The standard measure of information, H, is a summary score;
it is the average amount of information of a symbol in a sequence.
That average amount will depend on the number of different symbols
that occur and on their orderliness in the sequence.

For example, imagine that you wonder what the ith symbol in
a sequence is. If you know that the sequence consists of only one
kind of symbol (AAAAAAA...), then knowing the actual identity of
the ith sybmol reduces our uncertainty as to its identity not at
all (you were sure it would be an A), you have gained no information,
and the average information value of symbols in that sequence is
zero. If the sequence consists of two kinds of symbols, then you

would be somewhat uncertain about the ith symbol and knowing its actual identity would provide you with some information. The more different kinds of symbols the sequence contains, the more uncertain you would be about the identity of any particular symbol, and so the more average information value each symbol would have.

Information is usually measured by binary digits or bits (although other number base systems could be used). H, then, can be regarded as the number of yes-no questions required to determine the identity of the ith symbol. For example, consider the task of guessing a particular square of a checkerboard. It would take a minimum of 6 yes-no questions of the form "Is the target square in the left half?" to locate the square. Each answer provides *one bit* of information by reducing the remaining number of alternatives in half. The information is thus 6 bits

$$(2^6 = c = 64 \text{ squares}) \text{ or}$$

$$H = \log_2 c \, ,$$

where c is the number of equiprobable alternatives. (Hereafter log implies base 2.) Put another way, if each of the c possible events has a probability of

$$p = \frac{1}{c} \text{ then (because } c = \frac{1}{p} \text{)}$$

$$H = \log \frac{1}{p} \, .$$

The value of this information is that it suggests a way of determining the average information value when the possible events are not equally likely. The information value of a particular possibility would be

$$h_i = \log \frac{1}{p_i}$$

and the average of the two or more different possibilities would be the sum of the information value of each weighted by its probability. That is,

$$H = \sum_{i=1}^{c} p_i \log \frac{1}{p_i} = - \sum_{i=1}^{c} p_i \log p_i \, .$$

This is the classic Shannon-Wiener information measure.

If nothing is known about a sequence other than the number of different kinds of events encoded (c), then only a zero-order approximation of H is possible,

$$H_0 = \log c \, .$$

For example, if $c = 4$ then $H_0 = 2$ and if $c = 16$ then $H_0 = 4$. When the simple probabilities for the various events are known, however, the Shannon-Wiener formula gives a first-order approximation of H,

$$H_1 = - \sum_{i=1}^{c} p_i \log p_i .$$

If all events are equally probable, $H_0 = H_1$ and nothing is gained by the first order approximation. Normally, however, H_1 will have a value between zero and H_0. The more dissimilar the simple probabilities are, the lower H_1 is and the less average information value is attached to each symbol; that is to say, the less uncertain we would be about the identity of the ith symbol. In the extreme, H_1 would be zero if the probabilities for all events but one were zero.

The first order approximation assumes that we know no history. But if we know something of past events, better approximations of H should be possible. The second-order approximation of H then is simply the average information value of a symbol when we know the preceding symbol or, as Attneave puts it, "the new information added by each symbol in the sequence--new, that is, in the restricted sense that it was not contained in the immediately preceding symbol" (1959, p. 21).

To compute H_2 we first need to know the average information value of two-event chains. Above, the average information value of a symbol was computed. Likewise, we can compute the average information value of two-event sequences or digrams,

$$H(\text{digram}) = - \sum^{c^2} p(\text{digram}) \log p(\text{digram}).$$

(Because there are c^2 possible digrams, this value could be as high as $2H_0$). Computationally, the second-order approximation to H is

$$H_2 = H(\text{digram}) - H_1 .$$

That is to say, H_2 is the information added when the previous event is known; this is represented schematically in Figure 3. If an event were completely determined by the previous event, then H_2 would be zero; if an event were completely independent of the previous event, then H_2 would equal H_1. (The overlap or the difference between H_1 and H_2 can thus be thought of as the amount of information shared by pairs of events. This overlap is usually symbolized with the letter T, so that

$$T_n = H_n - H_{n+1} .)$$

Third- and higher-order approximations of H are computed in a similar manner and have a similar interpretation. In general,

$$H_n = H(\text{n-gram}) - H(\text{n - 1-gram})$$

where n is an order of approximation 2 or greater. In theory H_n should reach an asymptote, that is, there comes a time when knowing

TIME ⟶

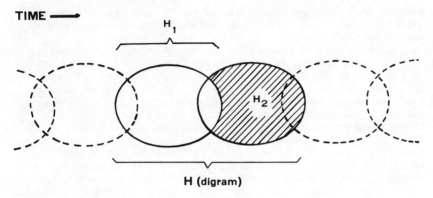

Figure 3. Successive events, overlapping in information content (from Attneave, 1959).

one additional previous symbol no longer reduces the average information value of symbols in the sequence. Descriptively this value of n is important because it indicates the depth of sequential constraint in some observed process. In practice, however, the number of symbols in the sequence limits the order of approximation possible. If a sequence is k symbols long, then the n order approximation H_n is based on H(n-gram) which in turn is based on the probability values of c^n n-grams. But a sequence k symbols long will contain only k-n+1 n-grams so for those probabilities to be reliably estimated, c^n should be some value considerably less than k-n+1. For example, above we had a sequence of 401 symbols and four possible codes. Thus there would be 64 possible trigrams and 256 tetragrams; in this case, a fourth order approximation · makes little sense.

If a process were completely random, were lacking any patterning or order whatsoever, then each successive approximation of H would equal H_0. The value of H_0 depends on the number of possible codes or events, of course, but can easily be transformed into a number that varies from zero to one by dividing each successive approximation of H by H_0. This is usually termed relative information or uncertainty. The complement of uncertainty is order or stereotypy. An index of stereotypy which varies from zero to one is

$$S_n = 1 - H_n/H_0$$

(see Miller and Frick, 1949).

Examples and Interpretations

The index of stereotypy (S) plotted for successive approximations describes the amount and nature of order or patterning in sequential data in a very simple and succinct way. Four examples are presented below.

Imagine that it were reasonable to compute a fourth order approximation for the data described above (we might pool sequences of 400 symbols for 20 dyads, say); the stereotypy profile might look like that presented in Figure 4a. At the level of one- and two-event sequences randomness predominates; not only are the events quite equally probable (as indicated by a low S_1), but knowing a previous event does not reduce our uncertainty much about the following event (the difference between S_1 and S_2 is small). However, when $n = 3$ there is a sharp increase in S, indicating that knowing the previous two events does decrease our uncertainty about the next event. The increase when $n = 4$ is relatively slight, and so we conclude that patterning in these data occurs to a large extent at the level of three-event sequences. Even so, that patterning is not overwhelming. The value for S_4 is only 0.4, which indicates that our guesses about the fourth event knowing the previous three, while somewhat better than our guesses about the third event knowing the previous two, will nonetheless be incorrect fairly often.

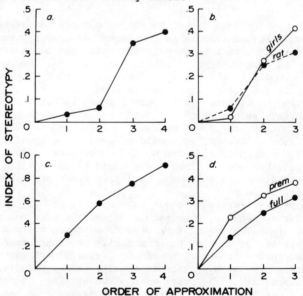

Figure 4. Four stereotypy profiles. Panel *a* is based on hypothetical data, panel *b* is from Miller and Frick (1949), panel *c* is from Altmann (1965), and panel *d* is from Bakeman and Brown (1977). Note that the scale of panel *c* is different from the other three panels.

Miller and Frick (1949) reanalyzed Hamilton's (1916) data concerning trial-and-error behavior in 7-year old girls and in rats (see Fig. 4b). All subjects were confronted with four doors only one of which would open and that one varied from trial to trial. The question was whether successive choices were made relatively randomly or whether they were stereotyped or patterned in some way. No particular door was favored (and so S_1 was nearly zero), but the preceding choice did affect the current one (S_2 represented a substantial increase over S_1). This was because both girls and rats had a tendency to try adjacent doors and not pass one by without trying it. But girls apparently had a better memory than rats and were unlikely to make their third choice either of the first two, and so S_3 was higher for girls. In this instance, stereotypy was a desirable characteristic; it facilitated problem solution. Indeed girls required about half as many guesses to complete 100 successful exits as did rats.

Altmann (1965) observed sequences of social communication in free-ranging rhesus monkeys (recording such behaviors as chases, smacks lips, grooms, grimaces, vocalizes, etc.) and selected for analysis those sequences which he felt represented completely observed interactions. All together 120 different behaviors were observed and 5507 discrete behaviors were recorded, from which 4572 digrams, 3639 trigrams, and 2863 tetragrams were extracted (Altmann's raw data consisted of many short sequences and not one long sequence and so the number of digrams is less than 5506, the number of trigrams is less than 5505, etc.); the stereotypy profile for these data is presented in Figure 4c. No simple patterning at the level of two- or three-event chains is evident; the increase in S is relatively constant for successive orders of approximation. As Altmann concluded, these results "are consistent with the theory that rhesus monkeys base their social behavior upon their memory for preceding events in their social group, and that this memory extends back beyond the immediately antecedent event" (p. 490). The value of S does approach one, however, suggesting that a few quite stereotyped four-event chains occurred with some frequency. But because in this case values of H were greatly underestimated (and so values of S were overestimated) this last interpretation is doubtful. With 120 possible behaviors there are 14,400 possible digrams, yet Altmann observed only 4571; with so few observed digrams, the probabilities of many will be underestimated as zero, consequently the value of H(digram) will be considerably deflated (as Altmann recognized), and H_2 will be underestimated. Needless to say, the situation worsens geometrically for each higher order of approximation. If more than a few behaviors are encoded, then, information measures cannot be reliably computed unless literally millions of observations are made. (For example, if c were only 10, there would be 10^5 tetragrams and a reasonably reliable fifth order approximation of H would indeed require about 10^6 observations.)

Finally, Bakeman and Brown (1977) observed premature and full-term infants interacting with their mothers during a feeding situation. Various behaviors of the mother and of the infant were defined as communicative acts (such as vocalizing, moving, rocking, etc.) and each successive five-second interval of the half-hour observation session was categorized as containing no such behaviors, only mother communicative behaviors, only infant communicative behaviors, or both mother and infant communicative behaviors. Since with four categories there are 64 possible trigrams, and for each dyad 360 successive intervals were encoded (and so 358 trigrams were observed), it is reasonable to compute approximations up to the third order but not beyond. S_0 through S_3 were computed for each dyad; mean values for the 31 premature and the 24 fullterm dyads are plotted in Figure 4d. These two stereotypy profiles indicate that premature dyads were more predictable and less varied in their behavior than fullterm ones ($p < .01$ for S_1, S_2, and S_3, by a two-tailed t-test); fullterms were about as stereotyped at the trigram as prematures at the digram level ($S_3 = 0.32$ for fullterms while $S_2 = 0.33$ for prematures). Still, for both premature and fullterm dyads, stereotypy increased less with each higher order of approximation, suggesting that the influence of sequential constraints did not extend much beyond the three successive time intervals examined here.

Testing the Order of Sequential Constraint

By definition, a first-order Markov process represents the current event as dependent on only the immediately preceding event. In general, if a sequence is generated by an ith order Markov process, then the current state or event is independent of all but the i previous states (that is, the focus is on sequences $i + 1$ sybmols in length). And, as noted in the preceding section, if the current state is dependent on only the previous i states, then the difference between H_{i+1} and H_{i+2} will be negligible. (Unfortunately for the sake of terminological consistency, a first-order Markov process and a second-order approximation to H both deal with two-event sequences.) Thus if a process is first-order Markovian, knowing the previous event will reduce uncertainty about the current event but knowing the two previous events, say, will not result in much further uncertainty reduction (and so the difference between H_2 and H_3 will be small). For example, in Figure 5b there is some evidence that trial-and-error behavior fits a first-order Markov model for rats but not for girls (for an additional example see Natale, 1976).

It would be helpful to have an index of the point at which the difference between successive approximations is no longer significant. The difference can be evaluated with a chi-square or similar goodness-of-fit test (see Attneave, 1959, pp. 28-30, Bishop, Feinberg, & Holland, 1975, Chap. 7; Chatfield, 1973; Chatfield & Lemon, 1970), although most procedures are computationally tedious. The simplest way is to use an approximate formula suggested by Attneave,

$$\chi^2 = 2(\log_e 2)kT_n = 1.3863kT_n$$

where k is the number of symbols in the sequence and

$$T_n = H_n - H_{n+1} \quad (df = c^{n-1}(c-1)^2);$$

For fuller discussion of degrees of freedom, especially if non-successive approximations are being compared, see Chatfield and Lemon,(1970). In any case, the accuracy of the computed chi-square depends on those factors which affect the accuracy of H as discussed earlier (either the number of codes is quite small and only a few low-order approximations are considered or the number of observations is astronomical). Because the chi-square approximations likely become successively worse as higher-order models are considered, Chatfield (1973) suggests that the graphical technique--simply examining the plot of H_n against n as discussed in the previous section--may often be more reliable than a series of significance tests.

DISCUSSION

The various techniques reviewed here can aid in the enterprise of detecting order in discrete sequences of behavior codes, but even together they form no panacea. Our own experience and the work of others discussed here convinced us, in fact, that there is no simple "single and sovereign" approach to the analysis of sequential observational data. Much depends on the type of data an individual investigator has. For example, the lag sequential approach to sequence detection works well for event sequence data, but works less well for timed-event sequence data (124, 1224, and 12224 are all seen as different sequences). Then, too, the lag sequential approach works best when the number of codes is moderate, more than 4 or 5, say, but less than 20. When the number of codes is quite small--4 or 5 or less--sequences are more convincingly detected by computing either conditional probabilities (the probability of C at time t given B at time $t-1$ and A at time $t-2$) or simple probabilities for 2-event, 3-event, and so on, chains (the probability of an AB sequence, for example, or of an ABC sequence). "Best" techniques, then, depend on local circumstances.

Still, a thorough knowledge both of the organisms observed and of the encoded sequences (the raw data) usually insures that analyses at the level of particular behaviors will be meaningful and sensible. More risky are analyses at the level of the behavior stream as a whole. Information measures, which can characterize an entire stream of behavior as more variable or random or as more predictable or stereotyped, are conceptually very appealing. But knowing that one interaction (or one group of interactants) is more stereotyped than another does not tell us how the more stereotyped interaction is put together--for this we need to look at particular behaviors-- nor does it tell us if a more stereotyped or predictable interaction is "desirable"--this is a matter of interpretation which should be based on the investigator's knowledge of the organisms involved and the situation in which they were observed.

The bulk of this paper has been concerned with describing discrete behavioral sequences; inference has received little attention. We believe that this reflects the current state of the field. Chatfield (1973) noted that although the probability theory of Markov chains has been extensively developed, relatively little

attention has been given to statistical inference concerning
Markov chain models. This comment could be extended to apply to
discrete sequences generally. Given the current interest among
various scientists in encoding and analyzing streams of behavior,
we hope it is only a matter of time until statisticians rectify
this neglect.

REFERENCES

Altmann, J. Observational study of behavior: Sampling methods.
    Behaviour, 1974, *49*, 227-267.
Altmann, S. A. Sociobiology of rhesus monkeys. II. Stochastics
    of social communication. *Journal of Theoretical Biology*,
    1965, *8*, 490-522.
Anderson, B., Vietze, P., & Dokecki, P. Reciprocity in vocal
    interactions of mothers and infants. *Child Development*, in
    press.
Attneave, F. *Applications of information theory to psychology*.
    New York: Henry Holt, 1959.
Bakeman, R., & Brown, J. V. Mother-infant interaction during the
    first months of life: Differences between preterm and full-
    term infant-mother dyads from a low income population (Tech.
    Rep. 5). Infant Laboratory: Georgia State University,
    Atlanta, 1977.
Bakeman, R., & Brown, J.V. Behavioral dialogues: An approach to
    the assessment of mother-infant interaction. *Child Development*,
    1977, *48*, 195-203.
Bakeman, R., & Dabbs, J. M., Jr. Social interaction observed:
    Some approaches to the analysis of behavior streams.
    Personality and Social Psychology Bulletin, 1976, *2*, 335-345.
Bishop, Y. M. M., Feinberg, S. E., & Holland, P. W. *Discrete
    multivariate analysis: Theory and practice*. Cambridge:
    M.I.T. Press, 1975.
Blurton Jones, N. (Ed.). *Ethological studies of child behaviour*.
    Cambridge: Cambridge University Press, 1972.
Bobbitt, R. A., Gourevitch, V. P., Miller, L. E., & Jensen, G. D.
    Dynamics of social interactive behavior: A computerized
    procedure for analyzing trends, patterns, and sequences.
    Psychological Bulletin, 1969, *71*, 110-121.
Box, G. E. P., & Jenkins, G. M. *Time series analysis: Forecasting
    and control*. San Francisco: Holden-Day, 1970.
Brazelton, T. B., Koslowski, B., & Main, M. The origins of
    reciprocity: The early mother-infant interaction. In M. Lewis
    & L. A. Rosenblum (Eds.), *The effect of the infant on its
    caregiver*. New York: Wiley, 1974.
Chatfield, C. Statistical inference regarding Markov chain models.
    Applied Statistics, 1973, *22*, 7-20.
Chatfield, C., & Lemon, R. E. Analyzing sequences of behavioural
    events. *Journal of Theoretical Biology*, 1970, *29*, 427-445.
Glass, G. V., Willson, V. L., & Gottman, J. M. *Design and analysis
    of time-series experiments*. Boulder: Colorado University
    Associated Press, 1975.

Goodenough, F. L. Measuring behavior traits by means of repeated short samples. *Journal of Juvenile Research*, 1928, *12*, 230-235.

Gottman, J. M., & Glass, G. V. Analysis of interrupted time-series experiments. In T. Kratochwill (Ed.), *Strategies to evaluate change in single subject research*. New York: Academic Press, in press.

Gottman, J., Markman, H., & Notarius, C. The topography of marital conflict: A sequential analysis of verbal and nonverbal behavior. *Journal of Marriage and the Family*, 1977, *39*, 461-477.

Hamilton, G. V. A study of perseverence reactions in primates and rodents. *Behavior Monographs*, 1916, *3* (No. 2).

Hinde, R. A., & Simpson, M. J. A. Qualities of mother-infant relationships in monkeys. In *Parent-infant interaction* (Ciba Foundation Symposium 33). Amsterdam: Elsevier, 1975.

Jaffe, J., & Feldstein, S. *Rhythms of dialogue*. New York: Academic Press, 1970.

Jaffe, J., Stern, D. N., & Peery, J. C. "Conversational" coupling of gaze behavior in pre-linguistic human development. *Journal of Psycholinguistic Research*, 1973, *2*, 321-329.

Kemeny, J. G., Snell, J. L., & Thompson, G. L. *Introduction to finite mathematics*. Englewood Cliffs, N.J.: Prentice-Hall, 1974.

Lewis, M., & Rosenblum, L. A. (Eds.). *The effect of the infant on its caregiver*. New York: Wiley, 1974.

McGraw, W. C. *An ethological study of children's behavior*. New York: Academic Press, 1972.

Miller, G. A., & Frick, F. C. Statistical behavioristics and sequences of responses. *Psychological Review*, 1949, *56*, 311-324.

Natale, M. A Markovian model of adult gaze behavior. *Journal of Psycholinguistic Research*, 1976, *5*, 53-61.

Patterson, G. R. A basis for identifying stimuli which control behaviors in natural settings. *Child Development*, 1974, *45*, 900-911.

Quastler, H. A primer on information theory. In H. P. Yockey, R. L. Platzman, & H. Quastler (Eds.), *Symposium on information theory in biology*. New York: Pergamon Press, 1958.

Raush, H. L. Interaction sequences. *Journal of Personality and Social Psychology*, 1965, *2*, 487-499.

Raush, H. L., Barry, W. A., Hertel, R. K., & Swain, M. A. *Communication, conflict and marriage*. San Francisco: Jossey-Bass, 1974.

Rosenblum, L. A., Coe, C. L., & Bromley, L. J. Peer relations in monkeys: The influence of social structures, gender, and familiarity. In M. Lewis & L. A. Rosenblum (Eds.), *Friendship and peer relations*. New York: Wiley, 1975.

Sackett, G. P. The lag sequential analysis of contingency and cyclicity in behavioral interaction research. In J. Osofsky (Ed.), *Handbook of infant development*. New York: Wiley, 1978.

Sackett, G. P. A taxonomy of observational techniques and a theory of measurement. In G. P. Sackett (Ed.), *Observing behavior*, *volume 2: Data collection and analysis methods.* Baltimore: University Park Press, 1978.

Selleck, J., & Bakeman, R. Procedures for the analysis of form: Two computer applications. *Journal of Music Theory*, 1965, *9*, 281-293.

Siegel, S. *Nonparametric statistics for the behavioral sciences.* New York: McGraw-Hill, 1956.

Shannon, C. E., & Weaver, W. *The mathematical theory of communication.* Urbana: University of Illinois Press, 1949.

Slater, P. J. B. Describing sequences of behavior. In P. P. G. Bateson & P. H. Klopfer (Eds.), *Perspectives in ethology.* New York: Plenum Press, 1973.

Stern, D. N. Mother and infant at play: The dyadic interaction involving facial, vocal, and gaze behaviors. In M. Lewis & L. A. Rosenblum (Eds.), *The effect of the infant on its caregiver.* New York: Wiley, 1974.

Wilson, E. O. *Sociobiology: The new synthesis.* Cambridge: Harvard University Press, 1975.

10.
Time-series analysis
of continuous data in dyads

JOHN M. GOTTMAN

Observational data are collected over time, and it is therefore sensible to view representations of dyadic interaction as realizations of bivariate time series. Unfortunately, this representation of social interaction data is very rare. This chapter is written to urge investigators of social interaction to represent a dyad's behavior over time as two graphs, each resembling the daily Dow Jones Industrial Average. This requires only that some continuous variable be plotted at discrete times for each member of the dyad; of course, the variables to be plotted must be experimentally interesting, but I expect from my own research and from the research presented at this conference that this is entirely possible. For example, Tronick, Als, and Brazelton (1977) cumulated behaviors for mother and infant such that increases were indicative of greater activity and stimulation of each person. Many researchers in this area seem reluctant to condense their categorical data, in fear that some essential mystery lurking in the data will elude their analyses. They should be reminded that these analyses do not foreclose other options. This chapter is intended as an introduction to analytic options with time-series, and a discussion is in order of various methods for generating time-series data from categorical data.

FROM CATEGORICAL TO TIME-SERIES DATA

Categorical data may be classified into several types, as discussed by Gottman and Bakeman in this volume. To review briefly, one data type is called *event sequence data,* which is a string of mutually exclusive and exhaustive codes representing the classification of a set of observed events. A second data type is called *timed-event sequence data,* which results when the duration of each

207

category and not just the event sequence is recorded. If there are
four behaviors, coded 1 to 4, an event sequence string might be
represented by a string of codes such as 12321413, whereas the same
sequence coded in timed-event sequence might have been 1112233333
211444133. Another data type is called *timed-multiple-event
sequence data* in which a set of concurrent, non-mutually exclusive
behaviors may be recorded during any time unit.

These three data types describe most of the data in the
observational literature on social interaction, though other data
types are possible. There are several ways to transform any of
these data types into a set of non-categorical observations which
would be called a *time series*.

First, it is possible to take a fixed window of k coding
intervals (not necessarily time based) and simply compute the
proportion (or the arcsine of its square root) of k intervals that
each code occupied at each location of the window. This procedure
has been followed to some extent by Mishler and Waxler (1975) in
studying family talk and silence patterns. Or, each code could
be numerically scaled on some particular dimension of interest,
such as activity, positiveness, or tension. This seems to be the
essential idea in Brazelton, Koslowski, and Main (1974). Or a set
of codes could be used to define a set of system states (e.g., 1 =
mother and infant both vocalize, 2 = one vocalizes, 3 = both
quiescent) which can be scaled on some dimension (e.g., activity).
For timed-multiple-event sequence data, the total number of codes,
or the total number in specific categories of codes (e.g., face
codes, touching codes, vocalizing codes) could be tallied.

These codes could also be weighted optimally to discriminate
various groups of dyads, or to discriminate specific types of
blocks of interaction. For example, Wills, Weiss, and Patterson
(1974) used a regression equation to discriminate love days and
regular days for distressed marriages; during love days husbands
were told by the experimenters to be particularly affectionate to
their spouses. However it is done, most investigators develop a
sense for the work their coding systems do in describing interaction,
and they should be able to create some univariate scaling of their
categories along one (or several) dimension(s).

At a recent conference Richard Vitale (personal communication)
suggested that researchers in the social sciences seem to have
developed a Victorian attitude toward their data--they do not think
they should manipulate data without the license of a hypothesis.
Vitale suggested that John Tukey's work on exploratory data analysis
advised researchers to study their data visually in as many
different ways as possible, in short, to plot, plot, plot. The
message is simple--time series analysis should be used to supplement categorical sequence analysis, not to compete as an alternative.

THE LANGUAGE OF TIME-SERIES ANALYSIS: ONE SERIES

Before we begin discussing the bivariate case, it will be
necessary to discuss the univariate case. There are two kinds of

time-series analyses--*time domain* and *frequency domain* analysis.
In time-domain analysis one series can be analyzed using the basic
"autoregressive question," namely, "how predictable is a series
from its past?" The goal is to construct a model, which could be
conceptualized as an infinite autoregressive process,

$$x_t = a_1 x_{t-1} + \ldots + e_t \tag{1}$$

Time series models are determined by estimating the parameters a_i
so that

$$[x_t - \text{MODEL}] = \text{a random, uncorrelated series (called "white noise")} = e_t$$

and such that $\Sigma\, e_t^2 = \text{minimum}$.

In frequency domain analysis the equivalent question is "what
are the component oscillations in the series?" The best way to
understand this is visually. Figure 1 shows how two time series
may be summed to produce a more complex series.   Once again a model

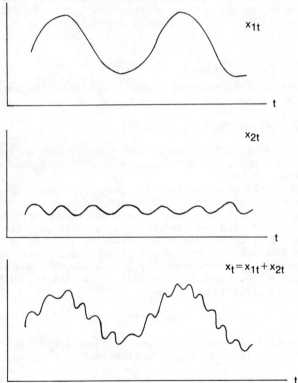

FIGURE 1.   Spectral decomposition of a time series composed of two
basic frequencies.

is constructed that is the sum of component oscillations such that

$$[x_t - \Sigma \text{ COMPONENTS}] = \text{WHITE NOISE}$$

For example, Whittaker and Robinson (1924) showed that the brightness of a variable star at midnight on 600 successive days could be fit perfectly by the sum of two periodic terms with periods of 24 and 29 days, i.e.,

$$x_t = 17 + 10 \sin \frac{2\pi(t+3)}{29} + 7 \sin \frac{2\pi(t-1)}{24}$$

(See Granger & Hatanaka, 1964), and they thus determined that the variable star was a binary star.

One central concept in the statistical analysis of time series is that an observed series is the realization of a particular process, i.e., it is sampled from a population of similar processes. A second concept is *stationarity*. A stationary time series varies about a fixed mean and has the same probability structure throughout.

To understand the meaning of the term "probability structure" we will need to define the notion of *autocorrelation*. Given a normally distributed time series, $\{ x_t \}$, pairs of points

$$(x_1, x_2), (x_2, x_3), \ldots,$$

are used to calculate the first-order autocorrelation coefficient, r_1; pairs of points

$$(x_1, x_3), (x_2, x_4), \ldots$$

are used to calculate the second-order autocorrelation coefficient, r_2, and so on. A plot of r_k versus the lag, k is called the "correlogram."

The term "the same probability structure" (for a normal process) means that the mean and the autocovariance is the same no matter what segment of the time series is sampled, which implies that r_k depends on only k, and not on time. For a stationary series, the correlogram dies out rapidly with increasing lag. Under the null hypothesis that the series is a realization of a white noise process, the variance of r_k is approximately 1/N, where N is the number of observations in the sample series (see Box & Jenkins, 1970, p. 35). Therefore, a correlogram that has

$$r_k > 2\sqrt{N}$$

(with increasing k) is nonstationary. Nonstationary series must be differenced to eliminate trend. A first difference

$$(x_t - x_{t-1})$$

will eliminate linear trend; a second difference (which is a first difference of the first differences) will eliminate quadratic trend, and so on.

This chapter will focus on frequency domain analyses, although transfer functions (which are time domain) will be used to introduce cross-spectral analysis. If a single time series is basically cyclic, consisting of some uncorrelated error, plus two component sine waves of different frequencies, there would be two cycles that contribute to the series with their appropriate amplitudes. If these two components were subtracted from the original series, an uncorrelated residual series (white noise) would result. The correlogram of the uncorrelated residual would be zero (i.e., it would lie within the two sigma confidence bands around zero). In frequency domain language, white noise, like white light, is an equal mixture of all frequencies. The reader might conjure up an image of Sir Isaac Newton using his prism to break white light into its component colors. This means that the "spectrum" of white light and hence of white noise would be uniformly composed of oscillations of all wavelengths. The spectrum should therefore be a constant.

It would be useful to have a way of calculating the spectral density of a time series. This function would have the following properties--it would peak at frequency bands that contribute important sources of variation to the series and it would be zero elsewhere. However, while the spectral density of the Whittaker and Robinson (1924) data would have peaks at two frequencies, and be zero elsewhere, in actual practice it will be more likely that a set of cycles around some particular frequency will contribute to the overall variance of the series, rather than just a particular frequency.

In the last decade of the 19th century Schuster proposed a particular function, called the *periodogram,* which in many cases had peaks at important frequencies that contributed to the variance of the series. Suppose that a series was obtained from the realization of a cyclic series, a cos(wt), plus a white noise series. Then the series would oscillate around one frequency, w, with a period (time from peak to peak) of $\theta = 2\pi/w$. The spectral density function, or periodogram, would have one spike at frequency w, and it would be zero elsewhere.

It is an amazing fact that the best least squares approximation of any function[1] x_t of period θ is the Fourier approximation, which is simply a sum of sine and cosine functions with appropriate weights:

$$X_N(t) = \sum_{n=0}^{N} \{A_n \cos(n \frac{2\pi}{\theta} t) + B_n \sin(n \frac{2\pi}{\theta} t)\} \qquad (2)$$

---

1. Any function that satisfies the Dirichlet conditions. See Gowar and Baker (1974).

Equation (2) is called a harmonic polynomial of degree N and period θ . The weights A_n and B_n can be uniquely derived from the least squares criterion (see Appendix 2). The periodogram of a time-series $\{ x_t \}$ is

$$I_n (w) = \frac{1}{\pi n} \{ (\sum_{t=1}^{n} X_t \cos wt)^2 + (\sum_{t=1}^{n} X_t \sin wt)^2 \},$$

where $w = w_j = {}^{2\pi j}/n$. The periodogram is a function plotted at these equidistant frequencies.

Unfortunately, the periodogram has some very poor statistical properties. Jenkins (1967) reviewed Bartlett's (1948) proof that the periodogram's variance does not decrease as the number of observations are increased. "In fact," Jenkins wrote, "for large n, the distribution of $I_n(w)$ is a multiple of a chi-square distribution with 2 degrees of freedom, independently of n. This means that in no statistical sense does $I_n(w)$ converge to f(w) [the spectral density function] as n becomes large. Thus, harmonic analysis which is the technique appropriate for the analysis of a periodic function breaks down completely when applied to a statistical fluctuation. Historically, this explains the existence of a theory of spectral estimates and also provides the starting point in the development of the theory" (p. 115, italics removed). Tukey (1967) wrote that, "if we dealt with problems involving the superposition of a few simple phenomena, as do astronomers interested in binary stars and related problems, we can learn much from the periodogram. Sadly, however, almost no one else has this kind of data. As a result the periodogram has been one of the most misleading devices I know" (p. 25).

Fortunately, Bartlett (1948) found that improved spectral estimates could be derived by partitioning the series, calculating periodograms for separate pieces, and averaging these periodograms. Jenkins (1967) showed that this procedure is identical to using techniques known as "spectral windows." The problems of the periodogram turn out to be a case of a general problem with the stability of the average value of any quadratic form derived from a stationary process.[2]

---

2. If Q is a quadratic form derived from a stationary process with power spectrum, $F(w)$, then it can be shown that

$$\text{average } [Q] = \int q(w) dF(w)$$

where q(w) must be a polynomial in cos w of degree less than the number of data points. Tukey (1967) wrote that, "as a consequence, all but a finite number of frequencies must contribute to any quadratic function of the data. Though we may wish to concentrate on only the frequencies of a certain band, nearly all other frequencies will leak in to some degree. The best we can do is to make q(w) large where we wish to concentrate and small everywhere else." (p.28)

The improved function that is of interest is called the *spectral density* of the series and it will have peaks at frequency bands that make large contributions to the variance of the series. Thus a series such as the one shown in Figure 1 is composed of two superimposed frequencies, a low frequency wave and a faster oscillation, and the spectral density would show peaks at W_1 (for the lower frequency) and W_2 (for the higher frequency).

There is an elegant link between time-domain and frequency-domain time-series analysis. The link is provided by a function called the Fourier transform by which the spectral density can be directly estimated from the autocovariances of the original series. Because the sample spectrum is the Fourier transform of the sample autocovariance function (see Jenkins and Watts, 1968, p. 215), all spectral estimates are of the form

$$f(w_j) = (\frac{1}{2\pi})\{\lambda_o C_o + 2\Sigma\lambda_k C_k \cos w_j k\}$$

where $w_j = (\pi j/\underline{n})$, $j = 0,1,2,\ldots,\underline{n}$, and C_k are the estimated autocovariances (see Granger & Hatanaka, 1964, p. 59). The usual choice of weights, i.e., the usual spectral window is the Tukey-Hanning window,

$$\lambda_k = \frac{1}{2}\{1 + \cos \frac{\pi k}{m}\}$$

The integer m represents the frequency bands for which the spectrum is estimated, though in practice m is usually less than $n/6$, where n is the number of observations (data points) in the series. The Fourier transform of a series is the distribution of signal strength with frequency, of the component oscillations of the series (Jenkins & Watts, 1968, p. 25). Confidence bands for these spectral estimates are given by Granger and Hatanaka (1964, p. 62 ff).

An intuitive understanding of the relationship between the autocovariances of the series and the spectral density can be obtained by considering a perfectly seasonal series such as vegetable prices plotted over several years (see Figure 2a). The autocorrelation of this series has recurring minor peaks at equal distances apart. This makes sense since vegetable prices should be more predictable in neighboring months, decline in predictability thereafter, but increase because of seasonal variation. The increase occurs because across years, prices in July months will be more highly correlated than months within a year that are not separated by seasons. This correlation composed by pairing the same months across years should also drop off with increasing years. As Figure 2c shows, the spectral density function will have one peak corresponding to a period of 12 months, or

$$12 = \frac{2\pi}{w}$$

months, so w at the peak equals 1.91, which is the number of complete swings or cycles in 2π months.

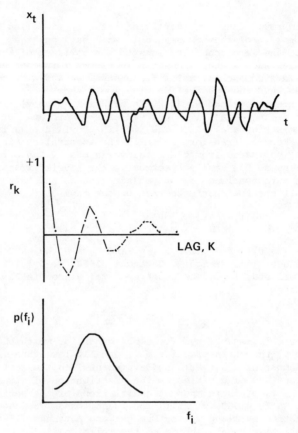

FIGURE 2.   A periodic time series, its autocorrelation function, and
its spectral density function.

EXAMPLES

Two examples will be considered, one in which the time-series
are fit by a first-order autoregressive process, with no cyclicity
and one in which the time series are cyclic. The data are taken
from the coding of videotapes of distressed and non-distressed
married couples resolving a marital issue. The first set of data
are taken from a distressed couple discussing a money problem,
and the second from a different distressed couple discussing a
sexual problem. The coding system and the method for computing
the continuous variable from discrete codes are both described in
Gottman, Markman, and Notarius (1977) and the procedures for the
study are described in Rubin (1977). In general, the graphs displayed in Figure 3 represent the cumulative overall positivity
or negativity of the interaction, and the unit on the abscissa is
the floor switch, that is, the set of utterances when one person
stops speaking and the other person takes the floor represent one
point on the graphs. Cumulative points are plotted because they

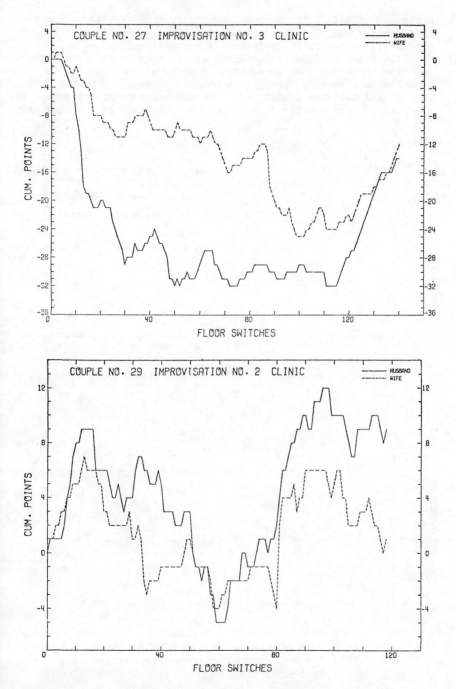

FIGURE 3.   Time series for two clinic couples.   a) Couple 27,
b) Couple 29.

are smoother and easier to read. However, they are, in general, unstationary and therefore the noncumulative series (i.e., the cumulative series first differenced) are analyzed.

The spectral density functions are plotted in Figure 4. In this case the one major peak in spectral density at low frequencies for cou 27 means that there is trend in the data. This trend should be removed and the data reanalyzed. The two major peaks for couple 29 means that there are two superimposed cycles, much as in Figure 1.

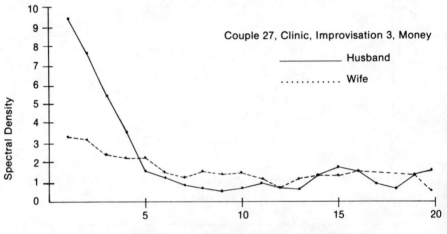

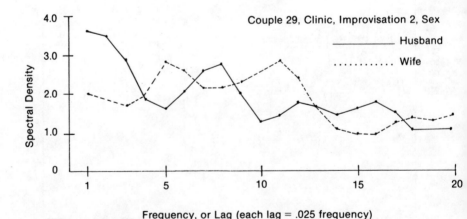

FIGURE 4. Spectral density functions for Couples 27 and 29.

In the case of couple 27, there is no evidence (Figure 3) of cyclicity, and there would not be after detrending the series. Ignoring nonstationarily, the process looks exactly like a first-order auto-regressive process, with positive autocorrelation (see Jenkins & Watts, 1968, p. 219). In this case the autocorrelation function

$$r_k = \phi^k, \ (|\phi|<1)$$

decays exponentially. However, for couple 29 the graphs of both husband and wife show peaks at both high and low frequencies. Examination of the graphs of couple 29 in Figure 3 shows that this is not at all surprising--there is strong visual evidence of these cyclicities. Hence, if there is some interest in detecting cyclicity, the spectral density function would be a useful tool.

CROSS TIME-SERIES ANALYSIS

The major focus of this chapter is dyadic processes, so we turn to a discussion of the relationship between two time-series. The two time series could be mother vocalization and infant smiles over time, or a husband's and a wife's positive or negative behaviors in a problem solving task, and so on. This chapter did not discuss the modeling of a single time series in much detail, nor will it discuss the analysis of interrrupted time-series experiments. For the former the reader is referred to Anderson (1976), Box and Jenkins (1970), and for the latter, Glass, Willson and Gottman (1975) and Gottman and Glass (1978). However, we should mention one potential application of the interrupted time-series experiment that has been suggested by Sackett (personal communication) for studying the effects of rare events. To assess the impact of one instance of a low frequency event, an interrupted time-series quasi-experiment on some variable of interest would be plotted before and after the rare event, and its impact as an "intervention" would be assessed. A computer program for this analysis has been written by Padia, Bower, and Glass[3] based on the mathematics developed by Glass, Willson, and Gottman (1975).

The analytic methods that are discussed in this chapter are currently available on most university computers as part of the Biomedical package (Dixon, 1974, pp. 517-582, Programs 2T, 3T, and 4T). The analyses presented in this chapter were performed by using program 2T of the Biomedical package.

The major analytic tool to be discussed will be *cross-spectral* time series analysis. However, this form of analysis will be

---

3. Computer programs, sourcedecks, and a manual are available for $25 from Gene Glass, Laboratory of Educational Research, University of Colorado, Boulder, Colorado 80302.

considerably clearer if it is preceded by a discussion of a time-domain analysis known as *transfer-function* analysis.

TRANSFER FUNCTION ANALYSIS

This chapter has discussed the possibility of transforming multiple event sequential data into a continuous time series. Howeve time-series data are derived, whether they be rates, intensities, or any other continuous variable, a series of numbers graphed over time are analyzed sequentially by attempting to predict the present value of the series from its past values. This "auto-regression," that is, the regression of the series on its own past, identifies a time-domain time series model (see Equation (1)).

We are often interested in predicting the future of one time series, $[Y(t)]$, from the past of another series $[X(t)]$. This problem is solved by defining the *cross-correlation* between $X(t)$ and $Y(t)$ as a function of lag. Economists also search for a *lead time* between $X(t)$ and $Y(t)$; for example, wholesale prices are a lead indicator of retail prices. The equation which makes the prediction between $X(t)$ and $Y(t)$ is called a *transfer function*. An example of a transfer function would be

$$Y(t) = v_0 X(t-b) + v_1 X(t-b-1) + \ldots + v_r X(t-b-r) + e_t,$$

where the v_j's are weights called the *impulse response function*, b is the *lead time,* and e_t is uncorrelated error.[4] Figure 5 illustrates this relationship. Because the mathematics of estimating the impulse response function is not well known, it is presented in an appendix to this chapter. The impulse response function tells us precisely how the series $X(t)$, at each lag, predicts the series $Y(t)$.

For example, if we try to predict a mother's stimulation of her infant from the proportion of time her infant's eyes are open in a particular time block, we might obtain the impulse response in Figure 6. This figure is interpreted as follows. For five lags there is essentially no predictability between the proportion of time the infant's eyes are open and his mother's stimulation. For the four lags after lag 5, the proportion of time the infant has his eyes open positively and strongly predicts the amount of mother stimulation. After lag 9 the relationship declines exponentially. In other words, if the infant spends a high proportion of his time with eyes open, we can predict that after

---

4. We may have to difference the input series $X(t)$ d times to obtain a stationary series. A first difference ($d = 1$) of $X(t)$ is $\nabla X(t)$ = $X(t) - X(t-1)$ and is used to eliminate linear trend. In the linear transfer function we assume that the series $X(t)$ has been differenced until it oscillates about a fixed mean level.

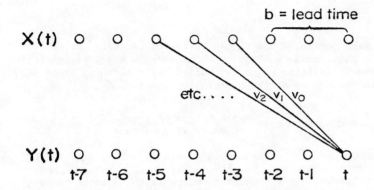

FIGURE 5.   The structure of transfer function analysis showing impulse response function $[V_i]$.

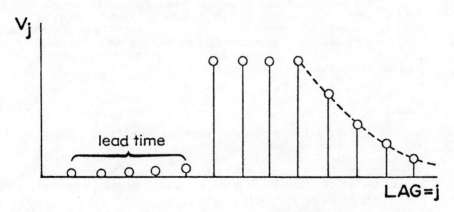

FIGURE 6.   Impulse response function for mother-infant example.

five lags, the mother will begin stimulating, and then stop.[5] An alternative transfer function equation that might be important would first subtract some part of Y(t) that is predictable from its own past, and then attempt to account for variation in the residual with the past values of X(t).

CROSS-SPECTRAL ANALYSIS

Two time series, X and Y, can be correlated with one another at various lags and an analogue with regression analysis can be constructed by defining a quality called the *coherence,* which is similar to the square of the correlation coefficient,

$$R^2 = \text{Coherence} = \frac{\left| \text{cross-spectrum of Y with X} \right|^2}{(\text{Spectrum of Y})\ (\text{Spectrum of X})}$$

We mentioned that the spectrum of a series is a function, called the Fourier transform, of the autocovariance of a series,[6] and it can also be shown that the cross-spectrum is the Fourier transform of the cross-covariance between the series. The Fourier transform is an important function in cross-spectral time-series analysis.

After the data of one series are used to predict the data of the other series, a residual series will be obtained, and if the prediction is good this residual should be white noise, which, like white light, will have a constant spectrum (i.e., be equal at all frequencies).

Either the coherence or the cross-amplitude spectrum can be used to study the strength of association in the two series at different component frequencies. The cross spectrum is the Fourier transform of the cross covariance function, and it is composed of two terms, the cross amplitude spectrum and the phase spectrum. Jenkins and Watts (1968) wrote,

---

5. For a description of computer programs for transfer function analysis see Box and Jenkins (1970), pp. 509-516.

A more efficient solution by a simple process called "prewhitening the input" would occupy too much space here because the preliminaries of time-series modeling using the shift operator would have to be presented.

6. The sample spectrum is the Fourier transform of the sample autocovariance function. The Fourier transform of the autocovariance of a series is given by the expression

$$\text{Spectrum } [w] = \int_{-T}^{T} \text{AUTOCOV } [u]\ e^{-2\pi i w u} du,$$

where $-\infty \leq w \leq \infty$ and $i = \sqrt{-1}$. See Jenkins and Watts (1968, pp. 213-216)

The cross amplitude spectrum shows whether frequency
components in one series are associated with large or
small amplitudes at the same frequency in the other
series. Similarly, the phase spectrum shows whether
frequency components in one series lag or lead the
components at the same frequency in the other series.
(p. 341)

The phase spectrum can thus be used to analyze which series leads
at a particular frequency. For one example of a physical meaning
of the phase spectrum, Gottman (in press) defined dominance in
marital interaction in terms of differentials in prediction of
one series from another. He wrote,

In a dyad, if B's future behavior is more predictable
from A's past behavior than conversely, then A is said
to be dominant. (Italics removed)

In this application the phase spectrum is used to operationalize
the concept of dominance, but it may have different meanings
depending on the variables and the research context.

INTERPRETATION OF THE PHASE SPECTRUM

This chapter will discuss one fairly general case of the phase
spectrum. Granger and Hatanaka (1964) suggested that the phase
spectrum be examined for trend, which would suggest a time lag (or
lead) equal to the *slope* of the regression line. If there is a
quadratic component in the phase spectrum, this would imply differential lead-lag relationships as a function of frequency. For
example, if the trend is positive but steeper at lower frequencies,
this would suggest that one member of the dyad responds more rapidly
to fast changes in the other member than to slow changes (since the
slope of the regression line equals the time lag or lead). A negative slope indicates that the second series lags (rather than leads)
the first series.[7] Granger and Hatanaka (1964) suggested using
every other point of the phase spectrum in the regression analysis
since neighboring values are strongly autocorrelated.

---

7. If the regression line varies about a nonzero constant, the
relationship is called a *fixed angle lag* by Granger and Hatanaka
(1964), which means that the *time* of the lag is the constant
divided by the frequency, i.e., high lags for low frequencies and
low lags for high frequencies.

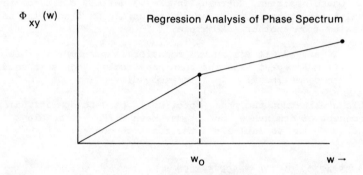

$\Phi_{xy}(w)$ Regression Analysis of Phase Spectrum

w_O $w \rightarrow$

FIGURE 7.   Phase spectrum showing different lead-lag
relationship at two frequency bands.

EXAMPLES: COHERENCE

Figure 8 is a plot of the coherence of both couples 27 and
29.   Note that, in addition to the peak of the coherence at zero,
there is an additional peak for the coherence of couple 27 at
around lag 10.   Frequency and lags are strongly related, so to
understand this idea visually, lagging one series ten floor shifts
should line up some peaks and valleys in the two series.   Note
that the coherence for the data of couple 29 show repeated peaks
in the coherence about every six floor shifts.   To understand this,
note that in Figure 3 at around floor shift 35, the wife is
dropping in positivity while her husband is rising; they seem
slightly out of phase by about six floor shifts.

This analysis of the covariation between two time series is
completed by an examination of the spectral density of the residuals, which, in the case of both series looks reasonably flat.
Confidence intervals for the coherence are given by Jenkins and
Watts (1968, p. 379 ff).

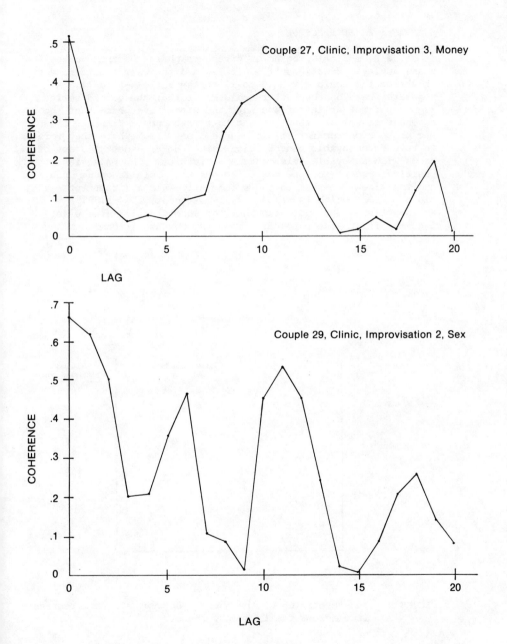

FIGURE 8.   Coherence for Couples 27 and 29.

EXAMPLE - PHASE SPECTRUM

The Biomedical program 2T gives the phase spectrum versus the phase angle in fractions of a circle, and the user should convert this from the scale given (0 to 1) to the scale ($-\pi$ to π). A negative phase on the latter scale means that the second series lags the first at that frequency, and a positive phase that the second series leads the first at that frequency. Figure 9 shows the phase spectrum for clinic couple 3 on a task where they were to have an enjoyable conversation using the "fun deck," a set of cards with enjoyable leisure time activities. The phase is positive, except for one point, across the whole frequency range, and the linear regression shows a negative slope (intercept - .95, slope - -.02) which is marginally significant, $t = -1.89$, $p < .10$. The negative slope indicates that the second series (the wife) lags the first (the husband). Thus the husband is dominant in this interaction.

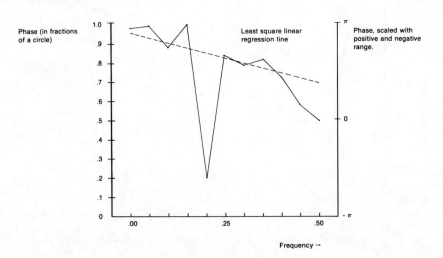

FIGURE 9. Interpretation of the phase spectrum using the regression line across the frequency range.

CONCLUSION

This chapter has focused on the analyses of the relationships between two time series. Transfer function analysis was suggested as one method in the time domain. In the frequency domain, spectral analysis of two time-series was suggested in this chapter for three purposes: To obtain an index of the predictability of one series from another using the coherence, to study the cyclicity of each series using the spectral density function, and to study lead-lag relationships using the phase spectrum.

Each investigator will have to discover his or her own physical interpretations of the analyses presented in this chapter. Dominance was given as one example of lead-lag relationships using the phase spectrum. However, interpretations of time-series statistics are by no means automatic, any more than it would be possible to suggest one physical interpretation for an F-ratio or a regression coefficient. Specific interpretations are as varied as the applications of the analyses and the imaginations of researchers. It was the intention of this chapter to stimulate the use of time-series analysis of observational data so that, with our collective imaginations, we will all eventually learn what these methods can teach us about social interaction.

REFERENCES

Anderson, O. D. *Time-series analysis and forecasting: The Box-Jenkins approach.* London: Butterworths, 1975.

Bartlett, M. S. Smoothing periodograms from time series with continuous spectra. *Nature,* 1948, *161,* 686-687.

Box, G. E. P., & Jenkins, G. M. *Time-series analysis: Forecasting and control.* San Francisco: Holden-Day, 1970.

Brazelton, T. B., Koslowski, B., & Main, M. The origins of reciprocity: The early mother-infant interaction. In M. Lewis & L. A. Rosenblum (Eds.), *The effect of the infant on its caregiver.* New York: Wiley, 1974.

Dixon, W. J. (Ed.) *Biomedical computer programs.* Berkeley: University of California Press, 1974.

Glass, G. V., Willson, V. L., & Gottman, J. M. *Design and analysis of time-series experiments.* Boulder: Colorado University Associated Press, 1975.

Gottman, J. M. *Experimental investigations of marital interaction.* New York: Academic Press, in press.

Gottman, J. M., & Glass, G. V. Analysis of interrupted time-series experiments. In T. Kratochwill (Ed.), *Strategies to evaluate change in single subject research.* New York: Academic Press, 1978.

Gottman, J., Markman, H., & Notarius, C. The topography of marital conflicts: A study of verbal and nonverbal behavior. *Journal of Marriage and the Family,* 1977, *39,* 461-477.

Gowar, N. W., & Baker, J. E. *Fourier series.* London: Chatto & Windus, 1974. Distributed in USA by Crane, Russak & Co., 347 Madison Ave., New York, N. Y. 10017.

Granger, C. W. J., & Hatanaka, M. *Spectral analysis of economic time series.* Princeton, N. J.: Princeton University Press, 1964.

Jenkins, G. M. General considerations in the analysis of spectra. In E. Parzen (Ed.), *Time-series analysis papers.* San Francisco: Holden-Day, 1967.

Jenkins, G. M., & Watts, D. G. *Spectral analysis and its applications.* San Francisco: Holden-Day, 1968.

Mishler, & Waxler, N. E. The sequential patterning of interaction in normal and schizophrenic families. *Family Process,* 1975, *14,* 17-50.

Rubin, M. E. Differences between distressed and nondistressed couples in verbal and nonverbal communication codes. Unpublished doctoral dissertation, Indiana University, Bloomington, Indiana, 1977.

Schuster, A. On the investigation of hidden periodicities with application to a supposed 26 day period of meteorological phenomena. *Terr. Magn.,* 1898, *3,* 13-41.

Tronick, E., Als, H., & Brazelton, T. B. Mutuality in mother-infant interaction. *Journal of Communication,* 1977, *7,* 74-79.

Tukey, J. W. An introduction to the calculations of numerical spectrum analysis. In B. Harris (Ed.), *Advanced seminar on spectral analysis of time-series.* New York: Wiley, 1967.

Wills, T. A., Weiss, R. L., & Patterson, G. R. A behavioral analysis of the determinants of marital satisfaction. *Journal of Consulting and Clinical Psychology,* 1974, *42,* 802-811.

Whittaker, E. T., & Robinson, G. *The calculus of observations.* London: Methuen, 1924.

APPENDIX 1:   TIME-SERIES ANALYSIS

A transfer function model suggested by Box and Jenkins (1970) is

$$Y_t - S_1 Y_{t-1} - \ldots - S_r Y_{t-r} = w_0 X_{t-b} - \ldots - w_s X_{t-b-s} + N_t$$

In words this ways that the part of Y(t) which is not predictable from the past history of Y(t) is predictable from the past history of X(t), lagged *b* time units to within a white noise process, N_t. Another way of expressing this is to say that X(t) is a lead indicator of the unpredicted part of Y(t).

Solution of the problem of estimating the parameters of the transfer function model proceeds by defining the sample cross-covariance function,

$$C_{xy}(k) = \frac{1}{n} \sum_{t=1}^{n-k} (X_t - \overline{X})(y_{t+k} - \overline{y})$$

Note that $C_{xy}(k) = C_{yx}(-k)$. The sample cross-correlation function is

$$r_{xy}(k) = C_{xy}(k)/_{S_x S_y}$$

Suppose that the linear transfer function can be written as

$$Y_t = v_0 x_t + v_1 x_{t-1} + \ldots + m_t,$$

where y_t, x_t, and m_t are stationary processes with zero means. Multiply the equation above by x_{t-k} for $k \geq 0$:

$$x_{t-k} y_t = v_0 x_{t-k} x_t + v_1 x_{t-k} x_{t-1} + \ldots + x_{t-k} m_t.$$

If we assume that x_{t-k} is uncorrelated with m_t for all *k*, and take expectations of both sides, we obtain the set of equations

$$\gamma_{xy}(k) = v_0 \gamma_{xx}(k) + v_1 \gamma_{xx}(k-1) + \ldots; \quad k = 0, 1, 2, \ldots$$

If the V_j weights are effectively zero after k = M, the equations can be written

$$\vec{\gamma}_{xy} = \Gamma_{xx} \vec{v} \quad \text{where}$$

$$\Gamma_{xx} = \begin{bmatrix} \gamma_{xx}(0) & \gamma_{xx}(1) & \ldots & \gamma_{xx}(M) \\ \gamma_{xx}(1) & \gamma_{xx}(0) & \cdots & \gamma_{xx}(M-1) \\ \vdots & \vdots & & \\ \gamma_{xx}(M) & \gamma_{xx}(M-1) & \ldots & \gamma_{xx}(0) \end{bmatrix}$$

$$
\vec{\gamma}_{xy} =
\begin{bmatrix}
\gamma_{xy}(0) \\
\gamma_{xy}(1) \\
\cdot \\
\cdot \\
\cdot \\
\gamma_{xy}(M)
\end{bmatrix}
\qquad
\vec{v} =
\begin{bmatrix}
v_0 \\
v_1 \\
\cdot \\
\cdot \\
\cdot \\
v_M
\end{bmatrix}
$$

Substituting the estimates $r_{xx}(k)$ of the autocorrelation function of the input and estimates $r_{xy}(k)$ of the cross-correlation function provides $M + 1$ equations for $M + 1$ weights.

APPENDIX 2:   TIME-SERIES ANALYSIS

Spectral analysis of time series is concerned with the study of a series in terms of its frequency content. The focus is on the oscillations that add together to generate the observed time series. Spectral analysis is a generalization of Fourier analysis to non-deterministic (i.e., stochastic) data. Any time-series, f(t) with period (which satisfies the Dirichlet conditions) can be approximated as closely as is desired as a linear combination of sine and cosine functions

$$f_N(t) = \sum_{n=0}^{N} \{A_n \cos(n \frac{2\pi}{\theta} t) + B_n \sin(n \frac{2\pi}{\theta} t)\}$$

In least square approximation we want

$$\int_0^\theta \{f(t) - f_N(t)\}^2 \, dt$$

to be a minimum, and this makes it possible to solve for the A_n and B_n as

$$A_o = \frac{1}{\theta} \int_0^\theta f(t) \, dt \qquad\qquad B_o = 0$$

$$A_n = \frac{2}{\theta} \int_0^\theta f(t) \, \cos\, (n \frac{2\pi}{\theta} t) \, dt, \; n > 0$$

$$B_n = \frac{2}{\theta} \int_0^\theta f(t) \, \sin\, (n \frac{2\pi}{\theta} t) \, dt, \; n > 0$$

The coefficients A_n and B_n do not depend on N. This is the Fourier series expansion of the time series f(t).

The amount of the total variance of the series contributed by each frequency in the Fourier expansion is simply

$$(1/2) \; (A_n^2 + B_n^2),$$

and a plot of this function with respect to the frequency

$$n \frac{2\pi}{\theta} = w$$

is called the sprectral density function. In the deterministic case when f(t) is exactly composed of a finite number of frequencies, the periodogram will have peaks at each frequency just as a line spectrum would if light were composed of only a finite set of wave lengths mixed together. The analogy breaks down for statistical time-series in which the observed series is assumed to be one realization from a population.

11.
Conceptualizing and quantifying influence patterns in the family triad

ROSS D. PARKE, THOMAS G. POWER, & JOHN M. GOTTMAN

A recent trend in early socialization research is the study of the infant's development in the family context. In contrast to the earlier emphasis placed on the mother-infant relationship (Bowlby, 1951; Ainsworth, 1973) and to more recent work on father-infant interaction (Parke & Sawin, 1976; Parke, 1978c; Kotelchuck, 1976; Lamb, 1976a), the importance of studying the family as a socializing unit is finally being recognized (Parke, O'Leary, & West, 1972; Parke & O'Leary, 1976; Pedersen, 1975; Lamb, 1976b; Pedersen et al., 1977; Clarke-Stewart, 1977). This realization, however, brings with it a host of methodological and conceptual problems. As opposed to the study of the parent-infant dyad, the study of the family involves the conceptualization and quantification of a myriad of direct and indirect influences individuals have on one another in this interacting system. The purpose of this paper is to offer a conceptual framework for understanding these influences and to illustrate ways in which these influences can be quantified.

CONCEPTUALIZING INFLUENCES IN THE FAMILY TRIAD

This section offers a scheme for conceptualizing direct and indirect influences in the family unit. As the number of influences increases geometrically with the addition of family members, only the mother-father-infant triad will be considered here. In addition, as this paper is concerned with family dynamics *within* the triad, the role of the wider social networks in which families are embedded will not be considered. Reviews of this topic are available elsewhere (Bronfenbrenner, 1977).

Certain assumptions underlie our conceptual scheme. First,

231

it is assumed that all members of the family triad can influence
each other. In contrast to more traditional formulations, most
modern theorists assume that infants and children play an active
role in modifying the adults in the family (Bell, 1968, 1974).
The relative degree of influence that any member of the triad
exerts on other members will vary with the task, the context, the
developmental status of the infant/child and a host of attitudinal
and prior history variables that each participant brings to the
triadic interactional setting.

Second, it is assumed that triadic interaction can be
conceptualized not merely as face-to-face interaction, but also
as interaction that takes place in the absence of one of the
members of the triad. Implicit in this assumption is the concept
that social control can be exerted through earlier interaction
patterns.

Third, it is assumed that a variety of data sources can
usefully be employed in understanding triadic interaction (Parke,
1978a). Direct behavioral observations represent only one source
of data. Other sources, such as interviews and questionnaires
that serve to tap attitudes and expectations of the interactors
are also useful. Underlying this assumption is a cognitive
mediational model of human social interaction, which posits that
parents and children bring cognitive sets to an interaction setting
which serve as filters through which objective behaviors of the
other participants are processed (Parke, 1978b).

Fourth, it is assumed that individuals within a triad can
serve either as initiators or recipients of any action. Fifth,
it is assumed that two types of influence can be distinguished--
direct and indirect. By direct influence, we mean the process
by which one individual influences another by directly acting on
the other. In contrast, indirect influence refers to the process
whereby one person influences another through the mediation of
another person.

To represent the various influences that occur in triadic
interaction contexts is the aim of the model diagrammed in Figure
1. In the figure, the letters A, B, and C represent members of
the triad. A is the individual whose influence is being studied,
while B and C are the other two members of the triad. By calling
each of the three family members A, three such "trees" of direct
and indirect influences can be generated (one for each family
member). One of these trees (the tree representing the influences
of the father) is worked out in Figure 2. Four types of influences
are illustrated in these trees: dyadic or direct, transitive,
circular, and parallel influences. In addition, four steps or
agents are also identified: influence source, primary recipient,
secondary influence source and secondary recipient. Each of these
terms will be considered below.

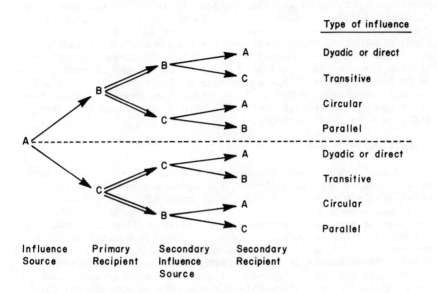

				Type of influence

FIGURE 1.   General Model of Influence Patterns.

CATEGORIES OF INFLUENCE

Dyadic or Direct Influences

Inspection of Figure 1 shows that there are two paths of
direct influence. These can be represented by two expressions:
$A \to B \rightleftarrows B \to A$ and $A \to C \rightleftarrows C \to A$. Before these paths are
considered, however, the expressions themselves require some
explanation. The single arrows in these expressions represent
behaviors or cognitions involving or directed at another individual.
For instance, $F \to I$ could represent a father's attitude toward his
infant, an observable behavior directed toward his infant (such as
a kiss) or even a style of interaction with his infant that is a
product of a long period of interaction. The double arrows point
to the consequences of such relationships. So, the case: $A \to B \rightleftarrows$
$B \to A$ represents a situation where the consequence of person A's
actions or attitudes toward person B is an action or attitude of
person B directed back to person A. For simplicity of communication

of these patterns, the individual's involved in these paths of
influence are given names that represent their respective position
in the paths. Person A is referred to as the *influence source,* the
person who is the direct recipient of A's behavior or attitudes is
called the *primary recipient,* the person who initiates the consequent
of the A → primary recipient relationship is called the *secondary
influence source* and finally, the ultimate influence recipient is
called the *secondary recipient.* With these definitions in mind,
then, direct influences represent the case where the influence
source is also the secondary recipient and the primary recipient
is also the secondary influence source. An example of such a dyadic
or direct influence is the case where a mother smiles at her infant
and her infant smiles back. Also notice that person A within the
triad can have direct influences on both B and C, and that these
influences are bidirectional.

Transitive Influences

     Transitive influences represent the case where A has an influence
on a member of the triad through the remaining individual in the
triad (Lewis & Weinraub, 1976). This represents the situation
where one member of the triad is the influence source, another is
both the primary recipient and the secondary influence source and
the third is the secondary recipient. Figure 1 shows that there
are two paths of transitive influence: A → B ⇄ B → C and A → C ⇄
C → B. Transitivity is possible with either of the remaining
individuals serving as secondary influence source or recipient.
An example of a transitive relationship is a case where the father
kisses the mother and the mother then nuzzles the infant.

Circular Influences

     Circular influences represent the case where A is both the
influence source and the secondary recipient and the primary
recipient and the secondary influence source are the other two
members of the triad. As in all other cases, there are two possible
paths of influence: A → B ⇄ C → A and A → C ⇄ B → A. An example
of a circular influence would be as follows: father tickles the
infant, who in turn vocalizes and then mother smiles at the father.

Parallel Influences

     Parallel influences occur when the primary and secondary
recipient are the same person and the remaining two individuals are
the influence source and the secondary influence source. The
simplest case of such a relationship is when the secondary influence
source models the influence source's behavior. For example, father
(influence source) tickles the infant (primary recipient) and then
mother (secondary influence source) imitates this behavior by
tickling the infant (secondary recipient). Although parallel
influences occur only when two individuals direct their behavior

toward the same person, this does not necessarily imply modeling.
For example, maternal compensation on the part of a mother whose
husband interacts little with the infant is also an example of a
parallel influence. As before there are two possible paths of
parallel influence: $A \rightarrow B \stackrel{\rightarrow}{\leftarrow} C \rightarrow B$ and $A \rightarrow C \stackrel{\rightarrow}{\leftarrow} B \rightarrow C$.

SOME GENERAL COMMENTS

Before illustrating the utility of this classification scheme
by going through a detailed example, a few general comments need to
be made. First, this scheme cannot classify all influences. Family
members' perceptions of the family as a unit (van der Veen, 1965)
and perceptions of relationships between two family members (for
example, the father's perception of the mother-infant relationship)
do not fit well into this scheme. This weakness is a function of
the classification scheme's emphasis on pairs of dyads within the
triad. Although a scheme consisting of triads and dyads is a
possibility, the representation gained would probably not justify
the resulting complexity. In addition, it is likely that only a
very small proportion of the multitude of influences derived through
such a system would be theoretically meaningful. Finally, most
relationships defined by such a system can, through slight modification, fit the dyadic model. For example, the latter perception
described above could be redefined as the husband's perception of
how good the mother is with the baby or *how good the baby is* when
with the mother.
A second point to be made about this system is that the nature
of the trees is quite different when different individuals are
defined as A. As mentioned earlier, mothers, fathers and infants
come into interaction situations with a diversity of backgrounds
and abilities. As this is the case, one must not assume that since
Figure 1 represents a general case, that the constitution of specific
cases are identical. Although the *direction* of certain influences
may be similar, this does not imply that other aspects of these
relationships share this commonality.
Finally, this system should not be thought of as a static one,
for as the infant and family develop, the importance of certain
influences will inevitably change.

DIRECT AND INDIRECT EFFECTS OF FATHERS:
AN EXAMPLE OF THE CLASSIFICATION SCHEME IN USE

In order to demonstrate the utility of the scheme for generating and conceptualizing triadic influences, a detailed example of
its use will be provided here. The example is chosen to demonstrate
that the kinds of influences defined by the proposed system do relate
to common patterns of influence under naturalistic conditions. The
direct and indirect influences of fathers on their infants and spouses
will be considered in this example. Underlying the choice of this

example was the assumption that, at least in traditional families, one would expect the indirect effects of the father to be more potent than those of the mother as the father has less time for direct interaction with his infant (Pedersen, et al., 1975). These influences are illustrated in Figure 2. All four kinds of influence (direct, transitive, circular, and parallel) will be considered separately for two cases. These influences will be considered for the case where the primary recipient is the infant (above the dotted line in Figure 2) and when the primary recipient is the mother (below the dotted line). In each case, examples of these influences will be offered either from the literature or from our own experience. We have also tried in each case to cite examples that represent a range of data sources including observable behavior, interaction history and cognitions (attitudes, expectations, etc.). When offering examples, those that deal with observable behavior will be considered first, followed by those involving prior interaction history and cognitions.

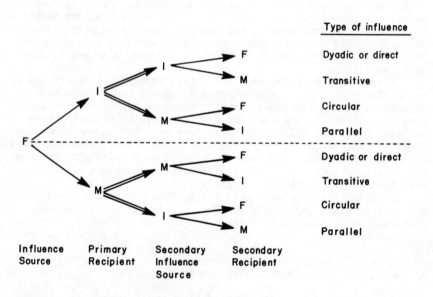

FIGURE 2. Model of Father Influences.

Influences: Mother as Primary Recipient

Dyadic or Direct Influences. This section deals with influences
of the father that are a consequent of the father's relationship or
interactions with the mother. Direct or dyadic influences will be
considered first. These influences are symbolized in the following
way: $F \rightarrow M \overset{\rightarrow}{\leftarrow} M \rightarrow F$. To understand the uniqueness of these dyadic
influences in a triadic context, a strategy of comparing the M-F
dyadic interaction alone (dyad) and in the presence of a third party,
such as a child (triad) has been frequently employed in recent
investigations (Lamb, 1976b; Parke & O'Leary, 1976; Rosenblatt, 1974).
The dyadic interaction patterns between spouses show systematic shifts
across dyadic and triadic contexts with the amount of social interaction decreasing in the presence of a third person. In a recent
observational study of couples interacting in a variety of settings
(shopping malls, the zoo, cemeteries, a university, etc.), Rosenblatt
(1974) found that adults accompanied by children were less likely to
touch, talk, or smile at each other than were couples unaccompanied
by children.

When comparing the dyad across these two contexts, not only does
the *amount* of social interaction change, but the type of social behavior is probably altered as well. The type of conversation topics,
the degree of physical intimacy and the complexity of the verbal
interactions would all be modified in the presence of a child. Just
as Shatz and Gelman (1973) demonstrated that adult→child speech shifts
in complexity to suit the developmental status of the child, a parallel
effect for adult→adult speech may occur when the child is a bystander
in a triadic context. Systematic examination of the role that children of different ages play in modifying adult-adult interaction would
not only increase our understanding of the role of situational factors
in adult dyadic interaction, but would contribute to our knowledge of
children's influence on adult behavior as well.

Transitive Influences. Transitive influences of the father
through the mother are illustrated in the following way: $F \rightarrow M \overset{\rightarrow}{\leftarrow} M \rightarrow$
I. Most of the research on indirect father effects concerns this
relationship. In fact, the early literature on the role of the father
in infant development (Bowlby, 1951) suggested that the father's primary role in infancy was a transitive one:

> "While continual reference will be made to the mother-
> child relation, little will be said of the father-child
> relation; his value as the economic and social support of
> the mother will be assumed" (Bowlby, 1951, p. 13).

The supportive role of the father probably begins during pregnancy or possibly even during the earlier planning stages when the
explicit decisions concerning the desirability of children are being
made. Although the literature is surprisingly silent on these
issues, some relevant speculations and a few findings can be offered.
For instance, the extent to which the father has been supportive of
his wife during pregnancy, labor and delivery and in the immediate
post-partum hospital period would probably determine the ease with

which women adjust to this new mothering role. In a relevant study,
Shereshefsky and Yarrow (1973) found positive relationships between
the wife's successful adaptation to pregnancy and the husband's
responsiveness to the wife's pregnancy. Similarly, husband support
during labor and delivery lessens maternal distress (Anderson &
Standley, 1976; Hennenborn & Cogan, 1975; cf. Macfarlane, 1977).
Finally, one would expect on the basis of observations of family
interaction in the early post-partum period (Parke & O'Leary, 1976)
that "post-partum blues"--a condition suffered by two-thirds of all
post-parturitional women (Yalmon, 1968) might be lessened by the
presence of a supportive other such as a husband or relative. In
addition, as Feiring and Taylor (1978) recently demonstrated, high
maternal-infant involvement was positively related to the mother's
perception of support from a secondary parent--in this study, 67%
of these secondary parents were fathers.

Support can, of course, take a variety of forms, including
direct instructions concerning appropriate caregiving or play,
making salient certain aspects of the infant's behavior and by
offering direct physical assistance in the execution of caretaking,
such as helping mother change diapers or feed. While support can
be provided directly in a face-to-face triadic context, the father
can also provide support by assuming responsibility for infant care
as well. More generally, the amount of caretaking responsibility
taken on by the father would influence to a great deal the number
and nature of opportunities the mother has with her infant. By
having the father relieve the mother of some of these routine
responsibilities, the quality of mother-infant interaction might
improve by permitting more time for playful and other non-caretaking
activities.

Economic support is another way that the father may influence
the mother-infant relationship. In addition to influencing the
mother's feelings of economic security and determining to a large
degree the nature of the mother's environment, the father's occupation also determines the amount and nature of the time he has available for his infant. As both the availability of time for leisure
(Orthner, 1975) and the nature of the shift that a father works
(Moore, 1963; Luce, 1973) appear to be related to measures of
family functioning, the father's work schedule seems to be an
important variable to consider. Other work-related factors include
the nature of the job in terms of person-orientation (Hurley &
Hohn, 1971) and organizational stress (Renshaw, 1976). Hurley and
Hohn (1971), when comparing responses to a child-rearing question-
naire taken in college and then approximately 6 years later, found
that male college graduates that went into person-oriented professions
(teacher, parole officer, social worker, etc.) increased less on
manifest rejection scores, but decreased more on overprotection
scores than those who went into more impersonal occupations (govern-
mental workers, policemen, attorneys, etc.). Renshaw's (1976) data,
demonstrated that different kinds of organizational stress (international transfer, extensive travel, and job change) were related
to measures of family functioning. These studies suggest that a
number of facets of the father's occupation could, in a variety of

ways, influence the mother's interaction with her infant; through the amount and nature of time for interaction, through the amount of economic and environmental support available, through the transmission of work-influenced child-rearing attitudes, and through factors surrounding job transfer.

The quality of the husband-wife relationship may affect the mother-infant relationship. Several studies have shown that measures of husband-wife relationships are related to measures of mother-infant or mother-child behavior. Johnson and Lobitz (1974b) found a negative relationship between marital satisfaction and parent negativeness while Pedersen (1975), for families of male infants, found a negative relationship between tension-conflict in the marriage and the mother's feeding competence. Similarly, Pedersen et al. (1977) found a positive relationship between fathers' verbal-criticism-blame directed at their wives and mother-infant negative affect.

The extent to which there is consensus between husband and wife concerning child-rearing, may, in turn, alter mother-offspring interaction patterns. For example, Feldman (1971) found that consensus between husband and wife on child-rearing attitudes was more significantly related to marital satisfaction than was consensus about the wife's career orientation. If indeed, marital satisfaction is related to mother-infant interaction patterns, then it follows the husband-wife disagreements about caretaking practices are an important example of an indirect influence. Moreover, discrepancies in the ways in which parents perceive their infant may alter their interactions with their infants. In a recent study, Pedersen et al. (1977) secured independent maternal and paternal characterizations of their infant and found that the degree of discrepancy between mother and father was positively related to negative affect displayed by the mother toward her infant in a dyadic interaction session. Although these data are correlational, and the direction of the effect is not clear, one explanation for this result is that the mother's negativeness toward her infant is a consequence of earlier disagreements with the husband about the infant's characteristics.

Discrepancies in attitudes toward infants and child-care are only one type of husband-wife discrepancy. Another recently documented way in which husband-wife discrepancies can alter parent-infant relationships is the bio-rhythms of the parents--as expressed by the "nightness" or "morningness" of family members. Cromwell et al. (1976) compared the family lives of "matched" and "mismatched" couples in this regard. In general, mismatched couples tend to have more marital problems than matched couples. Although it is not clear what is the cause and effect of this relationship, generalization to the cause of father effects in infancy is possible. A father's "nightness" or "morningness" could influence mother-infant interaction in a number of ways. A "morning" father may not climb out of bed for a midnight feeding, while a "night" father will rarely give his infant cereal in the morning. In addition, if a father's time schedule is mismatched with his infant's, it is likely that the mother will do a large proportion of the caregiving.

Another transitive influence to be considered involves the husband's perceptions of the mother's competence as a parent. These perceptions can be transmitted to the mother in subtle ways, thus influencing mother-infant interaction. One example of such a relationship has been reported by Pedersen (1975) who found that the father's esteem for the wife as mother was significantly related to the mother's feeding competence in an observation of the mother-infant dyad.

Finally, child-rearing attitudes are affected by the presence or absence of the spouse. This influence can occur in a variety of ways. Husbands can reinforce their own views whenever their wives may appear to follow them (Marsella, Dubanonski & Mohs, 1974) or the father's very presence can influence their wives to act in a certain way (Marsella et al., 1974; Putney & Middleton, 1960). At least two studies offer interesting illustrations of this latter case (Marsella et al., 1974; Putney & Middleton, 1960). In one study (Putney & Middleton, 1960), married couples were more strict in their answers to child-rearing questionnaires when they filled them out together (rather than alone). The second study (Marsella et al., 1974), a study of wives of nuclear submarine personnel whose husbands were at sea and at home for 3 months shifts, found that maternal child-rearing attitudes reflected more maternal domination during the periods their husbands were at home. Both of these studies suggest that the father's presence is associated with stricter child-rearing practices on the part of the mother. These results are consistent with both of the views suggested above. Fathers could be selectively reinforcing their child-rearing attitudes in their wives and their wives would most likely show similar views when the father is around (stimulus control).

In summary, there exists a sizable number of ways in which fathers can have indirect influences on their infant's development in a transitive way through the mother. These influences operate through information exchanged with the mother, the father's occupation, his physical support of the mother, his disagreements with her concerning a number of infant and non-infant related topics, his perceptions of the mother and through the nature of the husband-wife relationship in general.

Circular Influences. Circular influences of the father with the mother as the primary recipient and the infant as the secondary influence source are illustrated in the following way: $F \rightarrow M \not\rightleftharpoons I \rightarrow F$. Examples of this kind of influence are not as plentiful as examples of the previously discussed influences, especially in the infancy period. These influences do, however, become more important as the child grows older and develops greater representational abilities (Lewis & Weinraub, 1976). Hetherington's (1967) finding that boys in mother-dominant families are more likely to imitate their mothers than their fathers is an example of a circular influence ($M \rightarrow F \not\rightleftharpoons I \rightarrow M$) in families of older children. There are, however, a few examples of such processes in families of infants, and these will be considered below.

One example of a circular influence that can be observed in interaction sessions occurs in the case where a father in the family

triad talks to his wife and the infant responds to the sound of
the father's voice by smiling at the father. Another example can
be found in families with traditional caretaking allocations. In
this situation, the father may have arranged for the mother to do
most of the caretaking, so when the father actually does participate in the caretaking of the infant, his infant responds
more intently as he is a novel stimulus (Pedersen et al., 1975).

A final example is where a father's perception of his wife as
a poor playmate for the infant is communicated to the mother,
thereby reducing her confidence when playing with the infant.
In this situation, the infant may come to prefer playing with
the father, thus completing the circle.

Parallel Influences. Parallel influences of the father with
the mother as primary and secondary recipient and the infant as
secondary influence source are illustrated in this way: $F \rightarrow M \rightleftarrows I \rightarrow$
M. As in the case of circular influence, this pattern of influence
is generally found in families of older children. Examples of
such influences are when a child might compensate for his/her
father's poor treatment of the mother by treating the mother with
special kindness, and the finding that a child's perceptions of
his/her mother's satisfaction with his/her performance is related
to the marital integration of the parents (Farber, 1962). Examples
of parallel influences in families of infants include the situation
in which a father's gaze at the mother might influence the infant
to also look at the mother, or in the case where the father shows
the mother a new way of playing with the baby so that the infant
becomes more responsive to the mother in later play sessions.

Influences: Infant as Primary Recipient

Dyadic or Direct Influences. This section deals with influences
of the father that are a consequent of the father's relationship
or interaction with his infant. As before, direct or dyadic
influences will be considered first. These influences are symbolized
in the following way: $F \rightarrow I \rightleftarrows I \rightarrow F$. As was the case with the
father-mother dyad, this dyad needs to be considered both alone and
in the family triad. Two studies have shown differences between
father-infant interaction in these two social contexts (Parke &
O'Leary, 1976; Lamb, 1976b). Lamb (1976b) found that fathers
interacted with their infants more when in the father-mother-infant
triad, although parents in both situations were told to just
respond to infant initiations. Parke and O'Leary (1976) found
that fathers were more likely to touch and rock infants when alone,
but smiled more at their infants in the mother-father-infant triad.
Although Clarke-Stewart (1977) presents data that suggest that
triadic play situations may be rare in the home environment,
studies of the father-infant dyad in both contexts still appear
to uncover a number of aspects of family functioning. As there
exists a growing literature on the direct effect of fathers in
father-infant interaction that has been reviewed elsewhere (Parke,
1978c) direct effects will be given no further treatment here.

Transitive Influences. Transitive influences of the father

on the mother through the infant are illustrated in the following
way: F → I → I → M. As is the case with many of these paths of
influence, transitive influence through the child become more
important as the child grows older. Examples of this kind of
transitive influence in older children is found in Hetherington's
(1967) paper. Data from her paper that is relevant here is
concisely summarized by Lewis and Weinraub (1976):

> "Others have also emphasized the importance of the father
> in the daughter's acquisition of femininity. According
> to Hetherington (1967) femininity in girls is related
> to the father's approval of the mother as a model as well
> as the father's own masculinity and *his reinforcement of
> the daughter's participation in feminine activities*.
> The mother's femininity is not, however, related to
> the daughter's femininity" (p. 170--emphasis ours).

This excerpt illustrates several important points. First, the
italicized phrase represents the kind of transitivity being
discussed here: transitive effects of the father on the mother
through the child. One should also recognize that another phrase
in the paragraph ("father's approval of the mother as a model")
represents an influence discussed earlier: a parallel influence
of the father with mother as primary and secondary recipient and
the child as secondary influence source (F → M ⇄ I → M). Finally,
the final sentence shows the importance of studying indirect
influences in the family system--the mother's own femininity could
not explain their daughter's femininity (the dyadic influence
pattern), but several indirect influences of the father could.
   There are, however, a few transitive influences that can
operate in families of infants. For instance, a father providing
adequate or inadequate health care for his infant can indirectly
influence infant-mother interaction patterns through his control
over the infant's physical condition. Another example is the case
where the father manipulates the infant's behavior when the mother
is present so that the infant acts a certain way toward its mother.
Although no evidence for this kind of effect is available in the
infant literature, a study by Johnson and Lobitz (1974a) illustrates
similar effects with older children. In order to determine the
amount of control parents have over their children in observation
sessions, twelve families of normal 4 to 6-year-old children were
observed for six 45 minute sessions on six different days. On half
of these days, parents were asked to make their child look good for
the observer and on the other days were asked to make their child
look bad. Results showed that children had significantly higher
deviant behavior scores on the "bad" days than on the "good" days.
As parents can manipulate their children in such a way for an
observer, it is possible that fathers of infants might be able to
show similar manipulation of their infant's behavior when their
wives are present for any of a number of reasons (to cheer their
wives up on a bad day, to convince them that having a baby was a
good idea, etc.).

Although there appears to be no evidence in the infancy literature that directly addresses the issue of paternal control of infant behavior in a triadic situation, some evidence suggests that a father's interaction history with his infant can subsequently influence I → M behavior. A methodology for studying such effects comes from the early study of Rheingold (1956) who provided extra "mothering" for a group of institutionalized children. Later these infants who received the extra social stimulation were more responsive to an adult examiner. An intervention program with fathers offers further support. As part of an intervention program to facilitate infant-father attachment in low interacting father-infant dyads (Zelazo et al., 1977), twelve fathers were given a list of games to play with their infants each evening over a four-week period. A control group of eight low-interacting fathers received no such treatment. One measure of the effectiveness of this program consisted of pre- and post-intervention free play periods for mother, father, and infant in which parents were instructed not to initiate interactions, but to respond naturally to the child's behavior if he or she was distressed or approached them. A non-significant interaction discussed in the paper is relevant here. For the control group, proximity to the mother increased by the post-intervention session, but decreased in the experimental group. This suggests that the change in the father's involvement with their infants indirectly influenced their infants' involvement with their mothers (transitivity). A final example of such an influence pattern (transitive influences through interaction history) includes the case where irritable infant patterns may be reinforced by an impatient father which, in turn, alters the mother's feelings toward the infant.

Circular Influences. Circular influences with the infant as primary recipient and the mother as secondary influence source are represented in the following way: $F \rightarrow I \rightleftharpoons M \rightarrow F$. An instance of this kind of influence observable in interaction is the situation where a mother selectively reinforces subtle father-infant interaction patterns. A more drastic example is where less subtle, destructive father-infant interaction patterns (such as child abuse or neglect) lead the mother to separation or divorce. A less extreme case in the opposite direction is where a father's involvement with his infant might provoke jealousy in the mother leading to problems in the marital relationship.

Parallel Influences. Parallel influences of the father where the infant is both primary and secondary recipient and the mother is the secondary influence source is symbolized as follows: $F \rightarrow I \rightleftharpoons M \rightarrow I$. Examples of this kind of influence include maternal modeling of father-infant interaction styles, or compensation on the part of a mother whose husband interacts little with the infant. Another such influence is the case where the toys a father buys for the infant influences the nature of mother-infant interaction. Finally, Pedersen, Yarrow & Strain (1975) offer a pattern of parallel influence that involves parental emotions:

"If the father feels positively toward the infant, it is
likely that the mother's positive feelings and behaviors
may be enhanced. But at the pathological extreme, one
mother may be jealous of the father's affection for the
child and may be more demanding and harsh in her treatment
of the infant" (p. 3).

Summary and Conclusions. The preceeding section has illustrated
in a rather detailed way, the use of the classification scheme
offered in the first section of this paper. This illustration
points out how this system can generate and classify a wide variety
of influence patterns ranging from influences observable in mother-
father-infant interaction sessions, to influences involving the
family's interaction histories and to those tapping perceptions,
attitudes and other cognitions. Also illustrated is the distinction between direct influences in the dyad and those within the
triad and how the level of the child's development can influence
greatly the types of influences that are found in various family
groups. In fact, a review of this section shows that whenever the
infant acts as the secondary influence source, there are relatively
few indirect influences of the father ($F \rightarrow M \not\rightarrow I \rightarrow F$; $F \rightarrow M \not\rightarrow I \rightarrow M$
and $F \rightarrow I \not\rightarrow I \rightarrow M$). This occurs as the infant has yet to develop
the complex representational abilities that allow influences to
occur in the absence of all three family members. However, these
kinds of influences do occur when all three family members are
present, and to a lesser degree, when one parent is gone primarily
through the processes of stimulus novelty, generalization and
control. Examples of these latter processes include those cases
where the infant responds differentially to the father as he is a
more "novel" stimulus (stimulus novelty - circular influences),
where the infant has developed a certain pattern of interaction
in the father's or mother's presence (stimulus control - circular
influences and parallel influences), and where patterns of interaction that come out of interaction with one parent generalize to
interactions with the other (stimulus-generalization - transitive
influences).

In summary, this section has illustrated a number of features
of the proposed classification scheme: its ability to generate and
classify a wide range of influences, its ability to classify both
direct and indirect influences, and finally its ability to generate
hypotheses about the mechanisms underlying some of these influences.
Examination of some of the influences discussed above also points
out how generation of similar trees for the infant's and mother's
indirect influences would lead to very different sets of relationships.

QUANTIFYING INFLUENCES IN THE FAMILY TRIAD

This section will briefly illustrate how some of the influences
considered in the previous section can be quantified, and how casual
inferences about the direction of such influences can be drawn. As

the kinds of influences discussed above have ranged from those observable in face-to-face interaction sessions to those involving interaction histories and a variety of attitudinal variables this section will be divided into two parts. The first section will be concerned with the analysis of triadic patterns using only observational data, and the second will be concerned with integrating observed triadic patterns with the kinds of non-observational data sources necessary to tap less observable influences.

TRIADIC PATTERNS IN OBSERVATIONAL DATA

Assume that we have an observational coding system with a small number of codes, for example, FV (father vocalizes), FS (father smiles), MV (mother vocalizes), MS (mother smiles), IV (infant vocalizes), and IS (infant smiles). Although it is the case here, there is no need for the same codes to apply to each member of the triad. An observational record will be some string of codes such as:

(FV, IS, FS, IV, MV, IS, MS, IV, . . .)

For a discussion of the various types of such observational data, see Gottman and Bakeman (this volume).

It is possible to analyze the sequential dependencies in these data by applying the techniques of lag-sequence analysis (also discussed in the Gottman and Bakeman chapter). In effect, the conditional probabilities of each code, $p(X/C)$, following a criterion code, C, are compared to the unconditional probabilities of each code, $p(X)$, at each lag from the criterion, using the Z-score statistic described in the Gottman and Bakeman chapter. This produces a table such as Figure 3. Arrows are drawn between codes that are connected by significant lag-one Z-scores. This procedure was used by Gottman, Markman and Notarius (1977) in identifying sequences in marital interaction, but it can also be applied to triads. In Figure 3, three sequences have been identified:

(1) FV → FS → MS → FV
(2) FV → MV → IV → FV
(3) FV → IS

In addition, the conditional starting probabilities of each sequence can also be calculated.

Notice that only one of the above sequences in the interaction is triadic (number (2)). Analysis of this sequence illustrates the way in which such a sequential lag procedure can be used to investigate the kinds of triadic influences discussed earlier. Although this sequence is circular in one sense, (FV → MV → IV → FV), it does not necessarily qualify as a circular influence as discussed earlier in this chapter. As it is not clear who each person in the triad is talking to at what time, the first two acts of this sequence

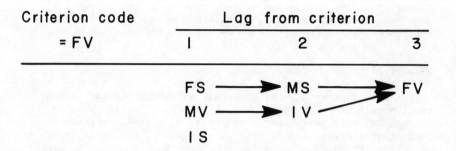

FIGURE 3.   Detecting Patterns in Triadic Interaction. (Significant
       codes listed.)

alone could represent a parallel

$$(F \overset{VOC}{\to} I \not\to M \overset{VOC}{\to} I),$$

a transitive

$$(F \overset{VOC}{\to} M \not\to M \overset{VOC}{\to} I),$$

or a direct

$$(F \overset{VOC}{\to} M \not\to M \overset{VOC}{\to} F)$$

influence. Therefore, a coding system that would adequately
represent such influences would have to identify the recipients
of different acts. One possibility would be to expand the coding
system as follows: FVM (father vocalizes to mother), FVI (father
vocalizes to infant), MVF (mother vocalizes to father), MVI (mother
vocalizes to infant), IVM (infant vocalizes to mother), and IVF
(infant vocalizes to father), with FS, MS, and IS as before. With
this system, the first two acts of sequence (2) could then represent
direct (FVM → MVF), transitive (FVM → MVI), or parallel (FVI → MVI)
influences, but in this case, the type of influence would be explicitl
spelled out. Subsequently, conditional probabilities calculated
at lag-one would identify those particular influence paths most
common in the data.

Analysis beyond lag-one would serve a quite different purpose. As the proposed model of influences is concerned primarily with influences transmitted in pairs of events (e.g., father voc. to infant ⇶ infant voc. to mother), sequential data adequately described by such a model would be characterized by indefinite elements intervening between these pairs. At the indefinite element, conditional probabilities have returned, temporarily for that lag, to unconditional levels (see Gottman & Bakeman, this volume). For example, the sequence: FVM → MVI ⇶ IVF → FVM could be identified if there were an indefinite element intervening at the double arrow. Furthermore, given the presence of indefinite elements, it would be possible to detect sequences of other influence patterns that don't fit the proposed model, such as:

$$FVM \rightarrow MVI \rightarrow IVF \overset{\Rightarrow}{} FVM \rightarrow MVT \rightarrow IVF.$$

In short, such a procedure offers a method of determining how adequately the model offered in the last section describes particular sequences of interest in the data.

Once the sequences for one code have been examined (as is done for FV in Figure 3), the complete set of sequences can be identified by using each code in turn as the criterion. The essential point in this discussion is that there is *nothing mathematically difficult about the fact that the data are triadic*. The analysis is blind to how the codes were generated; they could arise from one organism, a dyad, or a triad. The limitation is only one of practicality-- a large number of codes used for each member of the triad will produce an inordinate amount of sequential information, which can only be managed when there is an adequate amount of data. This problem is especially relevant in the case described above where the recipient of each act is identified. For example, with 20 codes per person, there are 60 distinct codes; an analysis carried out three lags has 60x60x60, or 216,000 possible combinations. Of course, most of these combinations will never occur, but for the Z-distribution to be a reasonable approximation to the binomial the number of instances of each pair of codes in p(XIC) must exceed 25. If only 20% of all the code combinations were to be examined to lag 3, there would have to be 1,080,000 observations. In most cases, however, only a few of the codes are the most frequent, so that a carefully chosen lumping scheme can often mitigate against such effects, making possible the investigation of sequential dependencies in the triad.

TRIADIC INFLUENCE MODELS

Since much of the non-observational data discussed in this paper could practically only be collected once for each triad (for example, only one attitude assessment may be taken), if these data are to be combined with observational data for the construction of models of triadic influence, data will have to be combined across

subjects. An excellent analytic tool for this form of model building
is *path analysis* (Duncan, 1975; Heise, 1975).

In path analysis a model is assumed between variables. For
example, if F = father, M = mother, and I = infant, and if the
model is:

$$\overset{\displaystyle p2}{F \to M \to I}$$
$$\quad p1 \quad p3$$

this implies that the father's influence on the infant operates
entirely through the mother (a transitive influence). The equations
for this model are:

$$M = p_1 F + p_2 I$$

$$I = p_3 M$$

The path coefficients can be calculated in terms of the correlations
and partial correlations between the variables.

If the variables are ordered in time, the path analysis will
yield a *time path model*. When observational and non-observational
data are mixed in a model this requires some assumptions about the
influence of variables upon one another. For example, if the
attitude measures are taken before the observations are collected,
we can assume that the attitudes influence the observations, unless
we have reason to suppose otherwise.

Time-path analysis was used by Bates, Lounsbury, and Klein
(1977) in constructing a model of mother-child interaction in
stores. Using factor scores[1] for each dyad at each point in the
interaction, they found evidence of bidirectional influences in the
interactions and wrote:

> "...the correlation between the first pair of child and
> mother statements indicates that the child's level of
> positivity (at time 2) may have induced some degree of
> reciprocal matching of permissiveness/warmth (at time 2)
> in the mother. In turn, the mother's permissiveness/warmth
> (at time 2) influenced the positivity of the second child
> statement...Apparently, the child's positivity (at time 2)
> and mother's permissiveness/warmth (at time 2) was recipro-
> cally influenced earlier in an interaction, but it later
> became resistant to new interpersonal influences." (p. 16,
> ms.).

---

1. The use of factor scores is not necessary. For example, lag
conditional probabilities at each lag to be considered can be used
in constructing the time path model.

Although this study only concentrated on dyadic influences, it is easy to see (through generalization of the earlier equation for transitive influences) that the path analysis model could be extended to consider many of the influence patterns discussed earlier. Not only does this procedure provide a means for the simultaneous consideration of both observational and non-observational data; it also allows for the generation of causal inferences.

SUMMARY AND CONCLUSIONS

This paper has offered methods for the conceputalization and quantification of influences in the family triad. In the first section, four types of influence patterns were discussed: direct, transitive, circular, and parallel influences. In addition, several aspects of the proposed conceptualization scheme were illustrated through a detailed example of the scheme in use: the conceptualization of father influences. The second section offered two statistical tools well-suited for the quantification of such influences: sequential lag analysis within subjects and time path analysis across subjects.

Although the analysis offered in this chapter suggests only preliminary steps in a virtually unexplored field, it is hoped that simultaneous use of the proposed influence scheme and statistical tools will provide researchers with an initial framework for the untangling of influences in the family triad.

ACKNOWLEDGEMENTS

Preparation of this chapter and the research reported here was supported by the following grants: NICHD Training Grant, HD-00244, and Office of Child Development Grant, OHD 90-C-900.

REFERENCES

Ainsworth, M. D. S. The development of infant-mother attachment. In B. M. Caldwell & H. N. Ricciuti (Eds.), *Review of child development research: (Vol. 3) Child development and social policy.* Chicago: University of Chicago Press, 1973.

Anderson, B. J. & Standley, K. A methodology for observation of the child-birth environment. Paper presented to the American Psychological Association, Washington, D. C., September, 1976.

Bates, J. E., Lounsbury, M. L., & Klein, A. R. Mother-child interaction in the store. Unpublished manuscript, Indian University, 1977.

Bell, R. Q. A reinterpretation of the direction of effects in studies of socialization. *Psychological Review,* 1968, *75*, 81-95.

Bell, R. Q. Contributions of human infants to caregiving and social interaction. In M. Lewis & L. A. Rosenblum (Eds.), *The effect of the infant on its caregiver.* New York: Wiley, 1974.

Bowlby, J. *Maternal care and mental health.* World Health Organization, 1951.

Bronfenbrenner, U. Toward an experimental ecology of human development. *American Psychologist,* July, 1977, *32*, 513-532.

Clarke-Stewart, K. A.   The father's impact on mother and child.
    Paper presented at the Biennial Meeting of the Society for
    Research in Child Development, New Orleans, March, 1977.
Cromwell, R. E., Keeney, B. P., & Adams, B. N.   Temporal patterning
    in the family. *Family Process*, 1976, *15*, 343-348.
Duncan, O. D.   *Introduction to structural equation models*.   New
    York: Academic Press, 1975.
Farber, B.   Marital integration as a factor in parent-child relations.
    Child Development, 1962, *33*, 1-14.
Feiring, C., & Taylor, J.   The influences of the infant and secondary
    parent on maternal behavior: Toward a social systems view of
    infant attachment. *Merrill-Palmer Quarterly*, 1978, in press.
Feldman, H.   Changes in marriage and parenthood: A methodological
    design.   Unpublished manuscript, Cornell University, 1971.
Gottman, J. M., Markman, H., & Notarius, C.   The topography of
    marital conflict: A sequential analysis of verbal and non-
    verbal behavior. *Journal of Marriage and the Family*, 1977, *39*,
    461-477.
Heise, D. R.   *Causal analysis*.   New York: Wiley, 1975.
Henneborn, W. J., & Cogan, R.   The effect of husband participation
    in reported pain and the probability of medication during
    labor and birth. *Journal of Psychosomatic Research*, 1975, *19*,
    215-222.
Hetherington, E. M.   The effects of familial variables on sex-typing.
    In J. P. Hill (Ed.), *Minnesota Symposium on Child Psychology*
    (Vol. 1).   Minneapolis, Minnesota: University of Minnesota
    Press, 1967.
Hurley, J. R., & Hohn, R. L.   Shifts in child-rearing attitudes
    linked with parenthood and occupation. *Developmental Psychology*,
    1971, *4*, 324-328.
Johnson, S. M., & Lobitz, G. K.   Parental manipulation of child be-
    havior in home observations. *Journal of Applied Behavior*
    Analysis, 1974a, *7*, 23-31.
Johnson, S. M., & Lobitz, G. K.   The personal and marital adjustment
    of parents as related to observed child deviance and parenting
    behaviors. *Journal of Abnormal Child Psychology*, 1974b, *2*,
    193-207.
Kotelchuck, M.   The infant's relationship to the father: Experimental
    evidence.   In M. E. Lamb (Ed.), *The role of the father in child*
    development.   New York: Wiley, 1976, pp. 329-344.
Lamb, M. E.   The role of the father: An overview.   In M. E. Lamb
    (Ed.), *The role of the father in child development*.   New York:
    Wiley, 1976a, pp. 1-83.
Lamb, M. E.   Effects of stress and cohort on mother- and father-infant
    interaction. *Developmental Psychology*, 1976b, *12*, 435-443.
Lewis, M., & Weinraub, M.   The father's role in the infant's social
    network.   In M. E. Lamb (Ed.), *The role of the father in child*
    development.   New York: Wiley, 1976, pp. 157-184.
Luce, G. G.   *Body time*.   New York: Bantam Books, 1973.
Macfarlane, A.   *The psychology of child birth*.   Cambridge, Massachuset
    Harvard University Press, 1977.
Marsella, A. J., Dubanowski, R. A., & Mohs, K.   The effects of father
    presence and absence upon maternal attitudes. *Journal of*
    Genetic Psychology, 1974, *25*, 257-263.

Moore, W. E. *Man, time and society.* New York: Wiley, 1963.

Orthner, D. K. Familia ludens: Reinforcing the leisure component in family life. *The Family Coordinator,* 1975, *24,* 175-183.

Parke, R. D. Interactional design and experimental manipulation: The field-lab interface. In R. B. Cairns (Ed.), *Social interactional analysis: Methods and illustrations.* Hillsdale, N. J.: Lawrence Erlbaum Assoc., 1978a, in press.

Parke, R. D. Parent-infant interaction: Progress, paradigms and problems. In G. P. Sackett (Ed.), *Observing Behavior (Vol. 1) Theory and applications in mental retardation.* Baltimore: University Park Press, 1978b.

Parke, R. D. Perspectives on father-infant interaction. In J. D. Osofsky (Ed.), *Handbook of infancy.* New York, 1978c, in press.

Parke, R. D., & O'Leary, S. E. Father-mother-infant interaction in the newborn period: Some findings, some observations and some unresolved issues. In K. Riegel & J. Meacham (Eds.), *The developing individual in a changing world: Social and environmental issues (Vol. II).* The Hague: Mouton, 1976.

Parke, R. D., O'Leary, S. E., & West, S. Mother-father-newborn interaction: Effects of maternal medication, labor, and sex of infant. *Proceedings of the American Psychological Association,* 1972, 85-86.

Parke, R. D., & Sawin, D. B. The father's role in infancy: A re-evaluation. *The Family Coordinator,* 1976, *25,* 365-371.

Pedersen, F. A. Mother, father and infant as an interactive system. Paper presented at the Annual Convention of the American Psychological Association, Chicago, September, 1975.

Pedersen, F. A., Anderson, B. J., & Cain, R. L. An approach to understanding linkages between the parent-infant and spouse relationships. Paper presented at the Society for Research in Child Development, New Orleans, March, 1977.

Pedersen, F. A., Yarrow, L. J., & Strain, B. A. Conceptualization of father influences and its implications for an observational methodology. Paper presented at International Society for the Study of Behavioral Development, Guildford, England, July, 1975.

Putney, S., & Middleton, R. Effect of husband-wife interaction on the strictness of attitudes toward child-rearing. *Marriage and Family Living,* 1960, *22,* 171-173.

Renshaw, J. R. An exploration of the dynamics of the overlapping worlds of work and family. *Family Process,* 1976, *15,* 143-165.

Rheingold, H. L. The modification of social responsiveness in institutional babies. *Monographs of the Society for Research in Child Development,* 1956, *21,* No. 63.

Rosenblatt, P. C. Behavior in public places: Comparison of couples accompanied and unaccompanied by children. *Journal of Marraige and the Family,* 1974, *36,* 750-755.

Shatz, M., & Gelman, R. The development of communication skills: Modifications in the speech of young children as a function of listener. *Monographs of the Society for Research in Child Development,* 1973, *38,* No. 152.

Shereshefsky, P. M., & Yarrow, L. J. *Psychological aspects of a first pregnancy and early postnatal adaptation.* New York: Raven Press, 1973.

van der Veen, F. The parent's concept of the family unit and child
    adjustment. *Journal of Counseling Psychology,* 1965, *12,* 196-200.
Yalmon, I. D. Post-partum blues syndrome. *Archives of General
    Psychiatry,* 1968, *28,* 16-27.
Zelazo, P. R., Kotelchuck, M., Barber, L., & David, J. Fathers
    and sons: An experimental facilitation of attachment behaviors.
    Paper presented at the Biennial Meeting of the Society for
    Research in Child Development, New Orleans, March, 1977.

12.
The effects of the social context on dyadic social interaction

MICHAEL E. LAMB

As the recency of most of the research cited in this volume attests, the study of social interaction has lately become remarkably popular within psychology, zoology, anthropology, sociology, and pediatrics. This is especially true of developmental psychology, where the popularity of interaction research has paralleled an interpretive shift from theorizing about parent effects on children, through a concern with child effects on parents, to speculations about the mutual influences of children and parents upon one another. With the last-named perspective there has emerged a widespread interest in the analysis of social interaction, partly because most researchers believe that the mutual influences occur in the course of interpersonal interaction.

In developmental psychology, most of the relevant studies have focused on mother-infant interaction (e.g., Schaffer, 1977; Lamb, 1977c), though several researchers have commenced consideration of father-infant interaction as well (e.g., Lamb, 1978d; Parke, 1978). Although investigators of mother- and father-infant interaction have directed their efforts toward somewhat different questions, there is a critical similarity between the two bodies of literature: In both areas, most researchers have formulated models that emphasize interaction within *dyads*. This has been true even when the social systems studied have been more complex. In some of my own studies, for example, I observed infants in the presence of their mothers, fathers, and two relatively unfamiliar investigators, yet in my analyses discussed the mother-infant, father-infant, and stranger-infant interaction separately (cf. Lamb, 1976b, 1977a, 1977b). This strategy--considering complex systems in terms of the component dyads--is imposed on researchers by the poverty of available statistical techniques, most of which are suited for the analysis of dyadic interactions. It is certainly not an unreasonable compromise. Without doubt we can obtain impor-

253

tant insights into the nature of social development with this
approach. On the other hand, we must acknowledge that the
adoption of such a strategy involves many simplifying assumptions, and may result in a failure to appreciate the rich complexity of social interaction and the effects thereof.

When using the "component dyad" strategy, furthermore, it
is important to consider all of the component dyads. In addressing many questions about infant-family interaction, for example,
it is important to appreciate that the mother-father dyad (explicitly ignored in my early studies) is worthy of attention.
It deserves study not only when one is explicitly interested in
marital interaction, but also because the nature of the relationship between the parents surely affects the type of interaction
each has with their infant. More simply, the mere presence of
the father, and what he is doing, may affect the nature of the
mother-infant interaction and vice versa. Stated in its most
general form, it is most unlikely that the various component relationships are independent of one another. Given that improba-
bility, it behooves us to investigate situations in which one individual (A) might affect another (B) through interaction with
him/her, whereupon B behaves differently in interaction with a
third (C), and thus changes C's behavior. In such a case, while
the *direct* effect is from B to C, A is having an important *indirect* effect on C.

Motivated by considerations such as these, I decided that
empirical investigation of the effects of the social context upon
dyadic interaction might permit us to use the "component dyad"
strategy more fruitfully. Thus I embarked on the series of studies
that are reported in this chapter. My concern with these issues
was heightened by the attention being directed to them by my
colleagues. Most important were Bronfenbrenner's (1974, 1975,
1976, 1977) appeals that developmental psychologists turn to focus
on "ecologically valid" problems. One issue that had been neglected
in conceptualizations of social development, argued Bronfenbrenner,
was the fact that many developmentally significant effects might
be mediated, not through direct interaction with the child concerned, but indirectly via another person. Such effects were labelled "second order effects" by Bronfenbrenner, and Lewis and
Weinraub (1976) have gone so far as to argue that the major impact
fathers have on their children is indirectly rather than directly
mediated. In our present state of ignorance, it is perhaps premature to attempt the quantification of relative importance. Suffice it to say that we need to consider the potential importance
of indirect effects more seriously than in the past.[1]

While the studies described below were designed to elucidate
indirect effects, the aims were rather modest. I was concerned

---

1. Lewis and Weinraub (1976) speak simply of "indirect effects"
rather than "second order effects". I shall use the terms inter-
changeably. In my earlier studies (Lamb, 1976a, 1976c), I had referred to "the cohort effect", but since this term was destined to
yield confusion, I now use the terminology proposed by Bronfenbrenner
and Lewis.

solely with determining whether and in what manner the presence,
identity, and behavior of persons present ("the social context")
affected interaction within focal dyads composed of the infant,
and its mother, father, or sibling. My concern throughout has been
with effects on immediate *interaction* rather than with long-term
effects on the child's personality. This is not because I am un-
interested in long-term effects, but because, like Hinde (1974),
I believe that we are unlikely to learn much about the effects of
early social interaction on development until we can describe, and
thus understand better, the nature of the formative interaction.
Even the simple experiments discussed in this chapter tell us important things about the nature of social interaction and the factors that affect it. This in turn increases the precision with
which more sophisticated questions (such as those concerning the
effects of specific experiences upon developing personalities) can
be addressed in the future.

My first studies in this area were focused on the effects of
a parent's presence on the interaction between an infant and its
other parent. The results of these studies are reported in the
next section, in the course of which I will describe the four
major cues that appear to mediate the effects that we find. Thereafter, I will discuss how the effects differ when the "intruder"
is not a parent but either a strange adult or the child's sibling.
The differences are consistent with other data concerning stranger-
reactions and sibling relationships in infancy. In the penultimate
section, I will present data concerning the effect that the infant's
age has on its responsiveness to the social cues described earlier
in the chapter. The final substantive section deals briefly with
attempts made by other researchers to explore the effects of the
quality of the marital relationship upon the type of interaction
each parent has with the infant.

EFFECTS INVOLVING PARENTS

Perhaps the simplest way of assessing whether the social context has an effect upon dyadic interaction involves observing the
dyad with and without a third person present. This was the strategy we adopted in the first studies, which were undertaken in an
attempt to assess what effect the mother's presence had on father-
infant interaction and what effect the father's presence had on
mother-infant interaction. We have consistently found that fathers
affect mother-infant interaction in exactly the same way that mothers
affect father-infant interaction. Thus we can speak simply about the
effect of one parent's presence upon the infant's interaction with
the other, without regard to the sex of the parent concerned. The
infants studied have been 1 year of age and older, which means that
they are quite capable of playing an active role in mediating the
effect. This contrasts with some early studies by Parke and O'Leary
(1976), in which the infants (who were newborns), could not monitor
the social context and be responsive to the cues we are concerned
with. My major interest has been in the infants' behavior, although
as the research has proceeded it has become clear that to understand
the infants' behavior, one must pay attention to what their parents
are doing.

The first studies in this series were conducted in laboratory playrooms at Yale University whereas the later studies took place at the University of Wisconsin. The dependent measures in these studies were the frequency of affiliative and attachment behaviors directed by the infants to their parents, and the frequency of adult vocalization to the infant. These measures are listed in Table 1; the definitions employed were published in Lamb (1976c). We chose the frequency of parental vocalization as our index of parental behavior because it could be recorded by observers without requiring that they take their eyes off the infant, and because it was the most frequently occurring parental behavior that was also objectively defined and reliably observed.

TABLE 1.   DEPENDENT MEASURES FOR STUDIES OF INDIRECT EFFECTS WITHIN
THE MOTHER-FATHER-INFANT TRIAD

Affiliative Behaviors	Attachment Behaviors	Parental Behavior
smile	proximity[a]	vocalize to infant
vocalize	touch[a]	
look	approach	
laugh	fuss	
proffer	ask to be held	

Note: [a]Duration measures. All others are frequency counts.

The procedure followed in these studies involved observing the infants with their mothers, with their fathers, and with both parents. The order in which the episodes occurred was counterbalanced. The study involving 24-month-olds had some additional episodes involving strangers which will be discussed in the next section. Although we have studied both mothers and fathers, and have included equal numbers of boys and girls in each experiment, no significant effects related to sex of parent or sex of child have been found, so I will not discuss these two factors.

All our studies have indicated quite clearly that the presence of either parent has a dramatic impact on the amount of interaction between an infant and the other parent.[2] Twelve-, 18-, and 24-month-olds directed fewer social behaviors to either parent when the other was present than when the child was with one parent only (Lamb, 1976a, 1977a, 1978e). For their part, the parents consistently spoke to their infants far more in the one parent-child situation. Table 2, 3,

---

2. In one study (Lamb, 1976c) we did not find this effect. In that study, however, changes in the social context were confounded with changes in the degree of distress to which the infants were subjected. When this confound was removed, the indirect effect was obtained (Lamb, 1978e).

TABLE 2.   MEANS ON ATTACHMENT AND AFFILIATIVE BEHAVIOR MEASURES IN
ONE- AND TWO-PARENT SITUATIONS:
12-MONTH-OLDS

Behavior	Spouse Present	Spouse Absent	Significance of Difference
Affiliative			
Smile	3.7	3.9	-
Vocalize	4.5	7.4	$p < .01$
Look	15.1	19.9	$p < .0001$
Laugh	0.4	0.1	-
Proffer	2.0	3.6	$p < .01$
Attachment			
Proximity[a]	151.2	276.9	$p < .01$
Touch[a]	46.0	78.0	-
Approach	3.3	5.0	$p < .05$
Seek to be held	0.6	0.7	-
Fuss	0.7	0.6	-
Adult vocalize	14.4	38.1	$p < .001$

Note: All entries represent the means per parent per 8-minute
episode. Data are taken from Lamb (1978e).
[a]Entries represent the number of seconds over which the
designated state extended.

and 4 present the relevant means obtained in the studies of 12-, 18-,
and 24-month-olds respectively. Inspection of these tables indicates
that the criterial behaviors were directed toward each parent more
frequently when the infant was alone with him/her. In general,
exceptions to this tendency occurred only when the frequency of occurrence was so low that changes could not be detected.
    There are two social cues that may account for this effect.
First, there is an additional potential interactant present in the
triadic (two parents and infant) situation, and the infant may simply
divide its attention between the two persons available. This would
reduce the amount of attention paid to each one by the infant. One
might refer to this as a distributional explanation, with the relevant
social cue (number of persons present) being labelled the *distributional* cue. Each parent, meanwhile, may divide his/her attention between
infant and spouse for the same reason. Since they would therefore
be paying less attention to the infant than when alone with it, they

TABLE 3.   MEANS ON ATTACHMENT AND AFFILIATIVE BEHAVIOR MEASURES IN
ONE- AND TWO-PARENT SITUATIONS:
18-MONTH-OLDS

Behavior	Spouse Present	Spouse Absent	Significance of Difference
Affiliative			
Smile	2.5	2.6	–
Vocalize	7.9	19.9	$p < .001$
Look	10.8	17.9	$p < .001$
Laugh	0.6	1.3	$p < .025$
Proffer	5.5	9.3	$p < .005$
Attachment			
Proximity[a]	15.3	22.7	$p < .01$
Touch[a]	1.3	5.0	$p < .005$
Approach	6.5	5.3	–
Seek to be held	0.3	0.7	–
Fuss	0.1	1.1	$p < .005$
Adult vocalize	18.3	44.6	$p < .001$

Note: All entries represent the means per parent per 9-minute
episode.   Data taken from Lamb (1976a).
[a] Entries represent number of seconds over which the
designated state occurred.

would be eliciting less interaction. This too may serve as an important social cue, inasmuch as a socially active partner invites
more interaction than one who is relatively passive. An active
partner is, presumably, more responsive to the infant's social bids
as well, and this is also likely to facilitate interaction. This
might be called the *invitational* cue.

If this invitational cue is important, there should be significant correlations between the levels of social activity of parent and
infant. Among 18- and 24-month-olds such correlations clearly exist
(Lamb, 1976a, 1977a). As a result, when we controlled for variations
in the level of parental activity by covariation, we severely reduced
the level of significance of the second order effect. Use of the
covariation procedure affected the results of many of the univariate
analyses as well as multivariate analyses of all the affiliative
behaviors combined. These results and their consistent replication

TABLE 4.   MEANS ON ATTACHMENT AND AFFILIATIVE BEHAVIOR MEASURES IN
ONE- AND TWO-PARENT SITUATIONS:
24-MONTH-OLDS

Behavior	Spouse Present	Spouse Absent	Significance of Difference
Affiliative			
Smile	1.1	1.4	-
Vocalize	10.7	27.3	$p < .001$
Look	7.9	12.1	$p < .001$
Laugh	0.4	0.7	-
Proffer	3.0	5.1	$p < .01$
Attachment			
Proximity[a]	9.0	18.3	$p < .10$
Touch[a]	1.3	1.9	-
Approach	3.5	4.1	-
Seek to be held	0.1	0.2	-
Fuss	0.1	0.2	-
Adult vocalize	16.5	33.6	$p < .001$

Note: All entries represent the means per parent per 7-minute
episode. Date taken from Lamb (1977a).
[a]Entries represent number of 15-second units during which
designated state occurred.

indicated that the invitational cue was being perceived and responded
to by the infants. In addition, the fact that significant second
order effects were evident even after the effects of variations in
parental activity had been controlled for statistically indicated
that the distributional cue was also important.

Strangely, however, there was no correlation between the levels
of parental and infant activity among 12-month-olds, and the results
of the analyses that revealed the second-order effect were unaffected
by the covariation procedure (Lamb, 1978e). The absence of correlation between indices of parent and infant activity was also found in
another sample of 1-year-olds (Lamb, 1976c), suggesting that a genuine, rather than spurious, age effect was involved. It appeared,
therefore, that the second-order effect observed among 12-month-olds
was mediated solely via the distributional cue, and that variations
in the amount of attention paid by the parents (the invitational cue)

were insufficient. Among older infants, by contrast, both of these
cues were being utilized. This suggested a limitation in the social
competence of 1-year-olds (Lamb, 1978e).

In the three studies just discussed, we have described only two
possible social cues, and we have considered only the presence or
absence of the third person. In fact, of course, when the third perso
is present, s/he is not only a target for the social behaviors of the
two members of the original dyad, but may also engage in interaction
with them. If we regard the third person as an active participant in
the social interaction, there are two types of effects we might expect
to find. First, the amount of interaction between the two adults
should be negatively correlated with the amount of interaction betweer
infant and either parent, since to the extent that they are interacti
with one another, the parents are less accessible to the infant. Seco
the amount of interaction between either parent and the infant should
be negatively correlated with the amount of interaction between the
infant and its other parent since an infant who is intensely involved
in interaction with one person is less available for interaction with
another. We are testing these predictions in a current study of 18-
month-olds who are being observed with each parent separately as well
as with both parents (Lamb, 1978b). Instead of recording only instanc
of parental vocalization to the infant, we are recording when the
parents vocalize to, smile at, offer toys to, or play with the infant,
and when they vocalize to, look at, and smile at their spouse. We
also record the infant behaviors listed in Table 1. We are hoping
that our analyses will show: a) that there is less interaction between infant and parent when the other parent is present than when
s/he is absent, b) that there are significant negative correlations
between the amount of interaction between the parents and the amount
of interaction between each of them and the infant, and c) that there
are negative correlations between the amount of interaction between
either parent and infant and the amount of interaction between the
infant and the other parent. Finally, even when all these other influences are statistically controlled via covariation, there should
be a residual effect--presumably mediated via the distributional cue
described earlier. This experiment, then, is designed to illustrate
the complexity of the ways in which the social context influences
dyadic interaction. We propose that within the mother-father-infant
triad, there are at least four cues to which infants are sensitive,
and that they utilize these cues in modulating their involvement in
parent-infant interaction.

It is important to note, however, that these second order effects
involve changes in the absolute levels of social activity. In none
of the studies have we found that the presence or behavior of the thir
person has different effects on some behavioral measures than on other
Both affiliative and attachment behaviors are directed toward either
parent more often when the other parent is absent than when s/he is
present. However, Clarke-Stewart (1978) found that when fathers were
present, mothers not only interacted less with their 15-, 20-, and
30-month-old infants but they were also less responsive to the infants
signals.

In closing this section, there are two issues to consider. First, it is of course quite possible for babies to interact as much with each parent when two are present as when one is present. The fact that they do not suggests that babies impose ceiling limits on their degree of involvement in social interaction. Second, the reader may wonder, as I did, how the observed frequencies of interaction with each parent in the triadic situations compare with the amounts one would obtain by halving the frequencies observed in the single parent episodes. Inspection of Tables 2, 3, and 4 reveals that among 12-month-olds, the obtained values were systematically greater than the expected values, whereas there were no consistent patterns evident among older infants.

EFFECTS INVOLVING STRANGERS

The results presented in the previous section illustrate that the presence of a third person had a qualitatively similar effect on all the measures we recorded. What would happen, we wondered, if the third person was a strange adult, rather than a parent? Theoretical considerations suggested that a rather different effect should be observed. Specifically, ethological theorists such as Bowlby (1969) and Ainsworth (e.g., Bretherton & Ainsworth, 1974) propose that the entrance of an unfamiliar adult should provoke wariness. As a result, infants should exhibit a shift from affiliative and exploratory behavior to attachment behavior until the stranger leaves or the wariness habituates. This is precisely what we found in a study of 2-year-olds (Lamb, 1977a). The entrance of a stranger and the entrance of a parent had indistinguishable effects on the amount of affiliative interaction within the focal parent-infant dyad. In both cases, the effect was mediated largely by the reduction in level of activity on the part of the parents (the invitational cue). This was demonstrated by using the analysis of covariance approach described earlier. The distributional cue also appeared to account for some of the variance on the affiliative behavior measures. On the other hand, "wariness" did not appear to have any independent impact on the occurrence of affiliative behaviors directed toward the parents, since their occurrence was affected similarly by the stranger's and by the parent's presence.

The effects on the occurrence of attachment behaviors, however, were very different depending on the identity of the third person. The entrance of the stranger caused an increase in the display of attachment behaviors directed toward the parent even though the low frequency of several of the critical behaviors ensured that significant changes were evident on only two of the measures used in this study. By contrast, a parent's entrance led to a reduction in or no change in the occurrence of these behaviors. The key factor here appeared to be wariness elicited by the stranger's presence. This confirmed a theoretically predicted relationship between the fear/wariness and attachment behavior systems, and (more important in the present context) it illustrated that the familiarity of the person joining a dyad was an important determinant of the effect that person's presence would have on interaction within another dyad. Not every person, then, has the same effect on dyadic interaction.

In fact, the familiarity of the person may not be the only salient factor when second order effects are concerned. In a recent study (Lamb, 1978c) we set out to determine whether the sex of the person might also be important. The design of this study differed from the procedure followed in the studies described earlier in that observations took place at home at a time when both parents were present, and each lasted about 1 hour. The visits were made by the same two persons--a male and a female--who took turns in serving as observer and visitor. It was the visitor's role to interact with the family and relieve their anxieties about being observed. Though neither the observer or the visitor knew it, the primary purpose of this study was to see whether the sex of the visitor affected the amount of interaction the infant had with its mother and father. My expectation was that the female visitor would be most likely to interact with the mother, and that the father would be more likely to interact with the baby in such circumstances. With a male visitor, the reverse should occur: father and visitor should converse, leaving the mother available for interaction with the baby.

Our findings were partially consistent with these expectations. When there was a female visitor, fathers spoke to the infants more than mothers did. When the visitor was male, mothers spoke to their infants more than fathers did. Both parents spoke to their infants more when there was an opposite-sex than a same-sex visitor. On the other hand, none of the other measures of parental or infant behavior were affected by the visitor's sex. In all, then, it seemed that the sex of the visitor had a relatively minor impact on parent-infant interaction patterns. Thus, it is unlikely that varying the sex of an investigator would have a major impact on the conclusions researchers might draw about parent-infant interaction

RESEARCH INVOLVING SIBLINGS

In addition to the familiarity and sex of the person or persons who comprise "the social context," another important variable is their age. We have investigated the effect of the age of the person in two studies involving preschool-aged siblings (Lamb, 1978a, 1978f). The infants in the studies concerned were 12 and 18 months of age.

In the first study (Lamb, 1978f), we were interested primarily in obtaining descriptive accounts of the amount and type of inter- action between 18-month-old infants and their siblings. To achieve this, we observed the sibling dyads in a laboratory setting. During 24 minutes of observations, the children were seen for 8 minutes with their mothers, 8 minutes with their fathers, and 8 minutes with both parents present. One of the analyses we conducted involved comparing the effect of the second parent's presence on the parent-infant and sibling-infant interaction. This analysis thus resembled those described in the section entitled *Effects Involving Parents,* and the results were predictable: infants interacted less with either parent or sibling when the other parent was present than when s/he was absent. Although the effects on parent-infant and sibling-infant interaction were similar in nature (i.e., both involved reductions in the amount of interaction) we found that the parent's entrance had a much greater impact on the parent-infant interaction than on the sibling-infant interaction. The likely meaning of this will become clearer after we discuss the results of the second study.

The latter study (Lamb, 1978a) involved a systematic comparison of the effects of a sibling's and a parent's presence on parent-infant interaction (Lamb, 1978a). Twelve-month-old infants were observed in either of two series of episodes: mother-infant / father-infant / mother-father-infant, or mother-infant-sibling / father-infant-sibling / mother-father-infant-sibling. The order of episodes within both series was counterbalanced. As in the studies described earlier, the dependent measures were the frequencies of affiliative and attachment behaviors directed by infants to parents, and the frequency of parental vocalization to infants and preschoolers.

Analyses revealed that the infants directed fewer criterial behaviors to their parents when either their siblings or other parents were present than when they were absent. This was consistent with the findings of several of the studies described earlier. More interesting was the fact that the siblings' presence did not inhibit the infants' behavior as much as the additional parents' presence did. Similarly, while the presence of preschoolers and the presence of spouses inhibited the amount of attention paid by the parents to the infants, the spouses' presence had a far greater impact on them than the preschoolers'.

The results of these two studies show that a parent's presence affects sibling-infant interaction less than parent-infant interaction, and that the sibling's presence affects parent-infant interaction less than the presence of a parent does. These findings bring to mind the distinction proposed by Harlow (e.g., Harlow & Harlow, 1965; Suomi & Harlow, 1978) between the parent-infant and peer "affectional systems". Substituting the word "interactional" for "affectional", but maintaining Harlow's claim that the child interactional and adult interaction systems comprise relatively independent modes of social interaction, one would predict that the presence of another adult would establish competition within the adult interaction system, which would lead the infant to distribute its attention between the adults present. That adult, however, would not 'compete' with a child interactant since a different interactional system would be involved and hence the effect on child-child interaction should be less. This, of course, is precisely what we found. A further test of the hypothesis regarding the independence of the child and adult interactional systems could be made by systematically varying the number of children present in order to monitor the effects on the amount of child-child and adult-child interaction. The hypothesis predicts that if two children were available as interactants, the focal child should distribute its attention between the two of them. If one then left, there should be an increase in the amount of interaction with the other child, but little if any effect on the amount of interaction between the focal child and any adults present. We are currently planning this study.

AGE OF THE INFANT

In each of the studies involving 1-year-olds, we have found
that they respond to the social cues somewhat differently than
older infants. These findings suggest that the "social competence"
of 1-year-olds is deficient in at least two respects. First, as
noted earlier, we find among 12-month-olds no significant correlation between the levels of activity of adult and infant in
either the one-parent or two-parent contexts. Thus although the
presence of a spouse causes each parent to direct less attention
to the infant, the information contained in this invitational cue
is, apparently, not perceived or acted upon by the infant. Stated
somewhat differently, the effects of another person's presence on
the parent-directed behavior of 1-year-olds appears to be mediated
via the distributional cue--the infant divides its attention
among the potential interactants available regardless of variations in the amount of attention paid by them to it. This finding
has now been replicated in three samples of infants (Lamb, 1976c,
1978a, 1978e).

During the study involving 1-year-olds and their siblings
(Lamb, 1978d), we encountered the second apparent limitation in
the ability of infants to take cues from the social context into
account. Specifically, we found that the entrance of a fourth
person had no greater effect upon the infants' behavior in dyadic
interaction than the entrance of a third person. Among 18-month-
olds, by contrast, the entrance of a fourth person did have an
additional impact on the amount of interaction within the parent-
infant dyads (Lamb, 1978f). This indicated a limitation in the
ability of 12-month-olds to utilize the distributional cue when
the number of persons among whom attention was to be divided was
greater than three. We do not know, at this stage, at what point
a similar limitation becomes apparent in the social sensitivity
of both older infants and adults.

The results indicate, in any event, that the social context
has differential effects upon dyadic interaction depending on the
age (and thus level of social competence) of the infant concerned,
even though we know little about the manner in which sensitivity
to the social context is developed.

NONEXPERIMENTAL STUDIES

Although some of these studies have been conducted in homes
rather than in the laboratory, and although correlational analyses
have played an important role in identifying the effective cues,
the program of research outlined above has been experimental in
nature. Rosenblat has reported several studies conducted in
naturalistic settings which substantially buttress the findings
described above. This independent replication leads me to be
cautiously optimistic about the 'ecological validity' of the
phenomena concerned.

Rosenblatt's (1974; Cleaves & Rosenblatt, 1977) studies have
involved the unobtrusive observation of families in public places.
The procedure is simple. Observers merely note the number of

persons in the group, and the amount of interaction or intimacy displayed. Rosenblatt (1974) has found that there is far less intimacy between spouses when they are accompanied by a child than when they are alone, and that the amount of interaction decreases as the number of persons in the group increases (Cleaves & Rosenblatt, 1977).

Meanwhile, Pedersen (Pedersen, Anderson, & Cain, 1977; Pedersen, 1975) has sought to elucidate the effects of *relationship* variables on interaction. Thus, for example, he has explored the effect of the quality of the marital relationship on the patterns of mother-infant and father-infant interaction. Pedersen's studies are especially important because of the obvious relevance of these variables. Unfortunately, however, Pedersen's findings did not support his prediction that parents who interacted affectionately with one another would express more positive affect towards their infants, although it was found that parents who were more critical of one another expressed more negative affect to the infants. Clarke-Stewart's (1978) data showed that husbands and wives tended to behave similarly with their infants. Thus when either parent spoke a great deal to the baby, the other tended to do so as well. Unfortunately, Clarke-Stewart did not attempt to evaluate the effect of the parents' relationship with one another upon their interaction with the infants.

Despite the disappointing yield thus far, it seems certain that relationship variables will dominate future research on the effects of the social context on family interaction patterns.

CONCLUSION

The data reviewed in this chapter and in the next illustrate that the social context has rather dramatic and important effects upon interpersonal interaction. Many of these effects are not surprising although they are seldom taken into account when designing studies of social interaction or when interpreting their findings. They are likely to be especially important considerations when comparing the results of different studies.

The most obvious way of assessing whether the social context affects interaction involves comparing interaction bouts that take place with and without the additional person(s) present. Several studies have now shown that as the number of persons present increases, the amount of interaction within any component dyad decreases. I suggested that three factors mediate this effect: the facts a) that each individual distributes his/her attention among the available partners, b) that each therefore receives from others fewer social bids that would have stimulated further interaction, and c) that the interaction between any two individuals limits the access of a third person to either of them. (This yields two social cues.) The data indicate that the ability to perceive and/or respond appropriately to the relevant social cues improves with age.

Certain characteristics of the persons who comprise the social context influence the type of effect they will have upon adult-infant interaction. The most salient variable thus far studied is the individual's familiarity to the adult and infant. Unfamiliar persons evoke wariness in the infant and thus their presence leads to an increase (rather than a decrease) in the occurrence of attachment behavior directed toward the parents. Whether the third person is familiar or strange, however, the effect on the occurrence of affiliative behavior is similarly inhibitory.

The age of the intruder is also important. There is some evidence for the existence of partially independent peer interactional and adult interactional systems. We find that the presence of a child does not affect the amount of parent-infant interaction as much as the presence of an adult does. Similarly, the entrance of a parent affects levels of adult-infant but not sibling-infant interaction. As yet, no studies have shown that the sex of an individual substantially influences the type of effect s/he has on parent-infant interaction.

Only recently have researchers turned their attention to the more complex task of determining how the quality of the relationships among individuals affects the interaction between them and influences the effect that the presence of one will have on the others' interaction. It seems reasonable to predict that these indirect effects are likely to prove both interesting and important.

Most of the studies described in this chapter have been focused on factors affecting immediate interaction. Consequently, they tell us how indirect effects might influence our observations and the interpretations we draw from them, but they do not elucidate the formative or developmental significance of indirect effects. Thus two of the major issues concerning indirect effects have yet to be addressed systematically by researchers.

ACKNOWLEDGMENTS

I am grateful to Stephen Suomi for his comments on an earlier draft of this chapter, to the Foundation for Child Development and the University of Wisconsin Graduate School for financial support, to Urie Bronfenbrenner for his catalytic encouragement, and to Cheryl Arbaugh, Hildy Feen, Sheila Huddleston, Jamie Lamb, Cindy Neff, Steve Neren, and Kinthi Sturtevant for their assistance in data collection.

REFERENCES

Bowlby, J. *Attachment and loss.* Vol. 1. *Attachment.* New York: Basic Books, 1969.
Bretherton, I., & Ainsworth, M. D. Responses of one-year-olds to a stranger in a strange situation. In M. Lewis & L. A. Rosenblum (Eds.), *The origins of fear.* New York: Wiley, 1974.
Bronfenbrenner, U. Developmental research, public policy, and the ecology of childhood. *Child Development*, 1974, *45*, 1-5.
Bronfenbrenner, U. Social change: The challenge to research and policy. Paper presented to the Society for Research in Child Development, Denver, April, 1975.

Bronfenbrenner, U. The experimental ecology of education.
     Educational Researcher, 1976, *5*, 5-15.
Bronfenbrenner, U. A theoretical model for the experimental
     ecology of human development. Paper presented to the
     Society for Research in Child Development, New Orleans,
     March 1977.
Clarke-Stewart, K. A. And daddy makes three: The father's
     impact on mother and young child. *Child Development*, 1978,
     49, in press.
Cleaves, W. T., & Rosenblatt, P. C. Intimacy between adults and
     children in public places. Paper presented to the Society
     for Research in Child Development, New Orleans, March, 1977.
Harlow, H. F., & Harlow, M. K. The affectional systems. In
     A. M. Schrier, H. F. Harlow, & F. Stollnitz (Eds.), *Behavior
     of nonhuman primates* (Vol. 2). New York: Academic Press,
     1965.
Hinde, R. A. *Biological bases of human social behavior*. New
     York: McGraw-Hill, 1974.
Lamb, M. E. Effects of stress and cohort on mother- and father-
     infant interaction. *Developmental Psychology*, 1976, *12*,
     425-443. (a)
Lamb, M. E. Interactions between eight-month-old children and
     their fathers and mothers. In M. E. Lamb (Ed.), *The role
     of the father in child development*. New York: Wiley,
     1976 (307-327). (b)
Lamb, M. E. Twelve-month-olds and their parents: Interaction in
     a laboratory playroom. *Developmental Psychology*, 1976, *12*,
     237-244. (c)
Lamb, M. E. The development of mother-infant and father-infant
     attachments in the second year of life. *Developmental
     Psychology*, 1977, *13*, 637-648. (a)
Lamb, M. E. Father-infant and mother-infant interaction in the
     first year of life. *Child Development*, 1977, *48*, 167-181.
     (b)
Lamb, M. E. A re-examination of the infant social world. *Human
     Development*, 1977, *20*, 65-85. (c)
Lamb, M. D. A comparison of "second order" effects involving
     parents and siblings. Unpublished manuscript, 1978. (a)
Lamb, M. E. The effects of parent-parent interaction on parent-infant
     interaction. Unpublished manuscript, 1978. (b)
Lamb, M. E. The effects of the investigator's sex on parent-
     infant interaction. Unpublished manuscript, 1978. (c)
Lamb, M. E. The father's role in the infant's social world. In
     J. H. Stevens & M. Mathews (Eds.), *Mother/child, father/child
     relationships*. Washington, D. C.: National Association for
     the Education of Young Children, 1978. (d)
Lamb, M. E. Infant social cognition and 'second order' effects.
     Infant Behavior and Development, 1978, *1*, 1-10. (e)
Lamb, M. E. Interactions between 18-month-olds and their preschool-
     aged siblings. *Child Development*, 1978, *49*, in press. (f)
Lewis, M., & Weinraub, M. The father's role in the child's social
     network. In M. E. Lamb (Ed.), *The role of the father in child
     development*. New York: Wiley, 1976.

Parke, R. D. Father-infant interaction. In J. D. Osofsky (Ed.),
    Handbook of infancy. New York: Wiley, 1978.
Parke, R. D., & O'Leary, S. Father-mother-infant interaction in
    the newborn period: Some findings, some observations, and
    some unresolved issues. In K. F. Riegel & J. Meacham (Eds.),
    *The developing individual in a changing world. Vol. 2. Social
    and environmental issues.* The Hague: Mouton, 1976.
Pederson, F. A. Mother, father, and infant as an interactive
    system. Paper presented to the American Psychological
    Association, Chicago, September, 1975.
Pedersen, F. A., Anderson, B. J., & Cain, R. L. An approach to
    understanding linkages between the parent-infant and spouse
    relationships. Paper presented to the Society for Research
    in Child Development, New Orleans, March, 1977.
Rosenblatt, P. C. Behavior in public places: Comparison of
    couples accompanied and unaccompanied by children. *Journal
    of Marriage and the Family,* 1974, *36,* 750-755.
Schaffer, H. R. (Ed.). *Studies in mother-infant interaction.*
    New York: Academic Press, 1977.
Suomi, S. J., & Harlow, H. F. Early experience and social develop-
    ment in rhesus monkeys. In M. E. Lamb (Ed.), *Social and
    personality development.* New York: Holt, Rinehart, &
    Winston, 1978.

13.
Monkeys in time and space

LEONARD A. ROSENBLUM

"The Sea rolls against a sandy beach; the waves subtly
corregate the sand. A painted wall cracks; the surface
becomes a web of fine lines. A car moves in the snow;
the tires leave deep tracks. Rope falls; it lies in
smooth curves on the ground. A board is cut; it shows
the marks of the saw. All these phenomena caused by
various processes can be understood as diagrams in
space representing forces acting upon the varied
materials plus the resistance of the materials to the
impact of these forces." (L. Moholy-Nagy, 1956, p. 36)

When the study of animal behavior emerged in the post-Darwinian
era, the behavior of animals was placed in a broad context concerned
with evolutionary adaptation to environmental demands. Nonetheless,
modern comparative psychology has focused primarily on intra-
individual capacities and interindividual behavioral interactions,
with little attention paid to the impact of broad environmental
factors. Particularly in laboratory situations, there has been an
attempt at minute cataloguing of the differential effects of highly
specified positive and negative reinforcing agents in influencing
specific behaviors. However, the global environmental context
within which the organism experienced these reinforcing events
has not received the same degree of attention, although current
efforts suggest the efficacy of this approach (Parker & Gibson,
1977). Until recent years, animal social behavior, and in particular that of the nonhuman primates, has been studied in the
absence of a conceptual organization of the situations within
which specific clusters of behavior have been observed. To be
sure, in most laboratory studies detailed descriptions of a number
of physical dimensions of the observational environment, including
spatial dimensions, hours and levels of illumination, etc. have

269

been offered. However, little effort has been directed towards providing the type of framework within which varied test environments could be compared and contrasted with respect to their likely impact on the behavior of the various species observed within them.

In recent years, students of primate social behavior have been confronted by a tremendous range of social and individual behavior patterns seen within members of the same species studied across several natural habitats. At the same time, we have been sensitized by the growing force of principles elucidated by the various disciplines subsumed under the heading of "Ecological Psychology". As a result, it seems appropriate that we now begin the task of conceptually differentiating and categorizing those environmental settings in which behavior is observed, to the same degree that has been directed towards the measurement of the behaviors observed within them. As Schoggen (1978) has recently remarked: "The most basic or fundamental suggestion arising from the ecological perspective is its insistence on abandoning the often unrecognized assumption, which has tended to dominate thinking in Psychology, that behavior is to be understood or explained primarily in terms of person-centered, "under the skin" personality factors. Instead, it would adopt as a guiding principle the concept of behavior in context, i.e., behavior and environment as interdependent elements in a unitary dynamic system" (p. 56). Although directed towards the study of human psychological processes and behavior, Schoggen's comments are equally applicable to studies of nonhuman primates as well.

Some attention to the role of environmental influences on animal behavior has, of course, emerged from time to time. Even as early as the turn of the century, some animal behaviorists began to emphasize the role of the environmental context in influencing various elements of animal social structure. Petrucci (1906), for example, concluded that spatial dispersion and group composition, as well as the interaction of individuals within such groups, would be directly responsive to various aspects of the environments within which the society functions. Moreover, he suggested that social behaviors of individuals lack the kind of consistency across time and setting which might allow them to be compared in the same way that biologists compared morphological features. In terms of human psychological and social functioning, it was the work of Brunswik and Lewin that laid the basis for a growing concern regarding the relationship between the psychology of the individual and the environmental setting within which psychological processes occurred. Lewin's (1951) concept of the "life space" best examplified these early efforts to understand a person's behavior in terms of both internal factors and the environmental context, as psychologically perceived by the person at the time the behavior emerged.

This notion of the effects of environmental circumstances on shaping the behavior of individuals and ultimately groups of individuals in the animal domain, was also incorporated in the ideas of von Uexkull (1921). He proposed that because various animals' sensory capacities differed widely, their perceived

environment (Merkwelt) differed accordingly. Hence, the elements
of their total surroundings (Umwelt) which could effect their
behavior differed as well and thus had to be assessed with
explicit regard to each animal's unique capacities. Thus, the
Merkwelt of man (the observer) could not be assumed to be the
functional, effecting environment of the other species under
study, for in general they were not the same.

Even within the study of human behavior, Yarrow (1968) has
emphasized that the definition of environmental stimuli independent
of the organism upon whom these stimuli act is likely to result
in the distortion of the role of various factors. Much as classical ethology (Tinbergen, 1951) suggested that specific types of
animals respond to particular portions of a total environment under
any given circumstances, perhaps because of genetically determined
specific sensitivities (the "releaser" concept), Yarrow argues that
in studying the human child it is vital, "...that the effective
environment be defined in relation to the organism's characteristics, capacities and sensitivities." Yarrow indicates in addition,
that, "This model has significant implications for research on early
experiences. It emphasizes that the measurements of a given experience at any point in time must be related to the characteristics
of the organism. It also emphasizes the dynamic changing chracter
of the environment throughout the development cycle" (p. 106).

When we turn our attention to the behavior of nonhuman primates,
the abundant research of the last 20 years clearly reflects the
diversity of behavior and social organization of various species
when viewed in broadly diversified natural environments. Indeed,
in recent years, considerable emphasis has been placed on the
behavioral plasticity in social organization of primates in response
to varying environmental demands; such plasticity is now viewed as
a key factor in primate evolution (Jay, 1968). Differences in
behavior and social organization emerge not only in comparisons
between disparate species observed in different settings, but
indeed, even in comparisons of closely related species or different
troops of the same species. Sussman (1977), for example, has
recently described the social structure of two closely related
species of lemur, *Lemur catta* and *Lemur fulvus*, in Madagascar.
Although observed within several forested areas on the island,
including areas of species' overlap, the two species showed clear
habitat preferences. Thus, during the day, groups of *Lemur fulvus*
spent over 70% of their time in the high canopy of the trees and
were observed on the ground in less than 2% of the daily observations. When *Lemur fulvus* groups traveled, they almost always moved
in the canopy of the trees, and indeed, observations suggested that
areas they may have necessitated ground locomotion were avoided
by these groups. *Lemur catta,* on the other hand, were observed
on the ground over 30% of the time, and about 70% of group travel
in this species took place on the forest floor. Sussman indicates
that *Lemur catta,* in distinction to *Lemur fulvus,* used almost all
the levels of the forest, moving and traveling on the floor, taking
daytime rests in the low trees, and sleeping in the closed canopy
at night. The social structure of groups in these two species also

differed quite dramatically. Although both species lived in multi-
male groups with an approximate 1:1 sex ratio, groups of *Lemur catta*
were nearly twice the total size on the average as those of *Lemur
fulvus* (18.8 vs. 9.5 members, respectively). In assessing the
outcome of agonistic encounters, there was evidence of a well-
defined dominance hierarchy in groups of *Lemur catta,* but no discernible hierarchy emerged in groups of *Lemur fulvus.* Perhaps as
a produce of these differences in hierarchical structures, Sussman
reports that *Lemur catta* groups were frequently divided into subgroups that separated while moving, foraging, and resting, whereas
groups of *Lemur fulvus* were very cohesive, and regular subgroups
were not seen. It is clear, from even these initial observations,
that indivduals living within social groups of these two species,
despite their occupation of the same forests on a relatively small
island, function within rather distinct physical and social environments.

Similar distinctions in social structure and behavior have been
described in several comparative studies of closely related species
in other parts of the world. Kummer's study of the so-called desert
and savanna baboons (*Papio hamadryas* and *Papio cynocephalus)* indicated
similar broad differences in social structure, which appeared to
correlate meaningfully with the different habitats within which
these species are found (Kummer, 1968). Gartlan (1968), in discussing
the relationship between environmental conditions and primate social
structure in the analysis of the behavior of two species of vervet
(*Cercopithecus aethips* and *Cercopithecus mitis),* has concluded,
"The results of these studies indicate that social structure in
many widespread primate species is largely habitat- rather than
species-specific." Comparative studies of various troops of the
same species, such as those of common Indian langurs (Yoshiba,
1968) or Japanese macaques (Frisch, 1968), have yielded results
that suggest a similarly broad range of variation in behavior and
social organization, which appear to relate to specific physcial
features of the environment confronted by various troops of these
species.

For those interested in the behavioral development of nonhuman
primates, it is important to note that various aspects of mother-
infant interaction and early phases of the socialization process of
infant primates also seem related to social and physical environmental dimensions. For example, the relatively more terrestrial
Lemur catta infants are more precocious than the infants of *Lemur
fulvus. Lemur catta* infants are observed to move onto the mother's
back and ultimately away from her at an earlier age. The social
structure differences in the two species also result in the fact
that during the first month of life, *Lemur catta* infants are not
shared by various nonmother females in the group, whereas *Lemur
fulvus* infants are not shared at all during the first month and are
shared only rarely thereafter (Sussman, 1977). In much the same
manner, Gartlan and Brain (1968) suggested that differences in
the intensity of the mother-infant bond emerge in verets observed
in different habitats.

Clearly, it is not the purpose of the present chapter to catalog

the wealth of currently available material on the diverse forms of
nonhuman primate social organization and behavior within various
environmental settings. The preceding examples are presented
simply to remind the reader that not only did the evolution of the
primate order emerge in response to various and changing environmental demands, but also that extant primate species, and even
groupings within species, often confront diverse environmental
circumstances and appear to adapt their behavior accordingly. The
transfer of these wild forms to various laboratory conditions must
of necessity impose a new range of environmental stimuli and
constraints. The relationship between species and individual
characteristics, the structure of the environment within which they
are observed, and the particular behavior patterns being recorded
must be sensitively assessed. The concept of a "synomorphic relation" between the behavioral patterns (which are usually the foci
of research, and the environment within which such patterns are
observed, has been critically discussed in the human literature
(Schoggen, 1978), but the concept has failed to evoke sufficient
attention in laboratory animal research still influenced by an
earlier, specific S-R, investigative tradition. Furthermore,
although considerable effort has been directed toward the specific
study of human environments and situations, as well as attempts
at conceptual categorization of the settings within which behavior
occurs (e.g., Fredrikson, 1972; Moos, 1973), work in this area has
not kept apace at the nonhuman level.

Laboratory studies of nonhuman primates have repeatedly
demonstrated the impact of gross environmental factors on the
behaviors of the subjects under observation. Indeed, it has repeatedly been pointed out that the act of bringing wild forms into
captivity, by the very nature of the massive changes in available
space, feeding sites, and daily environmental rhythms, alters
drastically the behavior usually observed in the wild. For example,
relative increases in fighting and related agonistic activity under
captive conditions have been described in several species where
appropriate comparative data were available (e.g., Gartlan, 1968;
Kummer & Kurt, 1965). One succinct description of the type of
effects imposed by a captive environment on the patas monkey
(Erythrocepus patas) is provided by Gartlan (1968).

> Hall (1965) stated that the spread of individuals of
> a wild patas group during foraging, masured along
> and at right angles to the direction of movement,
> was often of the order of 300-500 m. He also indi-
> cated that some animals might be foraging as far as
> 800 m. from the remainder of the group. In contrast
> the room in which the captive group was kept at Bristol
> measures 14' 6" x 20' 10" x 10'. Thus animals which
> normally spend a good part of the day up to several
> hundred meters away from other group members are con-
> fined to a room of which the longest axis is less than
> 7 meters. In addition to the stress inevitably caused
> in this manner and expressed, as has been noted previously,

by an increase in aggression, certain other behavior
patterns are also altered. Terrestrial primate species
such as baboons and patas monkeys spend the greater
part of the day moving slowly in the home range, foraging and feeding. Indeed most other behavior can be
considered as taking place against this background.
In captivity this basic daytime pattern is replaced
by one or two brief feeding periods which occupy at
most an hour or so. This leaves up to 11 hours or
more of daylight, which would normally be taken up
foraging, unoccupied and with animals abnormally
crowded. It is to be expected that behavioral changes
will occur. (p. 104)

The unquestionable impact of the shift from the range and
diversity of natural environments of a species to the spectrum of
laboratory situations should not act as an inhibition to such
laboratory research. Rather, we must come to grips with the fact
that each laboratory environment is not "neutral" with regard to
any aspect of behavior we wish to study, just as each field setting
is not "neutral". Each species we place in these situations, whether
acutely or chronically, whether as adults or as infants, will act
to shape and reshape the patterns of social and nonsocial behavior
that we observe.

Perhaps the most dramatic studies of environmental impact on
the behavior of nonhuman primates are the series of investigations
on the effects of social-isolation rearing conditions in rhesus
macaques (see Sackett, 1968). These studies initially demonstrated
generally sustained behavioral alterations in rhesus monkeys as a
function of the duration and extent of early environmental deprivation. In more recent years, however, these studies have served to
emphasize that assessment of the effect of even such gross environmental distortions must take into account the nature of the subjects
reared under such circumstances. Sackett, Holm, Ruppenthal, and
Farhrenbruch (1976) have recently shown that pigtail infants (*Macaca
nemestrina*), when reared under similar deprivation conditions, do
not show the same behavioral deficits as rhesus. Similarly, other
studies show that even in rhesus macaques, females are not as
severely affected by deprivation-rearing as are males (Sackett, 1974).
The interplay of phylogenetic, gender, and ontogenetic environmental
variables, so beautifully illuminated by this series of studies,
has led Sackett et al. to conclude, "Rhesus monkeys, as a species,
appear to be more susceptible to isolation rearing effects than
pigtails. On the other hand, a wealth of data attests to the idea
that males are more vulnerable than females to postnatal insult.
Thus, the relative insensitivity of pigtails to isolation-rearing
effects may decrease the magnitude of measureable sex differences
in pigtail isolates. The relative susceptibility of rhesus to
isolation effects may, conversely, serve to magnify sex differences
in rhesus isolates. Although complex, this interaction of genetic
variables with impoverished rearing conditions may yet prove to be
an excellent experimental model of the study of individual differences
in abnormal behavior" (p. 128).

A similar illustration of the relationship between environmental factors during rearing and the emergence or obscuring of sexual differences can be seen in a study of squirrel monkey (*Saimiri sciureus*) infant development carried out in our laboratory (Rosenblum, 1974). For this study, 21 squirrel monkey mother-infant dyads containing 11 male and 10 female infants were studied in one of two rearing situations. All pens were approximately 1 x 1 meter and 2 1/2 meters high, and identical in basic physical structure; they contained shelves, watering devices, mesh ceilings, and a large one-way vision mirror on the front wall, through which all observations were made. All groups contained four dyads, sex-balanced at any given time. The normative-control subjects were housed as stable groups, formed when the infants were born; they lived in the same pen throughout the period of study. The normative control pens contained smooth, uncolored aluminum walls. For these control subjects, neither the social nor the physical environment was manipulated in any way during the course of the infants' development. For those subjects reared in what was designed as the "complex environment", four standard pens were altered to enhance their complexity. Each pen, otherwise identical to those of the normative groups, was wallpapered in different, wildly patterned and colored plastic material around the side and back walls of the pen. These wall coverings were removed and replaced with different patterns every 5 or 6 weeks. In addition to the wall coverings, the complex pens contained three or four different complex manipulanda. Also, for the complex groups, at the beginning of each week of the study, the composition of the study groups was rearranged so as to maximize unfamiliarity of group members, while maintaining the two male, two female infant composition of each group. At the same time the groups were socially restructured, each newly formed group was moved to a new complex pen. Thus, for the complex groups, both the social and the physical environments were manipulated each week in order to enhance total environmental complexity.

Observations in the development of infant-independence from the mother, measured in terms of decreases in filial contact, showed that within the first 20 weeks of life, three phases of infant development could be discerned; moreover, these two dramatically different environments affected subjects differently in each of the three successive phases. For approximately the first 6 weeks of life, neither male nor female infants differed from one another in the two environments, nor were there any discernible effects of the environments themselves. From approximately 6 to 12 weeks of life, both male and female infants did not differ in the normative environment, and infants of both sexes in the more complex environment showed a relative enhancement of infant attachment during this period. However, from approximately 14 to 20 weeks of age, although infants of the two sexes in the normative environment did not differ from one another in the development of their independent functioning from the mother, striking sex differences emerged in the complex environment. Female infants in the complex situation continued to show relatively heightened levels of infant attachment to the mother, as compared to those in the normative setting. On the other hand, male infants during this period of life showed significant decreases in the amount of infant attachment, both with respect to males reared under the normative, stable environmental conditions, and with regard to the females of the complex condition. Thus, it was clear that the nature of the environment, the gender of the infants, and the age at which they were observed, all interacted to produce the range of behaviors observed. No simple scheme for the objective description of this experimental situation suffices to describe or predict the nature of the differences in behavior observed, nor will any simple description allow for potential generalization to other species, other ages, or other conditions under which these or other types of subjects may be studied in the future.

This sampling of material indicates clearly that observable behavior is a product of complex interactions between factors in the historical and present physical and social environment, and the species, gender, age, and prior experience of the subjects under study. Consequently, how can we even attempt to establish a particular "ideal" situation in which to carry out all, or even many, of our studies? Such an effort seems likely to fail and not only does not solve all problems, but may perhaps obscure many of them. The situation which appears constant to us as humans is not invariant in the sense that it is the same for various subjects of a given species, whose sensory-motor and cognitive capacities may differ widely, placed within it. It is not the same for different groups or species whose genetic heritage impels them to greater or lesser attention and sensitivity to various dimensions of that environment. Indeed, it may be argued that this diversity of response, and the varied and changing environmental conditions to which such diversity is adaptive, provided the impetus to the evolution of the primate order. In this perspective, assessment of behavior under diverse circumstances, in both the field and the laboratory, is critical to our ultimate understanding of the origins of the diversity of patterns of which these forms are capable.

Discussing the significance of environmental diversity and its study in our attempts to understand the nature of man, Rene Dubos (1968) has argued, "We must shun uniformity of surroundings as much as absolute conformity to behavior, and make instead a deliberate effort to create as many diversified environments as possible. This may result in some loss of efficiency, but the more important goal is to provide the many kinds of soil that will permit the germination of the seeds now dormant in man's nature. Insofar as possible, the duplication of uniformity must yield to the organization of diversity. Richness and variety of the physical and social environment constitute crucial aspects of functionalism, whether in the planning of cities, the design of dwellings, or the management of life." (p. 154).

It grows evident, however, that if we are to develop a science which establishes lawful relationships between the patterns of behavior we observe and the environmental situation in which they occur, we must create some organized conceptual schema within which to describe these situations. We must, of course, accept the need for replication of observations and the requirement for detailed descriptions of situations, using the dimensional elements that are most pertinent and which are currently communicable, regarding our human perceptions of the situation (e.g., size of the area in meters, population in numbers of subjects and sex-age classes, illumination in footcandles, and hours of light and dark). Nonetheless, we must attempt some coherent description of such situations, in terms of the elements that are most relevant to the particular subjects under study, as well as the congruence of such features with the tasks which confront the subjects we observe. (See Stockols, 1978, for a discussion of the concepts of "salience" and "congruence" in regard to human-environment interactions.)

What follows is an initial attempt to suggest a possible taxonomy for describing laboratory situations in which the social behavior of nonhuman primates may be studied. It is important to point out that this suggested taxonomy derives from several underlying assumptions, some of which have been explicated above. First, it was assumed that at present, when it is feasible to use them, these descriptive dimensions would serve to supplement more traditional, quantitative measurement systems, rather than substitute for them. Secondly, wherever possible, an attempt was made to dimensionalize the situation in terms likely to be salient to the subjects under study. Third, it was deemed useful for experimental studies of behavior, in which quantitative manipulation of variables might be instituted, to provide a roughly ordinal scaling of levels within each situational dimension described. Fourth, an effort was made to incorporate both social and nonsocial situational elements. The fifth, and perhaps most important, assumption rests in the idea that the usefulness of this initial taxonomic effort will be measured in terms of the speed with which it is replaced by more empirically based, and less clearly biased dimensionalizations, derived from many more types of subjects viewed in many more situations than could be drawn upon at this time. It is critical to note that the current suggestions are drawn largely from extended laboratory experience with three species of macaques, studies of squirrel monkeys and marmosets, and a reasonable familiarity with the basic laboratory primate social literature. I make no pretense at providing a "complete" list of possible dimensions, and if this effort evokes any interest at all, I am sure that the "lumpers" and "splitters" among us will have ample room for suggesting the constriction or expansion of the list of dimensions proposed in Table 1.

In order to give the reader an overall view of the taxonomic structure offered, an outline of the total framework will be presented first, followed by a more detailed description of the elements listed and the author's rationalization.

It must be said from the onset that many of the elements suggested for incorporation in this preliminary situational taxonomy lack empirical quantification at present. The issue of the utility of these elements is, of course, related to the degree to which such

TABLE 1. SITUATIONAL TAXONOMY

A. *Physical Space:*

1. *Restraining:* Essentially prevents locomotion.

2. One-dimensional (single resting-movement area; considerably less than *full locomotive potential* (FLP)).

3. *Multi-dimensional* (several resting movement areas; less than FLP.

4. *FLP:* Allows full locomotive potential to be expressed in X time units.

5. *Abundant:* area exceeds S's capacit to reach all parts in X time.

B. *Psychological Space:*

1. *Obstructed:* area beyond resting place is unavailable, i.e., provides no stimuli.

2. *Bounded:* unobstructed but sharply delimited visual and auditory space; distances are less than *full-flight distance* (FFD).

3. *Full-Flight:* distances about equal to the full-flight distance may be observed without obstruction

4. *Horizon:* essentially unlimited distances and areas are observable.

5. *Appended:* primarily auditory and olfactory stimuli from outside the visually available environment impinge on S.

C. *Social Array:*

a) All Ss of same class or type

b) Ss differ from one another.

1. *Solitary:* S is alone.

2. *Dyadic:* One other S is present.

3. *Triadic:* Two other Ss are present.

c) mixture of same and different subject classes.

4. *Groups:* From 3 to *MSSR* other individuals present. (MSSR = Maximum stable social relationships.)

5. *Crowd:* Exceeds MSSR.

D. *Nonsocial Stimulus Array:*

1. *Barren:* devoid of salient, discrete stimuli.

2. *Minimal:* fewer stimuli than S can effectively encounter in X time.

3. *Matched:* equal to S's capacity to encounter effectively in X time.

4. *Rich:* Exceeds S's encounter capacity.

5. *Excessive:* overwhelmingly exceeds S's encounter capacity.

E. *Density:* A derivative dimension based on the relationship of physical and psychological space with social array and nonsocial stimulus array.

F. *Constancy:*

1. *Static*
2. *Slowly changing*
3. *Rapidly changing*

a) *One-directional*

b) oscillatory (repeated changes between a limited number of values)

c) *"Random"*

G. *Familiarity:*

1. *Unknown:* not previously encountered.

2. *Encountered:* previously encountered, but not thoroughly explored, known.

3. *Familiar:* fully explored.

4. *Habituated:* fully habituated
    setting or stimulus which has be-
    come so commonplace as to become
    "background".

H. *Reinforcement Potential:*   1. *Nonreinforcing:* no positive or
    (The availability of   negative reinforcement available.
    stimuli of either a
    positive or negative   2. *Single:* one source of one type
    nature which relate to   of reinforcement.
    individual survival)
                                 3. *Multi-single:* one source for each
                                     of more than one type of reinforce-
                                     ment.

                                 4. *Multiple:* more than one source
                                     for more than one type of rein-
                                     forcement.

                                     a) *Clustered:* one locus for
                                         "3" or "4".

                                     b) *Dispersed:* more than one
                                         locus for "3" or "4".

I. *Reinforcement Effort:*   1. *Ad Lib:* no environmental work
                                     required; immediately available.

                                 2. *Work:* only through locomotor or
                                     other work on nonanimate aspects
                                     of situation.

                                 3. *Noncompetitive:* supply exceeds
                                     demand in X units of time.

                                 4. *Competitive:* demand exceeds
                                     supply in X units of time.

---

elements may in fact be measured. Certainly, some factors appear to
have heuristic value or apparent face-validity encouraging their
inclusion, but they may turn out to be too difficult or impossible
to measure in each type of subject to afford them a useful place in
a more developed taxonomy. Conversely, some suggested elements can
be measured, but may in fact fail to show consistent relationships
with those behavioral assessments we seek to obtain. A second characteristic of the proposed taxonomy is that the primary dimensions, such
as physical and psychological space, social and nonsocial arrays,
will, in general, all be required descriptors of any given situation,

for any subject or groups of subjects. In manipulative studies, it should be possible to hold many dimensions relatively constant, while systematically manipulating others; in most studies which have other central concerns, description of the situation in terms of all or most of these dimensions will be necessary, and only through the compilation of many studies, each varying one or more dimensions slightly, can we hope to determine the role of some specific situational features. This latter approach would approximate conceptually the efforts of those seeking to ascertain the specific portion of the brain that governs a particular behavior. To accomplish this goal, depictions of many lesions, each varying somewhat, are graphically overlaid. The determination of the locus of control of a specific response is made by specifying the area of overlapping destruction between different specimens showing similar responses. In the same fashion, a number of studies, conducted within varying degrees of situational overlap, should illiminate the role of specific factors.

One additional point of general significance: inasmuch as this taxonomy derives from a perspective in which the situation must be considered from the subject's point of view, it may well be necessary to describe a particular situation differently for each member of a group of subjects placed within it. Stated most directly, regardless of the distress which such consideration engenders in the scientist, two mothers and their infants, for example, placed into an observation pan, may well mean that four, similar, but nonetheless distinguishable situations have been created and should be assessed and described. Along with the reader, I shudder at such a prospect, but the idiosyncratic nature of subject-situation interaction effects is the basis of evolutionary adaptation, and we no longer can close our eyes to this phenomenon.

PHYSICAL SPACE

This descriptor, as proposed, incorporates two main ideas. Is the situation composed of a single uninterrupted area in which subjects can move and rest, or is the situation multi-dimensional in this regard? Subjects that must rest or sleep in a single suitable location (e.g., for their age, species) and whose every locomotive movement places them in immediate interface with others engaged in the same activities, regardless of the total space, are likely to be in a functionally different situation than occurs when that space has many separable areas for these purposes. Rowell (1967) states the case most clearly: "In fact probably more important than the total space available is its arrangement --the amount of three dimensional movement possible, and the extent to which the area is broken up into sections relatively separate from each other. One of the most striking differences between caged and wild baboons, for example, is that a caged group occasionally appears to "get trapped" in a cycle of agonistic interactions which goes on and on until the animals inflict serious damage on each other. In the wild these interactions do not go on too long, because one individual goes out of sight behind a bush until the other has forgotten about the incident. Where a cage is subdivided, such potentially dangerous interactions can usually be *broken* by one animal "escaping" to a different section; but if the same total area is left as a single unit and the animals are always in each other's sight, bad fights may be more frequent" (p. 228).

Recent studies of the social structure of squirrel monkeys in our laboratory have incorporated the use of a total area divided into two identical subpens separated by an opaque wall, but connected by a small tunnel at shelf-height. In addition, each subpen also contained a narrow, opaque barrier, partially obscuring one end of each subpen. Studies conducted over periods as long as 18 months in this situation indicated the successful employment of these subareas in a consistent fashion by adult males and females of these squirrel monkey groups. Thus, in these studies of the sexually segregated social structure of squirrel monkeys, major portions of the male and female subgroups were rarely found within the same subpen area, and when this did take place, males were most often hidden behind the partial barrier of the subpen area. In addition, significant effects in terms of crossing from one area to another took place during development in infants that were subsequently born to females in this situation (Rosenblum & Coe, 1977).

The second facet of this physical space dimension is the concept of "full locomotive potential". It is assumed that even with unlimited space, subjects do not normally run unceasingly, jump unlimited distances, nor continuously climb to the highest possible point. An area which allows a given subject the opportunity to reach all its salient features and, at least briefly, ascend to heights frequently sought, to run at full speed, and make approximately the full distance leaps of which it is capable, represents a situation in which a subject can express its *Full Locomotive Potential* (FLP). However, given the range of activity in which a subject may engage in any situation and the normal time constraints under which laboratory studies are usually undertaken, it was judged necessary to consider whether a given situation could allow FLP within a prescribed period of time, or if the area exceeded S's capacity in this regard. Thus, for example, a 6-foot square room with several shelves and perches, in which a subject is placed for a 5-minute test, may be "abundant" physical space, but the same subject living continuously in the same room may find this space equal to or less than its FLP.

PSYCHOLOGICAL SPACE

The first two levels of this dimension may be considered to be typified by the usual isolation and "home cage" situations, whereas "horizon" levels are typified by semifree-ranging arena situations. Subjects remain acutely aware of stimuli whose source can often be perceived, but to which access is prevented. Regardless of the physical dimensions of the constraining area, it is my impression that source-detectable stimuli from outside are generally responded to differently than those within the accessible portion of the situation, hence the proposed distinction between "bounded" and "appended" situations. While the latter situation may influence arousal levels, for example, and clearly alter ongoing behavior within the situation, specific orientation effects and discrete, outward-directed behaviors would usually be absent in the "appended" situation.

The concept of "Full-Flight Distance" (FFD) is an attempt to incorporate a psychological distance factor that may have broad applicability across subject types. In part as a function of the multi- or one-dimensionality of the available space, it is suggested that for each type of subject, the perceived availability of an unobstructed flight path, geared to the most active avoidance reactions of these subjects, may play a significant role in influencing ongoing behavior and social relations. As suggested above, in a multi-dimensional situation this FFD may be considerably less in absolute distance than in a one-dimensional situation. Similarly, the relationship between FFD and other psychological aspects structuring the situation, such as food distribution, may be quite complex. Nonetheless, there is an underlying assumption here that some degree of stress will be experienced when FFD is unavailable. Complicating matters further, however, it is worth noting that studies of mothers with their infants, during some early stages of infant development, suggest that for some aspects of their behavior, mothers may be more "relaxed" in situations offering less, rather than more, psychological space. Thus, mothers raising their infants alone in small cages may allow them to break contact earlier and for longer periods than mothers in larger enclosures.

SOCIAL ARRAY

The step from isolation to the presence of a single partner may be assumed to be profound for almost any type of subject. The shift to interaction with more than one other partner, the triad, is less self-evident a step on the way to larger groupings, but it does involve a considerably greater complexity of interaction possibilities than the dyadic situation and hence is worthy of separate categorization.

The concept of "maximum stable social relationships" (MSSR) is, however, a decidedly larger inductive leap in this taxonomic structure. Both field and laboratory observations of subjects in large groups suggest that although recognition of large numbers of group members may be possible, relatively consistent patterns of frequent interaction, stable over time, does not occur between all members of such groupings. Indeed, it may be possible, in some species at least, that this factor provides some constraint on the total size of the groups found under natural conditions (cf. Marler, 1976). Varying as a function of the discrimination and memory capacities of different subjects, the MSSR may differ accordingly, and hence the influence of different absolute numbers of subjects in the social array may vary in as yet unspecifiable ways. It is interesting to note that Esser and Deutsch (1978) have recently discussed the importance of this point in considering the relatively primitive pattern of social structures developed by chronic mental patients, held within institutions, who "...seem unable to focus attention upon all group relations simultaneously and thus often have to establish and protect their status in one-to-one dominance encounters with others."

As a second facet of this dimension, one must consider the relative homogeneity or heterogeneity of the social array with respect to any given subject. Again, the effects of the absolute number of subjects in the total array, or the behavior of any given subject, may differ as a function of their similarity or dissimilarity to the subject in question. For some purposes, for example, play in a 6-month-old, the number of same-species, and perhaps, same-sex, peers may be far more relevant than the number of adolescent females or heterospecific partners in the group. As a result of these considerations, it is suggested that the dimension of *Social Array* requires the inclusion of factors regarding both the number and homogeneity of the social group.

NONSOCIAL STIMULUS ARRAY

Two points should be made regarding the categories of this dimension. Each type of subject in a situation will attempt to reach, explore, or contact only a finite number of discrete, salient elements of the situation in a given period of time. Clearly, a number of factors, including the nature and complexity of the stimuli and the subject's familiarity with them or similar stimuli, will influence the pace at which it will actually encounter these elements. Thus, the possible influence of the number (and nature) of stimuli "available" must also be judged in terms of the time available to the subject in the situation. When a subject is able to make at least some degree of psychological or physical contact with all the major elements of the stimulus array in a given period of time, the environment is judged to be "matched" to the subject. Two subjects, for example, dropped into a bare room for a 5-minute test, may find the walls of the room itself a "matched" array. On the other hand, the same pen would emerge as "minimal" or "barren" with the passage of time. Thus, in terms of the direct effect on exploratory and play behavior, or the influence on social and other behaviors less immediately tied to specific features of the stimulus array, both the time dimension and the features of the array must be considered.

The usefulness of the distinction between "rich" and "excessive" arrays derives from the idea that a situation can contain many more salient stimuli than a subject can respond to in a given period of time. Such a situation may, in fact, produce a significant amount of stress and thus evoke agitation, avoidance, or arousal-reducing behavior, such as the flight of an infant to its mother. It is important to note, as Baldwin and Baldwin (1977) point out, that the perceptual awareness of the diversity of salient stimuli within a situation, will depend upon the discriminative capacity of the subject, and that "These discrimination skills vary with species' cortical capacity, age and history of learning" (p. 397).

CONSTANCY

It is clear that, except under unusually rigorous laboratory
conditions or under circumstances in which a subject is present in a
given situation for relatively brief periods, the situation which
confronts the subject often changes over time. These changes may
be controlled by the observer as part of the experimental paradigm,
they may occur as a result of factors outside of the observer's
control, or, in fact, they may be the product of the subject's own
efforts. As Stockols (1978) describes for humans, "Transactional
views suggest that any attempt to conceptualize the relationship
between environment and behavior must account not only for the
effects of the environment on people, but also for the reciprocal
impact of people on their milieu" (p. 279). The transactional or
bidirectional nature of the subject's relationship with a situation has not been the focus of much attention in studies of non-
anthropoid primates; however, as anyone who has observed the
systematic dismantling of a laboratory pen by a group of macaques
can attest, these animals clearly help to structure the situations
in which they live.

Moreover, the changes which occur in a situation may take place
more or less rapidly. Thus the subject may be confronted with a
slowly incrementing novelty which can be readily explored and
assimilated, or a rush of potentially overwhelming stimulus change.
However, the impact of the rate of change is likely to be affected
by the relative predictability of change from one point in time to
the next. In humans, it is clear in a variety of situations that
predictability (and, perhaps even more so, control) of salient
stimulus change can reduce stress effects (Stockols, 1978). "One-
directional" changes in various situations are not uncommon.
Increments or decrements in temperature or illumination or even
group size may change so gradually as to produce little detectable
change in behavior. Thus, because of the nature of the stimuli
undergoing change, the rate of change, and the discrimination
thresholds of the subjects, the effects of some one-directional
changes may be difficult to assess even during rather broad ranges
of shifting stimulus values. When situations do change perceptibly,
however, it is likely that the impact of such changes would be more
orderly and predictable (both for the animals and the observer) when
the changes oscillate amongst a limited number of conditions to which
the subjects can develop (over repeated shifts) a structured pattern
of responses. Random or unpredictable situational shifts, depending
on their salience, are much more likely to produce a general dis-
ruption of behavior and confound our best attempts to determine
systematic relationships between experimental variables studied
within that type of situation. It should also be noted that in
light of the importance of stable biorhythms of various sorts in
affecting primate behavior, the predictability of the time at which
changes occur, as well as the nature of such changes, must be
considered.

FAMILIARITY

This dimension pertains to all social and nonsocial aspects of the situation. The term "fully explored" is here intended to mean that the subject has reached the point in which a significant drop in the exploration of a stimulus has occurred; though perhaps still salient to the subject, the animal appears to have gained almost all available information about the stimulus that it is motivated or able to obtain. When stimuli no longer appear to hold any further sustained interest to the subject, these habituated stimuli provide a background for other factors. These stimuli can reemerge as important, however, when abrupt changes in these elements occur, and such changes can markedly effect behavior, although more gradual shifts in them may not be detected.

REINFORCEMENT POTENTIAL

It is hypothesized here that the perceived structure of the situation will influence the pattern of a subject's response as a function of the circumstances under which positive and negative reinforcement of various types are available. Needless to say, if a subject is to survive, the availability of food or water or the occurrence of painful or other aversive stimuli in the situation will be critical factors. Various subjects may respond differently as a function not only of the type of reinforcement potentially available, but whether alternate sources of the reinforcement are present, as well as the relative spatial dispersion of those various sources. The capacity of a dominant subject to control food access, for example, cannot be the same when only one food source is present, as compared to conditions in which food may be obtained from various sources. Similarly, the dominant subject's capacity to control food access will be affected by its own need to acquire water at a location close to, or distant from, the food source. Once again, observations of various species in the wild show the difference in various types of social behavior as a function of the dispersal of various resources (Rowell, 1967). It is important to note, however, that metabolic ingredients (e.g., food and water) are not presumed to be the only types of reinforcement possible in a situation; positive and negative social reinforcements, and the opportunities for exploratory activities, for example, must also be considered within this total scheme--again, as a function of the type of subjects under study.

REINFORCEMENT EFFORT

This "final" element of the taxonomy reflects two concerns. The first grows out of the idea that the situation in which subjects are observed may, in fact, leave subjects with "too much time on their hands". That is, subjects whose natural habitats, (i.e., those within which the species evolved) may require them to spend several or even

many hours a day to sustain themselves, may now find literally no
time required to obtain food, water, or shelter. On the other hand,
extremely time- or quantity-limited distributions of food or other
resources, or the requirement of high work effort to obtain these
"rewards" (such as a prolonged operant schedule), may quite literally
leave no time for anything but the pursuit of these incentives. This
latter circumstances, in which acquisition of vital incentives requires
protracted time and/or effort, can also occur naturally and has been
observed to have severe effects on ongoing behavior. As Rowell (1967)
says, "...if conditions are bad enough, social behavior almost dis-
appears". Finally, the total amount of significant resources, their
spatial dispersal, and the effort necessary to obtain them, must be
considered in a combined framework that considers both social and
temporal factors. Competition occurs in any situation in which demand
exceeds supplies in a given period of time, and its social and behavioral consequences follow. As with all other factors considered in this
taxonomic scheme, the absolute amount of food present, for example,
is not the sole issue. Who wants the food, how much they want, and
how much time they have in which to obtain what they want (not necessarily what they *need*) must be the basis on which the reinforcement
effort dimension of the situation must be conceptualized.

CONCLUSION

These nine dimensions, by which situations may be described, represent a range of features which are likely to influence behavior in
a number of experimental paradigms. The usual "objective" descriptions
of laboratory settings do, of course, provide some basis for comparisons across studies and study groups. However, such descriptions may
mask similarities between subjects, by failing to delineate the dissimilarities in the psychological dimensions of the situations in
which the subjects are observed. Consider, for example, the response
of pigtail and bonnet macaques to feeding situations in social groups.
As a by-product of their rather large individual distance pattern,
pigtails may be quite aggressive during feeding, if food is dispensed from a single or nondispersed set of sources. Multiple sources
of food, dispersed over their laboratory pen, will, however, allow
relatively placid feeding patterns to emerge. In bonnets, on the
other hand, small individual distances appear to be characteristic
of the species, and bonnets will contentedly feed together from a
single food-hopper. Thus, depending upon this dimension of food
dispersal, bonnets and pigtails may emerge as similar or dissimilar
in at least this aspect of their aggressive behavior.

Failure to delineate situational features from the perspective of
different classes of subjects may also mask dissimilarities as well.
Traditional studies of squirrel monkey infant development, for example,
were carried out in stable social groups and nominally unchanging or
static physical settings. Under these conditions, male and female
infants are virtually identical in the development of time spent off
their mother in the first 5 months of life. However, when the
situation is changed to one in which the social and physical environment changes abruptly and repeatedly during early development, male

and female infants differ dramatically in the pace of developing independence. Males in the changing situation were more independent of their mothers, whereas females remained somewhat more dependent (Rosenblum, 1974). Thus, in a sense, neither the *static* nor the *changing* situation was the same for the two sexes. There is reason to believe that because of sex differences in response thresholds, the *static* situation provided a *minimal* stimulus array for males, but a *matched* situation for females. Similarly, the *rapidly changing* situation may well have been *matched* for males, but *rich* or *excessive* for females. It is clear that we have only scratched the surface in our consideration of situational effects influencing primate behavior. If studies comparing species, males and females, or subjects of different ages or background are to have meaning, we must attempt to incorporate the objectively disparate conditions within which they are observed into an integrated conceptual framework. The preliminary taxonomy proposed here is a step in that direction.

In light of all that has been discussed above, it is unlikely that too many readers will perceive this taxonomic structure as does the writer. Some will see gaps where I see consistency, some will discern confusion where I perceive order, and doubtless many will see obscurity where I see profundity. If this preliminary effort arouses sensibilities, as well as sensitivities, to the area of situational constraints on behavior, so much the better. What is crucial is the recognition of the problem and the idea that some coherent effort must be made that conceptually organizes the disparate situational contexts in which we observe nonhuman primates.

REFERENCES

Baldwin, J. D., & Baldwin, J. I. The role of learning phenomena in the ontogeny of exploration and play. In S. Chevalier-Skolnikoff and F. E. Poirier (Eds.), *Primate biosocial development*. New York: Garland, 1977.
Dubois, R. Environmental determinance of human life. In D. C. Glass (Ed.), *Environmental influences*. New York: Rockefeller University Press, 1969.
Esser, A. H., & Deutsch, R. D. Private and interaction territories on psychiatric wards: Studies on nonverbal communication of spatial needs. In M. T. McGuire & L. A. Fairbanks (Eds.), *Ethological psychiatry*. New York: Grune & Stratton, 1978.
Fredrikson, N. Towards a taxonomy of situations. *American Psychologist,* 1972, *27,* 114-123.
Frisch, J. E. Individual behavior and inter-troop variability in Japanese macaques. In P. Jay (Ed.), *Studies in adaptation and variability*. New York: Holt, Rinehart & Winston, 1968.
Gartlan, J. S. Structure and function in primate society. *Folia Primatologica*, 1968, *8,* 89-120.
Gartlan, J. S., & Brain, C. K. Ecology and social variability. In P. Jay (Ed.), *Studies in adaptation and variability*. New York: Holt, Rinehart & Winston, 1968.

Jay, P. C. Primates. In P. Jay (Ed.), *Studies in adaptation and variability*. New York: Holt, Rinehart, & Winston, 1968.

Kummer, H. Two variations in social organization of baboons. In P. Jay (Ed.), *Studies in adaptation and variability*. New York: Holt, Rinehart, & Winston, 1968.

Kummer, H., & Kurt, F. A comparison of social behavior in captive and wild hamadryas baboons. In H. Vagtborg (Ed.), *The baboon in medical research*. Austin: University of Texas Press, 1965.

Lewin, K. Behavior and development as a function of the total situation. In D. Cartwright (Ed.), *Field theory in social science*. New York: Harper, 1951.

Marler, P. On animal aggression: The roles of strangeness and familiarity. *American Psychologist*, 1976, *31*, 239-246.

Moholy-Nagy, L. *Vision in motion*. Chicago: Paul Theobald, 1956.

Moos, R. H. Conceptualization in human environments. *American Psychologist*, 1973, *28*, 652-655.

Parker, S. P., & Gibson, K. R. Object manipulation, tool use, and sensorimotor intelligence as feeding adaptations in cebus monkeys and great apes. *Journal of Human Evolution*, 1977, *6*, 623-641.

Petrucci, R. Origine, polyphyletique, homotypie a et non-comparabilite direct des societes animales. (1906), cited by I. H. Crook in Social organization and the environment: Aspects of contemporary social ethology. *Animal Behaviour*, 1970, *18*, 197-209.

Rosenblum, L. A. Sex differences, environmental complexity, and mother-infant relations. *Archives of Sexual Behavior*, 1974, *3*, 117-128.

Rosenblum, L. A., & Coe, C. L. The influence of social structure on squirrel monkey socialization. In S. Chevalier-Skolnikoff & F. E. Poirier (Eds.), *Primate biosocial development*. New York: Garland, 1977.

Rowell, T. E. Variability in the social organization of primates. In D. Morris (Ed.), *Primate ethology*. Chicago: Aldine, 1967.

Sackett, G. P. Abnormal behavior in laboratory reared rhesus monkeys. In M. W. Fox (Ed.), *Abnormal behavior in animals*. Philadelphia: W. B. Saunders, 1968.

Sackett, G. P. Sex differences in rhesus monkeys following varied rearing experiences. In R. C. Friedman, R. M. Richart, & R. L. Vande Wiele (Eds.), *Sex differences in behavior*. New York: Wiley, 1974.

Sackett, G. P., Holm, R. A., Ruppenthal, G. C., & Farhrenbruch, C. E. The effects of total social isolation rearing on behavior of rhesus and pigtail macaques. In T. Walsh & R. Greenough (Eds.), *Environment as therapy for brain dysfunction*. New York: Plenum Press, 1976.

Schoggen, P. Ecological psychology and mental retardation. In G. P. Sackett (Ed.), *Observing behavior*. Baltimore: University Park Press, 1978.

Stockols, D. Environmental psychology. *Annual Review of Psychology*, 1978, *29*, 253-295.

Sussman, R. W.   Socialization, social structure and ecology of two
    sympatric species of lemur.   In S. Chevalier-Skolnikoff & F. E.
    Poirier (Eds.), *Primate biosocial development*.   New York:
    Garland, 1977.

Tinbergen, N.   *The study of instincts*.   London: Oxford University
    Press, 1951.

von Uexkull, J.   *Umwelt and innenwelt der tier*.   Berlin: Springer,
    1921.

Yarrow, L. J.   The crucial nature of early experience.   In D. C.
    Glass (Ed.), *Environmental influences*.   New York: Rockefeller
    University Press, 1968.

Yoshiba, K.   Local and inter-troop variability in ecology and social
    behavior of common Indian langurs.   In P. Jay (Ed.), *Studies
    in adaptation and variability*.   New York: Holt, Rinehart &
    Winston, 1968.

14.
General discussion of the methodological problems involved in the study of social interaction

EMIL W. MENZEL, JR.

I would draw three general conclusions from this conference. First, we do not yet have, and may never have, any single method for the analysis of social interactions that is ideal for everybody. Second, our basic problems lie more in conceptual considerations than in the lack of sophisticated technology. Third, despite these facts, the study of social behavior has never been more important, exciting and promising than it is today, and there is more than one ray of hope for the future development of better methods and the solution of increasingly complicated problems.

The present paper elaborates upon these themes. For the most part I shall concentrate on matters pertaining to the description and classification of behavior, rather than on problems of experimental or statistical analysis. Also, I shall try to avoid simply repeating what the other authors have said, especially since I agree with most of what they say and could not say it any better. Instead, I shall rise to a higher level of abstraction--cloud nine, no doubt--and try to take a bird's eye view of the forest through which we have been trying to hack our way. As one who is primarily interested in animal behavior, I am not sure how much of my discussion will be of interest to students of human social psychology; readers can judge this for themselves.

WHAT CHARACTERISTICS WOULD A METHOD HAVE TO POSSESS

TO BE IDEAL FOR EVERYBODY?

Each particular method develops as a tool for solving the theoretical or practical problems that seem paramount at a particular time in a particular area of research. Given the way in which the study of social behavior has expanded and diversified in the last

decades--not to mention the profound changes that have occurred
in psychology and the philosophy of science more generally--it is
hardly surprising that each method is eventually seen as having some
shortcomings. Rather than enumerate the shortcomings of particular
methods, it might be more useful and constructive in the long run
to ask ourselves what characteristics a method would have to possess
before we consider it ideal. Putting together all of the discussions
we had at this conference, I arrived at the following list.

Generality and flexibility. In order to be considered ideal,
a method should, at least in principle, be applicable to any species,
any system (ecosystem, society, group, dyad, individual-as-a-whole,
intra-individual) and any situation (including laboratory or field
and experimental or observational situation).

Non-procrustean nature. The application of an ideal method
would not distort the system under study nor require us to modify
the system in order to study it.

Simplicity. An ideal method would utilize the full complexity
of the real world in its very construction but at the same time be
extremely simple, intelligible and precisely defined.

Objectivity and reliability. The procedure for obtaining
information from any given sytem would be accessible to other
observers and readily replicated by them.

Parsimony. All of the data obtained by an ideal method could
be summarized succinctly, if not expressed in a single equation or
set of equations.

Adequacy. At the same time, nothing of fundamental importance
should be omitted from the analysis. As Fisher stated this ideal,
"A quantity of data which by its mere bulk is incapable of entering
the mind is to be replaced by relatively few quantities which shall
adequately represent the whole, or which, in other words, shall
contain as much as possible, ideally the whole, of the relevant
information contained in the original data" (Fisher, 1922).

Naturalism. The ideal method would obtain all of its information from the system under study, rather than appealing to outside
sources, especially those that might be inaccessible to other
observers.

Practicality. The hardware and software that are involved
would be cheap, portable and trouble-free; and the method would
render results rapidly, if not on-line.

Legality. Any method must of course not violate accepted legal
and ethical standards.

It may be seen that these various ideals are like Scylla,
Charybdis and their sister islands. Especially since the priorities
we attach to each are apt to fluctuate from time to time, it is
perhaps impossible to steer past all of them without getting knocked
about or smashed up at some point. Sackett is probably correct in
asserting that if any one characteristic (other than legality) is
absolutely necessary it is reliability. I would add, however, that
the ultimate and most general criterion of reliability is how well
one's basic findings or conclusions can be replicated, and more
specific measures are useful principally as estimates and facets of
this molar quantity.

In addition to the above nine ideals, which would seem to apply
in almost any area of science, we should probably add a tenth ideal
that is especially pertinent in the behavioral sciences, and call
it something like "correspondence with everyday knowledge or common
sense". (In some ways this amounts to broadening the ideal of
"adequacy" to include qualitative and phenomenological considerations as well as information that can be quantified in the Fisherian
sense. In other ways it might run counter to the ideal of "naturalism"
in that we might be making an appeal to sources of information other
than those derived solely from the system under study.) As Köhler
(1971, pp. 430-433) noted, there is a basic difference between how
we view the behavior of living beings and how a physicist views the
behavior of inanimate objects. The physicist observes only facts
of concomitance and sequence, and s/he can never tell us what a
causal connection really is. That is, causal connections are not
observed directly; they are inferred by indirect means, which we
call induction. But in psychology we have both: causal relationships and gestalt properties that we experience directly, and
causal relationships of which we know no more than physicists
know of connections in their field.

If our perception of a behavioral situation gave us only the
same kinds of information that a physicist obtains from his/her
observations, Köhler continued, such a situation would appear
to us as an array of functionally unrelated facts--until the scene
was studied with the techniques of induction--and the same would
hold for our perception of behavioral sequences. Instead, we
ordinarily feel quite capable of determining (for example) whether
animal A is actively approaching (or attracted by) animal B, or
withdrawing from (or being repelled by) something else that lies
in the opposite direction, or simply bumbling into B while oblivious
of its presence. Indeed, a vast majority of the terms that psychologists and ethologists employ to describe the behavior of people
or animals imply some such direct knowledge of functional or causal
relationships (cf. fighting, caressing, playing, grooming, avoiding)
and would scarcely be appropriate in a *purely* inductive, physical
science.

Köhler maintained that the possiblity of observing causal
relationships and gestalts directly gives psychologists a big
advantage over physical scientists, but also an obligation to relate
the sorts of information they obtain by classical scientific
induction to the sorts of knowledge they gain by direct experience.
Certainly such a position is still a theoretically controversial
one in psychology, and much current research consists of breaking
down molar actions and interactions into their components for closer
analysis (instead of accepting our "direct perception" uncritically).
At the same time, I see no evidence that any student of behavior
has ever avoided all inferences other than those established by
induction, or that such a feat, if it were possible, would tell
any student of behavior all s/he cares to know. In other words,
this tenth ideal is, at least implicitly, accepted by everyone;
what is controversial is how far we should carry it and how much
weight we should attach to it.

SOME PROBLEMS WITH CURRENT METHODS

The major problems with current methods probably lie less in hardware or software than in super-software. As Wittgenstein once said, "in psychology there are experimental methods and *conceptual confusion*.... The existence of the experimental method makes us think we have the means of solving the problems that trouble us; though problem and method pass one another by" (1968, p. 232). Although many exciting and important advances in science have come about as the result of technical inventions and procedural and statistical innovations, the opposite is just as likely to be true. Indeed, it seems to me that very often when a given area of research reaches the state where it can be fully automated or where professiona methodologists can tell everyone else precisely what to do, that area is likely to be scientifically moribund. In this regard it is worth noting that many of the major advances in current field research and research on social behavior stemmed from biologists and anthropologists who probably had not read enough about psychological methodology circa 1930-1960 to know that "good, sound, scientific research" in this area was just not possible (see, for example, Lorenz, 1971). Rather than trying to perfect an ideal method or general theory before looking for phenomena on which to test them out, they concentrated on the animals or the natural phenomena that they considered to be of intrinsic interest, and adopted or developed whatever methods and concepts seemed to provide the clearest insight into them.

My point here is not to argue for any one approach as such, but rather to stress that the *first* methodological problem, the *first* theoretical problem and the *first* naturalistic problem are one and the same: What is going on "out there" and what do we really want to account for? (The first applied and ethical problems, on the other hand, are: What can we do about this phenomenon, and what should we do about it?) In this sense, phenomena or events, and not our labels for them, are the ultimate measure of real things in psychology. Contrary to what some naturalists imply, merely sitting and staring does not always suffice as a method for gaining insight into events, nor is any method totally neutral, theoretically or ethically speaking. The methodologist is above all concerned with how to solve problems. And the first requirement here is obviously to recognize problems and to state them clearly enough to grapple with them. The more straightforwardly, clearly and completel one can specify what sort of problem it is that one is working with, the more obvious it will become that it is either solvable in principle or not solvable; and once one is certain on this score a methodologist's work is almost half finished. The difficulty of course is how to achieve such certainty; and this is not specifically a methodological problem.

What are we trying to account for? Many investigators would say that the central problem of social psychology is the same as the central problem of psychology in general: To account for (or to predict and control) the variance of behavior. In my opinion, such statements are not merely vague and uninformative but inaccurate.

The first question that immediately arises here is, *Whose* behavior?
What is the entity or natural system for whose actions we are trying
to account? In psychology this entity is the individual organism,
or more accurately the individual in interaction with a given
environment; but social psychologists may alternately focus their
attention here, or on dyadic interactions as such, or on somewhat
higher-order interactions (for example, mother-infant-father-
experimenter interactions) or on a "group as a whole" (in which
case an entire aggregate is treated, for purposes of analysis, as
if it were a single organism). Much discussion in the social and
behavioral sciences still centers around the question of which
focus of attention is the most appropriate one, and changes in
the general climate of opinion occur periodically. Since in any
situation consisting of N individuals, O objects and P experimenters
there are $2^{N+O+P} - 1$ possible combinations that might be considered
(including individuals, dyads, triads, quartets, and so on), such
discussions will undoubtedly continue unabated for many years unless
we can develop methods that permit us to deal with all components
of the ecosystem (or at least several of them) simultaneously.

The difficulty with taking individual behavior as one's central
problem is simply that, psychologically speaking, each individual's
view of the world is to some extent unique, idiosyncratic and inconsistent with those of other individuals. If one is trying to
deal with several such points of view simultaneously, there is no
known way in which one can achieve an overview of all of them that
does not do violence to any of them.[1] This is just as true for
current behavioral studies as it is true for phenomenologically-
oriented studies.

My own solution to this problem (Menzel, 1974, in press a,
in press b) is no doubt partial and dualistic. It involves
focusing on locational or spatial aspects of behavior and then
asking two different classes of questions: (a) Physicalistic
questions, such as, Where will this individual (or sub-group,
or group-as-a-whole) go next? (b) Mentalistic questions, such as,
What do the above facts suggest about the animals' perceptual,
cognitive or social-affectional organization? It is principally
when one gets into the latter sorts of questions that it is difficult to discuss various "levels of analysis" (i.e., individual,
dyadic, group) simultaneously.

A second problem in equating social psychology with the study
of "behavior as such" is that this term is so vague that in practice
it can mean just about anything. Classical ethology notwithstanding,
behavior is certainly not an object at which we can point as we
might point at a tree or a rock: it is an ongoing process, and

---

1. In everyday life, this problem is ordinarily solved by creating
a dominance hierarchy among the various possible points of view and
designating the point of view of a committee, court or outside judge
as the final authority. In psychology, the investigators appoint
themselves as the outside judges; they may or may not recognize that
alternative points of view are possible.

there are an indefinitely large number of ways to describe it--most
of which are in use today. Even if we were to consider behavior
as overt bodily movement per se, the contrast between a psychological
description of motion and the sorts of description used in classical
mechanics is quite striking. In classical mechanics, there is very
little confusion or disagreement about how to describe the behavior
of a given system. The total pattern of motion is considered to be
completely described once one can specify the position and velocity
of the various independent components of the system at any given
time and express these data in the form of equations. In psychology,
a comparable description would ordinarily be considered quite incomplete (some investigators would say meaningless), largely because
the interest of most psychologists is in larger functional, molar
units or chunks of motion, not motion as continuous process.

As Skinner (1953) once remarked, in psychology we chop the
continuous flow of behavior into rather arbitrary chunks
("operants"), and then we face the problem of putting these chunks
back together again and determining their overall organization.
Powers (1973) states the issue even more strongly. According to
him, behavior is not a directly observable thing that anyone can
see just by looking, for the point of view of the observer determines what s/he will see. Unfortunately, it is not the point of
view of the observer but that of the subject or the system under
study which should be of central interest. What we need, then,
are more general techniques which do not carve behavior into fixed,
a priori categories but which enable us to record events in such a
way that we can discover the correct point of view and the most
appropriate categories.

I believe that some of the methods of motion analysis that are
used in mechanics and biomechanics might be very suggestive here,
so long as we remember that, in contrast to behavioral science,
physical science is principally interested in objects rather than
subjects (do objects have any "point of view" in which we would
be interested?) and in "closed" rather than "open" systems. Other,
perhaps more useful, alternatives for the analysis of behavior-as-
continuous-process are the Eshkol-Wachmann system (e.g., Golani,
1976) and the systems under development by Johansson (1975) and
Westman (1977).

"Behavior taxonomy." Especially if one is interested in
quantal units of behavior (and what student of behavior is not?)
there is much that can be learned by using the highly sophisticated
classification system of classical biological taxonomy (see, for
example, Simpson, 1961) as a model of what we should be trying to
do. Unfortunately, it is rare to find any existing ethogram that
consists of anything more than a rather arbitrary list or catalogue
of items that strike the observer's fancy. In other words, there
is little by way of order or organization in such classifications,
and the basic rules or principles of classification bear no clear
relation to the principles of classical taxonomy. As Wilson puts
it, "...higher classifications of communicative acts [and social
interactions in general]... are a straightforward taxonomic exercise
limited by the built-in arbitrariness in the definition of unit

categories and clustering procedures. The difficulty is exacerbated
by the fact that social behavior is very far removed from the genotype and is unusually genetically labile. ... To collect behaviors
of different species in a single category is increasingly a matter
of judging analogy rather than homology, a largely subjective
procedure" (1975, p. 217).

The basic difference between "behavioral taxonomy" and the
taxonomy of organisms, other than the fact, noted earlier, that
the "objects" to be classified are not objects at all, and bypassing
the criticism of classical taxonomy that has been made by numerical
taxonomists such as Sokal and Crovello (1970), is that in the latter
field there is in principle a single ultimate criterion according
to which classifications are made. Two or more organisms are judged
to belong to the same class only insofar as they share the same
genotype or phylogenetic origin; and this criterion rests, of course,
on the neo-Darwinian theory of natural selection, which is viewed
as basic to all of biology. In behavioral taxonomy, on the other
hand, there are many different criteria that might be employed, and
no clear consensus as to which of these criteria are most fundamental.
Two or more behaviors may at times be said to be similar or to belong
to the same class if they appear similar to the observer in their:

   Morphology, topography or physical appearance;
   Function, consequence or effect upon the environment or upon
other individuals;
   Causation, or the factors which produce them (and these may
include internal and environmental factors);
   Ontogenesis, including maturational and learned factors;
   Phylogenesis, or evolutionary origin;
or if
   They occur in close sequential or temporal proximity to each other;
   They occur in similar situations or contexts;
   Individuals who score high (or low) on one behavior also score high
(or low) on the other; i.e., "individual differences" are the presumed
common cause;
   The subject or the observer can draw any analogy or metaphor that
relates them to one another (for example, Freudian equivalence, and
scientific models of various sorts). [For recent discussions and cri-
tiques of behavioral taxonomy, see for example Reynolds (1976), Wilson
(1975), Fagen and Goldman (1977). The above list is derived largely
from Reynolds.]

It should be apparent that these criteria are for the most part
complementary, and that behaviors judged "similar" in one respect are
not necessarily "similar" in other respects. Which criterion is the
fundamental one? I do not believe that this issue will ever be resolved merely by empirical demonstrations (such as determining which
sorts of units produce the smoothest graphs) or computer methods (such
as those employed in numerical taxonomy). Until such time as behavioral
investigators arrive at some theoretical or conceptual consensus--on a
par with the agreement of biologists about the importance of evolutionary considerations--the term "behavior taxonomy" should be used
in a hopeful rather than a factual sense.

This is not to say that the problem itself is unimportant.
Indeed, there are few if any methodological problems more fundamental

to an aspiring science than determining what one's basic units and principles of classification into higher categories are going to be. And lest it seems like an impossible dream to think that we can ever devise a satisfactory scheme for classifying all or most of the tremendous diversity of behaviors seen in humans, it might be remembered that there are several million organisms, all of which are presently classified according to the same basic principles--and this number is many times larger than the number of behavioral terms to be found in anyone' dictionary.

The uncertainty principle in behavior. In quantum mechanics the Heisenberg uncertainty principle asserts that one cannot simultaneously specify the exact position and the exact velocity of a particle. (Under ordinary conditions, where our observations are not very precise this is usually not a serious practical problem.) In trying to record the momentary location and ongoing behavior of young chimpanzees in a small indoor room, it became apparent to me that a precisely similar situation exists in psychology: the more precisely we tried to define the "instant" at which we made our observations so as to specify where the animal was (to the nearest 2 ft), the less we could say about its ongoing behavior. Indeed, at the point at which two observers could reach 95% exact agreement on locations, they could no longer even say with confidence whether the animal was standing, walking or running at the same instant; and, conversely, given enough latitude in the temporal interval they could use for their behavioral judgments to reach 90% or better exact agreement, their reliability on locational judgments dropped precipitously.

This finding is hardly esoteric and its basis should be obvious to anyone who has tried to take good still photographs conveying almost any molar action. In brief, every behavior in which we are likely to be interested has some appreciable duration and does not occur in its entirety in the time required to make a snapshot. Further, there is enormous variation in the typical duration of various classes of behaviors.

These facts are simple, but their implications for theory and method have not been recognized very clearly. Perhaps the most basic premise of behaviorism and ethology is that only behavioral units of a given size are directly and immediately observable; all else is inferred from the "directly observables". Simple extension of the uncertainty principle suggests, in contrast, that whether or not any psychological or behavioral event can be observed directly (and with high consensus between observers) depends in a very fundamental way upon the interval of time we allow the observer, and that our choice of this time interval which is to be a great degree arbitrary, immediately makes it difficult if not impossible to simultaneously observe other events whose temporal duration is much greater or smaller than the interval chosen. (Making film of an action sequence and scoring it twice does not, incidentally, solve the problem of achieving simultaneous judgments.) Conversely, whether or not any given behavioral description is thought to involve "unwarranted inference" on the part of the observer depends on our theory of (observer) perception and upon our current technical sophistication in rendering events "observable". It might even be that judgments to the effect that some species (reptiles, for example) "do nothing" most of the time and that other species (tigers, for example) are "nonsocial" depend in the last analysis upon our own metabolic rate and the consequent rates at which we move and interact with each other and the length of time we can watch other individuals whose temporal organization of behaviors is grossly different from our own without simply becoming bored. (To a creature that had a much higher metabolic rate than our own and a very poor capacity for temporal integration of information, would not human behavior look lethargic, unorganized and nonsocial?)

According to 19th century structuralistic psychology, no movement as such is observable, for it requires memory, inference and integration of the information from a series of instantaneous snapshots made by the retina. Thus even behavior categories such as approach-withdrawal, lever pressing, grooming and fighting must be viewed as inferential. The theoretical and methodological restrictions that behaviorism and ethology have placed upon us (that is, their claim that these categories are observables but that larger patterns such as migration and daily cycles of activity must be established by induction or inference and that most concepts used in everyday discourse are purely inferential) are in actuality a latter-day example of the same form of thinking--the main difference is that the size of the "elements" is on the order of 1/2 sec to 10 sec rather than, say, 1/16th sec.

What may be considered to be an observable in psychology, and what must be treated as inference? That is the question. On the theoretical level, the writings of the Gestalt psychologists (e.g., Köhler, 1929, chapter 6), Gibson (1966), Johansson (1975) and Polanyi (1958) are most pertinent here. On the practical level, high speed and time lapse photography give us particularly powerful tools for rendering "directly observable" that which was previously not (for example, the growth of a plant, or daily cycles in activity) and for examining the relation between different temporal levels of analysis. The ultimate solution to this problem, however, will not come about merely by using a large number of dependent variables that vary systematically in their level of analysis. Some lowering of our inhibitions about what constitutes "the" appropriate level is no doubt necessary; but multiple measures that are related to each other by no common metric or common underlying theoretical principles will more likely multiply rather than diminish our present confusion. In the physical and biological sciences, concepts such as energy and information, which apply at all levels of analysis, furnish an extremely useful sort of common metric, but at present it is difficult to see how they can be applied to the sorts of behavioral categories that students of social behavior are currently interested in, without losing sight of the categories themselves. The recent studies of investigators such as MacFarland (1977) are highly suggestive, however.

The zoom lens analogy (More on integrating various levels of analysis). In most of our everyday perceptions and verbal descriptions of everyday events subjects, objects, stimulus units and behavioral units come in no fixed sizes, shapes, or durations, and the borderline between subject and object and between object and context is a highly variable one: our momentary focus of attention shifts almost continuously from one level of analysis and one point of view to another, and the only time that such a procedure might result in confusion is if the shifts do not serve to advance our overall purpose, whatever that may be. Analogously, to film the same events a movie maker uses a variety of tricks of the trade such as zooming, panning, shooting from different angles and distances, changing focus, fading in and fading out, and filming at slow motion, normal and time lapse speeds. In the hands of an amateur, these techniques often result in total confusion on the part of a film viewer; but in the hands of a professional they ordinarily do not. Why is this so? Obviously, the professional does not use any technique for its own sake or in total isolation from others. S/he adapts each technique to his/her overall purpose (which is to convey some story or message or to accurately document some event). S/he has some fairly explicit rules for shifting from one technique to another and for integrating the various levels of analysis and the various points of view. Indeed, from a knowledge of these techniques and rules alone it is ordinarily very easy to determine the film maker's overall purpose; and one of the strongest indictments of a movie is that its maker had no apparent purpose, or that s/he included much material that is not relevant to the purpose.

In many respects the techniques and principles of scientific research are totally different from the above. Since our purpose is to achieve an accurate but impartial and objective perspective on the events in question, rather than some everyday individual or social end or an artistic masterpiece, it is very important to be as explicit and precise as possible about our methods, our units of measurement, our level of analysis and our point of view. And this ordinarily requires that we shift them only when it is necessary to do so.

Having rendered various details analyzable, however, there remains the task of integration or synthesis (methodologically, theoretically, or both). Here the problem and principles are precisely analogous to those employed in everyday life. Many investigators would, for example, argue that no theory of behavior can be considered complete unless it can not only deal with several levels of analysis simultaneously but also zoom in almost continuous fashion from one to the other without losing sight of either subject or context or going out of focus (see, for example, Dawkins, 1976; Menzel, 1969, 1975; Miller, Galanter and Pribram, 1960; Weiss, 1969). And this is not nearly so esoteric or profound as some theorists make it sound. The various "levels of analysis" or "levels of hierarchical organization" were never fixed or unalterable in the first place: such terms refer principally to the level of attention of the observer (or the theorist) whose attention has been attracted to certain regularities of patterns that seem to prevail there. The only thing that makes integration difficult is that we have not yet developed entirely satisfactory methods for specifying and quantifying the process of "zooming"--except in everyday terms or in metaphorical terms.

The zoom lens analogy is of course largely a spatial analogy

and it does not completely cover all of the problems that are
involved in synthesis, but it can easily be extended to the
temporal problems that were discussed in the preceding section
of this paper. (Coincidentally, it poses precisely the same
questions regarding the borderlines between observation and
inference.)

Zooming from one level of analysis should not, I believe, be
particularly difficult, methodologically speaking, so long as
one's data can be represented in purely spatiotemporal terms and
expressed with reference to some "absolute" zero point in space
and in time. It is principally when one must deal with other
forms of data or other forms of description (for example, verbally
defined categories) that the serious difficulties arise. Even
with categories such as geographical range, habitat, niche, home
range, territory, core area, home base and approach or escape
distance (which are clearly spatial concepts involving different
sizes of units), zooming is possible only in a metaphorical sense.
The central problem here, as in the case of our other unit categories, is that the rules by which the categories are defined are
varied, complex and in some cases unclear. Thus none of the
above terms can be defined in purely spatial terms; they vary
also with respect to the subject to whom they apply (species,
social group, individual animal), the length of the time interval
it would take to observe the phenomenon in question, and (in the
case of territory and approach and escape distance, for example)
verbally-defined behavioral considerations as well. If what we
are after is a fully quantified social psychology, such terms
should be considered useful principally at the level of "common
sense"--that is, they are devices for directing our attention to
aspects of life that we might otherwise overlook if we proceeded
in a purely inductive, quantitative fashion (Menzel, 1971).

IS THERE ANY HOPE FOR THE FUTURE?

Despite what I have written above, I am not at all pessimistic
about the prospects for the future development of more ideal
methods. Here, in very general terms, are my reasons.

No one knows, from everyday experience, what a quark, an
electron, a gene or even a species as such looks like, but no one
doubts that there are straightforward, objective rules for
identifying and describing and analyzing such phenomena. In
contrast, everyone is familiar with what people and animals do;
it is unlikely that either you or I would have any trouble in
giving someone an acceptable (everyday) answer if s/he were to
take us out into a park, point toward a group of children out
there, and ask us to describe (or predict) what was going on.
Any animal that is capable of surviving in the wild has, almost by
definition, a very respectable ability to predict, control and
understand the behavior of its peers, its prey and its predators.
Yet it is fashionable in some circles to maintain that adequate
behavioral classifications and behavioral analyses are just not

possible! There must, I submit, be something wrong with such reasoning.

Psychology's traditional answer here has been to claim that behavior is indeed orderly, but that you must bring your subjects into highly controlled laboratory situations and apply experimental procedures to them before you can demonstrate this. ("Real life" simply involves too many unknown complications.) Skinner (1969, p. 9) goes so far as to argue that non-laboratory methods alone are not even sufficient to specify what a pigeon is doing in a simple operant conditioning situation--and, if this is so, how can we ever hope to determine by the same techniques what pigeons, let alone people, are doing in complex, everyday situations?

Quite possibly, this is putting the problem backwards. First, how many investigators could design a useful scientific laboratory experiment if they had not already learned a good bit about what is going on in the real world via ordinary everyday experience? In fact, how many people would be able to master a scientific education at all without much prior everyday learning? Second, there is considerable evidence by now that observational data form a very powerful supplement to more traditional experimental data, even in operant conditioning situations (see, for example, Staddon and Simmelhag, 1971).

Admittedly, life is very complicated indeed, both inside and outside of the laboratory, and experimental analyses are probably necessary at some point if we wish to unravel all of the determinants of behavior. As a human being rather than a pure scientist, however, I find most descriptions of human societies, not to mention animal societies, at least as simple and intelligible as most descriptions of the structure of DNA or the nervous system of a cockroach and I can replicate my experience with people and animals at least as reliably as I got the "correct" results in my high school physics and chemistry laboratory classes. If anything, I find it easier to spot stable groupings and cliques of people in a park on Sunday than to identify the stable and obvious constellations in the sky. Indeed, in my experience one can make almost any subject matter about as complicated as one likes-- epistemologically speaking--and therefore how simple or complicated the "phenomena as such" *really* are seems to be an open question, if not indeterminate. The only limit to discoverable complexity is how much you really care, how closely you choose to look, and how much time, effort, grant money and IQ you can muster.

In any area of science, but especially in psychology, "The more you look, the more you see. Instead of selecting one truth from a multitude *you are increasing the multitude*. As you try to move toward unchanging truth... you actually do not move toward it at all. You move away from it! It is your application of scientific method that is causing it to change" (Pirsig, 1974, p. 109). Furthermore, as Norbert Wiener once said, "The social scientist has not the advantage of looking down on his subjects from the cold heights of eternity and ubiquity. It may be that there is a mass sociology of the human animalcule, observed like the populations of *Drosophila* in a bottle [cf. Alexander, 1975; Wilson, 1975], *but this is not a sociology in which we, who are human animalcules ourselves, are particularly interested*... In other words, in the social sciences we have to deal with short statistical runs, nor can we be sure that a considerable part of what we observe is not an artifact of our own creation" (1961, pp. 163-164, references and italics added).

The rules for discovering the complexities of social behavior seem to be fairly straightforward. It is far more difficult to specify the rules for discovering the underlying simplicities. One necessary but obviously not sufficient factor here is the simple faith, most eloquently stated by Einstein, that all of the basic "laws" of nature are indeed not only simple but also intelligible to men. The supreme goal of science, said Einstein, is to discover those universal elementary laws from which natural events can be arrived at by pure deduction. There is, however, no straight and narrow logical path to these laws. Only intuition, resting on sympathetic understanding of experience, can reach them. Nature as such does not provide us with the hypotheses that lead us toward these laws, Einstein continued; it provides only the data whereby our existing hypotheses may be tested and further ones formulated. Nor do we generate our hypotheses out of thin air. In spite of the fact that there is often no clear theoretical bridge between phenomena and their theoretical principles, in practice the world of phenomena uniquely determine our biological structure, our prescientific everyday knowledge and ultimately our scientific methods and theories.

With the above philosophizing in mind, it would be a serious mistake to limit our methods to those that meet the current standards of respectability in the natural and physical sciences. We need very much to develop and refine methods which explicitly recognize and exploit, rather than attempt to eliminate, the observer's prescientific, intuitive and global forms of judgment.

Let me give two concrete examples of the sort of research I have in mind here. First, Sackett (1970) found that rhesus monkeys that had never before seen each other tended to show strong preferences for those who had been subjected to the same early experiences. Analogously, Suomi, Harlow, and Lewis (1970), using the same preference technique, found that their monkeys, some of which were normal controls and others of which had been subjected to various types of brain lesions, could almost immediately pick out, from a group of strangers, whoever had had the same type of lesion (or sham operation) as their own. As the latter investigators point out, the monkeys were apparently better experimenters and diagnosticians than people, for any number of tests had previously been conducted to determine whether the various groups of lesioned animals differed from each other, and none of the tests had yielded significant results. Naturally one would like to know precisely how the lesioned animals differed from each other and from controls; but insofar as the "experimenter monkeys" were able to make reliable discriminations here, there can be little doubt that some reliable difference did exist and could be picked up by an outside observer. The task of human experimenters is either to look for the relevant cues themselves, or to ask the experimenter monkeys how they made their discriminations.

The second example is hypothetical, as no one (to my knowledge) has tried it. If one is interested in, say, the sequential analysis of behavior patterns, why restrict oneself to recording only what one's subjects are doing at any given time, and then looking for sequential dependencies after the fact? It might also be interesting and useful to have other observers (who are known to be skilled intuitive judges) attempt to predict ahead of time what the subjects will do, using whatever cues they care to use. If their predictions are recorded by voice on the audio track of a video recorder while the subject or subjects' behavior is filmed as usual, it would be simple not only to examine to some degree the basis on which these predictions are made, but also to get a clearer idea of what to look for in one's other analyses. Just as Alfred Binet used the judgments of teachers regarding their pupils' intelligence as the basis for validating his own tests and eventually for creating a test instrument that was in many ways superior to the teachers' judgments, so also the same procedure could be employed in the area of complex social inter-actions. It is conceivable that our present objective measures are already better predictors of what people and animals will do in some situations than are the intuitive judgments of woodsmen, naturalists and mothers. I know of no real evidence on this score. At least when contemplating going into a cage with an adult chimpanzee, however, I would be more inclined to trust a naturalist's judgment than a computer. In short, if it should be the case that one's purely inductive analysis suggests that behavior is not orderly when an intuitive judge's predictions were nevertheless quite accurate, we know that our inductive analysis must be incomplete and that it could be made better, if only we can discover the cues on which the intuitive judge was operating.

It may be that the judges cannot specify these cues; or they might have been operating on the basis of nonbehavioral cues. But these possibilities can be checked out, if we so desire, simply by experimentally varying the conditions under which they must make their predictions. Thus, for example, one might let them watch only a videotape of the original scene, rather than live action. If their predictive ability does not deteriorate, one might gradually reduce the information that is available from the tape—by rendering it impossible for the judge to discriminate the subjects' identities or genders, for example, or even by transforming the tape into an abstract cartoon, resembling those employed by Heider (1958) or Michotte (1963). Such an analysis could be made in as precise and detailed a fashion as one cared to make it. And if one is more interested in the psychology of one's (other) subjects than in the psychology of observers, there is no reason that similar tests cannot be carried out on them (see, for example, Menzel, Premack and Woodruff, in press).

In all, I think that the difficulties social psychology faces
in becoming a full-fledged science do not lie in our lack of
ability to *record* the behavior of our subjects objectively and
adequately. Indeed, this point seems totally noncontroversial,
if not trivial: even the most anti-behavioral person is ordinarily
satisfied with the record that is produced by videotape or sound
movies, and this is a man-made representation of events rather
than the real article. In precisely the same sense that Gibson
(1966) and Johansson (1975) would argue that all of the information
necessary for everyday judgments about talking, cooing, looking,
walking, playing and so on are available in the ambient patterns
of physical energy that are present when a live event occurs, it
can be argued that a very substantial portion of this information
is available in the ambient patterns of physical energy that can
be created by running a videotape of the live event through the
appropriate equipment.[2] Moreover, the amount of information lost
to a human observer can also be estimated fairly precisely, if we
so choose, by comparing the judgments of an observer who is present
at the original event with the judgments of an observer who is
present at the showing of the videotape. (By comparison with a
videotape record, Galileo's and Newton's record of the behavior of
inanimate objects was "crude" indeed! As a matter of fact, videotape and sound movies come about as close to an ideal single
method as one is likely to get. The one characteristic they lack
is parsimony.)

Now, if we possessed the appropriate sensory equipment or
the appropriate technology, we would not even have to play the
videotape through a tape deck and a monitor, for the roll of tape
as such contains a set of information that is completely isomorphic
to that which would appear in visual form on the monitor. The
dynamics of the original action are, in other words, captured in
a static form of representation, and we can process and analyze
it in this form without modification if we so choose. Furthermore,
any scoring of the tape into traditional behavioral categories
amounts in principle to nothing more than a recoding (that is, a
translation, a condensing and a discarding of "irrelevant" details)
of the same information.

---

2. The same thing can be said about a drastically reduced or
simplified videotape. Thus, for example, Johansson attached a
small set of lights (one light on each ankle, knee, hip, shoulder,
elbow and wrist) to each of two actors and produced a videotape that
showed only the locations and motions of these lights. Observers
who were shown a single frame of this tape, or (only) a sequence
during which the lights were stationary, could make no sense of it;
but if the lights were moving for as little as 1 sec, this sufficed
for the observers to perceive each constellation of lights as a
person (even when the actors were engaged in a social dance), and
to discriminate between many different behaviors on the part of the
actors.

If, then, it were possible to clearly specify the total information content of the videotape *and the rules of such recodings,* would it not be possible in principle to have the videotapes scored directly and automatically? This is a much more difficult task for live behaviors than for simple picture recognition; but given the rate at which computer analysis of pictures is currently progressing, such a hope does not seem far-fetched.

The simplest, most complete and most systematic form of recoding would undoubtedly be a physicalistic one in which (for example) the roll of videotape is considered as a two-dimensional space (the long dimension being the X axis and the other dimension being the Y axis) and a record is made for each possible point on this space of the magnitude of the magnetic charge. Such a recoding is quite feasible even today with the appropriate equipment.

Quite obviously, "this quantity of data is by its mere bulk incapable of entering the mind" of a human investigator. However, it should also be apparent that the principal tasks that remain are only two in number: First, to replace this quantity by "relatively few quantities which shall adequately represent the whole, or which, in other words, shall contain as much as possible, ideally the whole, of the relevant information contained in the original data" (Fisher, 1922), and second, to accomplish this task in a way that makes sense to us as human beings and does not totally fly in the face of the sort of common sense judgments the rest of humanity would make if they looked at the videotapes.

If we were content to ignore the second imperative and to state the first one in purely physicalistic terms, we would then have to account for the total variance of the above data (that is, how do the magnitudes of the magnetic charges vary as a function of one's position on the X and Y axes of the tape?) in the most parsimonious fashion possible. And this job too could quite possibly be handled by a computer. The only question is whether or not this would constitute psychology as we now know it.

SUMMARY AND CONCLUSIONS

Stated in its most general and elementary terms, the problem of method and of theory is to render observable, explicit and quantitative that which was previously only inferred, implicitly assumed or qualitatively described; to discover the order that in fact exists in any apparent disorder; to describe and explain what is really going on out there; and to make it equally clear how one arrived at one's conclusions. If one's analyses tell one nothing more than could be learned from everyday experience, it is doubtful that they should be called "science"; but, on the other hand, to view science as a world of its own or a complete substitute for everyday experience is to risk losing contact with social reality.

Many of the key difficulties in current methodology stem, I believe, from our failure to clearly recognize the impossibility of separating the observer from the system that s/he studies. To call this the problem of "experimenter error" is, however, unnecessarily pejorative and it involves one in a logical paradox. (To accept an experimental proof that all experimenters are in error, I must first of all be convinced that the experimenter who proves this is not in error. If I am convinced on the latter score, how can I also be convinced on the former score--or vice versa?) The key issue is not how to reduce the observer's role to zero (or even to an absolute minimum) but simply how to render it at least as explicit, as clear, and as quantitatively speci- fiable as any other aspect of the system under study--so that other observers will know how to look at the same phenomena from the same perspective, should they care to do so. A second major issue is whether such a perspective really answers the questions in which we are most interested. And the third major issue, which is not solely a methodological one, is, What are the questions in which we are most interested?

This last issue is, of course, the most important one, and until we can arrive at some general consensus here it will be impossible to arrive at some single general method that would be ideal for everyone.

REFERENCES

Alexander, R. D. The search for a general theory of behavior. *Behavioral Science*, 1975, *20*, 77-100.
Dawkins, R. Hierarchical organization: A candidate principle in ethology. In P. P. G. Bateson and R. A. Hinde (Eds.), *Growing points in ethology*. Cambridge: Cambridge University Press, 1976.
Fagen, R. M., and Goldman, R. N. Behavioral catalogue analysis methods. *Animal Behavior*, 1977, *25*, 261-274.
Fisher, R. A. On the mathematical foundations of theoretical statistics. *Philosophical Transactions of the Royal Society*, 1922, *222A*, 309-368.
Golani, I. Homeostatic motor processes in mammalian interactions: A choreography of display. In P. P. G. Bateson and P. Klopfer (Eds.), *Perspectives in ethology*, Vol. 2. New York: Plenum, 1976.
Heider, F. *The psychology of interpersonal relations*. New York: Wiley, 1958.
Johansson, G. Visual motion perception. *Scientific American*, 1975, *232*, 76-87.
Köhler, W. *Gestalt psychology*. New York: Liveright, 1929.
Köhler, W. *The selected papers of Wolfgang Köhler* (edited by M. Henle). New York: Liveright, 1971.
Lorenz, K. Z. *Studies in animal and human behavior*, Vol. 2. Cambridge, Mass.: Harvard University Press, 1971.
MacFarland, D.J. Decision making in animals. *Nature*, 1977, *269*, 15-20.
Menzel, E. W. Naturalistic and experimental approaches to primate behavior. In E. Willems and H. Raush (Eds.), *Naturalistic viewpoints in psychological research*. New York: Holt, Rinehart and Winston, 1969.

Menzel, E. W.   Discussant's comments.   In A. Esser (Ed.), *Behavior and environment: The use of space in animals and men*. New York: Plenum, 1971.

Menzel, E. W.   A group of young chimpanzees in a one-acre field. In A. M. Schrier and F. Stollnitz (Eds.), *Behavior of nonhuman primates, Vol. 5*. New York: Academic, 1974.

Menzel, E. W.   Communication and aggression in a group of young chimpanzees.   In P. Pliner, L. Krames and T. Alloway (Eds.), *Advances in the study of communication and affect, Vol. 2. Nonverbal communication of aggression*. New York: Plenum, 1975.

Menzel, E. W.   Communication of object-locations in a group of young chimpanzees.   In D. Hamburg and J. Goodall (Eds.), *Behavior of the great apes*. New York: Staples Press, in press (a).

Menzel, E. W.   Cognitive mapping in chimpanzees.   In S. A. Hulse, H. Fowler and W. K. Honig (Eds.), *Cognitive processes in animal behavior*. Hillsdale, N.J.: Lawrence Erlbaum Associates, in press (b).

Menzel, E. W., Premack, D., and Woodruff, G.   Map reading by chimpanzees. *Folia Primatologica,* in press.

Michotte, A.   *The perception of causality*. New York: Basic Books, 1963.

Miller, G. A., Galanter, E., and Pribram, K.   *Plans and the structure of behavior*. New York: Holt, Rinehart and Winston, 1960.

Pirsig, R.   *Zen and the art of motorcycle maintenance*. New York: Bantam, 1974.

Polanyi, M.   *Personal knowledge*. Chicago: University of Chicago Press, 1958.

Reynolds, V.   The origins of a behavioral vocabulary: The case of the rhesus monkey. *Journal of Theory of Social Behavior,* 1976, *6*, 105-142.

Sackett, G. P.   Unlearned responses, differential rearing experiences, and the development of social attachments by rhesus monkeys. In L. A. Rosenblum (Ed.), *Primate behavior: Developments in field and laboratory research, Vol. 1*. New York: Academic, 1970.

Simpson, G. G.   *Principles of animal taxonomy*. New York: Columbia University Press, 1961.

Skinner, B. F.   *Science and human behavior*. New York: MacMillan, 1953.

Skinner, B. F.   *Contingencies of reinforcement*. New York: Appleton-Century Crofts, 1969.

Sokal, R. R., and Crovello, T. J.   The biological species concept: A critical evaluation. *American Naturalist,* 1970, *104*, 127-153.

Staddon, J. E. R., and Simmelhag, V. L.   The "superstition" experiment: A reexamination of its implications for the principles of adaptive behavior. *Psychological Review,* 1971, *78*, 3-43.

Suomi, S. J., Harlow, H. F., and Lewis, J. K.   Effect of bilateral frontal lobectomy on social preferences of rhesus monkeys. *Journal of Comparative and Physiological Psychology,* 1970, *70*, 448-453.

Weiss, P. A.   The living system: Determinism stratified.   In A.
    Koestler and J. R. Smythies (Eds.), *Beyond reductionism*.
    Boston: Beacon, 1969.
Westman, R. S.   Environmental languages and the functional basis
    of animal behavior.   In B. A. Hazlett (Ed.), *Quantitative
    methods in the study of animal behavior*.   New York: Academic,
    1977.
Wiener, N.   *Cybernetics*.   Cambridge, Mass.:   MIT Press, 1961.
Wilson, E. O.   *Sociobiology*.   Cambridge, Mass.:   Harvard University
    Press, 1975.
Wittgenstein, L.   *Philosophical reflections*.   New York: MacMillan,
    1968 (3d edition).

AUTHOR INDEX

311

SUBJECT INDEX

DESIGNED BY EDGAR J. FRANK
MANUFACTURED BY THOMSON-SHORE, INC.
DEXTER, MICHIGAN

Library of Congress Cataloging in Publication Data
Social interaction analysis.
Includes indexes.
1.   Social interaction--Methodology--Addresses,
essays, lectures.   I. Lamb, Michael
II. Suomi, Stephen J.   III. Stephenson, Gordon
HM131.S585   301.11   78-53287
ISBN 0-299-07590-7